Contemporary A[merican]
Independent [Film]

D0665017

Since the explosion in low-budget filmmaking in the 1960s, the 'independent' film scene has produced some truly innovative and financially successful films, from *Easy Rider* to *Pulp Fiction* and *The Blair Witch Project*. But how independent is independent cinema today? And what are the artistic and economic concerns that separate it from Hollywood? To what extent does contemporary American independent film exist in a blurred zone no longer clearly represented by either the margins or the mainstream?

Contemporary American Independent Film is a comprehensive examination of the independent film scene. Exploring the uneasy relationship between independent filmmakers and the major studios, contributors trace the changing ideas and definitions of independent cinema, and the diversity of independent film practices. They consider the ways in which indie films are marketed and distributed, and how technologies such as video, cable and the internet have offered new opportunities for filmmakers to produce and market independent films.

Contemporary American Independent Film highlights the contributions of established indie and underground directors, such as Todd Solondz, John Sayles and Haile Gerima, indie icons, such as Parker Posey and canine star Benji, and distributors, such as Troma Entertainment. With such a wide focus and a particular emphasis on gender, sexuality and ethnicity, the anthology offers a true 'taster' of the richness and vibrancy of American independent cinema.

Chris Holmlund is Professor of Cinema Studies, Women's Studies and French at the University of Tennessee. She is the author of *Impossible Bodies* and co-editor of *Between the Sheets, In the Streets: Queer, Lesbian, Gay Documentary*. **Justin Wyatt** is Executive Director of Research at the ABC Television Network. He is the author of *Poison* and *High Concept: Movies and Marketing in Hollywood*.

Contemporary American Independent Film

From the margins to the mainstream

Edited by Chris Holmlund and Justin Wyatt

Routledge
Taylor & Francis Group

LONDON AND NEW YORK

First published 2005
In the US and Canada by Routledge
29 West 35th Street, New York, NY 10001

Simultaneously published
by Routledge
2 Park Square, Milton Park, Abingdon, Oxfordshire, OX14 4RN

Routledge is an imprint of the Taylor & Francis Group

Selection and editorial matter © 2005 by Chris Holmlund and Justin Wyatt
Individual chapters © 2005 copyright holders

Typeset in Perpetua and Bell Gothic by RefineCatch Limited, Bungay, Suffolk
Printed and bound in Great Britain by
Cromwell Press, Trowbridge, Wiltshire

All rights reserved. No part of this book may be reprinted or
reproduced or utilized in any form or by any electronic,
mechanical, or other means, now known or hereafter
invented, including photocopying and recording, or in any
information storage or retrieval system, without permission in
writing from the publishers.

British Library Cataloguing in Publication Data
A catalogue record for this book is available from the British Library

Library of Congress Cataloging in Publication Data
Contemporary American independent film : from the margins to the mainstream /
edited by Chris Holmlund and Justin Wyatt.
p. cm.
Includes bibliographical references and index.
1.   Motion pictures—United States—History. 2   Independent filmmakers—United States.
I. Holmlund, Chris.   II. Wyatt, Justin, 1963–

PN1993.5.U6C636 2004
791.43′0973—dc22
2004010036

ISBN 0–415–25486–8 (hbk)
ISBN 0–415–25487–6 (pbk)

For Dad and Jon, and in loving memory of my mother, Kerstin.
For Jeff, as always, and in loving memory of Alice Wyatt.

Contents

List of illustrations

Notes on contributors

José B. Capino has taught film studies at Northwestern University and Bowdoin College, and was recipient of the 2003 Dissertation Prize from the Society for Cinema and Media Studies. He writes on a wide variety of topics, including documentary film, pornography, postcolonialism, and national cinema.

Diane Carson is a Professor of Film Studies and Production at St. Louis Community College at Meramec. She edited *John Sayles: Interviews* (University of Mississippi Press, 1999). She has also co-edited *More Than a Method* (Wayne State University Press, 2004), *Multiple Voices in Feminist Film Criticism* (University of Minnesota Press, 1994), and *Shared Differences* (University of Illinois Press, 1995).

Ian Conrich is Senior Lecturer in Film Studies at University of Surrey Roehampton. He is an editor of the *Journal of Popular British Cinema*, a guest editor of *Post Script*, and co-editor of seven books, including *New Zealand – A Pastoral Paradise?* (2000), *New Zealand Fictions: Literature and Film* (2003), and the forthcoming *Horror Zone: The Cultural Experience of Contemporary Horror Cinema* and *Contemporary New Zealand Cinema*.

Robert Eberwein, Professor of English at Oakland University, is the author of *Sex Ed: Film, Video, and the Framework of Desire* (Rutgers University Press, 1999). He is completing a study of male sexuality and the American combat film, and editing an anthology on war films.

Joan Hawkins is an Associate Professor in the Department of Communication and Culture, Indiana University, Bloomington. She is the author of *Cutting Edge: Art–Horror and the Horrific Avant-garde* (University of Minnesota Press, 2000). Currently, she is working on a book on Todd Haynes.

Chris Holmlund is Professor of Cinema Studies, Women's Studies, and French at the University of Tennessee. She is the author of *Impossible Bodies: Femininity and Masculinity at the Movies* (Routledge, 2003) and co-editor of *Between the*

Sheets, In the Streets: Queer, Lesbian, Gay Documentary (Minnesota University Press, 1997). She is working on a book on action films.

Annette Insdorf, Director of Undergraduate Film Studies at Columbia University, is the author of *Double Lives, Second Chances: The Cinema of Krzysztof Kieslowski, François Truffaut* and *Indelible Shadows: Film and the Holocaust*. For the updated third edition (2002), she received the National Board of Review's William K. Everson Award in Film History.

David E. James teaches in the School of Cinema-Television at USC. His most recent book was *Power Misses: Essays Across (Un)Popular Culture* (London: Verso). He is currently working on a history of avant-garde film in Los Angeles.

Jon Jost has been making films since 1963. He's made fourteen feature-length works in film, eight long works in digital video, and numerous short subjects. In the past eight years, he has worked exclusively in digital media, branching into large-scale installation works.

Christina Lane is Assistant Professor in the Motion Picture Program at The University of Miami, Florida. She is the author of *Feminist Hollywood: From BORN IN FLAMES to POINT BREAK* (Wayne State University Press, 2000), and has articles in *Film and Authorship* and *The West Wing: the American Presidency as Television Drama*.

Ed Lowry was teaching film at Southern Methodist University when he died in 1985. His book, *The Filmology Movement and Film Study in France*, was published by UMI the same year. Essays include studies of the horror film, Kenneth Anger, and early film exhibition.

Gina Marchetti is an Associate Professor in the Department of Cinema and Photography at Ithaca College, New York. She is author of *Romance and the 'Yellow Peril': Race, Sex, and Discursive Strategies in Hollywood Fiction* (University of California Press, 1993) and *From Tian'anmen to Times Square: China on Global Screens* (Temple University Press, forthcoming).

Jonas Mekas's narrative, documentary, and 'diary' films have screened at festivals and museums around the world. Since 1954 he has also championed and critiqued avant-garde film as editor of *Film Culture*, columnist for *The Village Voice*, co-founder of the Film-Makers' Cooperative, and co-founder of the Filmmakers Cinematheque (now the influential Anthology Film Archives).

Diane Negra teaches film and television in the School of English and American Studies at the University of East Anglia. She has published *Off-White Hollywood* (Routledge, 2001) and is currently at work on an edited collection entitled *The Irish in Us: Irishness, Performativity and Popular Culture*.

Mark A. Reid directs the Film and Media Studies Program at the University of Florida. He is the author of *Redefining Black Film* (University of California Press, 1993) and *Postnegritude Visual and Literary Culture* (State University of New York Press, 1997), editor of *Spike Lee's 'Do the Right Thing'* (Cambridge University Press, 1997), and co-editor of *Le Cinéma noir américain* (Cerf, 1988).

Justin Wyatt is Executive Director of Research at the ABC Television Network. He holds a Ph.D in Critical Studies from UCLA. He is the editor for the Commerce and Mass Culture series at the University of Minnesota Press, and the author of *High Concept: Movies and Marketing in Hollywood* (University of Texas Press) and *Poison* (Flicks Books).

Patricia R. Zimmermann is Professor of Cinema and Photography in the Roy H. Park School of Communications and Coordinator of the Culture and Communication Program in the Division of Interdisciplinary and International Studies at Ithaca College, New York. She is the author of *Reel Families: A Social History of Amateur Film* (Indiana University Press) and *States of Emergency: Documentaries, Wars, Democracies* (Minnesota University Press).

Acknowledgments

Thanks for this book go first and foremost to the contributors for their insights, enthusiasm, hard work, and patience. And, of course, we are all grateful to those who have made such a range of independent films possible over the years.

A number of people have helped with this anthology. Chris thanks Charles Maland in particular for his encouragement and suggestions. Warmest of thanks, too, to Diane Carson, Krin Gabbard, Jon Jonakin, Karen Levy, Diane Waldman, and Dale Watermulder for providing ideas and counsel, on the phone, at the movies, in the mountains. Warm thanks, and much love, to my brother and my dad for their constant support and interest. Students at the University of Tennessee, especially those in a course on American independent film, provided invaluable, and often impassioned, feedback. The final compilation of this anthology was made possible by a semester's leave from teaching; sincere thanks to UT library staff for help with reprints and sources! I've had the pleasure to meet and work with several independent makers over the years, among them Su Friedrich, Ela Troyano, Jill Godmilow, Barbara Hammer, Gunvor Nelson, Yvonne Rainer, and Leslie Thornton: I take your creativity and your persistence as models. At Routledge, Kate Ahl, Alistair Daniel, Rebecca Barden, and Helen Faulkner have all been great. Justin Wyatt has been key to launching and designing this volume. I've learned a lot from and with him, and I always relish trading views on movies and life.

Justin would particularly like to thank Juan Morales, editor at *Detour Magazine*, and the numerous luminaries in the independent film world whom he interviewed for *Detour*, including Hal Hartley, Todd Haynes, Ted Hope, Marcus Hu, Lodge Kerrigan, Bruce LaBruce, Christopher Munch, Raoul O'Connell, Nicolas Roeg, Christine Vachon and Sande Zeig. His vision of the possibilities (and limitations) of independent film have been shaped by these individuals and their vivid war stories. Conversations with Matthew Bernstein, Jeffrey Clarke, Jon Lewis, Steve Prince, Hilary Radner, and Tom Schatz have also been extremely helpful in further refining my take on the 'indie world.' Finally, I owe my greatest thanks to my inspirational co-editor, Chris. Her endless enthusiasm, humor, all-around smarts, and generosity have shaped this project and our interactions as editors. I feel honored to call her a long-time friend and a valued intellectual colleague.

Photo credits are as follows: The stills from *The Gangs of New York, sex, lies & videotape, Heartland, The Doberman Gang, Stranger than Paradise, The House of Yes, In the Company of Men, Happiness, All Over Me, Gas, Food, Lodging, Fargo*, and *Boys Don't Cry*, and that of Andy Warhol appear courtesy of the Kobal Collection. The photograph of Lloyd Kaufman and Michael Herz and the still from *The Toxic Avenger* are courtesy of Troma Entertainment. The still from *Limbo* is courtesy of Columbia Pictures. The stills from *Bush Mama* and *Sankofa* are courtesy of Mypheduh Films. The images from *Bijou* and *Hotshots* are courtesy of Anthology Film Archives. The still from *Hide and Seek* is courtesy of Su Friedrich. The production still from *Girlfight* is courtesy of Sony Pictures. The stills from *Shopping for Fangs* appear courtesy of Quentin Lee. Website images from the Big Noise Film Collective are courtesy of www.bignoisefilm.com. Original cites and permissions (where possible to obtain) for the reprints are as follows: Annette Insdorf, 'Ordinary people, European-style: or how to spot an independent feature,' *American Film*, 6, 10 (September 1981): 57–60. David E. James, 'Alternative cinemas,' in *Allegories of Cinema: American Film in the Sixties*, Princeton: Princeton University Press, 1989 pp. 22–8. Jon Jost, 'End of the indies: death of the Sayles men,' *Film Comment*, 25, 1 (January–February 1989): 42–5. Ed Lowry, 'Dimension Pictures: portrait of a 1970s' independent,' *The Velvet Light Trap*, 22 (1986): 65–74; reprint courtesy of the University of Texas Press. Jonas Mekas, 'Independence for independents,' *American film*, 3, 10 (September 1978): 38–40.

Chapter 1

Introduction

From the margins to the mainstream

Chris Holmlund

From the margins to the mainstream

The popularity of independent films today is indisputable. 'Indies' – among them *Chicago* (Marshall, 2002), *Gangs of New York* (Scorsese, 2002), *Far from Heaven* (Haynes, 2002), *The Pianist* (Polanski, 2002), *Frida* (Taymor, 2002), *My Big Fat Greek Wedding* (Zwick, 2002), and *Bowling for Columbine* (Moore, 2002) – dominated nominations and awards at the 2003 Oscars.[1] Everywhere you look, you find independent features: in art-house miniplexes and special theaters; as videos and DVDs; on regular, cable, and satellite tv; increasingly on the web; more infrequently yet often prominently (as is the case with the above titles) in wide release.[2]

Admittedly, audiences for these movies vary – by age, across region, in size, because certain indie films target 'niche' audiences, while some tap diasporic populations, and others address trans-national communities. Each year, moreover, hundreds of other independent movies see no distribution, in part because – like production costs – price tags for prints and advertising have soared. Miramax's *Gangs of New York* surely tops the 'heavyweight' price list, with production costs rumored to be $100–120 million dollars (Oppelaar 2002: 62).

With so many expensive independent feature films now produced and released by mini-majors and the majors' own independent arms, independent films would seem to have moved squarely to the mainstream, away from the margins where historically they served to supplement studio production and often expressed 'outsider' perspectives. Has 'indie' become merely a brand, a label used to market biggish budget productions that aim to please many by offending few? What does the shift towards the mainstream entail, especially for those located on the margins?

This Introduction and the chapters which follow explore the economic and ideological consequences that attend the positionings of contemporary American independent features within the mainstream and on the margins. Most of us concentrate on feature films rather than on documentaries or shorts, as the

Figure 1.1 Amsterdam Vallon (Leonardo DiCaprio), William Cutting (Daniel Day Lewis), and Johnny Sirocco (Henry Thomas) in *Gangs of New York* (Scorsese, 2002). Courtesy of Miramax/Dimension Films/Kobal Collection/Mario Tursi.

former especially have been key to industry survival and expansion. Finally, by 'contemporary' American indies, we envisage primarily films made from the 1980s through the 2000s, though some of us explore independents made in the 1970s that helped inaugurate current trends.

But what exactly *is* an 'independent' film? *Who watches* independent films? *Which* independent films? Why does identification as an independent *matter*? Common as the term is, what it is that constitutes an independent film is ill-defined and hotly debated. For numerous critics, and many audience members, too, the label suggests social engagement and/or aesthetic experimentation – a distinctive visual look, an unusual narrative pattern, a self-reflexive style. The definition advanced in 2003 by the editorial board of *Filmmaker Magazine*, the journal of the Independent Feature Project and the Independent Feature Project/ West, is typical, and additionally acknowledges cross-over potential. In a yearly article introducing '25 New Faces of Indie Film,' *Filmmaker*'s editors posit that independent films are broadly associated with 'alternative points of view, whether they be expressed in experimental approaches or through crowd-pleasing comedies' (*Filmmaker* 2003).

Yet to say that personal vision or alternative perspectives characterize indies in general is to forget the hundreds of pulp actioners and horror flicks that every day jostle for space on video and DVD store shelves. Where, after all, would Dolph Lundgren or Jean-Claude van Damme be without straight-to-video indies? And let's not forget all those terrifying – and terrible – treats like *C.H.U.D.* (Creek, 1984)!

True, a director often sets his – still more rarely her – signature on an indie feature, making these films, as opposed to studio blockbusters, more genuinely the work of an 'auteur.' Occasionally – witness the success of Roger Corman or Troma Entertainment – a producer or a production company becomes a trademark. 'Thumbs ups' from leading, even local, critics count for more than they do with mainstream film. The presence of recognizable actors (more rarely stars) is often a salient factor fueling box office take and video/DVD rentals and sales. In contemporary art-house variants the performer him/herself may even serve as a marker of 'independence' – per the scores of independent films in which our 'cover boy,' the inimitable Steve Buscemi (there, in *Living in Oblivion* [Di Cillo, 1995], playing 'no budget' independent director Nick Reve), appears. A final complication involves identification of an independent film as 'American': many US studios happily distribute both foreign and American independent features, while foreign monies often help bankroll American independent productions.

Given the above – at times complementary, at times contradictory – definitions, many viewers fail to recognize that a big-budget, star-laden, film like *Gangs of New York* is actually an American independent, even though they may know that Miramax is the leading producer and distributor of independent work and even though they may also know that Martin Scorsese made a name for himself in 1973 with the far less expensive independent *Mean Streets*. We would however insist, with Chuck Kleinhans (1998: 308), that 'independent film' has always been a relational term: what's at stake is a continuum, not an opposition. Contemporary American independent films run the financial gamut, from 'no budget' (under $100,000) to 'micro' or 'low budget' (under $1 million) to – and, today, more frequently – 'tweeners' ($10–30 million) produced and marketed by mini-majors, even sometimes – as is the case with the Miramax–Paramount collaboration on *The Hours* (Daldry, 2002) – together with majors. Distribution as well may or may not be handled independently.

For us, the phrase 'from the margins to the mainstream' – subtitle both of this first introductory section and of the collection as a whole – thus takes on three, interconnected, meanings.

- As referenced here, argued in the next two introductory sections about indies past and present, and further explicated in the reprints and essays, independent and mainstream feature films are linked together on a sliding scale. Neither ideologically nor economically are they purely antithetical.

- Nevertheless, as also suggested by the first three sections of this introduction and developed in several of the original articles as well, in the last fifteen years key sectors of independent films have indeed migrated towards the mainstream, from the margins, with attendant effects.
- Finally, and precisely because the dominant trend has been away from the margins, towards the mainstream, many contributors choose to speak *from* the margins *to* the mainstream. As will be apparent both from the final two sections of this Introduction (overviews of our contributions and areas meriting additional research) and from several of the contributions which follow, such arguments are at times nostalgic, at times visionary – at times both, simultaneously.

That individual contributors emphasize different aspects and kinds of indie features testifies to the complexity that characterizes talk about contemporary American independent cinema. All of the contributors to *Contemporary American Independent Cinema* would nevertheless agree that to assess any of the many contemporary American independent cinema scenes, it is necessary to have some knowledge of the stages of American independent films *past* and some appreciation of the scope of independent films *present*. Accordingly, the next two sections sketch briefly the history of American independent film.

American independent film from the teens to 2000

With selection criteria that include 'original, provocative subject matter' and 'uniqueness of vision,' awards like the Independent Spirits fuel perceptions that independent film is synonymous with the 'hot,' the 'new,' and the 'now' (*Filmmaker* 2002).[3] But independent films are not strictly 'now' or simply 'new'; rather, they date back to the dawn of feature-length cinema time.

In the teens, ethnic, sexploitation, documentary, and avant-garde films made by independents provided welcome alternatives to output from the 'Big Three': Edison, Biograph, and Vitagraph. In the 1920s, race, exploitation, and ethnic films continued to prosper, even as studios became larger and more powerful. A few actors, like Harold Lloyd and Charlie Chaplin, started their own companies, while several famous studio directors, among them King Vidor and Maurice Tourneur, launched their careers in independent film.

In the 1930s the 'Big Five' (Warner Brothers, Paramount, MGM, Twentieth Century–Fox, and RKO) consolidated their control over big budget and 'programmer' production, contracting workers from directors and stars on down, and dominating a good deal of distribution and exhibition as well. Yet so great was the need for 'B' and specialized product that independent studios sprang up to fill the need, churning out cheap westerns, exploitation, ethnic, and black-cast films, often on Hollywood sets and sound stages.[4] As is the case today, these independent studios varied in size, from semi-independents like Monogram and Republic to the shoestring outfits of Poverty Row.

The 1940s through 1960s saw the gradual break-up of the studio system and the opening of new doors for independent producers, distributors, and exhibitors. The Paramount decision of 1948 was key, forcing the 'Big Five' to sell their theater chains. The number of contract players shrank dramatically, and many stars and directors – among them Burt Lancaster, Kirk Douglas, Robert Mitchum, George Stevens, Alfred Hitchcock, and Billy Wilder – set up their own productions. By the 1960s, the big studios had essentially become distributors, and the 'Little Three' (Columbia, Universal, and United Artists) had also become majors. Meanwhile the arrival of television created additional demand for films, while in theaters and drive-ins teen pix and exploitation flicks became 'must see' movies for the millions of postwar baby-boomers.

In the late 1960s and 1970s, the loosening of the 1934 Hayes Production Code and, in 1968, its succession by the modern Motion Picture Association of America (MPAA) ratings system paved the way both for a proliferation of porn movies and for the more personal, often confrontational, films that became known as 'American New Wave.' Independently produced (if often studio-released) youth-oriented and/or exploitation features, such as *Night of the Living Dead* (Romero, 1968), *Easy Rider* (Hopper, 1969), *Sweet Sweetback's Baadasssss Song* (Van Peebles, 1971), and *Billy Jack* (Laughlin, 1971), captured audiences' imaginations and raked in money. Art-house and adult theaters flourished. By the end of the 1970s, an alternative infrastructure of festivals, organizations, and distributors capable of supporting smaller features was in place. Prime among these were the US Film Festival, founded in 1978 and now renowned as the Sundance Film Festival, and the Independent Feature Project with its offshoot the Independent Feature Film Market, begun in 1979. Directors like Francis Ford Coppola, George Lucas, Martin Scorsese, Oliver Stone, Hal Ashby, Robert Altman, Bob Rafelson, and others became famous, first with independent, then often with semi-independent and studio productions.[5] But of all the iconoclasts making off-beat narrative films and moving between indie and studio work, John Cassavetes perhaps best embodies the spirit of resistance to what biographer Ray Carney has called 'happy-face, entertainment-obsessed, Hollywood-addled culture' (McKay 2001). Jack-of-all-trades Cassavetes assembled every crew and wrote each script, from his first film, *Shadows* (1959), on; he worked intensely and intensively with a core group of actors, coaxing them to remarkable performances in carefully crafted, complex roles; he experimented with camera position and movement; he fought to get his films into the theaters and noticed by critics.

Many of these 1970s films, festivals, and makers remain influential today. But American independent cinema really acquired its current shape in the mid-1980s and especially the 1990s, again thanks to changing relations in, around, and beyond Hollywood. Starting in the mid-1970s, production dropped off sharply as studios focused on big-budget 'event' movies. Costs surged upwards, and corporate buy-outs became common. The industry saw further concentration in the mid-1980s. Over the course of the 1980s, however, many independent auteurs made critically acclaimed and popular films, among them David Lynch, John Sayles, Gregory Nava, Wayne Wang, the Coen brothers, Jim Jarmusch, Spike Lee, Susan Seidelman, and John Waters. Thanks to the popularity of cable TV and home video, the number of films in distribution rose, jumping from 206 indies in release in 1983 to 316 in 1988 (Wyatt 2000: 149). The extraordinary success of big-budget, star-driven, indie action films, among them *First Blood* (Kotcheff, 1982), *Rambo* (Cosmatos, 1985), *Red Heat* (Hill, 1988), and *Terminator 2* (Cameron, 1991), catapulted independent production company Carolco to prominence in theaters and at home on video; other 1980s indie power-brokers included Cannon Group, DeLaurentiis Entertainment Group, and Vestron.

The year 1989 was a watershed, thanks to 26-year-old Steven Soderbergh's *sex, lies & videotape*, which won both the Palme d'Or and the Best Actor prize at Cannes. With an initial price tag of $1.2 million, *sex, lies & videotape* grossed $24.7 million in its initial domestic release. By 2001 it had earned over $100 million, proving beyond doubt that independent films could attract mainstream domestic and international audiences (Holt 2002: 304).

New Line was the first of the so-called 'major independent' companies, also known as 'mini-majors,' to move to a new level. Begun in the late 1960s as a non-theatrical distributor catering to art and exploitation-oriented college audiences,

Figure 1.2 Ann (Andie MacDowell) and Graham (James Spader) in *sex, lies & videotape* (Soderbergh, 1989). Courtesy of Outlaw/Kobal Collection.

during the 1970s and 1980s New Line added sexploitation and gay films, rock documentaries, and 'midnight specials' to its lists, thereby pleasing markets ignored by the majors. By the end of the 1980s, thanks to *The Nightmare on Elm Street* series and, especially, the wildly successful *Teenage Mutant Ninja Turtles* series and franchise (the first film, directed in 1990, grossed a whopping $135 million), New Line had struck it rich (Wyatt 1998a: 77). The success brought media mogul Ted Turner's attention: he bought New Line in 1993. Then in 1996 Turner Broadcasting Corporation merged with Time-Warner, bringing New Line and its Turner-designated specialist 'indie' arm Fine Line into the Warner Bros. family. And post 2000, in January 2001, Time-Warner's $112 billion merger with America Online created a veritable media behemoth.[6]

Miramax (formed 1979), too, moved mainstream with a vengeance in the late 1980s and 1990s. In 1993 it became the first mini-major to be purchased by a major, the once-upon-a-time indie Walt Disney Studies. Known for aggressive marketing around controversy (e.g. the skillful promotion of *sex, lies & videotape* and *The Crying Game* [Jordan, 1992]), all eyes turned to Miramax following the phenomenal success of Quentin Tarantino's 1994 *Pulp Fiction*. Winning the Palme d'Or at Cannes, nominated for seven Academy Awards, including best picture and best director (it won best original screenplay), *Pulp Fiction* grossed more than $100 million in US theaters and more than $200 million worldwide (Merritt 2000: 385). Tarantino imitators sprang up everywhere, all hoping for similar success. By the end of the decade, most of the major studios had – as earlier in the late 1970s and 1980s – again jumped on the indie bandwagon, creating indie arms like Fox Searchlight, Sony Picture Classics, and Paramount Classics. Many studios even 'injected [themselves] with some of independent film's DNA and created [their] own "indie" movies: *American Beauty*, *Being John Malkovich*, *Election*, *The Matrix*, etc.' (Kliot and Vicente 2002: 53).

Meanwhile the number of films submitted to Sundance zoomed upwards, from 60 dramatic features in 1987 (Merritt 2000: 354) to more than 849 competing for 16 slots in 1997 (Turan 2002: 32). Alternative festivals like Slamdance sprang up to accommodate directors whose films had been rejected. Begun in 1995, by 2002 Slamdance itself had 'over 2,000 films vying for slots' (Turan 2002: 33). And in a telling example of how much times have changed, in 1999 the IFP's Independent Spirit Awards were opened to *all* films made in a 'spirit' of independence: Paramount's *Election* won best film, best director, and best screenplay. Critics began to talk disparagingly of 'Indiewood' and 'dependies.' Final tally for the 1990s: contraction and, for smaller companies and films especially, an increasingly competitive market.

Bridging the millennium: today's indie landscape

As of 2003, all seven major studios – Disney, Warner Brothers, Twentieth Century–Fox, Sony, United Artists–MGM, Paramount, and Universal – have independent arms.[7] Only two really well-heeled independent production companies, Artisan and Lions Gate, still stand alone,[8] though the 2002 merger of Intermedia and Spyglass with the German Initial Entertainment Group, *Variety* reported, has created a kind of third entity, a company in 'a league of its own between the studios and the indie sector' (Dawtrey 2002: 14). With connections both to Disney distribution and pay-TV deals in Europe with Canal Plus, Sogecable and Kirch Media, Intermedia is poised to take greater risk on a few movies, for greater rewards: *Terminator 3* (Mostow, 2003) is one of its titles.

Vivendi–Universal's 2002 purchase of leading New York independent production company Good Machine is emblematic of the ongoing mainstreaming of influential margins. Launched in 1991 from a small loft space in lower Manhattan by writer–producer–Columbia professor James Schamus and his partner Ted Hope, Good Machine produced many important independent films over the years, among them *Safe* (Haynes, 1995) and *The Wedding Banquet* (Lee, 1993). The company survived by doing line producing for hire and keeping overhead costs low. Many films were commercially successful thanks to centrist marketing strategies which, as Wyatt and Marchetti have argued of *The Wedding Banquet*, in many ways reinforced, rather than questioned, cultural stereotypes.[9] The creation of a foreign sales company also gave Schamus and Hope greater control of Good Machine's products, increased financing sources, and provided information about what people in the international marketplace wanted.[10] Today renamed Focus Features, with Schamus and Good Machine sales partner David Linde aboard, Focus serves as Universal's indie arm, functioning 'as a magnet for talent, keeping filmmakers like Ang Lee, Steven Soderbergh, Spike Jonze, Neil LaBute, Mira Nair, and Todd Haynes . . . in the Universal fold, and creating an incubator for emerging filmmakers and stars' (Bing 2001: 1). True to expectation, Focus connections have been making money and garnering kudos. Focus's first acquisition was *The Pianist*, which cost France's Canal Plus $40 million to produce; their first title in distribution, the British–French co-production *Billy Elliot* (Daldrey, 2000), earned $100 million worldwide.

Since 2000 several American independents have made a considerable amount of money in theaters as well, among them: Miramax's *In The Bedroom* (Field, 2001), $36 million; Fox Searchlight's *One Hour Photo* (Romanek, 2002), $31 million; Lions Gate's *Monster's Ball* (Forster, 2001), also $31 million; and IFC-distributed mega-hit *My Big Fat Greek Wedding*, over $200 million (Glucksman 2003). Generally, however, theatrical profits are not large – if they even occur. Indicative of what is at stake – or, better, at risk – are the 2000 grosses of films acquired at Sundance.

While bigger box-office takers included New Line's *Love and Basketball* (Prince-Blythewood), $27 million, *Boiler Room* (Younger), $16 million, and Lions Gate's *American Psycho* (Herron), $15 million, only five other films – *The Tao of Steve* (Goodman), *Groove* (Harrison), *Urbania* (Shear), *Chuck and Buck* (Arteta), and *Girlfight* (Kusama) – even passed the $1 million mark (Glucksman 2001).[11]

Meanwhile, for those who are most on the margins, without production backing or distribution help from majors or mini-majors – i.e. the majority of documentarians, everyone who makes avant-garde work, and the many young and old hopefuls (in particular African Americans, Latinos, Asian Americans, and/or women) who helm short and feature fiction films – the situation today is far worse than when the current indie boom began in the late 1970s and early 1980s. State and federal funding have dried up, and although there are now literally hundreds of festivals screening independent films, only a few – Sundance and Toronto prime among them – net pickups.[12] Granted, Cannes has canonized a few indie auteurs – David Lynch, the Coen brothers, and Michael Moore regularly meet with critical and audience acclaim – but most independent films do not perform well in foreign markets. Compounding the problem is the fact that the more important festivals now serve as 'glitzy launching pads' for films specialty distributors have themselves produced (Bing 2001). In consequence, and as with studio films, multiple windows have become more important to marketing and exhibition.

Like Soderbergh, Tarantino, and others before them, some directors have capitalized on the buzz surrounding their indie debuts to move into studio productions or to move back and forth between studio and independent productions: David O. Russell, Darren Aronofsky, Wes Anderson, Paul Thomas Anderson, and Larry Clark are examples. But many find it hard to get a second feature off the ground, let alone into theaters. To reduce production costs and explore new options, both first-time and established indie makers have been turning to digital video, which the majors tend to use only for special effects or to check dailies. For those working on micro-budgets, digital video has several advantages. Because videotape and processing are inexpensive, directors can more easily shoot when they need or want to, and actors' performances can be more natural. Because directors own their cameras and do their own editing on computer, they can re-shoot and re-edit as desired. They can even take their feature to festivals without spending time and money on a blow-up, get feedback there, and further refine their movie.

For bigger budget digital productions, a current trend is to shoot with 24-frame high-definition cameras (also used for television production), then blow the picture up to 'pass' as 35mm: *Chuck and Buck* (Arteta, 2000), *The Anniversary Party* (Leigh and Cumming, 2001), and *Lovely and Amazing* (Holofcener, 2002) are cases in point.[13] In the last few years, digital production companies committed to making high-quality digital features have sprung up: among the more important count InDigEnt Film, Open City Films–Blow Up Pictures, and Agenda 2000 (the last can even guarantee distribution because its parent company is the Independent Film Channel).

But the biggest problem confronting digital movies remains theatrical distribution: reducing costs by no means guarantees pickup. Aggressive promotion by a studio or an independent distributor is still crucial, and, as mentioned earlier, marketing costs have skyrocketed. While digital video can readily be shown on broadcast, cable, and satellite television as well as on home video, theatrical exhibition generally involves transfer from video to film, a pricey process. Wide-scale roll-out of digital cinema in theaters is easily five years off. With 35,000 screens in the US and another 150,000 worldwide, NATO (National Association of Theater Owners) insists – and studios increasingly concur – that there must be worldwide agreement on format.[14] A second obstacle is cost: theater owners are reluctant to foot the bill for expensive equipment (as much as $150,000 per theater), when distributors stand to save up to $1 billion in print and shipping costs per year and a 35mm projector, which costs $30,000, can last two to three decades with proper care. Finally, there's the question of product: although there are three times as many digital theaters since Twentieth Century–Fox's 2002 distribution of Lucasfilm's $120 million *Star Wars: Episode II* (Lucas), digital releases have only doubled (Ellingson 2003a: 44). For exhibitors, mini-majors and studios and *not* smaller independents hold the answer to the current 'chicken and egg' conundrum. As Technicolor's Russ Winter puts it: 'Why should I buy systems when there are no digital films [being made]?' and 'Why should I make digital films when there are no systems in place?' (quoted, Dinglasan and James 2002: 40).

As a medium, film is therefore not (yet) dead, in spite of those like George Lucas who declaim: 'I love film, but it's a 19th century invention' (Romano 2002: 37). Acclaimed cinematographer John Bailey, who shoots on both film and video, predicts that 'it's going to be a long-time before film is replaced as a capture medium because it's so beautiful' (Bloom 2003: A4). Kodak and other companies are continuing to invest in, for example, alternative film formats that offer sharper images and more fluid motion.[15] Nonetheless, at the end of September 2003 Kodak announced that it is de-emphasizing film in favor of digital video.

Because theatrical distribution is so difficult to secure, after the success of *The Blair Witch Project* (Myrick and Sánchez, 1999), many smaller independents look to the internet as an alternative way to market and even distribute their movies. Bigger independents and studio arms are also interested. Yet here, too, there are problems: download times for large files are impossibly long for people with dial-up, i.e. the overwhelming majority of US households; and even cable TV brings no guaranteed audiences – different markets receive different bundles of programs, at divergent prices.

In a world where creativity and market are so thoroughly entwined, the challenges confronting lovers of independent films at the start of the new millennium are thus many. What does the future hold in store? Will the move towards the mainstream from the margins continue? How is the rugged appeal of indies to be rekindled?

Our 'takes' on names and networks

This collection offers an unprecedented look at the scope of indie options and the field of indie controversies. Though we differ in our approaches, we all feel passionately that *how* indies are defined, made, and shown makes a difference. We are thus keenly interested in the interface of economics, technology, aesthetics, and ideology. We recognize, of course, that in a world dominated by Hollywood product, independents are necessarily in positions of dependence. But even though constraints are multiple, we know that creative imagination, determination, and courage continue to be present.

Several contributors consequently speak to the mainstream from the margins, measuring contemporary American independent features in light of independent traditions encompassing earlier American feature, experimental short, documentary, and foreign films. Several explore emerging publics, new media, or novel marketing. Others look at more mainstream work, although we generally avoid detailed analysis of films produced and released by mini-majors or studios. A number of chapters survey audiences, distinguishing them by gender, generation (Generation X), sexual preference (Generation Q), ethnicity and race (GenerAsian X).

To set the tone for our investigations, we begin in Part I, 'Critical formations,' by reprinting four articles and one excerpt which discuss core antecedents of contemporary trends. As we see it, contemporary 'indie' origins are diverse, including unequal parts of:

- late 1960s–early 1980s identity politics (see David James' concept of counter-cinema);
- 1960s–1970s American and European art and experimental 'auteurs' (per Annette Insdorf, with scads of French directors, a handful of Germans and Italians, and select Swedes as models; witness also, however, Cassavetes, *et al.*, and see Jonas Mekas on the contributions of the American avant-garde); and
- 1970s–1980s exploitation flicks (via Ed Lowry's study of a leading 1970s' low budget action distributor).

Makers themselves, Mekas and Jost in particular, insist that community networking and public funding are crucial to artistic exploration.

Part II, 'Cult film/cool film,' showcases original essays, investigating the importance of 'eccentrics' and 'characters' to independent films and their audiences. Thanks to the indie film's outsider (commercial, institutional, social) status, it often connotes the hip, the cool, the transgressive. For Diane Negra, late 1980s' and 1990s' independent films signal and sell marketable 'hipness' thanks to actors, like 'Queen of the indies' Parker Posey, who seem to embody 'independence' by being more concerned with their craft than with being stars. Whether such performers appear exclusively in independent productions or, like Posey, cross over to mainstream movies – here think also of Harvey Keitel, Rosie Perez, Steve Buscemi, Christina Ricci, and Johnny Depp; the list is long! – their attention to manner and 'look' adds cultural cachet. In 'Dark, disturbing, intelligent, provocative, and quirky: avant-garde cinema of the 1980s and 1990s,' Joan Hawkins investigates the importance of 'downtown' location with respect to exhibition spaces and makers' and audiences' attitudes. Hawkins argues that the brutal, ironic films of Neil LaBute, David Lynch, Todd Solondz, and others marry avant-garde and exploitation traditions to postmodern convictions, thereby advertising bohemian resistance to middle-class values. Ian Conrich carries Hawkins' brief discussion of exploitation onwards, exploring the entrepreneurial success and nostalgic, small-town values that undergird what he terms the 'crusade of Troma Entertainment.' He documents the inventive approaches – from straight-to-video filmmaking to television series to internet sites to T-shirts to body art – that producer–distributor Lloyd Kaufman uses to enlist diehard fans for low-budget, burlesque, horror products like the *Toxic Avengers* series.

While 'star power' represents the major studios' most crucial marketing and advertising asset, independent films are often marked by quite a different set of movers and shakers. The three essays in Part III, 'Iconoclasts and auteurs,' study innovative producer–directors. Over the thirty-year span of his career, John Sayles has been dedicated to portraying marginal groups and exploring social issues, yet he maintains mainstream connections, financing his own films by writing and rewriting scripts. In 'Bet on yourself,' Diane Carson uncovers core themes in Sayles's diverse films and tracks his work with ever larger budgets, including, since 1997, studio (Sony Pictures) distribution. Ethiopian-by-birth Haile Gerima stands further outside the studio system. For three decades, he has managed – most recently with foreign as well as community funding – to produce, direct, and distribute his films. In 'Sacred shield of culture' Mark A. Reid focuses on two of Gerima's films, *Bush Mama* (1975) and *Sankofa* (1993), which foreground issues of importance to the African diaspora and to black women in particular. Gay producer–director–distributor Wakefield Poole – the subject of José Capino's 'Seminal fantasies' – also exemplifies indie ingenuity. Surveying Poole's arty porn films, Capino asks whether independents are defined by theatrical exhibition, stylistic, and financial models or whether they represent specific anti-Hollywood practices; boldly, he answers 'both.' Thanks to 'four-walling,' his second film, *Boys in the Sand* (1971), earned more per screen than did the then number one hit *Diamonds Are Forever* (Hamilton, 1971). And no one can say that Poole lacked personal vision: he even made a softcore porn adaptation of the Bible!

Historically independent films have offered a 'safe haven' for those ignored or neglected by the major studios, among them ethnic, racial, sexual, and political 'minorities.' Part IV, 'Identity hooks ⟺ cultural binds,' showcases independent feature films addressed to 'marginal' audiences who achieved demographic prominence (if not necessarily economic clout) in the late 1980s and the 1990s. In contrast to Part III's emphasis on individual auteurs, Part IV studies *groups* of makers. Chris Holmlund continues José Capino's interest in gay topics and audiences with 'Generation Q's ABCs,' looking at a set of 1990s' films featuring – for just about the first time – queer kid characters. Aiming to push queer representation further 'out there,' she notes that the life-and-death concerns of queer minors were backpedaled in much of the mini-major work; she also censures the MPAA for being tougher on queer than on straight sexuality. Yet she acknowledges that today's smaller *and* bigger independent features, like experimental shorts and foreign films, showcase a greater range of queer identities than do documentaries. Christina Lane is more concerned with issues of access than with questions of content or style. In 'Just another girl outside the neo-indie' she surveys the difficulties confronting women directors, charging that the 1990s were worse for women than were the 1970s or 1980s. Unsurprisingly, she finds that women of color have a tougher time completing a second film than do white women, though she hopes that cable TV, digital technologies, networking, and creative marketing will provide new options for all. Gina Marchetti's 'Guests at *The Wedding Banquet*' compares US and Chinese films, pointedly wondering just how *American* is American independent film? After studying three films directed by Asian Americans and Asian Canadians, co-financed with foreign funds and targeted to Asian diaspora, youth, and queer audiences, she concludes that 'at its best, American independent film exhibits the sign of the hybrid.'

Part V, 'Shifting markets, changing media,' tackles questions of industry and media, examining structures that shape contemporary independent features and studying emerging web work. In 'Revisiting 1970s' independent distribution and marketing strategies' Justin Wyatt zeroes in on two independents which pioneered novel release strategies: Joe Camp's highly successful family film *Benji* (1974), and George C. Scott's lesser known melodrama *The Savage Is Loose* (1975). Both Camp and Scott deserve places in the indie hall of fame, argues Wyatt, for their contributions to the business side of independent filmmaking. Patricia R. Zimmerman zips up to the twenty-first century, assessing the ways in which online festivals, Flash and streaming reconfigured relationships between shorts and the feature film industry in 2002, post 9/11 and the US invasion of Afghanistan.

Though she treasures the increased access the internet affords, she urges us in 'Digital deployment(s)' to remember that *progressive* change depends not on technology as such but on how technology is *used*. Finally, in 'Channeling independence,' Robert Eberwein reminds us just how important the Sundance Channel and Independent Film Channel now are to indie production, distribution, and exhibition. Guarded about the future, Eberwein applauds the channels' presentation of issues confronting people of color, gays, and women, and praises their broadcasting of foreign films, classics, contemporary features, and shorts. Yet he worries about the impact that media mergers may have, and warns that because not everyone has access or tunes in to these cable stations, a 'cultural class system tied significantly, but not solely, to economics' remains in place.

For the future

Always concerned with audiences, sites, and attitudes, all of the contributors to *Contemporary American Independent Cinema: From the Margins to the Mainstream* weave together reflections on history with assessments of the present and speculations about the future. To facilitate viewing, discussion, and debate, the majority of the chapters examine films that are readily available on video or DVD (occasionally also on laser disc), and those of us who invoke lesser known indie features typically provide information about rental and purchase. The grid established by our contributors is easily supplemented and enriched, for each original piece is accompanied by a bibliography that provides additional titles and websites, and most essays mention additional films as well.[16]

Thanks to their mix of in-depth investigations and broad surveys, these discussions thus constitute a cornerstone collection. Of course, no set of explorations or overview of trends could possibly encompass the diverse worlds that together comprise contemporary American independent film. Many indie arenas merit additional investigation in the future. Those undertaking classes in media studies, American studies, and cultural studies may wish to explore further the topics mapped out here, examining regional or local festival programming, following area cable broadcasts and theatrical releases, tackling coverage of mergers, pursuing fresh indie 'faces' and established indie icons.

We would love to see focused appraisals of how festivals now serve as, in Toronto Film Festival head Piers Handling's words, 'alternative distribution networks' (Turan 2002: 8), as well as more sustained engagement with global, not just European, art cinema. We would welcome concerted attention to critically disdained straight-to-video genres like pulp action, and we would relish evaluations of the work that indie directors are now doing for cable TV series.

Finally, what of the new cross-over audiences that are emerging, thanks, for example, to the extraordinary popularity of hiphop and the growing number of indie films that bring music and rap into play? With Patricia Cardosa's debut film *Real Women Have Curves* (2002) earning nearly $6 million at the box office,[17] will more Latinas have their films shown in theaters and will more be able to make second and third films, as have Miguel Arteta and a handful of Latinos? What does the future hold for African American indies? With the number of movies destined for kids on the rise – and with more and more indie 'players' now parents – do today's kiddie indies enjoy the same success, for the same reasons, as *Benji* and *The Teenage Mutant Ninja Turtles*? What is happening to smaller distributors like Strand Releasing? How are we to assess the contributions of festival organizers and programmers like Sundance's Geoff Gilmore?

One thing's for sure, independent films are alive and – at least reasonably – well, with a record number of indie films in theaters, on television, DVD, and video, thanks to the enthusiasm of both niche and cross-over audiences. We hope our work will fuel future studies of independent films, markets, and media. At the very least, we wish to push the margins and expand the mainstream: our goal is to increase enthusiasm for, deepen understanding of, broaden representation within, and widen access to a real range of contemporary American independent film. As media analysts *and* as film buffs who like lots of different kinds of movies, we are eager to extend the kinds of indie films people see, make, talk and dream about!

Notes

1 In 2003 Miramax had a hand in forty Oscar nominations, while Fox Searchlight ended up with no nominations for the first time since 1997 (Brodesser 2003: 55).

2 For box office tracker Nielsen EDI, 'wide release' means more than 600 play dates (DiOrio 2002b: 1).

3 Additional criteria are indicative of the slide of independent film towards the mainstream. They include not only 'economy of means with particular attention paid to total budget and individual compensation' but also 'percentage of independent financing' (*Filmmaker* 2002).

4 According to Brian Taves, about 300 films – roughly 75 percent of total output – were made annually by 1930s' indie or B studios (Taves 1993: 313).

5 See further Hillier 1994: 6–17, Wyatt 1998b, and Cook 2000: 301–36.

6 That AOL–Time-Warner dropped 'AOL' from its name in September 2003 acknowledges the merger's failure and initiates a new phase in what nonetheless remains a single media-focused mega-corporation.

7 Crucially, all these studio-owned independents use their own distribution system. There are, however, differences among them. To touch on the three biggest studio-owned indies: Miramax retains a good deal of autonomy and can hardly be called Disney's classics or art division. Though it increasingly makes 'tweeners,' it still competes for specialty screens, preserving its reputation for producing 'films no one else would make,' and relying on sister company Dimension Films to produce more family friendly fare like Robert Rodriguez's *Spy Kids* series. Like Universal's Focus Features, Miramax prides itself on nurturing talent, in Miramax's case Matt Damon,

Gwyneth Paltrow, Judi Dench, and Phillip Noyce (Oppelaar 2002: 1 and 62; Rooney 2003: 54). Known for not paying directors much but instead offering artistic freedom, Fox Searchlight has slowly adjusted its line-up to include genre films, while continuing to pursue 'elusive niches' (McNary 2002: 46). Sony Picture Classics 'has supported a slate of 12–15 art-house titles with the same low-overhead strategies for the last 13 years' (Brodesser 2003: 55).

8 Lions Gate is increasingly reliant on the films it makes rather than sells – a risky proposition (Bloom 2002: 56). The company has recently had a few $10 million plus grosses with *Monster's Ball* (Forster, 2001), *Frailty* (Paxton, 2001), *American Psycho* (Herron, 2000), *O* (Nelson, 2001), and *Dogma* (Smith, 1999), but seventy titles a year go directly to video (DiOrio 2002a: 10).

9 See Wyatt 2001 and Marchetti 2000. The strategy articulated by Jennifer Schaefer, vice-president of self-dubbed 'gay and lesbian studio' Funny Boy Films, reflects a comparable move away from identity politics. Producing and releasing low-budget independents 'shot on 24P Hi-Def video at budgets close to $850,000,' Funny Boy Films, she says, 'isn't about making "gay films." It's about making comedies and dramas and horror films for gay characters. . . . [N]ow we're living our lives, and we just want to relate' (Nguyen 2003).

10 See Holland 2000: 36 and Wyatt 2001: 61–71.

11 One should of course bear in mind that box office gross, which is highly dependent on advertising commitments and release patterns, is just one indicator of a film's overall financial performance, and that video/DVD, television, and foreign sales also factor into the equation.

12 Other key festivals include Berlin, New York, New Directors/New Films, Rotterdam and Venice. Citing books 'created specifically to keep track of [festivals],' Turan finds 400 and 500 festivals typically listed. Yet he admits that 'because there is less overlap in these listings than one might expect . . . it's possible that an outlandish-sounding *New York Times* estimate of more than a thousand fests around the world might not be as wild as it seems' (2002: 2).

13 Trade publications like *Filmmaker Magazine* and *Variety* frequently discuss the impact of video technology on aesthetic choices. See for example Bergmann 2001, Broderick 2002, Veselich 2002, and Bloom 2003. For interviews with key players, see Roman 2001.

14 No one wants to repeat the problems posed by the three competing, and incompatible, digital sound formats currently in place in many, though hardly all, theaters. Since a number of theaters, especially older ones or those in small towns, are not equipped for digital playback, prints must carry all three digital formats, and provide an analog track as well. See Südderman 2002.

15 See Ellingson 2003a.

16 A handful of book-length studies provide overviews of independently produced and/ or distributed feature fiction films, occasionally in conjunction with documentaries. See, for example, Emanuel Levy's survey of feature films made from 1979–1998, *Cinema of Outsiders*; Greg Merritt's history of American independent films from the silents to 1999, *Celluloid Mavericks*; John Pierson's investigation of key makers, films (including documentaries), and venues from 1985 to 1995, *Spike, Mike, Slackers & Dykes*; E. Deidre Pribram's study of foreign and US feature fiction films, *Cinema and Culture*; Geoff Andrew's analysis of ten male auteurs from the 1980s and 1990s; Richard K. Ferncase's investigation of ten 1980s films (including two documentaries), *Outsider*

Features; and Jim Hillier's compilation of recent *Sight and Sound* articles, *American Independent Cinema*.

17 According to www.imdb.com, *Real Women Have Curves* cost $3 million; by 30 March 2003 it had earned $5,844,929 in the US alone.

Bibliography

Andrew, G. (1999) *Stranger than Paradise: Maverick Film-Makers in Recent American Cinema*, New York: Limelight Editions.

Bergmann, M. (2001) 'DV Shootout,' *Filmmaker Magazine* (winter): 58, 61–3.

Bing, J. (2001) 'Cutting the Deck,' *Filmmaker Magazine* (winter), available online: www.filmmakermagazine.com (accessed 2 July 2003).

—— (2002) 'Will U's Focus Prove Blurry? H'wood Tries to Re-Invent Role of Niche Divisions,' *Variety*, 387, 7 (1–14 July): 1, 46.

Bloom, D. (2002) 'Art-house Party,' *Variety*, 386, 13, supplement (13–19 May): 55–6.

—— (2003) 'It's No Longer All or Nothing for Digital,' *Variety*, 390, 8 (7–13 April): A4.

'Box Office and Business: *Real Women Have Curves*' (2003), available online: www.imdb.com (accessed 1 October 2003).

Broderick, P. (2002) 'Ultra-Low-Budget Moviemaking – the 2002 All-Digital Model,' *Filmmaker Magazine* (fall): 6–7, 49, 51, 91–2.

Brodesser, C. (2003) 'Fox: A Brighter Searchlight,' *Variety*, 390, 8 (7–13 April): 55.

Cook, D.A. (2000) 'Orders of Magnitude I: Majors, Mini-Majors, "Instant Majors," and Independents,' in D.A. Cook (ed.) *Lost Illusions*, Berkeley, Los Angeles and London: University of California Press, 301–36.

Dawtrey, A. (2002) 'Indie Combo Creates Big League Player,' *Variety*, 385, 9 (21–7 January): 14, 21.

Dinglasan, F. and James, C. (2002) 'Present and Future,' *Boxoffice* (February): 40–1.

DiOrio, C. (2002a) 'Lions Gate Goes on Lean Diet,' *Variety*, 388, 3 (2–8 September): 10, 16.

—— (2002b) 'Bowling for Breakout Niche Pix,' *Variety*, 388, 14 (18–24 November): 1.

Ellingson, A. (2003a) 'Film Is Dead?,' *Boxoffice* 139, 2 (February): 40–1.

—— (2003b) 'Digital Debate,' *Boxoffice* 139, 6 (June): 44–5.

Ferncase, R.K. (1996) *Outsider Features: American Independent Films of the 1980s*, Westport, CT, and London: Greenwood Press.

Filmmaker Magazine (2002) 'Nominations Announced for 2003 IFP Independent Spirit Awards,' 18 December, available online: www.filmmakermagazine.com (accessed 1 July 2003).

Filmmaker Magazine (2003) '25 New Faces of Indie Film' (summer), available online: www.filmmakermagazine.com (accessed 1 July 2003).

Glucksman, M. (2001) 'The Balance Sheet,' *Filmmaker Magazine* (winter), available online: www.filmmakermagazine.com (accessed 2 July 2003).

—— (2003) 'Natural Selection,' *Filmmaker* (winter), available online: www.filmmakermagazine.com (accessed 1 July 2003).

Handy, B. (1998) 'Truly Independent Cinema,' *Time Magazine*, 26 October: 93.

Harris, D. (2003) 'H'wood Renews Niche Pitch,' *Variety*, 390, 8 (7–13 April): 1, 54.

Hernandez, E. (1999) 'Pixel Nation,' *Filmmaker Magazine* (spring): 31–2.

Hillier, J. (1994) *The New Hollywood*, New York: Continuum.

—— (ed.) (2001) *American Independent Cinema*, London: British Film Institute.

Holland, G. (2000) 'Filmmaking Year Zero,' *Filmmaker Magazine* (winter): 34–7.

Holt, J. (2002) 'Steven Soderbergh,' in Y. Tasker (ed.) *Fifty Contemporary Filmmakers*, London and New York: Routledge, 303–11.

Kleinhans, C. (1998) 'Independent Features: Hopes and Dreams,' in J. Lewis (ed.) *The New America Cinema*, Durham, NC, and London: Duke University Press, 307–27.

Kliot, J. and Vicente, J. (2002) 'Past Is Prologue,' *Filmmaker* (fall): 53–4.

Levy, E. (1999) *Cinema of Outsiders: The Rise of American Independent Film*, New York: New York University Press.

McKay, J. (2001) 'In Print: Jim McKay Talks with Ray Carney about John Cassavetes,' *Filmmaker* (fall), available online: www.filmmakermagazine.com (accessed 2 July 2003).

McNary, D. (2002) 'Searchlight: Low, Steady Beam,' *Variety*, 387, 7 (1–14 July): 46.

Marchetti, G. (2000) '*The Wedding Banquet*: Global Chinese Cinema and the Asian American Experience,' in D. Hamamoto and S. Liu (eds.) *Countervisions: Asian American Film Criticism*, Philadelphia, PA: Temple University Press, 275–97.

Merritt, G. (2000) *Celluloid Mavericks: A History of American Independent Film*, Berkeley, CA: Thunder's Mouth Press.

Nguyen, T. (2003) 'Out of the Celluloid Closet,' *Filmmaker Magazine* (summer), available online: www.filmmakermagazine.com (accessed 1 July 2003).

Oppelaar, J. (2002) 'Harvey Beefs Up, Slims Down: Miramax Gets Back to Basics,' *Variety*, 388, 13 (11–17 November): 1, 62.

Pierson, J. (1995) *Spike, Mike, Slackers & Dykes*, New York: Hyperion.

Pribram, E.D. (2002) *Cinema and Culture: Independent Film in the United States, 1980–2001*, New York: Peter Lang Publishing.

Roman, S. (2001) *Digital Babylon: Hollywood, Indiewood & Dogme95*, Hollywood: iFilm Publishing.

Romano, S. (2002) 'DLP: A Report from the Trenches,' *Boxoffice*, 138, 2 (February): 36–7.

Rooney, D. (2003) 'Mira Takes It to Max,' *Variety*, 390, 8 (7–13 April): 54.

Südderman, M. (2002) 'Sound Advice,' *Filmmaker Magazine* (winter): 48–50.

Taves, B. (1993) 'The B Film: Hollywood's Other Half,' in T. Balio (ed.) *Grand Design: Hollywood as a Modern Business Enterprise: 1930–1939*, New York and Don Mills, Ontario: Charles Scribner's Sons–Maxmell Macmillan Canada, 313–50.

Turan, K. (2002) *Sundance to Sarajevo: Film Festivals and the World They Made*, Berkeley, Los Angeles, and London: University of California Press.

Veselich, M. (2002) 'Let There Be Light,' *Filmmaker Magazine* (winter): 38–41.

Wyatt, J. (1998a) 'The Formation of the "Major Independent": Miramax, New Line and the New Hollywood,' in S. Neale and M. Smith (eds.) *Contemporary Hollywood Cinema*, London and New York: Routledge, 74–90.

—— (1998b) 'From Roadshowing to Saturation Release: Majors, Independents, and

Marketing/Distribution Innovations,' in J. Lewis (ed.) *The New America Cinema*, Durham, NC, and London: Duke University Press, 64–86.

—— (2000) 'Independents, Packaging, and Inflationary Pressure in 1980s Hollywood,' in S. Prince (ed.) *A New Pot of Gold: Hollywood Under the Electronic Rainbow, 1980–1989*, New York: Charles Scribner's Sons, 142–60.

—— (2001) 'Marketing Marginalized Cultures: *The Wedding Banquet*, Cultural Identities, and Independent Cinema of the 1990s,' in J. Lewis (ed.) *The End of Cinema as We Know It: American Film in the Nineties*, New York: New York University Press, 61–71.

Part I

Critical formations

Chapter 2

Introduction to 'critical formations'

Chris Holmlund

American independent films of the 1960s and 1970s blazed many of the trails followed by today's indie features. The essays reprinted in Part I identify and explore three – often overlapping – groups of films:

- 'auteur' films (including avant-garde work);
- identity-based/socially conscious films; and
- exploitation films.

Some essays additionally look back to films made in the 1930s–1950s; a few discuss 1980s' developments. Drawn from sources that range from the now defunct *American Film* to ongoing journals (*Film Comment* and *The Velvet Light Trap*) to academic monographs published between 1978 and 1992, each essay was written with a specific audience in mind. Necessarily, this marks *how* each was written; it also suggests how diverse were and are the arenas that showcase American independent film. Topics and optics vary as well, indicating the fervor with which critics – and audiences – champion and debate issues surrounding independent film. All five pieces nonetheless share core traits. Most highlight certain films and disregard others; all reference specific production and distribution networks; all invoke concrete political and economic trends. Most importantly, all insist that American independent films must be viewed *in relation to* other work. We also find it significant that each author acknowledges alternative approaches and categories, and that all somehow speak from the margins to the mainstream.

Annette Insdorf's 1981 *American Film* article 'Ordinary people, European-style: or how to spot an independent feature' begins by invoking a variety of independently produced and distributed films. For Insdorf, only (relatively) *non*-commercial independent features (i.e. not exploitation films) really count as 'independents.' Known for her work on (among other subjects) François Truffaut, Jean-Luc Godard, and Krysztof Kieslowski, Insdorf here argues that US 1970s' and early

1980s' independent features share with foreign art films elements like casting, pace, dialogue, and political stance. As she succinctly puts it, American independent filmmakers like Richard Pearce, Victor Nuñez, John Sayles, Charles Burnett, and Barbara Kopple treat 'inherently American concerns with a primarily European style.' A similar fondness for 'auteur' films that highlight quintessentially American settings and characters through a signature style pervades critical appraisal of independent films from the 1980s onwards – witness the popularity of makers like the Coen brothers.

Jonas Mekas's slightly earlier (1978) essay 'Independence for independents,' also published in *American Film*, similarly emphasizes the non-commercial nature of independent film. Unlike Insdorf, however, Mekas is concerned most with the definition and promotion of avant-garde cinema, a vital reference point for scores of contemporary directors, from Yvonne Rainer to Todd Haynes to David Lynch, and more. With Shirley Clark, Emile de Antonio, Robert Frank, and others, a founding member of the New American Cinema Group, Mekas has been a prolific and influential avant-garde filmmaker since 1963. As author, co-director of the Filmmakers' Cooperative, director of the Anthology Film Archives, editor of the journal *Film Culture*, writer for *The Village Voice*, Mekas has simultaneously – and surely as importantly – been a tireless polemicist and organizer on behalf of avant-garde independent film. In this article, he briefly describes the birth (in 1962) and growth (throughout the 1960s and 1970s) of the Film-Makers' Cooperative, then underlines the importance of alternative production and distribution networks to anyone who seeks to avoid Hollywood style, content, and formula in his or her films. In conclusion – and, as he puts it, more 'skeptically' – he nevertheless maintains that 'creative explosions' have been, and will be, more important to any 'genuinely independent' avant-garde film than any and every form of supporting infrastructure.

Ed Lowry's 1986 essay on Dimension Pictures engages with the manifestly more commercial sub-set of independent films mentioned – and refused – by Insdorf: 1970s' low-budget exploitation movies. Model and source for many of today's independent films (from straight-to-video porn, horror, and martial arts movies to 'tweener' neo-noirs and actioners), exploitation genres serve as a backbone for summer blockbusters as well. Where Mekas discussed 1960s' and 1970s' avant-garde scenes in light of 1940s' and 1950s' work, Lowry situates 1960s' and 1970s' exploitation movies in relation to the B movies of the 1930s through the 1950s. In the several essays (and one book) that Lowry produced in his too short life (he died at age 33), he engaged with each of the three strands we identify as core to contemporary American independent film; he also produced a series of influential program notes on classic films for Cinema Texas. In this study, revised by Dana Polan on the basis of Lowry's notes and published posthumously in *The Velvet Light Trap*, he investigates a small – and, he argues, typical – 1970s' independent exploitation studio, Dimension Pictures. Lowry positions Dimension Pictures in relation to 1950s' and 1960s' independent companies producing 'schlock' for the new youth niche market. He insists, however, that market conditions of the 1970s were quite different from those of the 1950s and 1960s: by the 1970s the gap between the six major studios and small independents like Dimension Pictures was immense. Nonetheless, thanks to alternative exhibition networks (drive-ins, inner-city theaters) and mostly R-rated genre films, for a brief period small independents thrived *outside* the mainstream industry. By the 1980s, even that window had closed: as Lowry says, 'increased uniformity in exhibition practices . . . enabled the majors to consolidate their control of distribution.' A nuanced, but crucial, observation occurs in passing: Lowry applauds Dimension's efforts to hire qualified women and suggests that Stephanie Rothman's films often critique dominant gender ideology. He acknowledges, however, that Dimension – and Rothman – consistently used women's bodies, and violence, to 'sell' their movies.

Vehemently opposed to commercial film, and since 1973 a staunchly independent filmmaker (and actor, composer, essayist), Jon Jost, in a 1989 *Film Comment* article titled 'End of the indies,' condemns 1980s' 'mainstreaming' of independent films. Because 'indie' became 'in' during the 1980s, by the end of that decade, Jost charges, there was little artistic, aesthetic, or ideological difference between most independent films and Hollywood product. He stresses, moreover, that already in the 1970s the term 'independent' united a diverse group of films under a single *marketing* banner. Some films (among them his own) were more marginal, influenced by the European art traditions referenced by Insdorf or the American experimental films promoted by Mekas. By the end of the 1980s, however, small distributors for such films had disappeared, exhibition options had shrunk, and funding sources had shriveled. Nevertheless, Jost gestures in conclusion towards factors (video, computers, foreign financing, etc.) that he hopes will provide new outlets and opportunities for 'the real independent,' the 'genuine artist.' Not surprisingly, then, one finds Jost among the many 'no-budget' and 'low-budget' indie makers who now use digital video. As he enthusiastically commented to *Filmmaker Magazine*'s Eugene Hernandez, DV allowed him to 'start all over as it were, and be more like the 19-year-old kid I was in 1963 walking around with a Bolex in hand, not thinking about money, and seeing and learning.'

In sharp contrast to Jost's animated polemics, David E. James's assessment of alternative and mainstream cinemas and sub-cultural and dominant ideologies is sober and densely written. His basic points are, however, crystal clear, and crucial:

1   relations between Hollywood and alternative cinemas and mainstream and subcultures change over time, prompted by specific historical conditions and needs; *but*

2   alternative and Hollywood cinemas are always somehow interconnected and interdependent, never simply opposites; *because*

3   aesthetics and politics, industries and ideologies are linked.

This excerpt is from the first chapter of James's 1989 *Allegories of Cinema: American Film in the Sixties*. (Other chapters center on independents who worked as avant-garde 'auteurs,' among them Stan Brakhage, Andy Warhol, Jonas Mekas, Carolee Schneeman, Jon Jost, and Yvonne Rainer; another book, published in 1992, studies Mekas and the New York Underground.) True to his insistence in this excerpt on the connections among various kinds of films, and to mainstream and subcultures, in later chapters James discusses also exploitation films, certain Hollywood movies, foreign art films, and documentaries. In effect, his theoretical insights and practical studies thus combine those presented by the other four essays of Part I. As importantly, they serve as 'critical *foundations*' for the original contributions of this collection that follow.

Bibliography

Hernandez, E. (1999) 'Pixel Nation,' *Filmmaker Magazine* (spring): 31–2.

Chapter 3

Ordinary people, European-style
Or how to spot an independent feature

Annette Insdorf

'When I think of independent features, I think of *Texas Chain Saw Massacre* and Russ Meyer,' says *Polyester* director John Waters. 'Why does independent film have to be about Rosie the Riveter instead of *Chain Saw*'s Leatherface?' Waters has a point. In Hollywood the term 'independent' brings to mind Orion, Lorimar, and Melvin Simon Productions. To punks queuing up for a midnight screening of *The Last House on the Left, Eraserhead*, or *Pink Flamingos* at the Roxie Cinema in San Francisco, it brings to mind Wes Craven, David Lynch, or Waters himself. Three thousand miles away, at the Museum of Modern Art or Film Forum, the term suggests Mark Rappaport's *Impostors*. Down at the National Endowment for the Humanities, in Washington, DC, independent conjures up Richard Pearce's *Heartland*, an evocative study of a pioneer woman in Wyoming, circa 1910, made with an NEH grant.

Often, the filmmakers are puzzled, too. 'I don't want to be an "independent" director. I don't want to be a "Hollywood" director. I just want to make movies I care about,' says Ira Wohl, who won an Academy Award last year for his feature-length documentary *Best Boy* [1979]. But there is nothing like a round trip to Hollywood to show filmmakers like Wohl that the kinds of films they care about often force them to make a choice, and guarantee that they will choose to remain independent.

After his Academy Award, followed by a successful commercial run of *Best Boy* at the Sutton Theatre in New York, Wohl began to get a lot of advice. 'Move to California, be visible, find a television movie to direct, and then move from television films to features.' Wohl did go to California, but he discovered that being the director of a 'documentary about a 52-year-old retarded man,' even of an Academy Award-winning documentary, did not prove to be a calling card that would open many doors. When, Oscar in hand, he tried to peddle a script about elderly people forced to pay up or move out by the condomania that is sweeping Miami, Florida, Wohl found himself on the next flight back to New York, an independent in spite of himself.

Figure 3.1 Jerrine (Megan Folsom) in *Heartland* (Pearce, 1979). Courtesy of Wilderness Women/Filmhaus Productions/Kobal Collection.

'As soon as I mentioned the words "old people" or "retired people," I was thrown out the door,' he confesses sardonically.

> When I said I wanted to make a movie with no murders and no rocket ships, people replied, 'If you don't have a character flying or dying, forget it.' And I found that agents don't really have an interest in looking for independent money.

Wohl still reads the scripts he gets in the mail, but insists that 'it doesn't make any sense to do some exploitation murder or horror picture to be a Hollywood director. Anyway, they don't need *me* to do that.' Wohl is completing his screenplay, despite no immediate hope of funding, on the assumption that the finished script will be produced one way or another.

Maxi Cohen and Joel Gold are encountering a similar problem. Having co-directed *Joe and Maxi* – a documentary that traces Maxi's relationship with her father, who was dying of cancer – has not exactly paved the way for their next project, a fiction feature called *Moving Violations*. With a rueful smile, Gold recalls the time

> we went to a studio executive to pitch the idea of *Moving Violations*. The way she explained things was not very appetizing to people who have been very much on their own, and have struggled to maintain their integrity. The kind of control the studio would have, from point A to

point Z, would render me helpless. That I had done a documentary meant nothing in Hollywood; they think you need a different sensibility for features.

John Hanson and Rob Nilsson, the directors of *Northern Lights* – winner of the Caméra d'or at the 1979 Cannes Film Festival – had been 'in conversation with the studios about development deals, but then we made the conscious choice not to go that route,' says Hanson. 'The studio system is set up to eat people like me. I would only consider a studio if I had control – like final cut and my choice of producer.'

The director of *Gal Young 'Un* has a sharpened sense of independence after his West Coast encounters. Victor Nuñez has taken

six or seven trips out there this year. So far, nothing there has seemed as interesting as what the potential of independent films could be. I've tried to stay open to the possibility of the 'big time' or 'real world' or whatever cliché you want to use, but there seems to be so much stuff that gets in the way for me. I'm used to a small crew and intimate situation; at this point I don't feel that's possible in Hollywood.

The films of these directors are in fact not commercial in the studio sense, and this distinguishes them from filmmakers like George Romero, Tobe Hooper, John Carpenter, and David Cronenberg, who to one degree or another exist outside the industry orbit, but whose affection for Grand Guignol, violence, and sex has attracted commercial money. *Northern Lights* and *Best Boy* are not 'portfolio' films made for the purpose of hopping to Hollywood.

What distinguishes *Northern Lights* and numerous other independent features from Hollywood products is a combination of such elements as casting, pace, cinematic style, and social or moral vision. Countering big stars with fresh faces, big deals with intimate canvases, and big studios with regional authenticity, these filmmakers treat inherently American concerns with a primarily European style. In their choice of form and working methods, and in their urgency to record subjects rarely seen in commercial films, these politically sensitive and geographically rooted directors resist Hollywood's priorities and potential absorption.

Northern Lights is a populist film about the 'rebel roots' of America. It recounts the story of North Dakota's Norwegian immigrant farmers who in 1915 organ-ized the Nonpartisan League to resist exploitation by the banks. Photographed in stark black and white by independent cinema's ubiquitous Judy Irola (and by Dolores Neuman), using local farmers in small roles and unknowns as leads, *Northern Lights* often feels like a documentary. According to Hanson, he and

Nilsson chose nonprofessional actors because North Dakota is 'a place where the dialect and history are so different from the rest of America that you can't pull in people from New York and Los Angeles.'

The visual inspiration for *Northern Lights* included the photographs of Walker Evans and Dorothea Lange, starkly moving records of America's dispossessed. This stress on the dignity of the poor is part of an American tradition which goes back to Emerson and Whitman, and the concern with art grounded in ordinary experience rather than escapism informs much of independent cinema. From John Cassavetes's early films, like *Shadows*, to contemporary feature documentaries, there has been a sense of a frame supple enough to let life seep in and spill out at the edges.

While the theme, concerns, and texture of *Northern Lights* are American, its directors confess that their sources are foreign. 'Bergman, Bertolucci, Fellini, but most of all *Les 400 coups, Jules et Jim*, etc.,' according to Nilsson. In fact, he finds that 'the notion of a wave – a group of people swapping juices, like Truffaut and Godard – has been a model for our vision, both political and artistic.' The slow pacing of *Northern Lights* is consistent with a European tradition that values a leisurely narrative over breakneck, television commercial-style pacing, reflection over action, and a depiction of political realities over sex and violence.

The abundance of dialogue – especially, intelligent dialogue – in many new independent features also invites comparison to European films, from Bergman to Jean Eustache's *The Mother and the Whore*. Like *Northern Lights*, John Sayles's *The Return of the Secaucus Seven* replaced typical movie action with a literate script, experienced actors with engaging newcomers, and brisk pace with a leisurely narrative unfolding. Like Renoir's *The Rules of the Game*, it reunites several characters for a weekend under one roof, accommodating shifting attractions and commitments, as well as the passing of an era (antiwar activism rather than aristocracy).

Independent features tend to illustrate Emerson's declaration: 'The invariable mark of wisdom is to find the miraculous in the common.' This requires a palpable sense of geography, evident in the rich images of the Midwest in Richard Pearce's *Heartland*, or the gritty textures of Watts in Charles Burnett's *Killer of Sheep*, or the hallucinatory ambience of New York's Soho in Jonathan Sarno's *The Kirlian Witness*. Unable and unwilling to create an artificial backdrop on a sound stage, directors like Victor Nuñez have grounded their films in the tones and rhythms of regional culture. Nuñez shot *Gal Young 'Un* in an area he knows intimately, rural Florida.

Based on a short story by Marjorie Kinnan Rawlings, Nuñez's first feature traces the unlikely relationship between Mattie, a widow of means (superbly played by Dana Preu in her acting debut), and Trax (David Peck), a young conman who courts and wins her. More precisely, he wins the chance to exploit Mattie and her property, first by building a whiskey still on her land and later by bringing home his young girl friend Elly (J. Smith). Mattie's skepticism and suffering are presented as quietly as the backwoods country of Florida; like her land, this woman can be accommodating but, if ignited, can blaze with a stunning fury.

The prevalence of creative directorial teams in independent American features also sets them apart from the studio mainstream. The direction of *Northern Lights* was a collaborative act: Nilsson worked with the actors, Hanson with the crew, but 'during a shot,' Hanson recalls, 'we'd both be huddling behind the camera, deciding together if it's a good take.' Documentaries in particular, from Barry Alexander Brown and Glenn Silber's *The War at Home* to Deborah Shaffer and Stewart Bird's *The Wobblies*, have come to rely on collaboration. According to Maxi Cohen,

> When you make a documentary where you really discover the story as you go along, the person behind the camera is in essence a director of what is happening. What and how he or she chooses to shoot formulates the story.

Independent features share preoccupations, as well as methods and sensibilities. Several recent films have dealt with 'hidden history' (material ignored by traditional textbooks) or subjects usually avoided by commercial films (aging, retardation, cancer). A fine example of revisionist history is *The Life and Times of Rosie the Riveter*, Connie Field's vivid portrait of women who worked during World War II at factory jobs traditionally reserved for men. The result is a heightened awareness of how women were seduced into these jobs when the government needed them, and how they were then forced back into the home when the government didn't.

Films like *Rosie the Riveter* and *The Wobblies*, about the Industrial Workers of the World, not only provide glimpses of bygone eras, but also offer a new image of old people. They are less senile 'senior citizens' than creatures of conviction who have stuck to their ideals with joyful fervor. Likewise, *Free Voice of Labor: The Jewish Anarchists* and *Image Before My Eyes* focus on the elderly but feisty survivors of long-dead movements.

In *Free Voice of Labor*, co-directors Steven Fischler and Joel Sucher chronicle the closing down of a Yiddish anarchist newspaper and move into an affectionate study of the Eastern European immigrants who brought a revolutionary dimension to New York life in the 1890s. Their delightful interviews with old Jewish agitators contradict the image of anarchists as crazy bomb throwers and reveal the paradoxical gentleness that infused their eccentric politics.

Similarly, *Image Before My Eyes* — a documentary on Polish–Jewish culture before the Holocaust which enjoyed a surprisingly successful commercial run in New York — 'brings to light the unpublicized, unsung threads of Jewish history,' according to director Josh Waletzky. The film interweaves photographs, rare home movies of the period, and interviews with Holocaust survivors. At a time when it often seems that the options for Jewish identity are polarized into assimilation or Zionism, *Image Before My Eyes* offers models of tradition and modernization which are not mutually exclusive.

The aged, the retarded (*Best Boy*), and the terminally ill (*Joe and Maxi*) are hardly the staples of conventional entertainment; consequently, the very decision to make such films can be seen as courageous. *Joe and Maxi* at least made it into commercial theaters; this has not yet been the case for *Pilgrim, Farewell*, Michael Roemer's devastating fiction feature about a tough and vibrant woman with terminal cancer. Although this unsentimental portrait took honors at the Venice International Film Festival, American distribution has not been forthcoming. Made primarily with German financing, the narrative is similar to Roemer's highly acclaimed *Dying*, a television documentary exploration of the same theme.

While many independent features have garnered excellent reviews and voluble supporters, their box-office performance has been so slack as to jeopardize the filmmakers' chances of making more films. Indeed, the grim realities of small audiences and smaller revenues have led a significant number of directors to make the move from documentaries to fiction.

For Stan Lathan, director of *The Sky Is Gray*, a film about blacks in rural Louisiana which won the grand prize at the 1980 American Film Festival, the movement into fiction came about because he found himself

> staging more and more, even if it was just sitting with the person to be interviewed, getting him to understand what the questions would be and how the answers could make the film better. I found myself reaching for specific answers from people, implanting my own prejudices and feelings. The next logical step was to make dramatic films that speak to the same kinds of issues.

The Dozens, Randall Conrad and Christine Dall's account of the experiences of a woman just out of jail, began as a documentary, but evolved into fiction when the filmmakers started to feel constrained by the documentary format. As Dall told writer Eric Breitbart:

> We didn't think we'd be able to follow one or two women around and capture on film the experience of being out of jail. We realized that if we did it fictionally and scripted it, we'd get in more information and more complexity.

Like Conrad and Dall, Barbara Kopple (*Harlan County, U.S.A.*) has already made the leap from 'recording' to 'inventing': she has completed a theatrical feature about a black Pentecostal preacher who works in a textile factory and the white organizer he meets. 'It's the story of their relationship,' reveals the 34-year-old filmmaker, 'and the risks and commitments that the people in the community take when they organize a union.' The film, based on a true story, was written by Horton Foote, who also wrote the script for *To Kill a Mockingbird*.

Unlike many of her colleagues, Kopple doesn't

> see Hollywood as an enemy. They're people with a tremendous amount of power; they make a lot of films that are very mediocre, but some of great quality. For example, an enormously talented director like Robert Young has been able to survive in that world. Hollywood hasn't stopped him from doing the things he wants to do.

Kopple has a development deal with Twentieth Century–Fox for *Peekskill*, a fiction film dealing with the Peekskill Riots of 1949.

> It's about three youths from different backgrounds – one who grew up in Peekskill all her life, one whose family goes there every summer, and one who works in a local gas station – coming together and coming of age with the backdrop of Paul Robeson's concert.

Kopple is working with Elizabeth Swados, who will do the music. 'We're definitely open to making the film any way we can,' Kopple says. 'The best thing I can do with the studio is to be very straightforward about what I want to do.'

And the directors of *Northern Lights* have moved in time and space, but not in spirit: Nilsson is preparing a film about a long-distance runner, set in the Bay Area, while Hanson's project is a contemporary story about a 30-year-old woman steelworker. He plans to give it

> the same kind of human richness and solid history as *Northern Lights*. Many people my age don't go to the movies any more. I'm committed to putting a different kind of American face on the screen, one that will bring adults back to the movies.

Chapter 4

Independence for independents

Jonas Mekas

The avant-garde filmmaker has progressed from a 'primitive' working at the margins of the commercial film to one whose work constitutes perhaps the very center of the art of the cinema. A look at the various terms used over the years by American filmmakers to describe the avant-garde film shows the progression.

Between 1930 and 1950 the terms *avant-garde film* and *experimental film* were in use. *Avant-garde* (in hyphenated form) described the European avant-garde film, and *experimental* described the American. But around 1950 filmmakers began to feel that *experimental* implied that their films were only experiments or tentative attempts, and in the next decade these terms were replaced by *personal film*, *individual film*, and *independent film*.

By 1960, however, the three terms were largely dismissed as inadequate. *Personal* and *individual* were invalidated by the advances of the auteur theory, which made it clear that not only the films of Maya Deren or Hans Richter were personal and individual but also the films of Robert Bresson and Alfred Hitchcock. As for *independent*, it was invalidated by Hollywood, where the term was used by 'runaway' directors like Otto Preminger. So in the early 1960s the terms *New American Cinema* and *underground film* came into use. The first was probably picked up from an article of mine and the second from a speech by Marcel Duchamp in which he declared that the artist of tomorrow 'will go underground.'

The terms were used interchangeably until approximately 1967 (a third term, *home movie*, was employed during the same period), when two usages – or directions – became apparent. One was the double-edged combination of *avant-garde–independent*. The other was the abandonment of all special terms and the use simply of *Cinema* (or the variation *formal Cinema*). This use, particularly stressed at Anthology Film Archives, amounted to a declaration of independence of all forms of cinema: all forms were seen as equal in the eyes of art, regardless of length, budget, the number of persons involved and regardless of what formal category or genre a film belonged to. Stan Brakhage was not making avant-garde films, he was making Cinema; Carl Dreyer was not making commercial films, he was making Cinema.

These changes in terminology and focus indicate a long and constant anxiety of filmmakers working in the avant-garde film mode to define their own identity, to understand where their art belongs within the art of cinema. It has been a slow movement away from the status of outcasts to the status of filmmakers whose work is far from marginal – perhaps, just the opposite. To paraphrase Peter Kubelka: It's the commercial film that is on the margin of the art of cinema and that needs a proper and clear term to describe it; avant-garde filmmakers do not need any terms to describe their work – their work is, simply, Cinema.

A similar process of growing and changing consciousness took place in the area of the distribution of avant-garde film.

Until approximately 1960, the distribution of avant-garde-independent films was conducted through the same companies that distributed most commercial films. Private companies that specialized in the distribution of independently made films were run the same way as those that dealt exclusively with commercial films. It was always the distributor whose taste determined which films were 'distributable' and which were not. The filmmaker had to sign a long-term exclusive contract and received only a fraction of the profits.

In 1960 a mixed group of independent filmmakers (including Shirley Clarke, Emile de Antonio, Gregory J. Markopoulos, Robert Frank, Adolfas Mekas, Harold Humes, Peter Bogdanovich, Ed Bland, Lionel Rogosin, and me) created the New American Cinema Group. Among its purposes was to propose new methods of production and distribution, and on January 19, 1962, the group created its own cooperative film distribution center, the Film-Makers' Cooperative. This has proved to be an event that most crucially affected the development of the avant-garde film in America.

The Film-Makers' Cooperative introduced six principles radically opposed to the practices prevalent in film distribution:

1   The cooperative will distribute every film submitted to it; it won't reject any film; it won't pass judgment on the quality and content of films distributed.
2   The cooperative is governed by the filmmakers themselves through their yearly elected representatives.
3   The filmmakers sign no contracts with the cooperative, remain the owners of their films, and can withdraw their films from the cooperative at any time. This also means that they can distribute their films simultaneously through as many other distribution centers as they wish.
4   All income from rentals goes to the filmmaker, except for twenty-five percent needed to run the cooperative.
5   All films are equal at the cooperative, and no one film is pushed above any other. All films are listed in a similar way in the catalog, and it's up to the

person who rents the film to know what's needed and who are the best filmmakers to fill that need.

6   Filmmakers' income/expense balance sheets are kept by the secretary of the cooperative, and copies are sent to the filmmakers. There is nothing more important for a cooperative (besides the proper physical upkeep of the films themselves) than to have the trust – a total trust – of its member filmmakers.

These principles have set a new standard for film distribution on which film-makers everywhere should insist. There are some who reproach the avant-garde filmmakers for their concern with economics. The artist's business is supposed to be art and nothing but art. But serious artists in all the arts and at all times have understood the necessity of having a grip on the economics of their art. We see it today as the only way of continuing our work on our own terms, not on the terms dictated by producers and distributors.

The creation of the Film-Makers' Cooperative came at a crucial time in the development of the avant-garde–independent film. The same fate that befell the filmmaking generation of the 1940s – a numbing of energies from lack of public interest and recognition – was threatening to befall the generation of the 1950s. The cooperative gathered the filmmakers together, brought their work to the attention of the interested public, and provided the filmmakers with perhaps a limited but nevertheless very often crucial income. This became the first gener-ation of avant-garde filmmakers for whom the avant-garde film was no longer an activity on the margins of their commercial work but their whole life direction.

The filmmakers had made their first attempts in 1953 to gather themselves together into an organization, but it had collapsed before it got off the ground. The main cause for the collapse, the way I see it, was the attempt to mix both aesthetics and economics. While various members seemed to agree on practical and economic needs, they totally disagreed on aesthetic questions. Seven years later, when the New American Cinema Group was being formed, the lessons of 1953 were remembered. It was made clear from the very beginning that no aesthetic discussions would be entertained during the meetings or included in the organization's final program. 'Here we'll deal with practical matters only,' we used to say. 'If anyone is interested in aesthetics – after the meeting we'll stop at a bar and there we'll pick up aesthetics.'

I credit this down-to-earth principle with much of the success of the Cinema Group and the cooperative. As a matter of fact, the only time that the cooperative was on the verge of collapse was in 1967 when Stan Brakhage, for a short period, believed it should abandon its open-to-all principle and adopt a policy of selectivity.

But there has been another serious threat over the years, what could be called the Desire for Success. The cooperative has needed constant vigilance to remain a neutral machine – that is, to serve purely as a source of films and not to engage in any promotion or advertising. To maintain this principle hasn't been easy. At each cooperative meeting, at least one filmmaker whose films haven't been renting comes up with a scheme of how to 'push the co-op films.' The cooperative has stood clear of such promotion work.

There was a period of two years, 1967–68, when there was an ambitious attempt to establish a 'commercial' branch of the cooperative, the Film-Makers' Distribution Center, which would actively go out and promote films. Some filmmakers felt that their films had enough commercial pull and would do well in commercial theaters. The experience was disastrous. In order to get into the commercial theaters and succeed there, we had to use the same competitive, shark techniques as were used by the commercial distributors. The values of films had to be blown out of proportion; the theaters stressed the secondary, often very marginal, aspects of the content, such as erotic references.

The lesson we gained could be summed up as follows: The genuine avant-garde film and the genuine formal narrative film by their very natures are noncommercial and appeal to limited audiences only. To succeed with such films commercially one needs to embrace not only the commercial distribution methods but also, eventually, the content, the styles, the formulas of the commercial film.

The avant-garde filmmaker has bypassed the commercial system and has created an alternative dissemination system, helped by the general movement away from the Hollywood circuits and toward the smaller, private, and community circuits of film presentation. According to figures from the Pacific Film Archive, there were 85,000 such noncommercial film showcases in the United States in 1973. The figure includes film societies, universities and colleges, galleries, museums, clubs, and so forth.

It's partly from this experience that avant-garde filmmakers have also taken a stand against competitive, commercial film festivals. Again and again our dealings with film festivals have shown us that the official festivals are primarily business and tourism affairs with interest in commercial cinema only. The avant-garde film is not presented as an essential part of the art of cinema but as a curiosity, 'cinéma libre,' 'cinéma jeune,' 'cinéma différent.' The works shown are usually works of desperate third-rate filmmakers who, no matter what the conditions, are willing to send their films just to get some exposure, real or unreal.

But there is support developing for film expositions such as the Montreux Exposition of 1974 (organized by Annette Michelson) or 'Une Histoire du Cinéma,' the exposition organized by Peter Kubelka at the Centre Pompidou in Paris, in 1976 – expositions of cinema without competition and without prizes but with an underlying idea.

The cooperatives have sustained the spirit and have brought to the filmmaker a minimal income. But that alone wouldn't have sustained the avant-garde filmmaker if another development hadn't taken place almost simultaneously: the growth of film departments in universities and colleges. The 1977 survey by the American Film Institute found 1,067 universities and colleges with film courses. Helped by the presence of a body of critical writing on the avant-garde film, and constantly under siege by traveling independent filmmakers, most of these institutions began to feel a need to balance their programs and courses with avant-garde–independent film.

This resulted in increased rentals to the filmmakers, and it created a demand for appearances by filmmakers themselves, thus enlarging the filmmakers' income to the point where they not only could live from their films and lectures but also could continue making films. When I say 'filmmakers,' I mean only two dozen of the best filmmakers working in the avant-garde film mode today. I do not mean the 470 filmmakers who belong to the Film-Makers' Cooperative in New York, or the 350 who belong to the Canyon Cinema Cooperative.

The second stage of this development started when colleges began to establish courses and chairs specifically devoted to the avant-garde–independent film, and when the avant-garde filmmakers found themselves among the most sought after properties on campuses. A recent semester found virtually all leading American avant-garde filmmakers teaching.

It's too early to tell whether this is a positive or a negative development. Stan Brakhage has repeatedly complained about constant disruption of his creative work because of his teaching at the School of the Art Institute of Chicago. He has proposed an alternative – appointing avant-garde filmmakers 'in residence,' but in residence at their own homes, accepting only calls and visits from students. Peter Kubelka has worked out his own procedure: he gives concentrated three-week courses, two or three every year, leaving him longer periods for his own filmmaking.

I'd like to end with a note of skepticism and maybe warning. The comparative difference between the situation of avant-garde film in the United States today and that of twenty years ago is immense. But when I look through the history of the American avant-garde film, I see that the main body of avant-garde work has been created without anybody's help and in spite of everything. It was created through great financial and spiritual struggle. Nothing could have prevented it from happening, neither lack of money nor lack of public interest. Economic structures such as cooperatives do not necessarily and vitally help the individual filmmaker and the individual works during the periods of intense creative outbursts. Rather, they help to bridge the periods between one creative explosion and another.

Still, whatever the reasons, for the first time in history avant-garde filmmakers, psychologically and practically, have freed themselves and their art from dependence on the public and commerce. The methods and procedures they used to achieve this state may not be transferable to other places and other times. But they have decommercialized film to the point where they can proudly say that they are working for no other reason but the greater glory of the art of cinema.

Chapter 5

Dimension Pictures
Portrait of a 1970s' independent

Ed Lowry

Late in 1971, *Variety* announced the formation of Dimension Pictures, a small film company which intended to produce films budgeted at around a quarter of a million dollars for the booming exploitation market.[1] The principal partners in this venture were Lawrence Woolner, a low-budget exploitation producer since the mid-1950s; Stephanie Rothman, a young woman who had already begun to attract attention as one of the few female writer–directors working in Hollywood; and her husband Charles Swartz, producer of the three films Rothman had directed since 1966. All three partners had left Roger Corman's independent New World Pictures (itself barely a year old) to go to work for themselves. Dimension was to provide them the opportunity to make their own low-budget features while turning a healthy profit from the same lucrative drive-in audience targeted by New World.

The recognition and exploitation of this specialized audience outside the mainstream of Hollywood production, distribution and exhibition, was hardly new to the 1970s. Certainly during the 1950s and 1960s, this stratum of the industry had been profitably mined by companies such as American-International Pictures and Allied Artists, which distributed cheaply produced or cheaply purchased films to a sectionalized market: primarily the 'youth' audience that attended drive-ins to see 'schlock' science fiction and horror films, and low-budget movies exploiting topical subjects in such newly molded sub-genres as beach party musicals, Hell's Angels' films and hippie drug-culture movies. Tacitly acknowledging that television, not cinema, had become the true mass medium of the period, these independents filled a gap left open by the majors, focusing on a target audience instead of the public-at-large to which Hollywood had traditionally appealed.

By 1970, successful AIP producer–director Roger Corman felt secure enough about the stability of this target audience to form his own production and distribution company, New World. The market seemed to be expanding: the number of drive-in screens had increased steadily since 1963,[2] and the establishment of the ratings system only two years earlier had introduced the possibilities of appealing to a sizeable audience interested primarily in films rated 'R' for nudity and violence. Corman's move also took place in the wake of *Easy Rider*'s phenomenal success, when the Hollywood majors had begun to eye with some interest the very youth market that was Corman's speciality. After a few abortive attempts to reach this audience via small 'counterculture' films, the majors turned their attentions toward milking bigger profits out of fewer films, focusing on the 'blockbusters' that came to symbolize Hollywood in the 1970s. Between *The Godfather* (1972), which surpassed all box office records back to *Gone With the Wind* (1939), and *Star Wars* (1977), the biggest blockbuster of the decade, the number of features released by national distributors decreased by 40% (from 312 in 1972 to 186 in 1977.[3] During the same five years, box office grosses for Hollywood films increased inversely, with the top ten grossing films of 1977 amassing $424 million in contrast to the $123 million accounted for by the top ten films of 1972 – an increase of nearly 345%.[4] Where nine films had grossed over $10 million each in 1972, some 28 films topped the $10 million earning mark in 1977.[5] Meanwhile, production costs for the average film during that period more than doubled, from an estimated $1.9 million in 1972[6] to around $4 million in 1977,[7] and by 1980, that figure more than doubled again, to about $8.5 million for the average film.[8] Such increases are far greater than the national rate of inflation, and represent a trend among the majors toward the increasing concentration of capital in fewer, more profitable productions.

Never before had such an enormous gap existed between Hollywood's majors and its independents. While the six majors had become broadly diversified corporations (in the case of Columbia, Twentieth Century–Fox) or subsidiaries of still larger conglomerates (as in the case of Warner Bros., Universal, Paramount, United Artists),[9] such independents as Dimension, New World and Crown International were personally owned businesses or partnerships. Producing fewer and fewer films themselves, the majors concentrated on the distribution of independent productions; but these independents had little to do with the low-budget fare of the exploitation market, and even less to do with the small films of the so-called New American Cinema of the late-1960s. Instead, they represented money from within the system employed by major producers with direct links, or at least distribution agreements, with the major companies. Thus, despite the increase of independent production, the six majors still dominated the market, accounting for 90% of box office earnings while producing only one-third of the films rated by the MPAA; this left the other two-thirds to compete for the remaining 10% of receipts.[10]

These are the trends responsible for what has been termed 'the notorious product shortage of the mid-70s'[11] which left exhibitors with fewer films than ever to show, and tended as never before to delineate 'specialized audiences' as the province of the independent companies. Here, outside the mainstream industry, existed a limited, highly competitive, but potentially profitable market character-ized by its own types of exhibition (mainly the drive-in and, by the 1970s, the inner-city movie theatre) and its own, mostly R-rated sub-genres (the softcore nurse/teacher/stewardess film, the women's prison picture, the graphic/erotic horror movie, the imported kung-fu actioner, and the whole range of blaxploit-ation). Dimension played a key role in the development and exploitation of this market during the 1970s.

The major stockholder of the fledgling company, Lawrence Woolner, had entered the movie business as owner of a New Orleans drive-in during the late 1940s boom in outdoor theatres. By the mid-1950s, he, like other regional exhibi-tors, had become involved in advancing money for the production of low-budget features which he could eventually exhibit. In 1955, he formed Woolner Brothers Pictures with his brothers Bernard and David, and co-produced *Swamp Woman*, Corman's third film as a director. Moving to Hollywood, Woolner continued to co-produce low-budget exploitation fare such as *The Human Duplicators* and *Mutiny in Outer Space* (both 1965); and in 1970 he became a partner in Corman's New World Pictures, serving as President in Charge of Sales and Distribution.[12] By the end of 1971, he had left with Rothman and Swartz, two of New World's most talented personnel, to form Dimension.

A veteran of exploitation films since the mid-1960s at AIP, Stephanie Rothman was the first woman to receive a Director's Guild Fellowship, which was granted her while she was studying film as a graduate student at the University of Southern California. In 1966, she began working on a variety of projects at AIP, and was given her first chance to direct with a beach party spoof called *It's a Bikini World*, produced and co-scripted by Charles Swartz. She and Swartz served as production executives on Corman's last AIP film *Gas-s-s-s* (1970), and left with him to begin New World. It was Rothman who directed and Swartz who produced one of New World's first releases, *The Student Nurses* (1970), a soft-core comedy of manners that initiated one of the new company's most successful sub-genres. Within the next year, they had made a second film for New World, *The Velvet Vampire* (1971), an R-rated erotic horror film centering around a female vampire in a hip southern California setting. As partners in Dimension Pictures, and the company's only in-house talent, Rothman and Swartz intended to continue producing the kind of commercial exploitation films which they found personally interesting, and to do so with even greater speed and less interference than they had encountered at New World.[13]

Charles Swartz, as Dimension's Executive Vice President in Charge of Produc-tion, and Stephanie Rothman, named Head of Project Development, were central to Dimension's initial plans to produce five low-budget films during 1972.[14] By February of that year, Dimension claimed to have three films in production. The first was a horror film, *The Twilight People*, directed by another AIP and New World veteran, Eddie Romero, and shot in the Philippines. The second was a women's prison camp film, first called *Sweet Sugar* and later *Chain Gang Girls*, produced by Swartz in Costa Rica. Non-union labor costs in such Third World locales more than made up for the expense of location shooting. The third film in production was actually a Mexican 'pickup' (that is, a film to which Dimension had purchased the US distribution rights) called *The Sin of Adam and Eve* which was partially re-shot and completely re-dubbed by Dimension. Such pickups quickly expanded the company's list of projected 1972 releases to fifteen.[15] The remainder of the year also saw the releases of *Group Marriage*, the first Rothman/Swartz film made for Dimension, and of the company's first genuine hit *The Doberman Gang*, co-produced with its writer–director David Chudnow's independent company Rosamund Productions.

By August, Dimension estimated a first year's gross of $8–10 million on an initial investment of only $1.5 million.[16] By November, Dimension's success served as the best example of new trends in low-budget production for *Hollywood Reporter*'s Ron Pennington in an article entitled 'Indies Taking Up Slack Where Majors Left Off.' Noting that 30% of playtime in the major US exhibition circuits was occupied by independent productions, he quoted Woolner's prediction that the percentage would soon reach 60%. 'The majors have lost control,' Woolner proclaimed boldly, 'to the extent that we can come in and demand and get preferred playing time.' Woolner accounted for the fact that Dimension was already 'in the black' with a weekly cash flow of $150,000 by pointing to the company's low operating expenses: 'What we do for $300,000, a major couldn't duplicate for $700,000 because of overhead. We do not allow one nickel to be wasted in production.'[17]

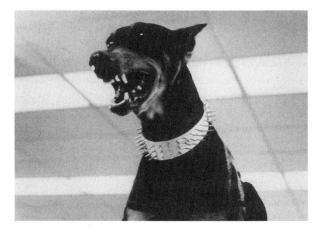

Figure 5.1 A star in *The Doberman Gang* (Chudnow, 1972). Courtesy of Rosamond Productions/Kobal Collection.

Woolner's remarks at the end of a first, successful, year indicate a sense of pride in what independent production, and Dimension Pictures in particular, represented in terms of creativity (the 'quality' of the company's first-year product notwithstanding). 'Majors today are hiring independents to produce pictures for them,' he comments, 'but they will never give a guy the freedom to make a picture in the way he wants. . . . We give people freedom to make pictures as they see it.'[18] A somewhat different, but related, sense of accomplishment can be seen in an earlier *Hollywood Reporter* article devoted to Rothman, entitled 'Dimension Pictures Opens Up Opportunities for Women.' Here Rothman declares that 'a concerted and unprecedented effort will be made to locate and hire qualified women in areas of filmmaking in which they are rarely if ever found.'[19] Rothman's statement, indicating a policy which she and Swartz seem to have followed enthusiastically, and Woolner's claims regarding creative freedom, highlight two of the frequently noted 'progressive' aspects of low-budget production which have drawn attention to the exploitation film. Unburdened by a corporate bureaucracy entrenched in a traditional studio hierarchy or by a need to appeal to the broadest possible audience, the exploitation film has served historically as a back door into feature filmmaking, offering young talent the opportunity to create and even to innovate, albeit within severe restrictions of budget and subject matter. Certainly Rothman has drawn attention from quarters that might normally eschew exploitation films as such – from the Sunday supplement of the local newspaper, where she was treated as a successful professional woman with feminist inclinations,[20] to the pages of *Screen* where her films were heralded as potential guide-posts toward a feminist discourse within the commercial cinema.[21] The desirability of viewing the exploitation film as an alternative to mainstream cinema capable of mounting a critique of prevailing film practices and dominant ideology must however be weighed against its simultaneous and consistent exploitation of talent, of women's bodies, and of violence as commodities. Not only does the exploitation film tend to adhere to the basic economic and representational practices of dominant cinema but in certain respects it intensifies them as a direct result of the often debilitating financial concerns bred on Poverty Row.

One of those concerns for Dimension involved its difficulty as a small producer in distributing its releases. Supplying a market outside the concerns of the majors, most independent exploitation films were distributed by regional exchanges. These sub-distributors most often handled films from a number of independent companies and exercised complete control over the bookings a film might receive. Despite Woolner's claims to the contrary, Dimension, as a new company selling a low-budget product, had less chance of demanding good bookings than a company with an established record or an inherently desirable slate of films (those with major stars or major national advertising). In addition, regional distributors were notoriously careless in the handling of prints (which represented a sizeable investment for a small company) and equally notorious for their slowness in paying rental percentages to the company owning a film. These practices could wreak havoc for a small company such as Dimension. Finally, regional exchanges generally received between 20% and 25% of the rentals paid by exhibitors, and that, too, was a major consideration for a company that did not waste a nickel.[22]

If Dimension were to continue producing films and releasing pickups, it would have to follow the lead of New World by setting up its own exchanges, asserting some measure of control over playdates, promotion, prints and cash flow. Therefore, at the end of 1972, Woolner announced plans to establish distribution offices in six of Dimension's key markets across the country: New Orleans, Charlotte, Memphis, Dallas, Minneapolis and Salt Lake City. These exchanges were to be jointly owned and operated by the General Film Corporation, a small film company owned by Don Gottlieb and Arthur Marks, a former television producer–director who had turned to the production of R-rated exploitation films.[23] Seeking a stake in distribution seemed both a logical and a wise way to invest the profits of Dimension's first successful year. Southern markets, where drive-ins operated year-round, were essential to the company's ambitious production plans. By March 1973, Dimension had opened three exchanges – in New Orleans, Dallas, and Memphis – but stopped plans for further expansion. And, although Woolner still proclaimed his intentions to open offices in 'every exchange center in North America,'[24] subsequent exchanges announced for Charlotte, Detroit, Miami, and Atlanta never seemed to have materialized.[25]

A major consideration in this respect is the high cost of distribution; for, while company-operated exchanges may give a producer more control, the expense of setting up such a network and of promoting films may far outweigh the advantages. It was estimated in 1975, for example, that a minor distributor like Allied Artists, with only 12 exchanges, ran on a yearly overhead of $3 million, and that it required over $12 million in annual rentals to support even this small network.[26] No matter how prosperous Dimension was by 1973, it could hardly guarantee yearly rentals of that magnitude (with rentals representing only a percentage of grosses), especially based on a slate of only eight or so low-budget releases.

Although 1973 saw the success of Rothman's *Terminal Island* and of *The Daring Dobermans*, a sequel to the first doberman hit, several of Dimension's eight announced releases for the year were pushed back to join the 15 films slated for 1974.[27] Nevertheless, Dimension enjoyed an unprecedented popularity during the mid-1970s, a result, as *Hollywood Reporter*'s Will Tusher slyly asserted in 1974, of 'the fact that even clunkers are clanking the cash registers at the box office.' In fact, this prosperity corresponded quite closely with the fall-off in product from the majors. At a time when mainstream Hollywood was seeking bigger profits from fewer films, Dimension was discovering that profits were to be made by filling the void with quantity rather than quality. 'Pictures that are not supposed to get money are getting more than they should,' Woolner commented happily in 1974, announcing an unprecedented $6 million budget for twelve 1974 releases and plans for 16 exchanges by the year's end.[28] Supplying product for this ambitious expansion into distribution would be a main concern for Dimension during the next several years; and though the additional exchanges were never realized, the release schedule was pursued in earnest. The company projected 25 new releases for 1975[29] and another 40 for the next two-year period, a release slate surpassing any of the majors except for United Artists.[30] Woolner sought product wherever available, from the pickup of foreign films such as the Italian film *Diary of a Female Prisoner* (1974) to the independently produced American documentary on the 1930s *Brother, Can You Spare a Dime?* (1975).[31] As for in-house production, two Rothman–Swartz films, *The Working Girls* and *Mama Sweetlife*, were planned for 1974,[32] but only the former was completed and released. By 1975, Rothman and Swartz had withdrawn from their partnership with Woolner and left Dimension. The precise reasons remain unclear, although Rothman later expressed her disappointment at finding it impossible to make the kinds of films she wanted in such an environment.[33]

In the period following the box office successes of such films as *Walking Tall* (1973), *White Lightning* (1973), and *Macon County Line* (1974), Dimension co-productions during the mid-1970s included a good many imitative backwoods sex-and-violence films. Among these were the commercially successful *Dixie Dynamite* (1976) and *Gator Bait* (1976), the latter produced and directed by the husband-and-wife team of Fred and Beverly Sebastian whose 1972 *The Hitchhikers*, a soft-core crime comedy shot in the California desert, was one of Dimension's first releases. In addition, 'blaxploitation' films made up an important part of Dimension's 1975 output, including such titles as *Boss Nigger*, *Tough, Dr. Black and Mr. Hyde*, and *Black Shampoo*. Reporting a 'steadily increasing market for black films in all parts of the country,' Woolner signed Steve Krantz, producer of the successful black film *Cooley High*, to a non-exclusive three-picture deal.[34]

It might be noted that the trends toward R-rated action films with rural settings, on the one hand, and 'blaxploitation' on the other, corresponded rather closely to Dimension's main target audiences: the southern drive-in crowd in the first case, and the inner-city movie-goer in the second. The decade-long rise in the number of drive-in screens prior to 1974 (at the moderate rate of about 26 per year) – a trend upon which Dimension's initial success had been partially based – underwent a major reversal in the mid-1970s with the startling loss of some 387 screens in 1976.[35] Rising real estate values in the suburbs which had grown up around the drive-ins had begun to make it more lucrative to sell the property than to show films there.[36] In addition, the propagation of suburban multiplex theatres, which corresponds historically to the decline in drive-in screens, had begun to compete for neighborhood audiences.[37] Increasingly in the 1970s, major urban areas (where most movie-going took place) were dominated by a few large theater chains, which tended toward the exhibition of mainstream Hollywood fare.[38] As a result, the bulk of Dimension's revenues during this period came from towns of 100,000 or less.[39]

If suburbanization had taken its toll on one of Dimension's major outlets, it had also contributed to the economic decline of formerly prestigious downtown theaters, which indirectly created another exhibition site for exploitation films. As the demographics of many inner-city areas shifted toward a larger minority population and lower income levels, downtown theatres often gave up trying to attract suburban audiences, choosing instead to book double bills of exploitation films to appeal to neighborhood patrons. While such theaters provided important venues for Dimension, they hardly constituted an expanding market, as such theaters tended to close throughout the decade. Urban renewal and the gentrification of such neighborhoods, of course, simply reversed the demographics upon which the appeal of Dimension's films were based.

By the end of 1976, it had become clear that if Dimension were to continue its expansion, it would have to find new outlets for its product. In a November issue of *Variety*, Woolner complained about the 'lack of cooperation from theater exhibitors in a shrinking market.' Decrying their lack of 'showmanship,' he added that exhibitors were 'destroying themselves with the high admission prices they are asking today. If a distributor or producer doesn't create box office excitement, there isn't any, because the distributor . . . won't spend money to help a film.' In response to these difficulties, Dimension announced plans to enter the production of features for television, emphasizing the type of exploitation fare with which the company had succeeded theatrically. By offering percentages of potential European theatrical releases of such films, Woolner hoped to attract major talent to such projects.[40]

Dimension's theatrical plans were expanding as well, with a record $12–$15 million budgeted for 1977–78 releases.[41] By mid-1977, the company would announce that it was enjoying its best year ever. 'We are on the brink of becoming a very important source of product,' Woolner proclaimed. 'The independent is important to the exhibitor . . . Dimension, Corman, and Crown. We are the three biggest independents.'[42] But being one of the biggest was still no guarantee of stability. 'We gamble with our money,' Woolner said proudly. 'We are not a stock company, and we do not go to a bank.'[43] In fact, since Dimension could offer no guarantee of major distribution agreements for its product, bank loans were virtually unavailable to the company.[44]

Having shifted with the market once again, Dimension's biggest releases of 1977 were horror films: *Kingdom of the Spiders*, a film about a town overrun by tarantulas, and the company's first production budgeted at over $1 million;[45] and *Ruby*, one of the films produced by Steve Krantz, starring Piper Laurie (fresh from her comeback in *Carrie*) as the owner of a drive-in haunted by a bloodthirsty ghost. After director Curtis Harrington was fired from the film, Stephanie Rothman was persuaded to complete it.[46] The result was Dimension's biggest hit ever, grossing more than $16 million.[47]

Spurred by this new property, Woolner was anxious to change Dimension's image to fit its newfound status as 'the fastest-growing independent.' Plans were made to move the company offices from a highrise on Sunset Blvd. to a 20,000 square-foot building providing room for the creation of a department to produce advertising trailers. Woolner also felt that it was time for Dimension to turn from quantity to quality in its releases, promising that 'even greater selectivity than has been exercised in the past will be used in deciding on a product pickup. . . . We want to give exhibitors better features – on a growing scale.'[48] Such changes seemed necessary if Dimension were going to compete for bookings in the multiplex theatres, especially in light of the rise in overall film production beginning in 1977.[49]

At the Cannes Film Festival the following year, Dimension officially announced its intentions to move from low- to medium-budget films, with three films planned, each in the $3 million range.[50] None of these projects was ever completed, nor did Dimension begin its production of television features. Although the company's expansion on every front, envisioned by Woolner as an aggressive response to an unpredictable market, was exactly the sort of gamble Dimension had taken again and again with great success, such actions could hardly be supported by a single hit like *Ruby*. They required a steady influx of capital which Dimension's sporadic release schedule could not provide.

By mid-1979, Dimension was cited in the first of a series of lawsuits that would spell the end of the company. The $1.6 million suit involved Saber Productions, co-producers of *Dixie Dynamite*, which charged that Dimension had violated the terms of its distribution agreement on the film and had lied regarding a deal to sell rights to another company.[51] In July 1980, Steve Krantz also filed suit against Dimension to recover $125,000 awarded to him in a settlement by the American Arbitration Association involving the release of *Ruby*.[52] Three months later, Dimension itself decided to sue David Chudnow and Rosamund Productions for $350,000, claiming that Chudnow had not paid Dimension its complete percentage for his re-use of footage from the doberman films that they had co-produced.[53] The suit seemed to be a last-ditch effort to postpone what by then seemed inevitable – a declaration of bankruptcy. Citing Dimension as the latest in the falling market for independent producers, *Variety* announced in February 1981 that the company had filed for bankruptcy under the provisions of Chapter VII, reserved for businesses 'hopelessly in debt.'[54]

The brief ten-year history of Dimension Pictures provides an excellent indication of the ups and downs of the independent film company struggling to survive the 1970s outside the mainstream of Hollywood production and distribution. While Corman's New World Pictures is most frequently cited as the prototype for this particular niche of the industry, it is usually chosen for its exceptional qualities: its prominence as the largest of the independents, its foray into the distribution of foreign art films, and Corman's virtually mythic role as the architect of the postwar exploitation film and talent scout for the New Hollywood. Dimension Pictures, it seems, may tell us far more about the marketplace itself. A production company formed to take advantage of the early-1970s boom in the exploitation field, it sought to gain control of its market by expanding into distribution. On the one hand, it proposed an ambitious production slate heralded by claims of creative freedom, while on the other hand it filled its release schedule with cheap foreign pickups and low-budget co-productions aimed at exploiting whatever trends were current. Buoyed by success in an industry climate more unstable than anyone suspected, Dimension attempted to make the leap from the shrinking exploitation market into the fringes of the mainstream, only to find itself faced with financial demands which few but the majors could meet.

The demise of Dimension Pictures marks the end of one of the 1970s' most interesting sub-chapters of film history: the one involving the exploitation film as a kind of alternative system flourishing in the gaps left open by the Hollywood majors. By the beginning of the 1980s, an increased uniformity in exhibition practices had enabled the majors to consolidate their control of distribution to the extent that those gaps had begun to close.

Notes

1 *Daily Variety*, 28 October 1971.
2 National Association of Theater Owners, *Encyclopedia of Exhibition* (1979): 42.
3 Gary Edgerton, 'American Film Exhibition and an Analysis of the Motion Picture Industry's Market Structure, 1963–1980,' unpublished Ph.D. thesis, University of Massachusetts, 1981: 50.
4 James Monaco, *American Film Now*, New York: New American Library, 1979: 35–8.
5 Edgerton: 74.
6 *International Motion Picture Almanac* (1976): 42A.
7 *International Motion Picture Almanac* (1978): 34A.
8 *International Motion Picture Almanac* (1981): 36A.
9 Monaco: 33–7.
10 Douglas Gomery, 'The American Film Industry in the 1970s: Stasis in the "New Hollywood",' *Wide Angle*, 5, 4 (1983): 53.
11 Monaco: 40.
12 *International Motion Picture Almanac* (1977): 308.

13 Terry Curtis Fox, 'Fully Female: Stephanie Rothman,' *Film Comment*, 12, 6 (November–December 1976): 46–50.

14 *Daily Variety*, 28 October 1971.

15 *Hollywood Reporter*, 16 February 1972.

16 *Hollywood Reporter*, 28 August 1972.

17 Ron Pennington, 'Indies Taking Up Slack Where Majors Left Off'. *Hollywood Reporter*, 1 November 1972.

18 *Ibid.*

19 Will Tusher, 'Dimension Pictures Opens Up Opportunities for Women,' *Hollywood Reporter*, 1 June 1972.

20 Kit Snedacker, 'Movies,' *California Living* (supplement to the *Los Angeles Herald-Examiner*), 20 September 1970.

21 Pam Cook, 'Exploitation Films and Feminism,' *Screen*, 17, 2 (Summer 1976): 122–7.

22 Lee Beaupre, 'How to Distribute a Film,' *Film Comment*, 13, 4 (July–August 1977): 48.

23 Allen Rich, 'Joint Exchange to Solve Distribution Woes,' *Hollywood Reporter*, 1 December 1972.

24 *Hollywood Reporter*, 26 March 1973.

25 *Daily Variety*, 18 June 1973; *Hollywood Reporter*, 8 August 1975.

26 Beaupre: 48.

27 *Daily Variety*, 1 October 1973.

28 Will Tusher, 'Box Office Bulge Inspires $6 Mil Spree on 12 Pics,' *Hollywood Reporter*, 10 January 1974.

29 *Daily Variety*, 21 April 1975.

30 Cobbett S. Steinberg, *Film Facts*, New York: Facts on File, 1980: 84.

31 *Daily Variety*, 21 April 1975.

32 Tusher, 'Box Office Bulge.'

33 Fox, 'Fully Female,' 50.

34 *Variety*, 25 February 1976: 25.

35 National Association of Theater Owners: p. 42.

36 Edgerton: 33–5.

37 Edgerton: 149.

38 Gomery: 54.

39 Frank Barron, 'Dimension Enjoying Best Year Ever,' *Hollywood Reporter*, 5 May 1977: 21.

40 *Variety*, 24 November 1976.

41 *Ibid.*

42 Barron: p. 21.

43 *Ibid.*

44 Gomery: 53.

45 Barron: 21.

46 Michael Weldon, *The Psychotronic Encyclopedia of Film*, New York: Ballantine Books, 1983: 598.

47 Ralph Kaminsky, 'Dimension Pictures Plans Expansion of Operations in '78, Woolner Says,' *Box Office*, 5 December 1977.

48 *Ibid.*

49 Monaco: p. 41.

50 *Daily Variety*, 15 May 1978.

51 *Daily Variety*, 25 July 1979.
52 *Daily Variety*, 24 July 1980.
53 *Daily Variety*, 24 October 1980.
54 *Variety*, 18 February 1981: 6.

Chapter 6

End of the indies

Death of the Sayles men

Jon Jost

It has been almost a decade since the Independent Feature Project proclaimed the existence of a 'New American Cinema,' a tag affixed to a crop of off-Hollywood features then being released: Robert M. Young's *Alambrista!*, Victor Nuñez's *Gal Young 'Un*, Rob Nilsson's *Northern Lights*, and John Sayles' *Return of the Secaucus Seven*. Since then, a long list of titles – ranging from the successful offbeats Wayne Wang's *Chan Is Missing* and Jim Jarmusch's *Stranger than Paradise* to the more mainline efforts of Paul Bartel (*Eating Raoul*) or Young – have jostled along with an even longer list of straight-out Hollywood product (albeit 'off-studio') to gather under the magically anointed 'independent' umbrella.

Ten years later, gathered beneath the Indie banner, one is more likely to find a list of studio execs, lawyers, distributors, and TV spin-off experts than an actual filmmaker, while discussions revolve around variants of Hollywood's favorite power-nosh topic – creative financing – rather than around the once-important aesthetics, or – God forbid – art. As we near 1990, we might wonder where Indie concerns might lie along the continuum from dollars and cents to film sense.

Looking back, the current situation might have been easily predicted: most films touted by IFP flagwavers and supporters were, from the outset, solid films of modest budget, liberal leanings, and minimal artistic wing-stretching. They accrued – some of them – modest box office, liberal kudos, and critical back pats proportionate to their artistic daring: just tepidly wonderful. Left to these films, the American indie would have gone, as quickly and mercilessly, the way of the Native American.

Instead, a series of quirks occurred disrupting this stew of PBS-flavored mush and rendering the indie scene as bizarre as sub-atomic particle physics: in the space of a few years a handful of films, each with its own charmed story, emerged to gather not only critical acclaim, but – most importantly in Reagan's America – also obtained decent distribution and box office clean-up.

John Sayles's $75,000 *Secaucus Seven* (1980) was among the starters that successfully tapped 1960s' nostalgia and made the box office buzz. Moguls took note; Sayles sailed. Wayne Wang's *Chan Is Missing*, a $25,000 ethnic comedy, lucked into a slot in New York's New Directors series and received a rave from the doyen of critics Vincent Canby. Snapped up by New Yorker, Wang was on his way.

In 1982, Susan Seidelman's downbeat SoHo sitcom *Smithereens* hit pay dirt, and in the surge of interest that attended this apparent New Wave, several new distributors coalesced into being. In 1985, Jim Jarmusch, with critical and financial support from Europe, weighed in with *Stranger than Paradise*, a formally refined parboiled comedy of New York 1980s' hip posturing. Again Canby raved, wheels and deals came, and *Paradise* grossed $1.25 million, never mind ancillary off-shore and video. This for a film that a few years earlier would have languished in the shriveling university and museum ghetto reserved for 'off-beaters,' as *Variety* invariably tagged them. Indie was In, with the bottom line matching the 1980s' ethos: this stuff makes money! At the jangle of serious cash, the eyes and ears of the biz swiveled to the indie sector.

Naturally, the premise of the phrase 'independent film' took on new meaning, the kind that attracted not only trend-hungry media scribblers, but also the deep pockets of the industry. Suddenly Seidelman shifted from self-proclaimed 'guerrilla filmmaking' to 40-foot trailers with *Desperately Seeking Susan*. Jarmusch's ante was upped from *Paradise*'s $125,000 to *Down by Law*'s nearly $1.5 million. Wang leapt from the modest proportions of *Dim Sum* to the slick Hollywood gloss of *Slam Dance*. And with them, new names, each carefully swathed in the indie banner, elbowed into the limelight: Spike Lee and Robert Townsend, Alex Cox and Oliver Stone. From Hollywood to the Lower East Side, from the Bayou to Puget Sound, film spilled forth.

Figure 6.1 Willie (John Lurie), Eva (Eszter Balint), and Eddie (Richard Edson) in *Stranger than Paradise* (Jarmusch, 1984). Courtesy of Cinesthesia-Grokenberger/ZDF/ Kobal Collection.

Budgets bloomed and, in equal proportion, likewise the promotional huzzahs. One could hardly turn a printed page without finding a glowing account of still another 'independent' in the works. Even the stodgy columns of *The Wall Street Journal* took up the cause. Robert Redford, using his high-profile star status, swung the spotlight onto his Sundance Institute, which offered the technical wizardry and professionalism of Hollywood to the indie initiate (as well as a shot at hobnobbing with moneymen).

Ironically, at the same moment the whole notion of 'independent' was mutating toward a total embrace of all things Hollywood, the chickens began to come home to roost. Even corporate money was not enough to compensate for weak script and Lee's, Seidelman's and Wang's projects nose-dived at the box office. Skewered by critics and abandoned by audiences that now expected more for the money, the indies wobbled. Wary distributors backed off. 'Independence,' warped and twisted by industry newspeak, had become, in reality (and Hollywood jargon), 'High Concept.' Bloated with generality and vagueness, its meaning devolved into little more than the jive and shuck of the con-artist.

From the outset, with its artificial baptism under the aegis of the IFP (which, in the best tradition of ad-hack, quite explicitly acknowledged the PR utility of a name tag), it became evident that the American Independent Feature has been little more than a bastard child of Hollywood, standing at the gates, yearning for legitimacy. While its embryonic forms have been but runt apings of the studios, the most successful birthings have been quickly snapped up by the mogul fathers. All too quickly did Seidelman, Wang, Lee, Amos Poe, the Coen brothers, *et al.*, opt for the glow of Sunset Strip, giving away the game: the rubric of this manu-factured tag was but another ad campaign of the inflated artifice of the Reagan legacy, a sham on the cultural credit card. Except in the most venal of senses, little of the American indie wave staked out anything that could legitimately claim any kind of independence from the Hollywood aesthetic model, its motives, or the preponderance of lawyers, deal-makers, and money talk, which fills those sem-inars dotting the film world landscape.

In high-1980s' fashion the real topic is money: how to raise it, borrow it, spend it, make it. Left far behind in the rush of this discourse is any concern for the kind of film, aesthetics, or content. At best, a trembling murmur from IFP tongues mentions 'humanism,' that catchall vacu-word for sentiments that dare not speak their name: wishy-washy left liberalism. Little wonder, then, that the films eman-ating from this confluence are virtually inseparable from their Hollywood counter-parts. The 'independent' wrapping is but a subterfuge, a PR angle for the dim wizards of the press, asserting a difference that is not there. Except, perhaps, in greenbacks. The claim of independence will buy from Siskel and Ebert a nod, which MGM pays for with freebies.

And what, then, beyond the hoopla of the media circus of an American cinema (even if circumscribed by the criterion 'feature'), that can make any reasonable claim to 'independence?' For those who choose not to succumb to the lure of big bucks and its concomitant market economy of aesthetics and ethics, the picture has – with an ominous sense of 'natural' ease – darkened considerably. Where the 1970s saw the emergence of a small body of works built on both American experimentalism and the European 'part film,' and which staked out space far from Hollywood (Yvonne Rainer, Jim Benning, Rick Schmidt, Mark Rappaport, myself . . . shortly followed by Bette Gordon, Charles Burnett, Andrew Horn, Lizzie Borden, Jim Jarmusch, and Sara Driver, among others), the 1980s have witnessed their decline.

While this may in part be attributable to the natural ebb and flow of creative surges, there are also more definable factors. On the most pedestrian level, the drastic change in the 16mm film industry, in which bread-and-butter jobs of TV news, industrial, and educational films have been shifted to video, has resulted in the curtailing of available film materials and services. In addition, prices have risen, and the quality of service has plummeted, all leaving the independent with far less room to maneuver, both aesthetically and fiscally. (For example, effects that are easily and inexpensively accomplished in reversal stocks – such as super-imposing titles over images – are made much more complex and costly in negative originals.) And it even appears likely that within the next few years 16mm will collapse as a viable medium.

Simultaneously, there have been changes in the exhibition circuit, and to ill effect. The list of museums, universities, and film societies that had been open to such work has been cut at least in half. And with the shrinking of even this marginal market, the few distributors and co-ops have either closed down or been reduced to a symbolic presence. Likewise, those cultural mechanisms that for-merly nurtured such work – if only by the encouragement of print – have shifted their attentions. Thus James Benning released *Landscape Suicide* (perhaps his best film), and Yvonne Rainer debuted *The Man Who Envied Women* to scarcely a breath of critical comment outside the pages of the most esoteric of specialist magazines. Previously supportive critics busy themselves with twisting clichés around the latest dross from Hollywood or extolling the latest Hollywood calling card as true creative genius.

The money-mindedness that dominates film production has well-afflicted the Pooh-Bahs of the press who presume to stand guard at the gates of culture. A $30 million turkey from Hollywood will command columns of explication in the pages of *The Village Voice, The New York Times* or *American Film*, while a $20,000 masterpiece will pass utterly without notice. And the picture stands only to worsen: the National Endowment for the Arts, for example, in line with Reagan-ite policy, recently announced a new $25,000 grant restricted to track-proven producers, intended only to help pull together a package for the production of a film for theatrical – read 'commercial' – release! A real independent could make a whole film for that.

And so the wind blows. As labs phase out 16mm or at best reduce it to a for-masochists-only format, the choice becomes 35mm, with its increases in costs and pressures to 'go commercial,' or, for better and worse, to work in consumer-level video where technological advances now offer virtually professional-level technical standards at down-home prices. Barring a sudden change in the country's cultural climate, it seems safe to predict that the small niche previously occupied by the truly independent filmmaker will reduce to an untenable toehold, with production dropping off to the occasional European-financed film – like Jarmusch's *Down by Law* – or the odd all-American item done against all reason.

It is likely fair, then, to write the obit of the American independent on the wall in any form distinguishable from Hollywood – if not today, then tomorrow. The energies that found expression there will either have to bow to the demands of 'the market' or, more likely, move into other forms more amenable to the artist–outsider. My own bet would be on a combination of video–computer synthesis, done on home-level equipment such as the Super VHS, Beta ED, or video 8 formats interfaced with Amiga or Atari or the new generation Macintosh computers for graphics and music. These tools, utilized with the same iconoclastic mind-set that distinguishes the real independent, offer the same aesthetic elasticity and room for creative cost-cutting that formerly made 16mm film such an advantageous format. As this shift occurs, doubtless pressures for developing channels for distribution and exhibition will give rise to electronic equivalents to the film co-ops of the 1960s. And in the change to this different format, the nature of the relationship between artist and viewer will also shift, with the genuine artist finding avenues far removed from either the routine of network television or the flash of MTV.

To think that such a development would happen autonomously from the general drift of our culture would be naive: art seldom materializes out of a vacuum. And while it may be prematurely optimistic, one senses a certain dismay, an uneasiness with the cultural (not to mention social/political) offerings of the past years and present. As yet unfocused and unsure, this nevertheless promises a future eruption of pent-up energies and ideas. The action, when it comes, will be somewhere far from the cynical canyons of LA. Or so one might hope.

Chapter 7

Alternative cinemas

David E. James

The present argument that the cinemas of disenfranchised social groups are the truly populist ones disputes both the naive celebration of the democracy of Hollywood and the apotheosization of the avant-garde; neither position can account for the diversity of non-studio film practices or the political transactions they involve. The categories of the avant-garde and the industry must be dismantled, and their blank polarization opened to the play of heterogeneity and interdetermination within the field of practices the terms otherwise simply divide. In place of the single transhistorical self-regulating avant-garde tradition appears the spectrum of alternative practices which develop and decay with historically specific needs and possibilities. And far from being categorically defined against a monolithic, uncontradictory industry, these alternatives emerge from (and in certain circumstances merge with) a similar plurality of practices constructed in the margins of the industry or even as mutations within it.

In this total field of continuously changing practices, the binary distinction between industrial product and modernist aestheticism retains only a much reduced role, that of marking theoretical extremes rarely approached in practice. *Mothlight* and *2001* would appear to be as close as any films to occupying exemplary positions. But even here the degree to which *Mothlight* must exist in a system of commodities and the signature of the modernist author in *2001*, with its use of the underground trope of the interior trip and of avant-garde technologies (like the slit-scan processes in the Stargate Corridor sequence developed years before by John Whitney), immediately qualify the polarization. Brakhage's *Reflections on Black* against a 'B' noir of the same period and *Tom, Tom, The Piper's Son* by Ken Jacobs against Billy Bitzer's film of the same name are other instances of different kinds of invocation of industry by art at the latter's most extreme reaches. But though the force of the heuristic evaporates whenever its defining limits are approached, still the great variety of ways in which all practices

© David E. James, 2005. All Rights Reserved.

negotiate with industrial functions and film languages allows the polarity a second function, that of organizing gradational scales that enable local instances within the entire range of production to be differentiated.

The replacement of a categorical bifurcation by multidirectional gradational scales allows the different practices otherwise yoked together or entirely obscured by the modernist polarity to be returned to their specificity in the gestalt of mutually determining practices that forms the general field of production. Industrial cinema takes its place in this field, but, itself neither unified nor stable, it is not confronted by a single contrary but surrounded and interpenetrated by many different kinds of filmmaking. The distinctiveness of each of these appears initially as a matter of form – as the use of a non-standard gauge and film length and the deployment of unorthodox profilmic and filmic codes. But these are only the traces of more fundamental innovations in the mode of film production that derive from the film's functions in the social unit that produces it. Constituting an alternative film practice as an alternative cinema, this register of functions determines filmic form, with alterity to the dominant mode being but one component in it.

This model of alternative film as subcultural practice organized around unorthodox modes of production makes possible the materialist investigation of the relation between aesthetics and politics. Attention to the specific practices that produce the dominant ideology and to those that enact resistance to it allows us to avoid the scholasticism of idealist generalizations about cultural autonomy (or semi-autonomy) that propose transhistorical conditions applicable uniformly to all forms of art; and it allows us to clarify the social origin of art and its functions in daily life without falling into an abstract reflectionism which can designate culture only as an epiphenomenon of a historical reality existing independent of it. Attention to the socially active group as the area where general historical possibilities achieve a concrete form, on the one hand, and as the origin of cultural practice, on the other, makes visible the social transactions where determination is lived and fought, where history is made.

When analysis takes its terms of reference from the material level of production (the sphere of cinema), filmic form may be understood as the product of social necessities and aspirations, as they engage the cinematic possibilities of their historical moment. A given stylistic vocabulary is never merely itself; rather it is the trace of the social processes that constitute a practice. Films are only the form of appearance of the cinemas they organize. All models of filmic distinctions, and especially all formalist models that propose distinctions between an alternative film style and the codes of the feature industry, must then be doubled to include the social determinants of each; they must be returned to social practice. And any alternative practice, whether it be black film, underground film, or women's film, may be understood as a response to the three other spheres of activity: the alternative social group, the dominant society, and the hegemonic cinema (see

Table 7.1 Alternative film as a response to three main spheres of activity.

Alternative film practice	Hegemonic film practice
Minority social or interest group	Dominant society

Table 7.1). To take the example of underground film, which will be our most comprehensive illustration of this complex of determinations, the films of the beat generation were shaped simultaneously by the beats' own aesthetic principles and social uses for film, by their situation in respect to the commercial cinema, and by their situation as a dissident subculture in respect to the surrounding social forma-tion. Underground film thus represents the modification of previous uses of the medium to produce a film practice formally consonant with its functions in beat society and capable of negotiating, symbolically and practically, the relations between the subculture and the social whole. Though a major procedure in underground film is the documentation of beat life, its function is not just the representation of beat society, but also the production of beat society.

But while underground film developed from previous marginal alternative film practices and continued to interact with other contemporary alternatives (such as the European New Waves), as well as adapting the innovations of poetry, jazz, and other art forms and cultural practices, its major determinant, both positive and negative, was Hollywood. Even as the dominant mode of material production in a given social formation influences and assigns ranks to other modes of production which may coexist with it, so the dominant mode of cultural production positions and inflects minority cultural practices. In the modern period, the media indus-tries inhabit all alternative cultural practices and so, for even the most recalcitrant avant-garde film, the film industry 'is a general illumination which bathes all the other colours and modifies their particularity . . . a particular ether which determines [their] specific gravity' (Marx 1973: 107). The underground's codes emerged, then, as mutations and mutilations of industrial codes, and its practices were carried on either in the spaces between industrial practices or as modifications of them.

In the late 1950s film was still the single most important agent of acculturation, with Hollywood the source of a national fantasy life, the vocabulary of its imagin-ation, and the matrix of its art. As John Clellon Holmes summarized, in 1965: 'The movies of the 1930s constitute, for my generation, nothing less than a kind of Jungian collective unconsciousness, a decade of coming attractions out of which some of the truths of our maturity have been formed' (Holmes 1965: 55). So while a tradition of working-class criticism of Hollywood may be traced back through such figures as Howard Lawson and James T. Farrell (e.g. Farrell 1944) to the Workers' Film and Photo League and Harry Potamkin in the 1930s, still in the popular mind Hollywood was distinguished *against* high art precisely by virtue of its accessibility and general appeal. Despite their ideological and material work in monopoly capitalism, the movies had always retained some populist affiliations, standing 'slightly aslant' of mainstream values (Sklar 1975: 267), and only recently had they been freed from the stigma of specifically working-class associations and even of a supposed communist orientation. On the other hand, while the studios were increasingly relying on independent production, conditions were still sufficiently rigid and over-centralized that young artists had little chance of self-expression before depleting themselves in years of mechanical apprenticeship.[1] Surrounding this situation and the aesthetic innovation it forced on the beats was a social crisis, the fragmentation of the postwar hegemony and the growth of dissent and contestation, which appears in underground film as a social content, the beats' elaboration of their social alternatives and their critique of American society. All these processes cross and recross in the text of each underground film, a total exegesis of which would clarify its determinations in all these areas: its function within the beat subculture; its filmic embodiment and production of beat values; its marginality in general cultural production; its critique, positive and negative, of the American consensus; and its critique, again positive and negative, of Hollywood.

But even such a hermeneutic is only a beginning of a social *history* of cinema; precisely because it does make provision for other inter-determinations – for the effect of underground film *on* Hollywood and *on* the dominant society, as well as for its role in producing and disseminating the beat subculture – this model makes possible the understanding of all these diachronically and historically. The social formation and each of its various cultural practices were all continually in the flux of their adjustment to developments in the others; and, in the cultural totality they jointly make up, each was constantly negotiating and renegotiating various degrees of autonomy and control, each continuously fracturing and reforming under the stress of internal contradictions and external pressures. Each was constantly in a state of production. Though the dominant industry generally reproduces the ideology of the dominant society, which is always itself the site of competing social groups and classes, it too is the scene of conflict. And of course the various subcultures were themselves continually in process, mediating between different desires and social possibilities. What we think of as the 1960s was a period of especially energetic activity in all these areas. The present concern is with the history of those social groups whose pursuit of their own interests or attempts to change America brought them into an engagement with film. These alternative cinemas must be contextualized, then, by a summary of the history of the film industry, for when it was not their ambition, it was their antagonist.[2]

The crisis in Hollywood

The postwar crisis for Hollywood peaked in 1960. Although in both 1946 and 1948 the average weekly attendance at movie theaters equaled the early depression high of 90 million, by 1950 a third of this had been lost, and the figure subsequently fell to record lows of 40 million in 1959 and 1960, the number of movie theaters in the country declining by a third in the same period. Since the price of tickets rose, annual box-office receipts declined less precipitously, from $1.7 billion in 1946 to $1.3 billion in 1956. The reasons commonly adduced for this decline are the changing social patterns that followed the end of the war, the preference for domestic entertainment explained by the sharp increase in the birthrate, and especially the commercial expansion of television. Though box-office receipts had begun to fall before television made a significant impact – around 1949 – after that time the number of sets rose quickly, from 1 million to 32 million 5 years later, and by the end of the 1950s only 1 home in 10 was without television.

The difficulties these developments occasioned were exacerbated by the antitrust suits and by the effects of the Supreme Court decision in the Paramount case in 1948, which forced Paramount, Warner Brothers, MGM–Loews, RKO, and Twentieth Century–Fox, the five major studios, to divest their control over first-run theaters, thus breaking apart the vertical integration that had sustained the studios' monopoly since the twenties. And just at this point, when innovative leadership was necessary to develop new markets, the industry instead, after the citation of the 'Hollywood Ten,' capitulated to the Red Scare, beginning ten years of blacklisting which essentially ended whatever responsiveness to progressive causes, whatever distance from mainstream values, Hollywood had been able to sustain.

The postwar reorganization of industrial production, completed by the purchase of the major studios by corporate conglomerates in the late 1960s[3] led to the confused retrenchment of the 1950s, with innovations largely restricted to attempts to capitalize on spectacular effects that television could not match. While nothing worthwhile came from the various wide screen and 3-D projects, the influence of television was not entirely negative. As television took over center stage in the mass culture, some elements in Hollywood began to redirect production toward selected minority audiences. The decentralization of production in the 1950s had made the studios more and more the distribution apparatus for independently produced features, which by 1967 amounted to 51.1 percent of all features released (Jowett 1976: 481). In the last third of the decade, this greater flexibility allowed the innovative directors of the New Hollywood – Arthur Penn, Mike Nichols, Francis Ford Coppola, George Lucas – to cement a relationship between the industry and a new audience, though even before that time there had been some responsiveness to the social changes of the period. John Ford's reversal of the Indian/white dyad in *Cheyenne Autumn* (1964), the spate of 'problem' movies dealing with race relations, Roger Corman's message movies, the emergence of cynical non-heroes like Paul Newman's early 1960s' roles (*The Hustler* in 1961 and *Hud* in 1963), and even Sean Connery's James Bond all variously indicate some redefinition of values and adjustment to social discontent.

Stimulated by the national cinemas, the various New Waves of the 1950s, and the growing popularity of the art film circuits, such developments also drew heavily on the 1960s' underground. Formal innovations such as overt reflexivity that fractured invisible narration passed into the commercial vocabularies of both film and television as the industry began to represent hippies, Blacks, and eventually women and the war (though this last, until the mid-1970s, only in allegorical displacement), and to confront the violence of some of these causes. The desire and the ability of the art or the political cinemas to maintain autonomy from the industry was, with few exceptions, entirely eroded by the late 1970s.

A component in the larger history of the industrial media and essentially shaped by the pressures of television and industrial music, this history of industrial cinema describes a crisis in its capacity as a means of capital valorization. The cinemas discussed here emerged from that crisis; but their history is the contestation of cinema as commodity production. From that of the solitary 'poet' to the cooperative efforts of large groups, the various interventions they inaugurated call into question the functions that constitute capitalist cinema. Deriving from the conditions of capitalism and its alternatives, their various aspirations produced different articulations of personal production and public consumption. The expressive possibilities that became available – and in them semiology was always imbued with and surrounded by politics – may be summarized as being hinged between authenticity and irony.

The interruption between signifier and signified that is the condition of signification separates signs, not only externally from their referents, but also internally from themselves. Constituted in difference, all images are thus inhabited by an otherness that erodes the affirmation of their apparent presence. In the case of the film image, whose history is redolent with myths of its indistinguishability as such, the duplicity of the simulacrum has been seen as both the source of its particular pleasures and the stigma of its mendacity, with the antinomy between 'the representation of reality' and 'the reality of the representation' summarizing what has also been a history of anxiety. This semiological contradiction extends through the various realms of cinema, with the various alienations of its industrial production and consumption joining with the alienation of modern life in general.

The horizon of modern consciousness, such systemic alienation was felt peculiarly forcefully in the 1960s, and indeed it forms the context for the period's characteristic political movements, the contrary articulations of dissent and counter-aspiration, whose post-Heideggerian and post-Sartrean existentialist vocabulary recurred to a gestalt of mutually ratifying terms: authenticity, the self, bad faith, free speech, self-realization, the politics of experience, the personal as political, and so on. From the Third World to the domestic rhetoric of liberation, from the Port Huron Statement to situationist *détournements*, such concepts are primary. Their force, even their tenability, has of course been so thoroughly impugned that what once seemed axiomatic political postulates now resonate with nostalgia and naiveté. Whatever the ultimate standing of the critiques of them (and it is here necessary to remark only that the conditions of the production and circulation of the ideologies of the postmodern are no less determined by the historical moment than were the ethics of presence they have displaced), their preoccupations are not new. Rather, the ideals of the 1960s were always tempered with their opposites, and, from the constructivism of perpetual revolution to the irreverent debunkings of the mass media, the cults of authenticity were always conducted through the cultures of fabrication.

In film no less. On the one hand, the drive for authenticity summarizes so many of the practices discussed here: the urgency with which film was inserted into the optical physiology or phenomenology of the individual; the social urgency of the revolutionary interventions in cinema; and the semiological crises of the image itself leading to the reduction to the essentially filmic. But all these were inter-penetrated, sometimes overwhelmed, by their opposites, by the recognition of difference, by a pleasure in the inauthentic, or by despair at its inevitability. If the alternative cinemas were typically powered by obsessions with authenticity, they were as often steered by the perspectives allowed by the rear-view mirror of irony.

The most convenient point of entry into these alternative cinemas is through the concept of authorship. Pried out of the anonymous bedrock of mass culture by the *politique des auteurs*, what initially appeared as an impregnable site of authen-ticity was almost immediately returned by subsequent theory to the social circula-tions of textuality and survived only in the reduced and ethereal form of the 'author-function.' But between these points the concept did provide a ledge where the romantic, idealist panoply of expressive individualism was forced into confrontation with the materialist and the social, with the specific potentials and limits of film, and with the public operations of cinema. The alternative possi-bilities of the reintegration of an independent authorial cinema into the industrial economies of the spectacle or its total liberation from them are paradigmatically exemplified in the work of Andy Warhol and Stan Brakhage, the 'slow and the quick' of the avant-garde (Mekas 1972: 158).[4] Though these were the most infamous avatars of the underground, their programs for independent film, for the optical events it could conjure and the social events it could organize, were entirely contrary. Where Brakhage's use of the medium as the scene of obsessively

Figure 7.1 Andy Warhol. Courtesy of the Kobal Collection.

personal vision demanded the innovation of practices antithetical in all respects to the industry, Warhol's project allowed him to redirect the artisanal mode and its visual splendors back toward industrial practice. Thus, they manifest two of the extremes between which other, less uncompromising practices steered.

Notes

1 In France, to take the most significant counter-example, the distribution of production among hundreds of small companies and the system of government grants made it relatively easy for young filmmakers to begin work in 35mm feature production; the *loi d'aide* allowed Godard, for example, to borrow the money for *Breathless*. Stephen Dwoskin notes that in Europe, domestic film was accepted 'as an activity open to anyone . . . like any other profession,' a factor which, with the greater political freedom there, allowed the Europeans to build upon what they had, whereas 'the New American Cinema started with film from scratch' (Dwoskin 1975: 76). Similarly, Sitney notes that 'without a chance to make the kind of films they wanted to make commercially, [American filmmakers] immediately set about doing what they could within the limitations of their circumstances' (Sitney 1970: 4).

2 On Hollywood in the sixties, see Baxter (1972); Sklar (1975); Balio (1976); Jowett (1976); Cook (1981); and Schatz (1983).

3 'In 1969, MGM was taken over by Kirk Kerkorian, a hotel magnate; Warner Brothers was purchased from Seven Arts by Kinney National Service, Inc., which operated parking lots, construction companies, and a comic book empire; Embassy was controlled by the AVCO Corporation, which built aviation equipment; Paramount was in the hands of Gulf and Western, a multifaceted conglomerate; Universal Studios went from Decca Records to MCA, Inc., the monolithic talent agency, and large television

production company; while United Artists was owned by TransAmerica Corporation, which also controlled banks, insurance companies and oil wells' (Jowett 1976: 436).

4 For other comparisons of Brakhage and Warhol, see Tyler (1969: 27), Sharits (1972: 34), and especially Arthur (1978).

Bibliography

Arthur, P. (1978) 'Structural Film: Revisions, New Versions, and the Artifact,' *Millennium Film Journal*, 2 (spring): 5–13.

Balio, T. (1976) *The American Film Industry*, Madison: University of Wisconsin Press.

Baxter, J. (1972) *Hollywood in the Sixties*, London: Tantivy Press.

Cook, D.A. (1981) *A History of Narrative Film*, New York: Norton.

Dwoskin, S. (1975) *Film Is: The International Free Cinema*, Woodstock, NY: Overlook Press.

Farrell, J.T. (1944) 'The Language of Hollywood', *Saturday Review of Literature*, 5 (August): 29–32.

Holmes, J.C. (1965) '15c Before 6:00 p.m.: The Wonderful Movies of "The Thirties,"' *Harper's* (December): 51–6.

Jowett, G. (1976) *Film: The Democratic Art*, Boston: Little, Brown.

Marx, K. (1973) *Grundrisse: Foundations of the Critique of Political Economy*, New York: Vintage.

Mekas, J. (1962) 'Notes on the New American Cinema.' *Film Culture*, in (Spring): 6–16.

Schatz, T. (1983) *Old Hollywood/New Hollywood: Ritual, Art, and Industry*, Ann Arbor: University of Michigan Press.

Sharits, P. (1972) 'Words Per Page,' *Afterimage*, 4 (autumn): 27–42.

Sitney, P.A. (1970) *Film Culture Reader*, New York: Praeger.

Sklar, R. (1975) *Movie-Made America: A Cultural History of American Movies*, New York: Vintage.

Tyler, P. (1969) *Underground Film: A Critical History*, New York: Grove Press.

Part II

Cult film/cool film

Chapter 8

'Queen of the indies'

Parker Posey's niche stardom and the taste cultures of independent film

Diane Negra

Introduction

One of the ways in which American independent cinema conventionally differentiates itself from big-budget Hollywood is in its rejection of genre and performer typologies. Yet the legitimacy of this presumption has been increasingly tested by the emergence of a set of performers (Steve Buscemi, John Leguizamo, Liev Schreiber, Lili Taylor, Christopher Walken) who, while perhaps not fully meeting the criteria for stardom in the conventional sense, nevertheless generate personae that operate as legible, functional trademarks. For the kind of independent film with the highest cultural and economic profile, the sort exhibited in a growing number of upscale art-house settings, the lure of a performer's name brand may, in fact, be a key feature of audience attraction. Bearing these concerns in mind, this article investigates the aesthetic categories engaged by discourses of recurrent performance in independent film. A case-study of stardom in the independent realm will focus on Parker Posey, the actress *Time* magazine designated 'queen of the indies,' referring to her ubiquitous presence in low-budget independent features (Corliss and Ressner 1997: 82–3).

For the new 'picture personalities' like Posey, recognizability functions to guarantee that the films in which they appear will support a certain aesthetic and status economy with which independent film-goers are likely to affiliate. Posey's success is crucially tied to her ability to perform the reconciliation of bohemian and bourgeois sensibilities that, as David Brooks has argued, now widely characterizes the privileged class of taste-makers (a disproportionate segment of the independent audience) in American culture.[1]

In exploring how independent film attempts to constitute oppositional gender and class rhetorics, I look at the filmography of Posey, the long-time 'indie ingenue' whose film roles have mobilized her excessively energized demeanor and trademark balance of girlishness and cynicism.[2] While the majority of her film roles would seem to grant her a subversively knowledgeable relationship to the narrative, I question the extent of Posey's seeming transgressiveness and identify films in which her oppositional status is thoroughly recuperated. This is not to deny that many of Posey's film roles genuinely endow her with an unruly and unconventional femininity; in fact, Posey's career in independents reveals both the freedoms within and constraints on this category of American film.

Reviving the 'picture personality'

Well-recognized 'indie' performers such as Posey are best understood not as embodying *stardom* in the contemporary sense of the term but as re-activating performance discourses from the era of the *picture personality* embodied by actors such as Florence Lawrence and Francis X. Bushman. The picture personality, which as Richard DeCordova (1990) has argued, was the principal site of product individuation prior to 1914, differs significantly from the star in terms of scope of celebrity and the limits of extrafilmic discourse. The foundation for such a histori-cally based comparison is fortified by Chuck Kleinhans's observation that the period before the 1920s was essentially one of independence: 'independent pro-duction and diffusion . . . was the norm when cinema was starting' (1998: 311). According to DeCordova, discourses on a picture personality while seemingly comprehensive, tended to reveal very little about them:

> In fact, many of the aspects of the actor's existence that we find most compelling today were never systematically addressed. . . . Extrafilmic discourse insisted on the personality's real-world identity, to be sure, but in describing that identity it merely referred readers back to the evidence of the films in a kind of tautological loop (1990: 91).

Press coverage of Parker Posey consistently bears out this tendency: seldom the subject of extensive interviews or feature pieces in the national press, the actress is most likely to be represented in the mainstream by a blurbed photo, such as one in *People* that informs the reader: 'Word on the street is that Parker's just as downtown as the funky characters she plays.'[3]

Bearing in mind Barry King's contention that 'stars transcend the demands of situated characterization' (1986: 161), we can observe that press coverage of Parker Posey does not quite pitch her as a star. Coverage of the actress in major mainstream entertainment publications such as *People* gives her only glancing attention, frequently in a critical vein (she may be cited for a fashion *faux pas*, for instance).[4] More extensive coverage of the actress notably congregates in upper-end publications such as the *New York Times, Harpers*, and *New York* where she is more approvingly evaluated. Even in such feature coverage, however, those elem-ents of the actress' life that we would expect to be thoroughly delineated remain nebulous. Brief biographical details recur (the fact that Posey grew up in Laurel, Mississippi, that she had a role in the CBS soap-opera *As the World Turns*, that her roommate at SUNY–Purchase was the actress Sherry Stringfield) but very little elaboration of her private life is provided. It is often suggested that Posey is fundamentally indistinguishable from the characters she plays; that she is, in certain essential ways, a personality both originative of film roles and retentive of them after a film has been produced. Thus, a *New York Times* review of *Party Girl* (1995) quotes the film's director Daisy von Scherler Mayer describing how she became interested in Posey for the starring role of Mary: 'A number of casting directors told me, "There's this girl running around town with this great wardrobe. She *is* Mary." ' (McGee 1995: H18). Where celebrity press coverage tends to focus heavily on the authenticity of a private life that grounds fictional perfor-

Figure 8.1 Publicity still of Mary (Parker Posey) in *Party Girl* (Von Scherler Mayer, 1995).

mativity, feature coverage of Parker Posey suggests that she remains a *character* in real life. Consequently, a feature piece exploring Posey's style preferences through an interview with her at her Chelsea apartment notes, for example, that 'her entire wardrobe consists of costumes . . . unlike so many actors who shed their costumes in favor of Gucci shoes and jeans between films, the lines between art and life blur with Ms. Posey' (Steinhauer 1997: 1). Similar constructions recur in a 1997 feature piece which profiled the actress' current projects and observed: 'Even when Posey is not making a movie, there's a dose of "let's pretend" in her life' (Smith 1997: 39). In this sort of coverage, just as in an earlier era of picture personalities, publicity and promotional coverage operate to heighten the power of onscreen characterization by endowing it with the status of *reality* rather than supplementing it through knowledge of the performer's offscreen identity.

The relative advantage of being a picture personality and not a star rests in the growing attraction of semi-anonymity in an era of routine overexposure and an apparent heightening of star disposability. Stardom now proliferates in a variety of forms that scarcely existed ten years ago, and it is very seldom grounded in a single medium. There is an inherent disposability in the kind of stardom generated by reality programming, for example, and an intensified malleability in the digital stardom of figures such as Lara Croft.[5] In crucial ways, as Paul McDonald has argued, the internet has decentered the production of star discourse, dispersed star authorship, and expanded the uses of star image (2000: 114–15). In such an environment, the reclaiming of craft is stabilizing on a number of levels.

Importantly, an emphasis on discourses of craft centers press coverage of 'indie' niche stars, helping to differentiate them from Hollywood stars increasingly vulnerable to tabloidization.[6] Indeed, independent film performer discourse may be linked to a wave of current middlebrow cultural forms that seek to recuperate stardom from the intense tabloidizing and scandalizing trends of the 1990s.[7] Television programs such as *Biography* (A&E) and *Inside the Actors' Studio* (Bravo) retrieve a more respectful approach to stardom by highlighting discourses of craft, while print publications such as *InStyle* achieve the same end by emphasizing discourses of celebrity good taste. Picture personalities who are not household names but rather performers associated with *quality* material, whether they are Marcia Gay Harden or Bradley Whitford, are not only insulated from tabloidization but come to represent attractive exceptions to a mainstream tabloid culture the class connotations of which run counter to the current demographic mandates of independent cinema. Additionally, given the widely acknowledged confusion about what *makes* an independent film even as the category has acquired greater marketing mileage and upscale class associations, it may well be that the uncertain mandate for independent film content is accompanied by a heightened need for performer recognizability. In the 1990s, a time when 'a snowball effect ensued in public awareness of films produced outside Hollywood' (Kleinhans 1998: 307), indie film 'regulars' were well situated to attract public attention beyond the level of character and bit-part acting but below the level of stardom. In other words, the discourse of and around 1990s' independent film generated a more active transactional site for niche stardom than has generally been acknowledged.

The sweetheart of Sundance

Parker Posey's omnipresence in American independent film has been explained in a variety of ways: sometimes she is cast as muse to indie auteurs, sometimes as an essential member of what amounts to a director's – Hal Hartley, Richard Linklater, Christopher Guest – stock company: often she is represented as the very lifeforce and spirit of independent filmmaking itself. Press anecdotes, such as a report that Posey once lent her credit card to a producer on a micro-budgeted film shoot, further this image – in this instance by implicating the actress in the kinds of narratives of improvisational funding that have consistently provided promotional fuel in indie marketing.[8] Posey's coronation as 'queen of the indies,' 'independent film goddess,' and 'sweetheart of Sundance,' bespeaks similar tendencies to inscribe her at the heart of the independent film mission.

Posey's career dovetails with a period of global film-festival proliferation, in which a growing number of cities and even towns have perceived the public relations value of hosting an event emblematic of affluence and high cultural capital. Parker is prominently associated with the preeminent Sundance Film Festival held in Park City, an event that according to Kenneth Turan 'has become more than just the mother ship for the American independent movement, more than the premier showcase for films that don't march to Hollywood's drum' (2002: 34–5). The film culture of Sundance remains studiously 'alternative' (even, according to Turan, to the point of being unproductively anticommercial), and this obviously provides an appropriate setting for an embrace of Posey as icon of alternative cool.

The embrace of Posey at Sundance – symbolized by the special jury prize she was awarded for her performance in *House of Yes* (Waters) in 1997 – miniaturizes in important ways her larger embrace within the independent film marketplace. This embrace may also stem from her usefulness to indie filmmakers, providing them with, in effect, an idealized image of themselves and their aspirations. As Alissa Quart argues, 'Posey herself was ultimately a stand-in for the indie film-makers who conjured her, and in so doing flattered themselves – directors who imagined that they, like Posey, were creatures of the demi-monde, just waiting for the world to understand their inordinate fabulousness' (2002: 42).

Mingling the aristocratic and the democratic

The highest profile and most profitable independent and 'art' films in America occupy a different aesthetic and class positionality than they did ten years ago.[9] The scope of their status transformation is symbolized by a dramatic change in the conditions of their reception in theaters. In the recent past, such 'smaller' films were the province of cinemas in decline – the older, non-multiplexed, less comfortable theaters where poor projection quality confounded spectators. The last several years, however, have witnessed the invention of the 'art-house miniplex,' a space devoted to screening art, foreign and independent films in conditions of previously undreamt-of comfort. Characteristically screening 6–10 films at once, the new art miniplex provides choice and comfort, yet avoids the lowbrow status of the gargantuan, 30-screen mega-multiplex. Tailoring itself to the affluent, it offers high-end concession items such as gourmet coffees and imported mineral water (the very newest have liquor licenses and may sell wine and beer), and will often have an on-premises restaurant or café. The art miniplex will not attach itself to a mall, nor encircle itself with a vast orbit of asphalt; rather it makes its home in carefully designed mixed-use sites that fuse together residential and upper-end retail space to denote nostalgia, retreatism and good taste. Such miniplexes are likely to be designated 'film centers' rather than 'cinemas' and will occasionally host local film festivals or visiting directors. Most importantly, the art-house miniplex has brought the experience of viewing independent film more fully in line with other high-status leisure pursuits such as museum visits or concert attendances. Its existence, such as in the form of the Angelika Film Centers in Houston, Dallas and New York, has the power to confirm a local or regional community's taste values and economic profile.

Given that the very term 'independent film' denotes not so much alterity as a highly marketable hipness, we can begin to identify Parker Posey as the right kind of icon for a category of film increasingly attuned to the display of class credentials. Since Posey is often constructed as, in effect, a prism through which the qualities and attributes of independent film itself can be glimpsed, it is perhaps fitting that she is the subject of a class-polarized discourse. Posey represents an intriguing example of a persona in which aristocratic hauteur and downtown street style become felicitous terms. Accordingly, press coverage tends to celebrate in the same breath her 'lanky' body and 'rolling' gait, and a seemingly innate elegance. Likewise, Quart describes her as having a highly functional 'air of discarded social class – think Katherine Hepburn on *a lot* of methamphetamines' (2002: 42). As I have suggested, the reconciling of apparent class disparities Posey achieves is in keeping with the current marketing mandates of independent film itself, as it bids for both bourgeois and bohemian artistic credentials. In this sense, the widespread identification of Posey as the 'poster girl' for American independent cinema is more than a convenient tag for a familiar performer: it is rather an oblique recognition that she incarnates the functional paradox currently centering this category of filmmaking.

As independent film-going has become more and more an act of 'hip consumerism,' it accords more fully with what Thomas Frank has deemed 'the marketplace as a site of perpetual revolution' (1997: 227) The apparent iconoclasm of cult figures like Posey is not necessarily detrimental to mainstream commercial viability. Rather, as Frank points out, 'in contemporary American public culture the legacy of the consumer revolution of the 1960s is unmistakable. Today there are few things more beloved of our mass media than the figure of the cultural rebel, the defiant individualist resisting the mandates of the machine civilization' (ibid.: 227). Seen in this light, we can better understand Posey as a highly functional icon of hip consumerism; in an environment of intensified niche marketing her recognizability tracks toward the art miniplex consumer who is more likely to read InStyle than People, more likely to turn on Bravo than Fox. Accordingly, a great many of the actress's film roles emphasize an unconventional yet elite sense of style (in Party Girl she must painfully sell off some of her couture clothing) and she is increasingly cited in publications like InStyle and The New York Times as an exemplar of good taste (albeit of the quirky, individualized sort). Thus with countercultural icons more and more likely to be recuperated into mainstream commercial ventures, we may well wish to temper any celebration of Posey as a transgressive free spirit with an awareness of her apparent marketing magnetism among key demographics.

There is little doubt that Posey is at her best when portraying characters who embody powerful and pleasing reconciliations of conventionally disparate attributes and experiences. In Party Girl, for instance, Posey's Mary is a downtown club fixture who becomes an expert librarian. Through the film's accumulation of diverse attributes and experiences Mary emerges as a young woman who simultaneously maintains her joy in the club scene, negotiates the cultural differences inherent in her romance with Mustafa (Omar Townsend), a Lebanese falafel vendor, and embraces the virtues of the Dewey decimal system, finally referring to an all-night cataloguing and shelving spree at the library as 'the wildest night of [my] existence.'

One of Posey's most 'democratic' roles is surely that of Margaret, the unofficial leader of a quartet of Manhattan office temps whose social and economic invisibility is the primary subject matter of Clockwatchers (Sprecher, 1997). Schooling her friends in small acts of resistance and subversion, Margaret rails against the petty tyrannies of the corporate workplace at Global Credit. Following a series of office thefts, scrutiny immediately shifts to the subcaste of female temporary workers, in particular the unruly Margaret. When, in the interests of improved surveillance of their activities, the group is deprived of even cubicle privacy, it is Margaret who voices the perception: 'We're like corporate orphans. We're like corporate call girls.' Margaret's willingness to buck the system is finally her undoing at Global

Credit; exhorting the other three to join her in a one-day strike, she is the only one who keeps to the bargain and is fired for her absence. Removed from the workplace under armed guard, Margaret is last glimpsed kicking and screaming at a supervisor who does not know her name (on noticing her absence, she queries the remaining three workers: 'Where's the other one?').

If Parker Posey's persona is equally charged by the democratic and the aristocratic, and her film roles run across a spectrum in this regard, then clearly *The House of Yes* represents the opposite end of the continuum to that of *Clockwatchers*. Posey's Jackie-O represents the aristocratic alternative to the working-class Leslie in a black comedy narrative that centralizes a contest for the affections of Marty (Josh Hamilton), Jackie-O's brother. A gothic-tinged comedy of familial dysfunction *The House of Yes* sketches a wealthy family whose secrets are repressed and displaced through the thematics of re-enactment. Jackie-O relies on her brother's role as JFK to her First Lady in an eroticized assassination scenario that simultaneously re-enacts both the shooting of the president and their mother's murder of their father. The film proposes that violence and incest are the family's aristocratic legacy, and it is only Marty's fiancée, Leslie (Tori Spelling), who interrupts Jackie's plans for perpetuating what she refers to as their 'heritage.' A Donut King waitress from working-class Pennsylvania whom Marty describes as smelling 'like powdered sugar,' Leslie is unable to compete with Jackie's high-culture credentials, displaying her ignorance of wines and foreign languages as well as fashion when she appears in a dowdy velvet-and-lace dress for Thanksgiving dinner. To Marty, Leslie represents the normalcy he craves – at one point he tells Jackie: 'I'm tired of being above everybody' – yet this does not prevent him from joining with his sister in mocking her in an exchange that turns on Leslie's economic and class inferiority:

> *Jackie-O*: Does your fiancée work in a donut shop?
> *Marty*:   A Donut King, actually.
> *Jackie-O*: A Donut King. So is she like the Queen? Are we
>   entertaining royalty?
> *Marty*:   She would be more like a Donut Lady-in-Waiting.

At the film's conclusion Jackie fulfills her mother's prediction that 'Jackie can have everything her way, she always has,' and a triumphant Jackie chronicles (in voiceover) Leslie's departure 'all the way back to Pennsylvania.'

Posey's stardom and New York in the national imaginary

One of the salient features of Posey's persona is her status as a quintessential New Yorker. As of this writing she has made ten films set in Manhattan or Long

Figure 8.2 Marty (Josh Hamilton) and Jackie-O (Parker Posey) in *The House of Yes* (Waters, 1997). Courtesy of Bandeira Entertainment/Kobal Collection/Wren Maloney.

Island, in the vast majority of which New York is far from an incidental location for the fiction. Indeed, Posey often appears in the films of writers and/or directors like Hal Hartley, Greg Mottola, and Nora Ephron who are overtly interested in New York and use it as a recurrent setting in their work. Whether playing real-life Manhattan art dealer Mary Boone in *Basquiat* (Schnabel, 1996) or archetypal New York women who are temps (*Clockwatchers*), novelists (*The Misadventures of Margaret* [Skeet, 1998]), or editors (*You've Got Mail* [Ephron, 1998]), Posey's persona has been distinctively regionalized, and this without recourse to the accent or ethnicity that so often characterizes performers associated with New York.[10] Posey's ability to guarantee a kind of regional authenticity is on display even in television guest parts, such as appearances on the NBC sitcom *Will & Grace*, in which she played a Barney's sales manager who covets a date with Will. As I have briefly suggested, New York-based publications such as the *New York Times* and *New York* have embraced the actress in ways the national press has not. A 1997 *New York* article, for example, uses Posey as the defining figure in a wave of talented young actors choosing to make their home in the city, characterizing her as 'the young film star who chooses to hold court in New York' (Smith 1997: 37).

Certainly one kind of associative tradition that would seem to ground Posey's persona is that of the quintessential New York 'girl' — the exuberant, but worldly-wise spirit of the city who may be seen in everything from 1930s' 'gold-digger' musicals to Audrey Hepburn's Holly Golightly and Diane Keaton's roles in Woody Allen's films to Carrie Bradshaw of HBO's *Sex and the City*. Posey's fusion of cosmopolitanism and a certain vulnerability both draws from and extends this type, symbolically negotiating contrastive images of New York itself.

Posey becomes an emblematic figure for New York at exactly the time when its regional meanings were split. On the one hand, New York was undergoing a sanitizing process under Mayor Rudolph Giuliani, designed to bolster the city's attractiveness to tourists. With the remaking of Times Square as a theatrical Disneyland, campaigns for public courtesy and the marketing of New York personalities through such forms as pre-recorded welcome messages in taxis, the city had seldom extended itself as consistently and aggressively toward securing tourist business. The sustained 'bull market' and its inauguration of the personal finance boom in the later 1990s also solidified a positive perception of New York as the financial center that grounded the nation's prosperity. On the other hand, New York still figured in the national imagination as a key site for the bizarre, the abject, the violent, and the dysfunctional, and maintained an ongoing tabloid identity furthered by scandals including the abuse of Abner Louima, the Haitian man brutalized by New York police officers while in custody and the 'Long Island Lolita' case involving Joey Buttafucco, whose very name became a catchphrase for the spectacle of lurid 'blue-collar' crime. In the cycle of mid-1990s' blockbuster disaster films devoted to the spinning of apocalyptic fantasies about the destruction of American cities, New York was a frequent target.

The function of a personality like Parker Posey during this phase of New York's history, much like that of *Seinfeld*, the hit sitcom that provided the highest profile and most consistent imaging of New York in this period, was to make compatible these two facets of urban identity. The comically bitter tone of the sitcom is matched in certain respects by the caustic, blunt, yet also playful and exuberant, sensibility that Posey consistently exhibits. Functioning in ways analogous to her status as an icon of/for independent film, Posey serves to stabilize and draw together the disparate meanings of a site crucial to the taste economies of affluent late twentieth-century culture.

Cameo-ing and crossing over: the limits of independent niche stardom

How can we speak of Parker Posey sustaining stardom when she appears pre-dominantly among ensemble casts, often occupies minimal screen time, and seldom carries above-the-title recognition or even any particular visual differen-tiation in promotional materials?[11] If, perhaps, Posey does not meet conventional definitions of stardom developed through/for Hollywood celebrity, her presence in films is nevertheless frequently highlighted using the kinds of techniques associ-ated with brand-name performers. One such technique is the cameo appearance, a 'technology of characterization' that presupposes the value and status of a featured performer.[12] When Posey cameos in big-budget star vehicles such as *The Sweetest Thing* (Kumble, 2002) we need to ask what meanings (if any) she carries into the fiction. Is she presumed to be unrecognizable? Vaguely recognizable but unnamable? These are the sorts of ambiguities that accrue to performers at the level of what I am calling 'niche stardom.'

Posey has made a large number of brief but dramatic appearances in films, but her cameo value differs significantly according to whether the film defines itself as an independent or a mainstream project. As she has amassed a track record, and become lionized as 'indie queen,' Posey has become more and more likely to cameo in an independent to give it an imprimateur of artistic credibility; she is the icon of independent filmmaking, therefore her appearance certifies any new film's 'independent' legitimacy. For instance, in Gregg Araki's 'heterosexual movie' *The Doom Generation* (1995) Posey makes a brief but intense appearance in an elaborate blonde wig and heart-shaped sunglasses as Brandi, declaring her love to the film's protagonist Amy Blue (Rose McGowan) and wielding a machete in an attempt to remove the penis of Jordan White, Amy's boyfriend. This sort of over-the-top cameo is far from atypical in a film which repeatedly stunt-casts countercultural icons in small roles (in addition to Posey, Margaret Cho, Perry Farrell, and Christopher Knight, the one-time child actor who was 'Peter' in *The Brady Bunch*, all make appearances). Yet it is part of a pattern in which the independent status of a particular film is bolstered through Posey's appearance – in this way her presence trademarks a film as having certain qualities expected of it.

In big-budget films such as *The Sweetest Thing*, in which Posey unquestionably makes her most lackluster and uninteresting cameo to date as an anxious bride-to-be who calls off her wedding, she is more likely to embody an alternative feminin-ity deficient to that of the protagonist(s). Certainly not all of Posey's mainstream film cameos serve the same function: for instance, as I discuss in greater detail later, in *Josie and the Pussycats* (Elfant and Kaplan, 2001) she enters the world of the film in order to infuse it with a sense of irony and high style that will later be discredited. But all Posey's mainstream cameos are connected in the sense that she inevitably serves as a referent to subversive femininity – this could even be said to be true of *The Sweetest Thing*, a film whose raunchy female *joie de vivre* is cast aside in a conclusion that caters to 'chick-flick' expectations for marriage and where Posey's contrastive role is as a woman who cancels her own wedding and goes to Bali.

Another question (and one I adapt from Chris Holmlund) has to do with the star characteristics and cultural conditions which make some performers eligible for 'cross over' from the category of independent to big-budget filmmaking while restricting others.[13] Not only have performers as varied as Anne Heche, Billy Bob Thornton, Ashley Judd, Matthew McConnaughey, and Renee Zellwegger crossed over from independent film into big budget filmmaking, but it is becoming increasingly common to 'commute' between the two realms as the industrial and economic lines between them become increasing difficult to draw.[14] Consequently, independent film has emerged as a productive site for Hollywood stars to either accumulate artistic capital (Tori Spelling), pursue uncommercial vanity projects (Al Pacino) or rehabilitate waning stardom (John Travolta, Marisa Tomei).

Parker Posey, though she increasingly plays small roles in big-budget films, has not crossed over in this fashion, and a recurrent concern in her press coverage asks why not? Some such coverage is anxious (*Time*'s feature article fretted openly 'Parker Posey seems to be in every alternative film. Is that enough?' and noted that 'Hollywood has yet to fall in love with her'), while some is complimentary, praising the actress for not selling out, and retaining her integrity. In this vein, a 1997 *Entertainment Weekly* article refers to Posey 'merrily transgressing a different taboo here: that hyperselectivity particular to contemporary actors that frowns upon taking any part that doesn't promise significant career advancement' (Willman 1997: 51).

One potential impediment to cross-over success for Posey is the fact that her roles have frequently tied her to a satire of the famous. Her character in *Drunks* (Cohn, 1997) wishes to be Janis Joplin, the small-town Dairy Queen employee she plays in *Waiting for Guffman* (Guest, 1996) dreams of a bigger theatrical stage on which she will become a star, and in *The House of Yes* Posey plays a (hilariously) unbalanced woman who channels the style and (a warped version of) the spirit of Jackie Kennedy Onassis. Reported to have once written an article decrying the behavior of 'bad stars' (Dicker 2002), Posey has also been relatively forthright about her own dissatisfactions with Hollywood typecasting in ways that are surely detrimental to cross-over success.

Posey has not received, for example, the kind of coverage accorded to Rose McGowan, an actress of nearly comparable longevity in independent films, though perhaps best known as rock star Marilyn Manson's ex-girlfriend. In a telling 2002 photospread in the *New York Times Magazine* McGowan's cross-over potential was anxiously visualized through a series of photos in which she was styled to resemble famous Hollywood 'bad girls' from Clara Bow to Lana Turner to Sharon Stone. By writing her into the history of Hollywood in this way, the piece enacts an assimilation process that demonstrates her casting potential and reassuringly anchors McGowan's 'bad girl' persona to Hollywood representational tradition.[15]

Posey's most high-profile role to date, that of Patricia Eden in You've Got Mail, exemplifies her tendency to be cast in unflattering caricatures of highly strung professional women when she appears in big-budget films. It would seem that Posey's tartly ironic presence has little representability in a Hollywood environment increasingly devoted to blockbuster action/adventure and family film categories.[16] In ways that are telling of the ideological economies of independent and mainstream filmmaking, the qualities of energy, irony and wit that play sympathetically in films like The House of Yes, Clockwatchers, and Party Girl take on negative connotations in bigger budget moviemaking. Auditioned for role of Annie that made Sandra Bullock a star in Speed (De Bont, 1994), Posey proves a little too arch to be 'America's sweetheart.' Now in her mid-thirties, Posey increasingly faces the usual age-related Hollywood casting restrictions for actresses, and she is ill-suited for the kind of mainstream 'chick-flicks' that are gaining both market force and commercial (if seldom artistic) credibility. As Peter William Evans has argued, the heroines of contemporary romantic comedies center a formula of 'consoling values in uncertain times' (1998: 191). For Evans, Meg Ryan is the quintessential performer of the genre, a figure who 'promotes love as a refuge from modern alienation and solitude' (ibid.: 193). Posey, by contrast, is a figure of irony, ambiguity, and truthfulness, and she is fittingly contrasted with Ryan in You've Got Mail, a film that reads Posey's intensity as a form of selfishness that disqualifies her from romance.[17] Unusually candid in its depiction of the moral anxieties of corporate predation, You've Got Mail offers up a therapeutic romance between Kathleen Kelly (Ryan) and Joe Fox (Tom Hanks) designed to alleviate Fox's moral guilt and naturalize the inevitability of big-business takeovers through both Fox Books' eradication of Kathleen's small bookstore and her acceptance of him as a partner for romance. Posey's Patricia Eden, a book editor so highly strung Joe complains she 'makes coffee nervous,' cannot alleviate Joe's guilt for she is his neo-machiavellian counterpart.[18] As the two discuss Kathleen's career prospects upon the demise of her bookstore, Patricia bluntly indicts Joe, saying: 'I love how you've totally forgotten that you've had any role in her current situation. It's so obtuse. It's so insensitive. It reminds me of someone. Who? Who does it remind me of? Me!' Patricia's failure to compensate Joe with the fantasy of innocence violates one of the most basic job descriptions of the contemporary romantic heroine.

Another impediment to 'crossing over' into a mainstream film market devoted to propagandizing family values is that Posey's body of work consistently places her as a member of a dysfunctional family (either literal or symbolic). This is certainly the case in what many independent film fans would see as the actress's most definitive film role, as Jackie-O in *The House of Yes*, and would be true also of her roles as Fay in *Henry Fool* (Hartley, 1997) (in which her husband sleeps with her mother), Margaret in *The Misadventures of Margaret*, and Jo in *The Daytrippers* (Mottola, 1996).

Distressingly, Posey has most recently appeared in two mainstream films that are essentially impersonator 'chick-flicks' where a superficial discourse of female empowerment serves as a gloss over plots in which women are demeaningly sexualized and trivialized. This is, indeed, a very dubious version of 'crossing over' for Posey as she is moved from the center to the margin by films that seem to want to implement her as a token of indie credibility to authenticate their ersatz concerns with female identity. Yet in both *The Sweetest Thing* and *Josie and the Pussycats*, Posey foils 'authentic' female friendship groups and operates as the 'bad object' embodying the wrong kind of unruliness for films that crudely co-opt notions of female power and individuality.[19] In *The Sweetest Thing* Posey's Judy is the woman who conveniently breaks off her wedding to the heroine's male love interest, but her value to the plot is perhaps secondary to the larger need to demonstrate the neutralization of an empowered female figure in order to highlight the ultimately non-threatening verve of the female protagonists.

In *Josie and the Pussycats* Posey's Fiona is a caricature of female professional power put in place to camouflage a sense of social inferiority. At the close of the film, Fiona's crisp professional authority as the head of Mega Record unravels and she is revealed as the desperate 'Lisping Lisa,' a woman who seeks to compensate for her social and physical inadequacies through pathetic schemes for power.[20] Here, the aristocratic is unmasked as the democratic. Posey's mainstream film roles up to this point seem to characteristically include such a moment in which her agency is dismantled, and we might well speculate that such scenarios have the cumulative effect of depreciating the power of Posey's 'indie' persona.

Although Posey's casting of late tends increasingly toward the cartoonish, it is important to note the considerable constraints against her as she moves into a new phase of her career (potential overexposure as an indie cliché, an empowered image unsuited for the fictions of gender conservatism released by Hollywood). These constraints would appear to be having some impact. A recent article quotes the actress discussing the difficulty of finding work, maintaining that 'the prolific times for Posey, 33, have ended as quickly as they began. Posey's bit on *The Sweetest Thing* was one of two weeks she worked in 2001' (Dicker 2002).[21] Given its raised cultural profile, proliferation of higher quality exhibition venues, and growing critical clout as evidenced in the 'indie' tallies at recent Academy Award ceremonies, American independent cinema would appear to have 'crossed over' more fully and meaningfully than has its 'Queen.'

Conclusion

In this chapter I have argued that figures who would not qualify for *stardom* under the conventional terms of film studies can serve important functions in non-mainstream film and that the study of film would be well served by an attentiveness to different degrees of stardom. Taking note of the category of niche stars who populate the worlds of independent film enables us not only to shed the mistaken assumption that name recognition holds drawing power only in big-budget filmmaking but facilitates exploration of some of the complexities of performance in indie filmmaking. In particular, Parker Posey's persona can be understood to allegorize the current contract between independent film and its audiences. The upgrading of the material conditions of independent film reception through the invention of the art-house miniplex is expressive of the dramatic transformation of 'indie' social capital. Given that independent film-going in America is largely a status-conferring leisure activity it qualifies as one of a range of activities that now denote 'hip consumerism.' Promotional coverage of 'indie queen' Parker Posey in the late 1990s paints her as a representative hip consumer whose aristocratic taste does not compromise her fundamentally democratic status. It is hard to imagine a fantasy better suited to secure the interest of the upscale contemporary film-goer.

Notes

I wish to thank Bonnie Blackwell, Gabriel Wettach and my colleagues and students in the University of East Anglia Film and Television Research Seminar for their enthusiastic and generous feedback during the writing of this chapter. It was Andrew Higson who suggested the term 'niche stardom,' and I thank him particularly.

1 See Brooks' 2001 work of 'comic sociology' *Bobos in Paradise: The New Upper Class and How They Got There*.
2 These qualities are played for quite different effect in mainstream Hollywood films such as *You've Got Mail* (Ephron, 1998) in which Posey's Patricia Eden is a caricatured neurotic and narcissistic career woman who we first see bolting down her morning espresso and last see shrilly crying out for her Tic-Tacs and contemplating plastic surgery in a stalled elevator. I discuss the re-orientation of Posey's performer attributes in big-budget filmmaking later in this chapter.
3 This blurb accompanied an undated, unspecified photo of Posey ordered from ebay.
4 Such discourses of negative evaluation also characterize Posey's roles in mainstream film.
5 See Flanagan 1999 for a discussion of the star system of electronic gaming.
6 At this writing, one-time Oscar nominee Winona Ryder can be glimpsed on CNN attempting to make her way through a throng of reporters as she sought to enter a Los Angeles court for a hearing related to the shoplifting charges filed against her. Ryder contends that she was jostled so severely her arm was broken.

7 Though it must be said that niche stars occasionally generate mini-scandals of their own: Lili Taylor's restraining order against ex-boyfriend Michael Rappaport and Steve Buscemi's stabbing in a bar brawl while in North Carolina to shoot a film both garnered fleeting press attention.

8 This report is included in Solomon 1999: 68.

9 For an account of this transformation see Sconce 2002. Parker Posey's persona is in striking accord with the features of the 'smart film' as Sconce details them (irony, black humor, playability to a sociocultural formation dedicated to disaffectedness).

10 Here we might look to the examples of stars like Woody Allen, Jerry Seinfeld, Fran Drescher, Rosie O'Donnell, Rosie Perez or Marisa Tomei. Nearly all of these figures are coded as loud, colorful, sarcastic, and ironic, and all are associated with rapid delivery of speech. Posey would be similarly constructed with respect to language, although her clipped WASP speech patterns also set her slightly apart.

11 Two particular exceptions would be *Party Girl* and *The House of Yes* — for both films, Posey is the central promotional image. In the former, she is a figure of offbeat downtown chic, posed against the backdrop of the New York skyline; in the latter she is attired in the 'Jackie-O'-style pink suit and pillbox hat she wears in the film.

12 Goble puts this phrase to use in his 2001 article.

13 See Holmlund's discussion of Lupe Ontiveros, Rosie Perez, and Jennifer Lopez in the chapter entitled 'Latinas in La-La Land: From Bit Part to Starlet in "Indie" and Mainstream Films' (Holmlund 2002: 109–22).

14 Apropos of this trend, Daryl Chin (1997: 65) observes that 'what seemed like insanity in the 1980s has become the paradigmatic career of the 1990: from Nicolas Cage to Al Pacino to John Travolta, everyone is taking a stab at the independent market.'

15 Blunter still is the text that accompanies the photos. Elvis Mitchell (2002: 48) writes 'The truth is, McGowan is an actress waiting for a great movie to serve her star-ready persona.' For those who want the accessories for bad girlhood, the article provides a list of brand-name items available at major Manhattan stores, including lingerie, stiletto pumps, and bust-firming cream.

16 On the importance of the family film to contemporary Hollywood see Allen 1999: 109–31 and Kramer 1998: 294–311.

17 It is worth pointing out that Posey 'warmed up' for her role as foil to Ryan in another film by Nora Ephron, *Sleepless in Seattle* (1993). Posey's role as Tom Hanks's neighbor in that film was cut during editing.

18 The requirement that Posey's trademark energy be pathologized in a mainstream romance is illustrated by her representation here as suspiciously dependent on both espresso and sleeping pills.

19 In fact, *The Sweetest Thing*'s version of 'gender equity' entails frequent rationalization of misogyny. Late in the film a nude female mannequin is struck by a car in an utterly gratuitous plot point that symbolically and starkly illustrates the superficiality of the film's 'girl-power' claims.

20 Interestingly, in order to effect this transformation it is not the actress's physical appearance that is altered, but her speech, one of Posey's trademark 'indie' attributes and a presumed intolerable sign of her empowerment. This film's toothless critique of the calculation of corporate culture (as if the film itself were not fully complicit in such calculation) stands in stark contrast to *Clockwatchers* which generates authentic critique of similar subject matter and uses Posey as a figure of unruly and blunt speech to do it.

21 Emblematic of Posey's declining capital in 2002 was her 'descent' to one of tele-

vision's lowest-status genres, the made-for-TV movie, when she appeared alongside Shannon Doherty and Shirley McLaine in *Hell on Heels: The Battle of Mary Kay* on 6 October 2002. McLaine and Doherty's 'post-peak' celebrity is meaningful here and doubtless impinged on the depreciation of Posey's stardom as she 'traded-down' from independent film to CBS Sunday night movie. As this chapter was completed, however, it appeared that Posey might be poised for critical rehabilitation, as reviews lauded her performance as Greta in Rebecca Miller's independent film *Personal Velocity*.

Bibliography

Allen, R.C. (1999) 'Home Alone Together: Hollywood and the "Family Film," ' in M. Stokes and R. Maltby (eds.) *Identifying Hollywood's Audiences: Cultural Identity and the Movies*, London: British Film Institute, 109–31.

Babington, B. (ed.) (2001) *British Stars and Stardom: From Alma Taylor to Sean Connery*, Manchester: Manchester University Press.

Brooks, D. (2001) *Bobos in Paradise: The New Upper Class and How They Got There*, New York: Touchstone.

Chin, D. (1997) 'Festival Markets, Critics: Notes on the State of the Art Film,' *Performing Arts Journal*, 19, 1: 61–75.

Corliss, R. and Ressner, J. (1997) 'Queen of the Indies,' *Time*, 149, 7 (17 February): 82.

DeCordova, R. (1990) *Picture Personalities: The Emergence of the Star System in America*, Urbana and Chicago: University of Illinois Press.

Dicker, R. (2002) 'For Posey, Fame Isn't Fortune,' *Toronto Star*, 18 April: A35.

Evans, P.W. (1998) 'Meg Ryan, Megastar,' in P.W. Evans and C. Deleyto (eds.), *Terms of Endearment: Hollywood Romantic Comedy of the 1980s and 1990s*, Edinburgh: Edinburgh University Press, 188–208.

Flanagan, M. (1999) 'Mobile Identities, Digital Stars, and Post-Cinematic Selves,' *Wide Angle*, 21, 1 (January): 77–93.

Frank, T. (1997) *The Conquest of Cool: Business Culture, Counterculture, and the Rise of Hip Consumerism*, Chicago: University of Chicago Press.

Gleiberman, O. (1997) 'Sibling Ribaldry: Parker Posey Plays a Girl Who Just Can't Say No in *The House of Yes*, a Dark Comedy of Forbidden Love,' *Entertainment Weekly*, 401 (17 October): 44.

Goble, M. (2001) 'Cameo Appearances; or, When Gertrude Stein Checks into *Grand Hotel*,' *Modern Language Quarterly*, 62, 2: 117–63.

Hillier, J. (2001) *American Independent Cinema: A Sight and Sound Reader*, London: British Film Institute.

Holmlund, C. (2003) *Impossible Bodies: Femininity and Masculinity at the Movies*, London: Routledge.

Hu, W. (1998) 'For Parker Posey, a Zany Dance in the Sun,' *New York Times*, 59 (6 September): 29.

King, B. (1986) 'Stardom as an Occupation,' in P. Kerr (ed.), *The Hollywood Film Industry*, London: Routledge & Kegan Paul, 154–84.

Kleinhans, C. (1998) 'Independent Features: Hopes and Dreams,' in J. Lewis (ed.), *The New American Cinema*, Durham, NC: Duke University Press, 307–27.

Kramer, P. (1998) 'Would You Take Your Child to See This Film? The Cultural and Social Work of the Family-Adventure Movie,' in S. Neale and M. Smith (eds.), *Contemporary Hollywood Cinema*, London: Routledge, 294–311.

Levy, E. (1999) *Cinema of Outsiders: The Rise of American Independent Film*, New York: New York University Press.

McGee, C. (1995) 'Don't Be Fooled: This Is No Dazed and Confused Party Girl,' *New York Times*, 4 June: H18.

McDonald, P. (2000) *The Star System: Hollywood's Production of Popular Identities*, London: Wallflower Press.

Mitchell, E. (2002) 'Goodness Has Nothing to Do With It,' *New York Times Magazine*, 24 February: 41–8.

Negra, D. (2001) *Off-White Hollywood: American Culture and Ethnic Female Stardom*, London: Routledge.

Peters, A.K. and Cantor, M.G. (1982) 'Screen Acting as Work,' in J.S. Ettema and D.C. Whitney (eds.) *Individuals in Mass Media Organizations: Creativity and Constraint*, Beverly Hills and London: Sage, 53–68.

Pierson, J. (1995) *Spike, Mike, Slackers & Dykes: A Guided Tour Across a Decade of American Independent Cinema*, New York: Hyperion.

Quart, A. (2002) 'Who's Afraid of Parker Posey?' *Film Comment* (November–December): 42–4.

Sconce, J. (2002) 'Irony, Nihilism and the New American "Smart" Film,' *Screen*, 43, 4 (winter): 349–69.

Smith, C. (1997) 'East of Eden,' *New York*, 30, 38 (6 October): 36–43.

Solomon, H. (1999) 'Parker Posey: The Very Big Star of Small Films,' *Biography*, 3, 1 (January): 68.

Spines, C. (2002) 'Who Let the Underdogs Out?' *Premiere*, 16, 2 (October): 84–9, 108–12.

Steinhauer, J. (1997) 'Life's a Ball: Dress for It – Unpacking (and Repacking) with Parker Posey,' *New York Times*, 9 (12 October): 1, 6.

Sullivan, R. (2002) 'Best in Show,' *Vogue* (November): 337.

Travers, P. (1998) 'Summer's Power Babes,' *Rolling Stone*, 790–1 (9 July): 146.

Turan, K. (2002) *Sundance to Sarajevo: Film Festivals and the World They Made*, Berkeley, CA: University of California Press.

Willman, C. (1997) 'Parker Posey,' *Entertainment Weekly* (November–December): 50–1.

Chapter 9

Dark, disturbing, intelligent, provocative, and quirky

Avant-garde cinema of the 1980s and 1990s[1]

Joan Hawkins

Not much has been written about avant-garde cinema of the past twenty years: *The Village Voice* writer Amy Taubin still reviews the avant-garde, in specialist columns; a few journals like *Millennium* and telnet listservs like 'Frameworks' provide information and viewing news for those already in the know. In terms of general film history, however, the impression all too often is that the avant-garde somehow died after Warhol. Not only are there few specialist publications about avant-garde cinema, but general works on cinema of the 1980s and 1990s have tended to focus on either popular multiplex titles or on mainstream independent productions. Books like William J. Palmer's *The Films of the Eighties: A Social History* (1993) make no mention of avant-garde film culture, an omission which suggests that the downtown art scene has no impact on 'social history.' And books like Emanuel Levy's otherwise excellent *Cinema of Outsiders: The Rise of American Independent Film* take 'the decline of radical [avant-garde] film practice' as a 'given' (Levy 1999: 6). Even authors like Robert Siegle and Greil Marcus, who have written on other aspects of radical punk-inflected culture – literature, art, music – have tended to omit discussion of contemporary avant-garde film (it's interesting that Marcus writes about situationist film, but very little that comes after, even though he knows the club environments in which many of these films originally played).

The one scholarly book that has come out on punk film, Jack Sargeant's *Deathtripping: The Cinema of Transgression* (1995), focuses on transgressive cinema – the in-your-face, gross-out branch of punk avant-garde cinema. Represented movies like Nick Zedd's *They Eat Scum* (1979), *The Manhattan Love Suicides* (1984), and John Spencer's *Shithaus*, this is the branch of recent avant-garde production that has the closest ties to porn, psychotronic, and splatter films. In terms of total avant-garde output, the films that Sargeant discusses represent just one small (albeit important) sector of downtown film culture. The rest of contemporary downtown cinema has received scant scholarly treatment. In a sense, then, avant-garde cinema of the 1980s and 1990s exists as almost a repressed term within the larger cultural–film history of the *fin-de-siècle*. And while there certainly will not be time in the course of this discussion to completely redress that balance, I propose to lay out some of the defining features of what I call 'downtown film culture' and trace its connections to more mainstream independent cinema.

I start with the mid-1970s and close with the end of the 1990s, in part because this is the period in which avant-garde cinema more or less disappears from the existing histories. But I am also concerned with this era because it is the time when American independent cinema seemed to come into its own, and there are interesting overlaps between the two cultural formations (downtown cinema and indie cinema). Several filmmakers who later became indie filmmakers – Todd Haynes and David Lynch, for example – started as downtown filmmakers. And many of the more provocative independent films of this period have been heavily indebted to downtown cinema and downtown film culture. Two such films – *Happiness* and *In the Company of Men* – are analyzed in the second half of the chapter. These films deserve special merit because they belong to what Emanuel Levy has called 'the new trend in indie cinema' (1999: 151). Ironic in tone, cynical, and emotionally brutal, these films mark both a special trend within independent cinema and illustrate the degree to which some of the more disturbing indie films have traded on the themes and stylistic tropes of late twentieth-century experimental film culture.

What draws together avant-garde cineastes and cinephiles of the late twentieth century is a common urban lifestyle, a shared commitment to formal and narrative experimentation, a view of the human body as a site of social and political struggle, an intense interest in radical identity politics, and a mistrust of institutionalized mechanisms of wealth and power. Politically, the filmmakers run the gamut from anarchist to libertarian, and many of them have roots in punk underground culture. They find literary parallels and, occasionally, inspiration in the works of J.G. Ballard, Louis-Ferdinand Céline and William S. Burroughs, and are theoretically indebted to the writings of Georges Bataille, Jean Baudrillard, Gilles Deleuze, Michel Foucault, Félix Guattari, Karl Marx and Friedrich Nietzsche. In terms of cinematic style, they seem to draw equally from surrealism, European art cinema, and the avant-garde tradition of Andy Warhol. But they also borrow heavily from 'low' culture – erotic thrillers, horror, sci-fi, and porn, and the adjectives most frequently used to describe their work are 'dark,' 'disturbing,' 'intelligent,' 'provocative,' and 'quirky.'

The first downtown films – Alexis Krasilovksy's *Blood* (1975), David Lynch's *Eraserhead* (1976) and Amos Poe's *Unmade Beds* (1976) – appeared in the mid-1970s, but the impetus for a new underground cinema really took hold in the 1980s when, as Robert Siegle notes, the US economy 'turned mean' (Siegle 1989: 9). In the face of recession and, later, the threat of an AIDS pandemic, some US artists and filmmakers began moving downtown: to the East Village in Manhattan, the warehouse district in Chicago, the South of Market area (SOMA) in San Francisco, depressed areas where rent was low and studio space was available. Once there, they got day-jobs and lived in what Chris Kraus (1997: 196) has called 'independent poverty' so that their real energy could go into cultural production. The cultural products they made reflected the neighborhoods they inhabited – burned-out areas which stand, Robert Siegle (1989: 1) writes, 'as one of the most potent demystifiers of the illusions in which most of us live.' It was the neighborhood itself which provided a sense of artistic cohesion, and it is perhaps for that very reason that both the artists and the work they produced were labeled with geographical epithets – 'downtown,' 'East Village,' 'SOMA.'

In addition to being united by a sense of community or place, the filmmakers are united by a clear sociopolitical agenda. Like the Dadas and surrealists, they attempt 'to shake up reified relations' (ibid.: 3) in both the art world and in society at large. Their work challenges received ideas about gender, race, class, and sexual preference; it attempts to destabilize the existing social order through direct intervention in that social order's spectacle. But downtown artists are not naively utopian. They know 'no structure will escape reification, no legislation fail to repress and normalize, no specification avoid replacing the "reality" it was intended to approach' (ibid.: 3). Despite these odds, however, downtown artists persist 'in a sort of hit-and-run guerrilla action' designed to make the consumers of their art confront the skeletons in our cultural closet (ibid.: 3). In film, this often takes the form of disturbing documentaries and nonfiction essays in cinema. Jennifer Montgomery's *Home Avenue* (1989), for example, is a seventeen-minute nonfiction film, shot, in a nice neighborhood, on a quiet street walking along which, 8mm camera in hand, the filmmaker retraces the events of a night when she was raped at gunpoint, not far from her parents' house. 'It is mock TV news,' Bill Nichols notes, 'mock "vérité" as Montgomery points out the actual spot in the dispassionate, upbeat manner of a TV street reporter, as if this happened to someone else. There are no screen tears of remembrance which only adds to the disturbance' (Nichols and Peary 1996: 36–7).[2]

Like Montgomery's film, many *fin-de-siècle* experimental movies attempt to lay bare the dark underside of middle-class and middle-American life. One nonfiction film of particular interest is *Seventeen* (1987) by Joel DeMott and Jeff Kreines. Originally produced for the PBS Middletown series, *Seventeen* was banned from television for its brutally honest portrayal of a girl's turbulent last year in high school. Now shown mainly on the downtown film festival and specialist house circuit, the film documents in raw, uncompromising style the class barriers that exist in the Indiana town where *Seventeen* is set. Like other downtown films of this era, it presents what would ordinarily be depicted as a socioeconomic problem – or even tragedy – quite unapologetically, so that this troubled life emerges within the bounds of the film as the *norm*. We see kids struggling at school and at home:

tumultuous classroom scenes, boozing parties, pot-smoking, preparing for a neighborhood race war, an unexpected pregnancy, a fatal car accident, and romance. I don't believe I've ever seen a movie about white teens that's so brutally devoid of any reference to the American Dream. The last day of school the black sociology teacher tells his senior class that life is half hard work and half luck; and that even if you've gotten straight As in school that's no guarantee of success. The best you can do, he tells them, is just *try* to do what you can, and be a good husband or wife or parent. Quite a bit different from the 'you-can-do-any-thing-you-want' and 'be-anything-you-want-to-be' message that most prime-time and mainstream Hollywood film kids are told.

Fiction films, too, take an uncompromising view of middle-American life. Todd Verow's *Frisk* (1996) is a case in point. Based on a novel by downtown writer Dennis Cooper, *Frisk* details a young man's growing fascination with snuff imagery (to which he's introduced by his brother and an adult male friend) and his concomitant desire to see what the opened body has to teach us. Walking a fine line between porn and horror, the film plays with many of the issues raised by such theoretical writers as Carol J. Clover (*Men, Women, and Chainsaws* [1992]) and Linda Williams (*Hardcore* [1989]). But its elliptical style and dark humor place it firmly within the 1980s–1990s downtown film movement. Well-written and acted (Parker Posey is terrific as the angel-faced co-conspirator in the murders which Michael Gunther stages), *Frisk* forcefully calls into question what's con-sidered low culture and what's considered 'art.' Incorporating images from S&M porn magazines and adult videos, it raises the unsettling question of the roles which pornography and the media play in shaping an individual's psyche. Like *Home Avenue*, the film stages all its violence in nice neighborhoods, and its mon-sters could be any number of clean-cut college-kids-next-door. What do upper-middle-class boys do when they get together with their friends, the film asks? You don't want to know.

All of these films reject sentimentality. Grim episodes are recounted or, in the case of the fiction films, acted out, with irony and with a certain sense of matter-of-fact detachment and cool. Perhaps more disturbingly, violence is often exploited in the interest of provoking real sensation in the audience. Directly engaging the body of the spectator, the films frequently use the visuals and the-matic tropes of 'low' genres like horror and porn to make their point.[3] Even here they push the envelope of audience response. Vampire films show large, gaping, ragged-edged wounds where the victim has been bitten, rather than the neat pinpricks and clean incisions used in Hollywood movies. Graphic depictions of sexuality are often cinematically motivated and cued by violence. Addiction is depicted – as Burroughs depicted it in *The Naked Lunch* – as the dominant organizing metaphor for life under late capitalism.

In the sense that they directly challenge the viewer, downtown films participate in the same kind of aesthetic practiced by Brecht and Godard. They form a 'counter-cinema,'[4] one that, like real political encounters, can take you 'by the shoulders and shake you out' (Kraus 1997: 156). Unlike the works of Brecht and Godard, though, these films are rarely overtly polemical,[5] and they rarely try to disrupt the narrative or block traditional processes of spectator identification. Rather, as Todd Haynes has noted, they attempt to reveal the way narrative and traditional processes of cinematic identification work, 'without nullifying the process of identification' itself (1999).

Not all of the downtown filmmakers are young and not all of them live down-town, though all of them do share what Jennifer Montgomery has called a 'punk underground aesthetic' (Nichols and Peary 1996: 36), a sensibility that Haynes labels 'East Village' (Haynes 1999). The stories they tell – about hustling in the sex industry, about drug addiction, about alienation, racism, homophobia, environmental illness, cultural malaise, and AIDS – frequently are not the stories mainstream film-goers want to see. There is a raw grittiness here, which often extends to the formal elements of filmmaking. In Eric Mitchell's 1978 film *Kid-napped*, for example, actors step carefully over exposed extension cords in a lower Eastside apartment, and perch on the side of a dirty clawfoot bathtub to write a ransom note. Amos Poe and Ivan Krul's's documentary of the emerging punk rock scene, *The Blank Generation* (1976), does not even try to use synch sound; instead, a soundtrack of songs by Patti Smith, The Ramones, *et al.* is simply juxtaposed with moving images of the performers. And many of the films made during the 1980s look as though they were filmed in the same blue-walled New York apartment.

Partly this is due to budget constraints; but, even when they have a budget, many downtown directors prefer their films to have a grainy, black-and-white look, which borrows equally from early Italian neo-realism and George Romero's *Night of the Living Dead* (1968).[6] They shoot on location, and many of them make extensive use of real time (if there is a dominant aesthetic that holds the films to-gether, one might say it's that of the long take, an aesthetic which seems indebted to both Antonioni and Warhol). If there is a beauty here, it is, as Andrei Codrescu notes, a 'savage beauty' marked by the 'sophistication and brutality' (Rose and Texier 1988: back cover) of both the historical avant-garde and film noir.

Despite the frequent references to historical antecedents, downtown culture is not simply a reworking of previous avant-garde and popular styles.[7] Many of the works have strong links to postmodern theory, to a discursive strategy which Steven Shaviro has identified as no longer 'a theoretical option or a stylistic choice,' but rather an endemic part of contemporary *fin-de-siècle* culture (Shaviro 1997: Preface) Many of the artists working downtown went to graduate school, and their works often explicitly reference the very theories which will be used to critique them. Writer–filmmaker Chris Kraus is one of the editors at

Semiotext(e), the leading US publisher of Jean Baudrillard and Félix Guattari. Furthermore, as the editor of the press's Native Agents series – a series of American prose works (fiction and essays) – she has a certain economic stake in demonstrating the degree to which downtown *artistic* culture enacts a kind of radical postmodern theory.[8] Todd Haynes studied feminist film theory at Brown University and has talked about the conscious manipulations of 'the gaze' in his films. Novelist–screenwriter Kathy Acker studied with Herbert Marcuse and frequently references philosophy in her work. Downtown cinematic culture positions itself, then, not only somewhere between 'high art' and 'low culture' (drawing equally from avant-garde and popular sources) but somewhere between official academic theory and a theory-savvy, streetwise, 'lay'-avant-garde style. If the surrealists opened a space for Marx and Freud's ideas within avant-garde art, downtown film and literature have reconstituted theory as radical chic. In that sense they comprise what may be described as a postmodern or poststructuralist avant-garde, an avant-garde which is heavily indebted to and informed by academic culture.

Perhaps the most extreme cinematic example of this is *Blue Tape* (1974), a videotape Stephen Sondheim made in collaboration with Kathy Acker (recently restored by Buffalo-based video artist Tony Conrad). Here, serious discussions of theory, writing, and art are juxtaposed with graphic depictions of masturbation and oral sex. Abel Ferrara's *The Addiction* (1994) similarly mixes theory with body genres as a philosophy graduate student slowly realizes she is turning into a vampire. And Bette Gordon's *Variety* (1983) tackles feminist theory head-on, as it boldly explores the feminine response to pornography.

Graphic sex and horror aside, there are connections between avant-garde films of this period and the 'independent film' movement of the same period, but most of the films we might call 'avant-garde' do not get the kind of distribution that mainstream indie films get. Downtown filmmakers often consider themselves artists and identify more with the downtown art scene than they do with Sundance. Their films play in alternative festivals,[9] clubs, galleries, museums, academic settings and cinémathèques, rather than art houses. Some of them are distributed through specialist mail order rental and purchasing outfits – the Monday/Wednesday/Friday video club in New York, Electronic Arts Intermix, Frameline, and Strand are the main distributors for the most offbeat stuff, but you can also rent videos from Facets Multimedia in Chicago. A lot of the filmmakers I consider 'downtown' speak quite derisively about so-called independent films, which they call 'Indiewood.'

That said, there *has* been a lot of cross-over, and many of the films have had a larger influence on mainstream independent film culture than one would think, given their limited distribution. Thanks largely to television (particularly community access cable), video, and now the internet, they've been seen – by midnight-movie fans (for whom some films, like *Eraserhead*, became cult hits), by people who scan the shelves of local independently owned video outlets looking for video boxes which promise 'something different,' by kids who read collectors' catalogues and surf the net, by middle-class Home Film Festival patrons who rent their videotapes by mail, and by insomniacs who happen to turn to the right cable channels late at night. Because they encroach so vigorously on horror, porn, and erotic thrillers, the films have reached a much larger video audience than most avant-garde film ever reaches; and because the individual titles tend to revolve around narratives, people who would ordinarily shy away from experimental media watch these films all the way to the end. Thus, they have had a much greater impact on US culture than their limited theatrical distribution would suggest, and their impact on more widely distributed independent cinema ('Indiewood') can be seen in such recent titles as Todd Haynes's *Safe* (1995), David Lynch's *Lost Highway* (1997), Neil LaBute's *In the Company of Men* (1997), Todd Solondz's *Happiness* (1998), and Lisa Cholodenko's *High Art* (1998).

Neil LaBute's *In the Company of Men* and Todd Solondz's *Happiness* belong to what Emanuel Levy has called 'the new trend in indie cinema.' Replacing Quentin Tarantino's 'profane, ultraviolent movies,' they stand as 'cynical, nihilistic exposés of social relationships, where the violence is more behavioral and emotional than physical' (Levy 1999: 151). Like the *fin-de-siècle* experimental movies I described earlier, they attempt to lay bare the dark underside of middle-class American life; and, like the experimental films of this period, they reject sentimentality. Grim episodes are recounted or acted out, with irony, with a certain sense of matter-of-fact detachment and cool, that is both disturbing and unsettling.

In the Company of Men begins in an airport courtesy lounge. Two men – Chad (Aaron Eckhart) and Howard (Matt Malloy) – who work for the same company are being sent to an unnamed midwest branch office for six weeks, in order to oversee an unspecified installation and training program. Chad and Howie are old college friends, and they begin exchanging stories of slights at work and humiliating experiences with women. 'Seems like everything: work, these women. Feel like they're getting out of balance, don't they?' Howie asks. 'Yeah,' Chad agrees, 'they really do. We ought to do something about it.' The men decide to wreak their vengeance on women by playing a cruel hoax on some woman they assume they'll meet in the heartland. The idea is that both men will target and seduce a woman from the local office, someone vulnerable – preferably 'deformed,' Chad says – who doubts that she can ever have a meaningful relationship. After a whirlwind courtship, during which they presume the woman will blossom ('start wearing makeup again'), they'll both dump her, and laugh about it, Chad says, 'until we are very old men.'

The woman they choose for this scheme is the lovely, deaf Christine (Stacy

Figure 9.1 Howard (Matt Malloy) and Chad (Aaron Eckhart) in *In the Company of Men* (LaBute, 1997). Courtesy of Fair and Square Productions/Atlantis/Kobal Collection.

Edwards), and both men start romancing her with dates and flowers, as planned. The twist comes, however, when Howard finds himself actually falling in love with Christine. In an unnerving scene, he tells her about the 'game' he and Chad are playing; then, producing a slightly used engagement ring, offers to 'make it right' by marrying her. But Christine has been badly hurt and will have nothing to do with him. A few weeks later Howard realizes that he has been as much a dupe of the game as Christine: not only did Chad win the competition for Christine's affections (Howard tells her about the game when she finally confesses to him that she loves Chad) but he has quietly undermined Howard's position at work, as well – in the penultimate scene, we learn that Chad has moved 'upstairs,' while Howard has been demoted to customer relations. At the same time, Chad reveals that his account of mistreatment by a lover – the story he had used to convince Howard to play the seduction game – was a lie. As Paul Arthur notes in his review for *Cineaste*,

> the suggestion is that, despite an overarching viciousness and anger directed at the social order in general, Chad's ulterior motive in concocting the seduction scheme has been status envy, the subversion of Howard's superior position in the corporate hierarchy. In other words, the manipulation of sexual power has served as a cloak for intrafraternal warfare: boys hit on girl, boys fuck each other up, boys exchange job descriptions (Arthur 1997: 2).

In a film that is so much about men, it makes sense that Christine remains something of an unknowable character. For the most part, the film maintains a strict perspectival focus on Chad and Howard. Scenes shift between the two men alone and their dates with Christine. She is given no independent life (we do not see her outside her relationship with the men). In this way the film seems to follow Chad and Howie's lead in cordoning off 'her subjectivity' (*ibid.*: 2) and treating her simply as a pawn in the men's scheme. At the end, however, the film seems to back away from its own chilly and chilling structure, and renders explicit its full sympathy for Christine. When Chad tells Christine that Howard's revelation about the 'game' is true and leaves the hotel room where he and she had been talking (leaves the frame), the camera lingers on a two-minute overhead close-up of Christine crying. This is the first time we have seen Christine alone and it is also the only shot in the film in which a character simply emotes, simply feels, outside a social encounter. This same sudden shift of perspective (where we are now suddenly *with* Christine) is 'repeated and amplified' in the final scene as, weeks later, Howard barges into the bank where Christine is now working and demands that she 'listen' to him (*ibid.*: 2). As he repeatedly yells 'Listen to me,' his voice abruptly disappears from the soundtrack, giving us – quite literally – the deaf woman's view.

In the Company of Men definitely belongs to mainstream independent cinema, but it is not quite the 'Indiewood' for which downtown filmmakers criticize it. Like narrative downtown films of this period, *In the Company of Men* is relentless in its portrayal of emotional violence. There is no traditional Hollywood ending, in which Chad would either learn a valuable lesson and change (the redemption motif) or get his comeuppance (the justice motif). Instead, as so often in real life, he merely ascends the corporate ladder; and at the end of the film we can only assume that he will play the same game again, if and when he finds a suitable 'mark.'

More importantly, unlike most 'Indiewood' films (films that are independently made but seem to follow many of Hollywood's formulae), *In the Company of Men* is less about individual morality than it is about systemic behavior. Throughout the film, Chad and Howard are shown to be products of the corporate world they inhabit. In fact, milieu plays almost as great a role here as it does in downtown cinema, which – as I said earlier – is often largely about neighborhood. Most of LaBute's film is shot against the elegantly nondescript background of corporate offices, hotel rooms and restaurants, and the male behavior depicted appears to be dictated to a certain extent by corporate environment and culture: 'I mean we're like ten years out of University,' Chad tells Howard early in the film. 'That's all. Just ten. And I've got a whole crop of these young dudes after my desk.' The corporate message is clear, at least according to Chad: eat or be eaten.

In this realm, Chad is the superior corporate man, a fact which is underscored in the final scenes of the film, when we finally see his apartment. While Howie says that the décor shows 'a woman's touch,' it really doesn't look much different from the corporate offices we'd seen earlier. The sofa is leather and there's an *American Gigolo* (Schrader, 1980) poster on the wall, but for the most part the apartment shows the same color scheme and minimalist style of the corporate lobbies we have seen throughout the movie. Chad is so at home in the corporate world, the *mise-en-scène* tells us, that he literally brings home the office.

I should stress that the corporate world depicted in this film is mainly that of the white male. The only women in this unnamed corporation appear to work in the secretarial pool, and the African American men who work there are subject to a kind of racial hazing that seems to be as much about machismo as it is about corporate culture. In fact the film goes a long way to collapsing the two – so that corporate culture is seen to be corrupt *because* it is such an 'intrafraternal' environment. What happens when women join the executive ranks is not explored, and their very absence seems to undercut Chad and Howie's complaints about feminism. If women are taking over, it is hard to see in this film exactly where that is happening.

If, as the title suggests, the film is largely about corporate *men*, it is also about the way in which all corporate men are the same at heart. Throughout the film, Howie seems like the nicer guy: he does not make fun of Christine behind her back; nor does he engage in the cruel body jokes that Chad likes to play (in one scene Chad makes an African American intern unzip his pants; in another he makes fun of Christine's voice by doing 'Flipper' imitations). In a touching pair of scenes, Howie even tries to sign, demonstrating that he is sensitive to issues of deaf culture. But when Christine tells him she loves Chad, he lashes out at her, saying things that are just as cruel as the things which Chad has said behind her back. 'You are fucking handicapped,' he tells her. 'You think you can choose? Men falling at your feet?' In the face of rejection, Howie reveals that he is just as biased ('able-ist') as his friend. No matter how beautiful or charming they are, people who are physically different are 'deformed' (in both Chad and Howie's view), and they should be grateful for any able-bodied attention they get.

The bleakness of the film's message – corporations corrupt; at heart all corporate men are the same; a dog-eat-dog world is what is out there – as well as its detached, matter-of-fact style, links *In the Company of Men* to downtown cinema. In addition, the film's visual style is reminiscent of downtown experimental narrative productions. While LaBute does not give his film the grainy, raw, gritty look that downtown filmmakers like Nick Zedd and Jennifer Montgomery seem to favor, he does make extensive use of the long take (as I said earlier, if there is a dominant aesthetic that holds downtown films together it is that of the long take, an aesthetic which seems indebted to both Antonioni and Warhol). There is very little virtuoso camera movement in this film; instead, scenes are mainly tightly framed two-shots, which are held for an extended period of time: people sit or stand, and talk. And while *In the Company of Men* does make more extensive use of shot–countershot than do most downtown films, the dominant look of the film is that of a high-budget downtown movie.

Todd Solondz's *Happiness* makes similarly extensive use of close-ups and long takes. The film has similarly been called a cynical, nihilistic exposé of social relationships, 'where the violence is more behavioral and emotional than physical' (Levy 1999: 151). Yet *Happiness* plays with identification in a way that LaBute's film hints at (the two scenes in which our focus is on Christine) but does not fully explore. While initially the film is so ironic, so detached, that identification with any of the adult characters would seem impossible, it ends up fostering strong audience identification with the most troubled of the male protagonists. Like downtown filmmaker Todd Haynes's films, then, *Happiness* attempts to reveal the way narrative and traditional processes of cinematic identification work, 'without nullifying the process of identification' itself.

The film follows Solondz's earlier film *Welcome to the Dollhouse* (1996) in both skewering middle-class suburban family life and in presenting a sensitive portrayal of adolescent insecurity. But *Happiness* is a much more complicated film – both in narrative terms and thematically – than is *Welcome to the Dollhouse* – and, for my purposes, it definitely has more of a downtown edge. The film is structured, as Cynthia Lucia and Ed Kelleher (1999: 2) note, like a spider's web. The narrative revolves, more or less, around three sisters and their interconnecting lives. Trish (Cynthia Stevenson) is a relentlessly perky suburban soccer mom, who continually assures her sisters and husband that she has 'it all' – three kids, a nice house, a successful husband (who no longer sleeps with her), and a dog. Her eldest son, Billy (Rufus Read), is in a crucial stage of pre-teen development, anxious to learn about sex and manhood from his father, Bill (Dylan Baker). And – as several critics have noted – his conversations with Bill play like a pastiche of the bedtime chats that *Leave it to Beaver* dad Ward Cleaver used to have with his son, the Beav. 'Dad, what does "come" mean?' Billy asks on one occasion; and, on another, 'How long is your penis?' Being an enlightened dad, Bill reassures his son that it is width, not length, that makes things 'a little more intense,' and he offers to show his son how to masturbate more effectively. What Bill does not tell his son is that he has his own concerns about sexual 'normalcy.' A psychologist, Little League dad, and involved community member, Bill is also a pederast. Early in the film, we see him drive to a convenience store, buy a magazine showing pre-teen boys, and masturbate. When he later molests two of Billy's classmates, Bill is exposed as a 'serial rapist' and 'pervert' (words that are spraypainted on his house), and Trish is forced to acknowledge that her husband really is – as he tried to tell her – 'sick.'

If child molestation is presented as the 'dirty secret' of American suburban life, it is also represented as the titillating ploy of the art world. Trish's sister Helen

(Lara Flynn Boyle) is a successful poet whose work is, as she herself admits, 'exploitationist and shallow.' ' "Rape at eleven," "Rape at twelve," what the hell do I know about rape?' she says. 'Oh, if only I'd been raped as a child! Then I would know authenticity.' Helen's conception of poetry and 'authenticity' as a never-ending exploration of 'wound culture' (Seltzer 1998) is meant as an ironic commentary on a culture industry that often confuses 'authenticity' with violence and pain. Yet Helen's longing for rape without trauma also links her to Bill (who always drugs his victims so that they have no memory of the actual event). And the fact that Helen makes money from what is essentially a violent sexual fantasy links her both to Bill, who is paid to listen to the sexual fantasies of his patients, and to the patients themselves, who long for an intense experience they've never had.

The third sister, Joy (Jane Adams), is a would-be folk singer who quits her day-job after a man she had dated commits suicide and leaves a note blaming her for his death. She then takes a job teaching English to immigrants. Even here she attracts hostility: 'I am not a scab,' she tells her outraged students the first day of class, 'I am a strike breaker.' While Joy might be miserable, her role as the underachiever in the family serves only to help her sisters to bond. When they meet for lunch, Helen and Trish engage in an elegantly understated, but nasty, game of oneupmanship, as each tries to reassure the other that *she* has the busier and more fulfilling life. 'Listen to us,' Helen tells Trish. 'We who have everything, while Joy – what does she have?'

In addition, there are the sisters' parents, Lenny and Mona (Ben Gazzara and Louise Lasser), a loveless couple who have moved to a Florida retirement

Figure 9.2 Allen (Philip Seymour Hoffman) and Helen (*Lara Flynn Boyle*) in *Happiness* (Solondz, 1998). Courtesy of October Film/Kobal Collection.

community, and Bill's patient, Allen, who initially loves Helen, but finally settles with his overweight neighbor, Kristina. Most of the characters want someone they cannot have, objects of desire 'far beyond their reach' (Lucia and Kelleher 1999: 2). And most of the characters in Solondz's film are depicted with a kind of ironic detachment that makes identification with them difficult: Joy seems almost to invite the hostility which, as she rightly notes, is so often directed at her; Trish is vapid to the point of caricature; Helen seems like a cartoon rendition of the pretentious poet; while Allen is a broadly played version of the sexually troubled and hapless nerd. Even genres are subject to irony here. The opening restaurant scenes between Andy and Joy almost always evoke audience laughter, as they unfold like a *Saturday Night Live* parody of sentimental romance. The point to the broad humor and irony, however, is not merely to stroke the audience's vanity, to let us laugh at the characters, from a position of feeling superior to them: rather the intent of the film is to make the audience question the culture which has produced such a striking assemblage of oddballs, and to do so through the distancing use of ironic comedy. The result, as *Sight and Sound* reviewer Xan Brooks notes, is an 'almost surreal' film, one in which suburbia is presented as a type of 'peripheral hell' (Brooks 2001: 146) – but one in which nobody, not even the audience, is let off the hook.

Of all the relationships which unfold – or never get started – in *Happiness*, the only one that seems to have real depth is that developed between Bill and Billy. This is doubly striking since Bill is represented as such a subversive character. Early in the film he recounts a recurring dream to his own psychologist, a dream in which he goes into a park where people are playing sports and having a good time. While a lilting refrain plays in the background, Bill opens fire with a machine-gun and massacres everyone. 'And how is this different?' the therapist asks. 'I don't kill myself at the end,' Bill answers.

From the start then, Bill is represented – the way monsters in horror films often are – as a character whose secret mission is to destabilize society, a character who is troubled by antisocial urges, and who still manages to garner at least some audience sympathy. As critics have noted, while the distribution controversy of *Happiness* 'centered, in large part, on the subject of pedophilia, it seems more likely that this controversy has arisen less from the subject itself than from the manner in which Solondz elicits audience sympathy' for the pederast (Lucia and Kelleher 1999: 3). In part, Solondz retains audience sympathy for Bill by discreetly pulling away long before the moment of rape itself, so that we never see Bill trying to penetrate a pre-pubescent child. Similarly, because Bill always drugs his victims, there is no traumatic aftermath to bring home the reality of child abuse. Johnny Grasso has what seems to be the 'flu after his comatose encounter with his friend's dad. When he later notices blood in his stools, he sees it as only an excuse to stay home from school. Trauma in this film, then, is linked not to the act itself but, in biblical and psychoanalytic fashion, to knowledge of the act (the knowledge of good and evil).

As a result, all the trauma caused by Bill's cumulative perverse acts is displaced on to his relationship with Billy. The final conversation that Bill has with Billy is the most painfully *real* moment in the film – no stock character acting or irony here. It is this conversation which renders the film – as the video box advertises – 'deeply disturbing' and 'subtly savage.' Emblematic of a relationship characterized by Bill's frank responses to Billy's sexual questions, this scene seems almost brutal as Bill gives painfully candid answers to his son. When Billy hesitatingly asks his dad what, exactly, he did to his friends, Bill answers: 'I touched them . . . fondled them . . . I couldn't help myself . . . I fucked them.' When Billy asks 'Would you ever fuck me?' Bill responds: 'No, I'd jerk off instead,' as both break down in tears. As several critics have noted, it is not clear in this scene whether Billy is crying because he wants Bill to desire him in the same way he desired Billy's friends, or whether he's relieved that his dad at least recognizes certain sexual bounds. What is clear is that Billy will now be thrown back on a set of unsatisfying relationships with cartoon-like people – not a very promising prognosis for a pre-teen trying to make sense of the world.

The sexual trauma and the destruction of the nuclear family which serve as *Happiness*'s climax seem initially to link the film to an avant-garde tradition, which from the nineteenth century onward has been critical of the patriarchal family as a social institution. But while the film appears to take a profoundly anti-family, anti-suburban, stance, at the end it seems to lose its avant-garde nerve, and to retreat to a more conservative and traditional posture. By making Bill the most sympathetic adult character in the film, Solondz insures that we will feel bad when he goes. Even as Trish packs the car the morning after Bill and Billy's critical talk, the audience wishes there was some way – draconian behavior-modification therapy for Bill, perhaps – to keep the family together. This is hardly the stuff of which true avant-garde drama is made: and it is exactly this kind of retreat to mainstream values that leads Emanuel Levy (1999: 6) to define indie cinema according to what it's not – 'it's not avant-garde, it's not experimental, and it's not underground.'

While *Happiness* is not avant-garde, it still shares a great deal thematically with the downtown films discussed earlier, and, in some ways, it has a similar cinematic attitude. The use of irony and a certain amount of detachment certainly links it to the early work of David Lynch, Todd Haynes, and others. Furthermore, the cultural critique mounted by the film – the implied criticism of a materialism gone poisonously crazy in a society where even love seems to operate according to a market economy – is remarkably similar to the cultural critique mounted by downtown cinema. The depiction of Helen – an uptown artist (she interrupts a phone conversation with Joy to take a call from Salman Rushdie) who is much more irritating and vicious than Vlad, the good-natured criminal – is reminiscent

of the downtown art scene's scathing depiction of the commercialized art establishment. Finally, the refusal of any norm-based sexuality (all the adult characters
seem sexually dysfunctional) and the honest depiction of pedophilia are remin-
iscent not only of films like Todd Verow's *Frisk* but of the novels of Dennis Cooper
and Kathy Acker, writers important to downtown culture.

Solondz himself seems to acknowledge a certain indebtedness to downtown
culture and, especially, to transgressive film. Two moments which Lucia and
Kelleher single out for criticism in the movie play like something of a direct
homage to the transgressive gross-out cinema of Richard Kern and Nick Zedd: the
film is 'often hampered,' they write (1999: 2–3), 'by Solondz's falling back on
cheap jokes . . . for example, when Allen's overweight neighbor Kristina . . .
casually orders an elaborate ice cream sundae in the midst of confessing to murder
and dismemberment.' While Lucia and Kelleher read this as 'playing the fat-lady-
joke card in an all too obvious and cruel manner,' I read it as something of a
homage to the kind of shock humor and bad taste that characterizes the work of
John Waters (whose films feature a number of disgusting scenes of eating), as well
as downtown cineastes like Zedd and Kern. It is a deliberately punk–transgressive
moment in a film which otherwise presents itself as classy satire.

Even more pointed, however, is the film's ending. When Billy finally ejaculates,
his emission lands on the balcony railing of his grandparents' condo. We see it for
a minute, dripping from the balcony rail, before it's greedily licked up by Kooki,
the family dog, who then runs happily into the dining room to lick Trish's face.
Called 'cartoonish' by mainstream critics, this is exactly the kind of gross-out
scene that transgressive cinema relies on for its affect. The unwavering close-up
on Billy's cum, the long-ish take of Kooki lapping it up, all the seemingly perverse
gross-out effects link it clearly to a cinema where gross-out effects became part of
an avant-garde arsenal of tricks, the attempt to 'attack the audience in audacious
rituals of broken taboo' (Sargeant 1995: 28). And like transgressive cinema, it
refers back to the world of low body genres – the 'money-shot' of porn. Viewed
in this light, the final scene of the film can be read as a homage to the avant-garde
tradition out of which more mainstream 'indie cinema' grew, and which some
critics – like Levy – say it has forgotten, the avant-garde tradition of *fin-de-siècle*
downtown culture. Like *In the Company of Men*, which has the look and feel of a
high-budget downtown movie, *Happiness* resembles an avant-garde film that had
the good fortune to get funding.

Notes

Special thanks to Tony Conrad, Skip Hawkins, Chris Holmlund, Mark Jancovich, Chris
Kraus, Sylvere Lotringer (and the Kathy Acker Foundation), Justin Wyatt, and the Roxie
Cinema in San Francisco, where I saw so many of these films for the first time.

1 Parts of the introductory section of this chapter also appear in Hawkins 2000.
2 Jennifer Montgomery's *Home Avenue* is distributed by Women Make Movies (website: www.wmmm.com). Distribution information for some of the other experimental films mentioned in this article is as follows: Joel DeMott and Jeff Kreines's *Seventeen* is part of the Middletown series, distributed by First Run–Icarus Films, 33 Court St. 21st Floor, Brooklyn, NY 11201; (718) 488–8900. Todd Verow's *Frisk* is available from Todd Verow's website (www.bangorfilms.com) and also from Strand Releasing's website (www.strandrel.com/home_video). At the time of writing, Tony Conrad's remastered version of *Blue Tape* is not in commercial distribution. To see the film, contact Tony Conrad directly (e-mail:conrad@acsu.bu). Bette Gordon's *Variety* is available from Kino (www.kino.com). For films by Eric Mitchell, Amos Poe, and other downtown filmmakers, see the Monday/Wednesday/Friday video club website (www.brickhaus.com/amoore/MWFdoc1.html).
3 I have used the quotation marks pointedly here: as my book *Cutting Edge* (2000) demonstrates, I believe that 'high art' and 'low culture' are closely related and inter-twined terms.
4 The term 'counter-cinema' here comes from Peter Wollen's 1985 essay 'Godard and Counter-Cinema: *Vent d'Est*,' in which he identifies seven Godardian 'cardinal virtues' in terms which seem to be drawn directly from Brecht's 1930 essay 'The Modern Theatre Is the Epic Theatre.'
5 I'm thinking here of such Godard films as *La Chinoise* (1967), *Tout va bien* (1972), *Letter to Jane* (1972), and *Numéro Deux* (1975) in which characters quote Marx and directly discuss class oppression.
6 This is not always the case, of course. Both Bette Gordon's *Variety* and Lawrence Fessenden's *Habit* (1997) use such lush, saturated color that my students find it distracting.
7 Downtown culture is careful to acknowledge and pay homage to those who went before, and it is very self-reflexive about its place in cultural history. Joel Rose and Catherine Texier's *Between C&D* (1985), for example, is dedicated to the French writer Céline. In terms of film, Eric Mitchell's 1978 *Kidnapped* is a re-make of Andy Warhol's *Vinyl*; and, in the early 1990s, filmmaker Keith Sanborn took time away from his own independent production to lovingly restore and retranslate Guy DeBord's film *Society of the Spectacle*, which is (thanks to him) now available on a subtitled video from Ediciones de la Calavera.
8 For Kraus's comments on this, see Schwarz and Balsamo 1996 and Kraus 2001.
9 They mainly play in alternative festivals like the Chicago Underground Film Festival, the New York Underground Film Festival, and Mix: The New York Experimental Lesbian and Gay Film Festival.

Bibliography

Arthur, P. (1997) '*In the Company of Men*,' *Cineaste*, 23, 2 (December): 40–4; text taken from EBSCOhost, online: http://ehostvgw17.epnet.com/fulltext (accessed 14 June 2001).
Brecht, B. (1930) 'The Modern Theatre Is the Epic Theatre: Notes to the Opera *Aufstieg und Fall der Stadt Mahagonny*,' in J. Willett (ed. and trans.), *Brecht on Theatre*, New York: Hill & Wang, 1964 33–42.

Brooks, X. (2001) 'Happiness,' in J. Hillier (ed.), *American Independent Cinema: A 'Sight and Sound' Reader*, London: British Film Institute, 145–7.

Clover, C. (1992) *Men, Women, and Chainsaws: Gender in the Modern Horror Film*, Princeton, NJ: Princeton University Press.

Hawkins, J. (2000) *Cutting Edge: Art–Horror and the Horrific Avant-Garde*, Minneapolis and London: University of Minnesota Press.

—— (2003) 'Midnight Sex–Horror Movies and the Downtown Avant-garde,' in M. Jancovich, L. Reboll, J. Lyons, J. Stringer, and A. Willis (eds.), *Defining Cult Movies: The Cultural Politics of Oppositional Taste*, Manchester: Manchester University Press, 223–34.

Haynes, T. (1999) 'Risks of Identity,' paper delivered at *Knowing Mass Culture / Mediating Knowledge*, Center for Twentieth Century Studies, Milwaukee, WI, May.

Kraus, C. (1997) *I Love Dick*, New York: Semiotext(e).

—— (2001) 'Ecceity, Smash and Grab, The Expanded I and Moment,' in S. Lotringer and S. Cohen (eds.), *French Theory in America*, New York and London: Routledge, 303–8.

Levy, E. (1999) *Cinema of Outsiders: The Rise of American Independent Film*, New York and London: New York University Press.

Lucia, C. and Kelleher, E. (1999) 'Happiness,' *Cineaste*, 24, 2–3: 80–4 +; text taken from EBSCOhost, online: http://ehostvgw17.epnet.com/fulltext (accessed 14 June 2001).

Marcus, G. (1989) *Lipstick Traces: A Secret History of the Twentieth Century*, Cambridge, MA: Harvard University Press.

Nichols, B. and Peary, G. (1996) 'Children, Art, Sex, Pornography: Jennifer Montgomery's Art for Teachers of Children (An Interview),' *Camera Obscura*, 39 (September): 35–51.

Palmer, W.J. (1993) *The Films of the Eighties: A Social History*, Carbondale and Edwardsville: Southern Illinois University Press.

Rose, J. and Texier, C. (eds.) (1988) *Between C&D: New Writing from the Lower East Side Fiction Magazine*, London and New York: Penguin.

Sargeant, J. (1995) *Deathtripping: The Cinema of Transgression*, London and San Francisco: Creation Books.

Schwarz, H. and Balsamo, A. (1996) 'Under the Sign of Semiotext(e): The Story According to Sylvère Lotringer and Chris Kraus,' *Critique*, 37, 3: 205–21.

Seltzer, M. (1998) *Serial Killers: Death and Life in America's Wound Culture*, New York and London: Routledge.

Shaviro, S. (1997) *Doom Patrols: A Theoretical Fiction about Postmodernism*, New York and London: High Risk Books.

Siegle, R. (1989) *Suburban Ambush: Downtown Writing and the Fiction of Insurgency*, Baltimore, MD, and London: Johns Hopkins University Press, 1989.

Williams, L. (1989) *Hardcore: Power, Pleasure, and the Frenzy of the Visible*, Berkeley and Los Angeles: University of California Press.

Wollen, P. (1985) 'Godard and Counter-Cinema: Vent d'Est,' in B. Nichols (ed.), *Movies and Methods*, Berkeley and Los Angeles: University of California Press, Vol. 2, 500–9.

Chapter 10

Communitarianism, film entrepreneurism, and the crusade of Troma Entertainment

Ian Conrich

Working under the slogan of 'Movies of the Future,' Troma Entertainment – founded by Lloyd Kaufman and Michael Herz – has been producing and distributing low-budget films since 1974. One of the longest surviving American independent film studios, it has been drawn to the practices of do-it-yourself guerrilla filmmaking developed within the exploitation trade, while simultaneously acquiring for its 'Tromaville Library' a medley of obscure and disregarded films which are then branded and marketed as Troma's own. There are, therefore, essentially two types of Troma film – those produced and those purchased (known as pickups) – which constitute the Library's 'veritable smorgasbord of scintillating, psychopathic, and surreal movies.'[1] Some unity is attempted with titles partnered in improvised collections – the 'Troma Strong Redneck Series,' 'Troma Strong Woman Series,' and 'Troma Strong Flesh-Hungry Zombies Series.'[2] But it is the trash aesthetic, the genre mutation and burlesque style, which identifies a Troma release and which is present in such provocatively titled films as, *Fat Guy Goes Nutzoid* (Golden, 1986), *Stuff Stephanie in the Incinerator* (Nardo and Jones, 1987), *Rabid Grannies* (Kervyn, 1988), *Horror of the Hungry Humongous Hungan* (DiNinni, 1991), and *Killer Condom* (Walz, 1997); and the cult movies *Surf Nazis Must Die!* (George, 1987), *Chopper Chicks in Zombietown* (Hoskins, 1989), and *Cannibal: The Musical* (Parker, 1996).

The films which have been the most commercially successful and revered by followers of the studio have been Troma's own productions: *Sgt. Kabukiman N.Y.P.D.* (Kaufman and Herz, 1993), *Tromeo and Juliet* (Kaufman, 1996), the *Class of Nuke 'Em High* series (1986–94 [three parts]) and, in particular, the *Toxic Avenger* series (1984–2001 [four parts]). It is the latter, the Toxic tetralogy, which will be the focus for this chapter. The Toxic Avenger, also known as Toxie, is a fighter of crime, a mutant superhero, who employs excessive violence to defeat evil and restore community harmony. The films effectively establish the transparent values of the Troma Universe, which Roger Corman has described as 'extreme yet idealistic, violent yet romantic' (Kaufman and Gunn 1998: xiv). This chapter

argues that behind such idealism there is a discernible communitarianist social
philosophy – a belief in community, justice, and democratic citizenship – which is
most developed in Troma's own productions, and the Toxic Avenger films. It is a
Troma vision that appears to inspire much of the studio's activities, persisting
even in the moderated anarchy of the *Toxic Crusaders* (1991), a thirteen-part
television cartoon series for children, that will be considered here as just one
example of Kaufman and Herz's entrepreneurism.

Neo-independence

Kaufman, the studio's president, is Troma's guiding spirit; Herz, studio vice-
president, is responsible for the financial and legal side of the company. Many of
Troma's own movies are directed by one or both of the filmmakers, but it is
Kaufman, a self-proclaimed family man, who is the public representative of the
studio, its showman. Roger Corman is the filmmaker who is cited as an early
influence:

> Michael and I were mimicking Roger when we first started Troma. We
> had the concept for a small studio that could turn out unique, quality
> films at a time when theaters actually needed them. . . . As a new studio,
> we would produce and distribute films that had predefined audiences –

Figure 10.1 The entrepreneurial Lloyd Kaufman and Michael Herz promoting Troma
productions. Courtesy of Troma Entertainment.

horror, sex, and science-fiction. If you made a romantic comedy, there was a chance that absolutely nobody would see it. But if you made a monster movie or a movie with lots of breasts, there would be some sort of audience no matter what (1998: 80).

The studio first established itself with the sex comedies *Squeeze Play!* (Kaufman, 1979), *Waitress!* (Kaufman and Herz, 1981), *Stuck on You!* (Herz and Kaufman, 1982), and *The First Turn On!* (Herz and Kaufman, 1983). The success of *The Toxic Avenger* (Herz and Kaufman, 1984) – a film which was apparently made after Kaufman had been roused by a story in *Variety* headlined 'Horror Films Are Dead' – moved Troma towards films packaged with nudity, gore, and comic book violence. What has subsequently marked Troma as a neo-independent producer are the diverse and inventive ways in which it has attempted to market a body of films which have been critically discredited. These are films that exhibit a distinct counter-aesthetic and which belong to what Jeffrey Sconce has argued is a sub-cultural paracinema that exists in opposition to the institutions of Hollywood industry and standards of popular taste (1995: 371–93).

Troma's market exposure is dependent on exploitation, showmanship, and stunts. Interestingly, for a neo-independent exploitation filmmaker, the studio values foremost the cinematic experience – Troma, as Kaufman and Gunn (1998: 180) state, 'continues to pride itself on creating films meant to be watched in an actual cinema' – and has all of its own productions shot on 35mm. But the studio has not been concerned with just the exhibition of its films in theaters: it has focused on the retail industry, television and the internet for the maximizing of the media opportunities and commercial potential of its products. Troma's contemporaries in the exploitation film market – companies such as Fred Olen Ray's American International Productions (AIP) and Sam Sherman's Independent International Pictures (IIP) – have been associated mainly with a monomorphic approach to film distribution. AIP has concentrated on the video market for the release of its films *Hollywood Chainsaw Hookers* (Ray, 1987), *Beverly Hills Vamp* (Ray, 1988), and *Bad Girls From Mars* (Ray, 1989), while IIP was dependent on the movie drive-ins, before they declined in the 1980s, for the exhibition of films such as *The Dynamite Brothers* (Adamson, 1974), and *Blazing Stewardesses* (Adamson, 1975).[3]

Olen Ray has been described as the 'direct-to-video king' (Quarles 1993: 79), yet those of his titles that were released for the domestic market were not distributed with a recognizable brand identity that established the film as an AIP product.[4] Troma, in comparison, created Troma Team Video in 1995 for the rental and retail distribution of its films. As Kaufman and Gunn observe, it allows Troma to control 'how our films are marketed, spread the use of Troma as a brand name, and take the profits ourselves' (1998: 194). In the UK, for instance, Troma videos have been marketed with distinctive brightly colored packaging stamped with the Troma Entertainment logo. The titles of the films themselves distinguish the product from most other videos in the stores, but it has been through marketing devices such as video stands and displays that the Troma release has been emphasized. An effective method of marketing, it has given the studio exposure, while within stores sectioning the videos, creating the notion of a video collection, and further encouraging a cult appreciation of the films. Kaufman's in-person visits to video shops and departments for signings and the promotion of new titles have added to the publicity.

Kaufman and Gunn acknowledge that Troma 'started a video company right when the video market plummeted,' although 'the company hasn't been doing too poorly' (1998: 194). Television, particularly the growth in cable channels and pay-per-view, has become an important area for new film sales. And it is here that Troma has been able to distribute a number of programs, headers and fillers for the home entertainment market. In Britain, many of Troma's films were first shown on Bravo, the cable channel devoted to exploitation, the bizarre and cult television. Troma shot for each of these screenings a special introduction and produced a similar series of support programs, *Tromaville Cafe – The Laughs*, for the overseas market. The studio's eccentric mix of ideas and values has been most noticeable on television in the series *Troma's Edge TV*, launched in 1997 in Scandinavia and the Benelux countries, with twenty new episodes commissioned in 2000 by the British broadcaster Channel 4.

Troma's Edge TV is a pseudo-media news and public information service pro-gram. It distinctly adopts the style of public access cable channels and is remin-iscent of the narrative format employed by *The Kentucky Fried Movie* (Landis, 1977): a fragmented series of skits which parody TV reportage and commercials, interspersed with extracts from movies that are either hoaxes or are genuinely bad. The programs, introduced by Kaufman – who at times critically responds to his own material ('Can you believe this shit?') – establish periods of humor which many would consider puerile (repeated flatulence jokes), grotesque (jokes regard-ing emesis and obesity, often with Michael Herz erroneously as the subject), and offensive (a concerted parkland search for pedophiles, complete with onscreen flashes of 'Pervert Alert'). Body humor is most evident in the fabricated adverts for merkins, dildos, piles ('Rhoid-Away'), and an aerosol spray for vaginal odors ('Twinkle Twat').[5] There is also frequent promotion of www.troma.com – the official Troma website.

Community access: TromaDance and the internet

Troma's use of the internet is significant. With Hollywood productions becoming increasingly dependent on huge promotional budgets for the successful release of a film, and the inter-media relationships of global corporations defining market exposure, existing independent filmmakers have struggled to establish publicity space for their new titles:

> The final tap on the wooden stake in the heart of independent films was skyrocketing advertising costs. . . . The days of low-budget, by-the-seat-of-your-pants, grassroots, dance hall, grindhouse distribution were over. To make matters worse, TV networks owned by Disney, Warner, etc., continually do so-called 'news stories' that amount to billions of dollars of advertising [sic] for the big studios. Independent films are ignored. Joel Siegel [critic for ABC's Good Morning America] confirmed to me that he 'doesn't review Troma movies.' Gene Shalit [critic for NBC's Today Show] has the same policy (Kaufman and Gunn 1998: 188).

Against such tough cultural and economic conditions, Troma has energetically developed a succession of alternative approaches for both publicizing its films and maintaining the exposure of the studio. In January 2000, it began the TromaDance Film Festival as a direct challenge to the perceived imperiousness of Sundance, the principal festival for independent filmmakers, from which it felt excluded: 'Give Independent Film Back to the People!' declares the TromaDance publicity.[6] Entrance to TromaDance screenings is free, filmmakers whose entries are 'truly from the heart' are not charged a submission fee, and there is no preference given to individuals or VIPs for reservations, panels or parties. The TromaDance statement declares:

> The official selections of TromaDance have been made with nothing more than passion, courage, integrity, and raw talent. Everyone at TromaDance is treated as an equal. . . . TromaDance is an opportunity for everyone who's ever picked up a camera to have their work seen without the compromises required by elitist cartel interference. TromaDance is proud to be the first and only film festival of the people, for the people, and by the people.[7]

Such community values are evident on the internet where a seemingly vast commonwealth of Troma fans is being catered for by an array of sites devoted to the studio and which have been developed in, for example, Britain, France, Spain, and Japan.[8] The studio's own website offers a Troma chatroom, a Troma tour, and a series of 'Troma Universe' links and 'Troma Galleries.' Under the latter, the link to 'Gallery of Tromatic Tattoos' displays the body art of male and female fans who have proudly submitted photographic evidence of their devotion to, in particular, the Toxic Avenger. Another gallery link to 'The Museum of Tromatic Arts' exhibits fans' varying artistic achievements, including Picasso-inspired interpretations of the Toxic Avenger's face, green glow-in-the-dark sketches, and a film poster concept for 'Toxie Driver.' Sconce's argument for paracinema is that 'it represents the most developed and dedicated of cinephilic subcultures ever to worship at "the temple of schlock" ' (1995: 372). Beyond the fanzines that form part of Sconce's discussion, these tattoos and drawings by Troma fans appear as the most vital examples of a paracinematic community's self-expression of regard for trash culture: a personalized virtual gallery of alternative taste that is counter to the established displays and public spaces for legitimate art.

The Troma website also offers the chance for unpaid internships at the studio, with such 'Opportunities in Tromaville!' open to those 'who wish to work in an energetic and challenging environment . . . [and who want] to learn about the film business and even work along side [sic] Lloyd Kaufman!'[9] Asked to 'apply early,' as 'there are only a few positions available,' new Tromites or Tromettes would assist at meetings and on publicity tours, where they could be invited to portray a Troma character. Fans can also assist the Troma community and be good citizens by directly approaching or asking friends to call local theaters and request that Troma films are shown – 'Tell the theater managers to contact us at . . .' the site advises. Another part of the site asks fans to petition Joe Hernandez, manager of licensing at McFarlane Toys. McFarlane is a producer of collectable models and figurines of characters and moments from horror cinema, including David Cronenberg's Brundlefly creation (from *The Fly* [Cronenberg, 1986]), and the shark and the fishing boat from *Jaws* (Spielberg, 1975). The production of figures based on the popular Troma characters would be a good business opportunity for Troma Entertainment: the one page petition headed 'We Want Troma Action Figures!' ends 'We, The Undersigned, are asking that you please consider producing an action figure line based on the Troma characters.'[10]

Troma merchandise, or Tromabilia, is available at the 'Tromaville Maul,' the studio's extensive official store. Products offered include the usual masks, posters, T-shirts, hats, and buttons/badges, and the practical mouse pads and binders. The site www.toxicavenger.com advises that Troma's Homie hats and Ho shirts offer 'the fastest way to get laid.' The Tromaville Maul also offers Toxic Crusader rarities – boardgames, action figures and vehicles, puzzles, candy-filled dispensers from Topps, party cups and kids' sneakers ('only mix-matched pairs' remaining), which were more widely available in the early 1990s when the cartoon series was first transmitted. Among the less predictable products offered is a range of jewelry which includes at discounted prices a 14-carat gold Tromaville bracelet at $1,416 and a 10-carat gold nipple ring of the Toxic Avenger's head screaming for $143.20.[11] Deprived of the more traditional areas for publicity, Troma's relationship with its audience has grown through the promotion of the studio on the internet. Crucially, internet users will gain differing cultural value from access to the sites, though many fans will have, perhaps through the films, prior knowledge of the Troma Universe. Here, the shopping 'Maul' may be a virtual retail area, but it caters for consumers able to recognize its location within the fictitious Tromaville community.

Tromaville and communitarianism

Central to the narratives of the *Class of Nuke 'Em High* and *The Toxic Avenger* series is Tromaville, New Jersey – 'The Chemical Capital of the World' – with a population of 15,000, the town's welcome sign advises. Throughout the two series various businesses and institutions are established, such as the Tromaville Health Club, Tromaville Video, Tromaville Optical, Tromaville Tattoo, Tromaville High School, Tromaville Institute of Technology, Tromaville School for the Very Special, Tromaville Center for the Blind, Tromaville Memorial Hospital, and Tromaville Nuclear Utility. This imagined community exhibits the characteristics of the American small town featured in the films of directors such as Frank Capra, William Wyler, Delbert Mann, and Preston Sturges.[12] Kaufman and Gunn (1998: 165) write that it was the 'small town ensemble atmosphere' in the films of Sturges that inspired the creation of the first Tromaville for *The Toxic Avenger*. Raised in Manhattan, Kaufman imagined the non-cosmopolitan nature of suburban New Jersey, considering it to be 'true America' (1998: 165). He had also been informed through his grandmother of the work of sociologist C. Wright Mills which, Kaufman says, 'defined the politics of Tromaville.' Mills, whose key works appeared in the 1950s, 'harped on the conspiracy of elites. These elites have effectively joined forces to cut off the common people from any sort of wealth, comfort, or power. It is these elites Toxie battles to emancipate the little people of Tromaville' (Kaufman and Gunn 1998: 167–8). The social politics of Tromaville are, however, closer to being a form of communitarianism,[13] an area of social and political philosophy that has attracted a range of opinions:

> The exact nature of the communitarians' positive proposal is not easy to specify. According to some, a revitalization of the feeling for tradition and community is needed in the face of the erosion of tradition and the fragmentation of our value horizon after three centuries of liberal hegemony; others emphasize a participatory politics. On a theoretical level, the common denominator is the affirmation of . . . the validity of norms and principles of justice, as well as an emphasis on the role of judgment and the need to mediate what modern thought has differentiated: facts and values, rules and application, the right and the good, the individual and the community (Ferrara 1995: 14).

Tromaville is a community of paradoxes and incongruities, most noticeably in

The Toxic Avenger films in which figures the belief that Troma villains must be punished for their extreme actions, yet where the brutal behavior of the ever-grinning superhero Toxie is accepted in his fighting of crime. Moreover, Toxie is committed to eradicating from Tromaville unsociable behavior and immorality, yet within the wider Troma Universe – where Toxie has an iconic status and seems inseparable from the image of Troma – the studio produces films which many would view as vulgar and offensive. There is, though, a deep belief in Tromaville, Troma's model of the American small town, in the value of community, the family, and the environment. As communitarianist texts, Tromaville films are *for* justice and democracy, good citizenship, and social solidarity, and *against* crime, corruption, greed, pollution, and the excesses of capitalism. The ethical views of Troma regard the community as paramount and as benefiting from the spirit and pioneerism of the entrepreneur, who stands against the large corporations.

The Toxic Avenger

Troma's philosophy is clearly influenced by Kaufman. Moreover, a reading of Kaufman's opinions reveals that he has much in common with the Toxic Avenger. Such a view is supported by Kaufman's wife, Pat, who sees that

> deep down inside Lloyd IS Toxie. Toxie is a creature of deep and abiding principle, loyalty and love. That's Lloyd! Toxie is devoted to his mother and loves his girlfriend/wife. Toxie is loved by little kids. And Toxie ALWAYS stands up for the little guy . . . [Lloyd is] the only one who really stands up for [the filmmaking] little guys who are true independents (Kaufman and Gunn 1998: 280).

Throughout the Toxic Avenger series and the publicity for the films, there are constant written and verbal reminders that Toxie is 'the first superhero from New Jersey,' and that he is a 'hideously deformed creature of super human size and strength.' The series is best conveyed as a jumble of Peter Jackson's style of splatstick horror, the absurdity and vulgarity of *South Park*, the physical comedy of the Three Stooges, the inventive executions of the slasher films of the 1980s, the vigilantism of the *Death Wish* films (1974–94), and the spoofing of film moments, narrative conventions, and media events perfected by Jim Abrahams, David Zucker and Jerry Zucker in films such as *Airplane!* (1980). The series also draws on superhero mythologies, especially those depicted in comics, which, as Scott Bukatman argues, 'present body narratives, bodily fantasies, that incorporate (incarnate) aggrandizement and anxiety, mastery and trauma' (1994: 94). Bukatman is interested in the tormented superhero, whose unfamiliar

body-form and ability, marking an earlier accident or natural abnormality, com-
plicates social relationships. The monstrous seven-foot tall tutu-wearing Toxie was
once young Melvin Junko, an imbecile and '98 pound weakling' employed as a
health club janitor, who as the result of a prank fell into a vat of toxic waste and
mutated. Toxie's new crime-fighting powers place him as a heroic figure central
to the stability of Tromaville's harmonious community, yet his distorted appearance requires that he be removed to the boundaries of society, where he con-
structs 'Toxie's Shack,' a domestic space of bricolage that utilizes material from
the surrounding toxic dump.

Residing largely in isolation (though a blind girlfriend later moves into the
shack), Toxie remains the friendly neighbor and a model citizen. His body might
signify chemical pollution and his home might be contaminated, yet Toxie is
essentially law-abiding and clean-living – he does not drink, smoke or take drugs,
and in *The Toxic Avenger Part II* (Herz and Kaufman, 1989) is shown vigorously
maintaining his personal hygiene while abroad, in Japan. Within Tromaville,
Toxie works with the blind, helps the elderly cross the road, rescues a dog
stranded in a tree and, even more mundanely, assists a housewife to open a tight
jar lid and a mother to feed her obstinate child. Tromaville's public spaces, the
streets and parklands populated by old and young, illustrate community equality,
membership, and allegiance. Toxie can walk freely through Tromaville despite his
unconventional appearance. Here, on the busy sidewalks, other expected social
outsiders, for instance the homeless (who are evidently happy to be destitute),
are valued representatives of the street culture. Furthermore, Tromaville's main-
tenance of worthy institutions – its School for the Very Special and its Center for
the Blind – indicate a caring community that appears to have concentrated social
funds on those who are disadvantaged. The citizens of Tromaville – as they are
referred to in the films – are repeatedly seen moving through the community,
dancing in groups; they enjoy abundant leisure time which is spent dog-walking
and taking picnics; horse-drawn carriages are an optional mode of transport, and
flower-sellers are ever-present; while well-behaved children cycle and play in the
roads free from any passing traffic, eating a seemingly endless supply of
ice cream.

Communitarianism is built on more than just strong neighborhood values, a
shared social identity, and good citizenry: at its basis are the traditional union
established by the family, and the love and support which it can offer. The number
of children and babies within Tromaville suggests a safe and benevolent community ideal for family growth. In *The Toxic Avenger* a corrupt town official who
wants to turn open spaces into dumps for radioactive waste complains that
Tromaville offers an environment so positive that 'new families are moving
into town everyday' – a fact which is reinforced by the voice-over narration:
'Tromaville was safe. Tromaville was happy. Tromaville was prosperous.' Toxie

Figure 10.2 The good citizen. Toxie (Mitchell Cohen) halts a car and assists an old lady (Margaret Riley) in crossing the road in *The Toxic Avenger* (Herz and Weil/aka Kaufman, 1984). Courtesy of Troma Entertainment.

may be from a single-parent family, but his relationship with his mother remains strong even after he has mutated and is no longer recognizable as Melvin. 'Mom' is enraptured by Toxie's importance to the community and walks arm-in-arm with him along the streets, her motherly love emphasized in the framed pictures positioned close to Toxie's bed. The strength of the family notion is extended in *The Toxic Avenger Part II*, in which Toxie's search for his father takes him to Japan, a journey which culminates, back in Tromaville, with the discovery of his true father. Toxie, himself, becomes a father in *Citizen Toxie: The Toxic Avenger IV* (Kaufman, 2001), albeit only after a blood-soaked fight with his doppelganger, the Noxious Offender, a battle to the end which is mirrored within the womb of Toxie's girlfriend who is carrying good and evil fetuses, the result of impregnation by both Toxie and Noxie.

Citizen Toxie, the fourth instalment in the series, begins by stating that it is 'The Real Sequel' to *The Toxic Avenger* part 1; parts 2 and 3 were 'rotten.' The film is certainly the most inventive of the series, but it is also the most outrageous and offensive; Lisa Nesselson, in a review for *Variety*, described it as 'politically incorrect on the same scale that Hiroshima was explosive.'[14] In the film, Toxie is transported, via intra-dimensional travel, to the opposing community of Amortville. As the disabled scientist Dr Flem Hocking (a crude parody of Professor Stephen Hawking) advises, for every dimension there is 'a diametric opposite of that dimension.' Amortville is the reverse of the communitarianist Tromaville, a place where the joyous society of the latter has been replaced by rampant sleaze and crime: a dysfunctional community of drug dealers, pimps, and prostitutes, racists and fascists. Meanwhile, in Tromaville, the evil Noxie, with whom Toxie has switched dimensions, finds the utopian Tromaville to be nauseating, and he sets about destabilizing the community. Toxie is able to return home by clicking together the heels of a pair of red shoes, while repeating 'There's no place like Tromaville' whereupon he immediately begins to 'clean up' the community he has missed from the corruption and the fascistic New Order coordinated by a member of the local police.

Industrial capitalism, political greed, corporate corruption, and the criminal actions of gangs constantly threaten Tromaville's utopia. Such counter-communitarian behavior challenges the moral rights of the community, its need for choice, and for an environment devoid of intimidation. Tromaville, as *The Toxic Avenger Part II* informs us, is 'a little town, with little buildings, little businesses, and little people,' who were happy 'with no criminal or oppressive politicians around.' In the first Toxic Avenger film, the obese Mayor Belgoody (Pat Ryan Jr.), and other town officials including the Germanic Chief of Police (David Weiss), were furtively trying to create toxic-waste dumps in areas of wildlife and conservation. In the second and third films, the industrial giant in nuclear production Apocalypse, Inc. forcibly attempted to acquire large areas of Tromaville for its operations – a desire for 'total ownership of everything and everyone' – including the plan to build a power plant in place of the park.

Such transgressions are eradicated by Toxie who, as a citizen, is committed to the common good of the community. He symbolizes the collective will of the Tromaville citizens whose actions are capable of shaping the social future of the town. Toxie's defense of the 'little guys' against corporate and organized crime may appear to be a solo effort – rarely is Toxie physically assisted in his fight – but he continually enjoys a rallying of local support. Tromaville citizens, portrayed via an array of community figures and tradespeople, stand firm behind Toxie in (static) crowd scenes that function partly as a demarcation of the arena of conflict between good and evil. In other instances, such as the opening scene at Tromaville Video in *The Toxic Avenger Part III: The Last Temptation of Toxie* (Herz and Kaufman, 1989), and the fight in the restaurant in *The Toxic Avenger*, the good Tromaville citizens cower as Toxie savages the villains, their bodies beaten and ripped apart, before the horrified eyes of his supporting public. Yet still he is hero-worshipped and, with the last villain defeated, he is acclaimed and embraced by those he has rescued. In many crowd scenes multiple flags of the stars and stripes are waved; a large version of the flag hangs behind the sofa in Toxie's shack; and the flag is featured on the poster art for the first two Toxie films. Moreover, on the poster for *The Toxic Avenger Part II*, the American flag flies from the pole of Toxie's raised mop – in his clean-up of crime, Toxie's primary weapon is his janitor's mop, a utensil which is used effectively to purge the community of arguably its greatest threat: contamination. Where the mop and flag are conjoined, the notion of communitarianism is extended beyond the values of family and neighborhood to those of the State and the nation.

The Toxic Crusaders

By the early 1990s, Toxie's cultural value had broadened, especially following the transmission of the syndicated series of cartoons *The Toxic Crusaders*, intended for children. A Saturday-morning program in America, it apparently 'penetrated 96% of the U.S. television market' (Kaufman and Gunn 1998: 150).[15] The first transmission of the program in the UK was in 1993, and if children's response could be gauged by those who entered a competition or submitted artwork which was displayed prior to the start of later episodes, then *The Toxic Crusaders* seemed to appeal most to boys aged between five and eight years old.[16] Yet this was a series based on a group of adult-rated movies which, *The Toxic Avenger* in particular, had been heavily censored in various film markets. Interestingly, much of the myth of the Toxic Avenger, and the initial storyline of the first film in the series, remained in *The Toxic Crusaders*. The most noticeable change was a new move towards science-fiction, with the introduction of cockroach-like aliens from the planet Smogula, whose base on Earth, the fume-filled Island City (which could be read as Manhattan), is a short distance by water from Tromaville, the last unpolluted town in New Jersey. With Earth operations led by Dr. Killemoff, the ultimate plan in each episode is to pollute Tromaville, or at least to weaken the community, thus enabling the Smogula cockroaches to mount an invasion. Toxie still resides in a shack on the edge of the community, but he now shares the space with Blobbie, a furry and pink protoplasm pet, and his Toxic Crusaders, an all-male gang of mutant superheroes named Major Disaster, Nozone, Junkyard, and Headbanger. Due to the toxic waste, Toxie's mop is able to act on its own, in a manner not unlike that of the Sorcerer's Apprentice in Disney's *Fantasia* (Algar and Armstrong, 1940), while Toxie's girlfriend, who is now just a visitor to the shack, has her own home and is no longer blind, but poor-sighted – she initially could not see Toxie due to the loss of her contact lenses. The success of the *Teenage Mutant Hero Turtles* (also known as the *Teenage Mutant Ninja Turtles*) animated children's series (a program referenced several times in *The Toxic Crusaders*) led to an offer by the animation company Murikami Wolf to make such a similar series for Toxie.[17] The company effectively cleaned-up Toxie, sanitizing *The Toxic Crusaders* by removing the violence and vulgarity of the films, at the same time magnifying Toxie's communitarianist concerns for the environment.

The mutant superhero team-up of the Toxic Crusaders borrows from the established comics and cartoons of the X-Men and the Fantastic Four. In their environmental fight, the Crusaders (referring to themselves as Environmental Superheroes) focus not just on the macro hazards created by Killemoff, but on

Tromaville's micro issues. In the episode 'Tree Troubles,' Arbor Day is being celebrated with citizens encouraged to plant trees, but Killemoff has managed to reverse the process of photosynthesis, so that plants now produce smog; in 'The Making of Toxie,' Killemoff releases a giant oil-slick creature on the town; and in 'This Spud's for You,' a chemical is added to growing potatoes so that the fries sold at the McDonaldsesque 'Burpo Burger' will transform consumers into forgetful and clumsy geriatrics. It is in the episode 'The Pollution Solution' that the Crusaders develop grime-busting projects such as pooper-scooping (encouraged by Junkyard, who is half-man and half-dog), graffiti removal (using the letter-getter, developed by Headbanger, who is a two-headed mutant, part scientist and part surf dude), the collection of aluminium cans (coordinated by Nozone, an aircraft pilot who became a mutant due to the hole in the ozone), and the tackling of noise pollution (led by Major Disaster, who is half-soldier and half-plant-life). In the Kaufman and Herz co-scripted episode 'Still Crazy After All These Shears,' there is a 'Beautify Tromaville' week dependent on a 'Just Say Grow' campaign in which citizens are encouraged to plant free seeds; and in the episode 'Invasion of the Biddy Snatchers' the elderly members of the community form the 'Biddy Committee to Keep Tromaville Pretty.' Kaufman and Herz, creative consultants for the series, co-scripted two Toxic Crusader episodes, but Kaufman also had script clearance on all the others, and his environmentalism which he has discussed elsewhere[18] is evident throughout.

In this series of kids' programs, Tromaville demographics appear to have altered, so that there is a much higher community ratio of children. The Crusaders help mostly the young (and the old), with Toxie pausing at times to preach. 'What good does it do anybody to poison the environment?' he asks, standing against a background of the American flag. In the series, new environmental superheroes join the Crusaders by taking an oath (as in the 'Club Fred' episode) with such a team-up becoming – what Bukatman, in his work on comics, has described as – a 'kind of superhero popular front movement' (1994: 103). The availability of Toxic Crusader merchandise enabled children to create their own allegiance to Toxie and the series, and packaging (made of 'partially recycled paper') provided variations of the Crusader oath – 'de-tox tips' such as 'DON'T BE A BOTTLEBRAIN – RECYCLE GLASS!' A young environmentalist group in Brooklyn subsequently called themselves 'The Toxic Avengers' (Kaufman and Gunn 1998: 151), while Troma publicly supported the US presidential campaign of Ralph Nader, the Green Party candidate.[19] The Toxic Crusade is Troma's crusade within the studio's greater communitarianism. And with initial royalties for *The Toxic Crusaders* 'enormous' (see Kaufman and Gunn 1998: 263), this exposure of the studio's iconic Toxie was a brief yet significant moment in which a neo-independent filmmaker was brought into the mainstream.

Conclusion

The populist nature of Troma's own productions disguises the extent of its social and political philosophies, and of those circulating within Tromaville, the fictitious community built with the values of the studio. As a model community, Tromaville may have influenced the community beliefs (especially those related to environmentalism) of Troma's younger viewers attracted to *The Toxic Crusaders*. But it is unlikely that Troma's communitarianist approach would have been absorbed to any degree by, the adult viewers of, in particular, *The Toxic Avenger* films, who would have valued the productions for their disposable style.

It is notable that an independent producer of low-budget exploitation films should incorporate such ideologies into its productions. Troma's communitarianism is, however, not without its complications: The acts of violence in *The Toxic Avenger* films are part of Toxie's fight for community justice, yet they are clearly unethical, and contradict the values of communitarianism; similarly, the vulgarity of the films themselves within a context of cultural reception has lead to many challenging their cultural worth. Troma's form of communitarianism is far from complete, though it is not without its moments of irony and eccentricity. However, beneath such frivolity, there is the deeper concern that Troma's view is but a reflection of American contemporary social anxieties and a community desire redolent of US conservatism. In today's societies of complex identities, such a desire to recapture traditional values and to create harmonious communities of good citizens, functional families, and shared social identity seems untenable. Furthermore, Tromaville is a simplified community which looks back to a mythical period of 1950s' America, one which for many never existed.

Notes

I wish to thank Fraser King, Estella Tincknell, Henry Swindell, Roy Smith and Debs Marsh for their invaluable comments and advice.

1 Online: www.troma.com/movguide.html (accessed 10 June 1996).
2 See Kaufman and Gunn 1998: 314–36.
3 See Ray 1991 and Quarles 1993.
4 A few of Olen Ray's films are distributed by Troma: *Demented Death Farm Massacre* (1986), *Haunting Fear* (1990), and *Wizards of the Demon Sword* (1990).
5 A merkin is a pubic hair wig, generally manufactured for women with pubic hair loss.
6 See Troma's other own website and the links: 'Read What the Tromadance Organizers Think of the Sundance Festival!', 'Learn Some of the Tactics Sundance Uses to Try and Stop Alternative Film Festivals like Troma Dance [*sic*] from Happening!' by Doug Sakmann, and 'Sundance Politics and Conspiracy Against the Spinoff Festivals,' by Kent Bye. Online: www.tromaville.com/Tromadance/index.asp (accessed 26 May 2002). The official TromaDance website is at www.tromadance.com (accessed 26 May 2002).

7 See www.tromaville.com/Tromadance/index.asp (accessed 26 May 2002).
8 The official British Troma fan website is www.toxie.com; the official Spanish Troma fan website is http://inicia.es/de/fester; and the main French site is www.sud07.com/plan9/tromaville-france/main.html. A Japanese site worth visiting is www.clydefilms.co.jp/test/dokudoku, while the home of Tromaniax Japan is at http://home.interlink.or.jp/%7Ei-burt/TROMA/tromaindex.html. See also the official US fan website www.tromamovies.com and Troma's own site, 'Dedicated to the Fans of The Toxic Avenger,' at www.toxicavenger.com (accessed 20 March 2002).
9 See www.troma.com/FAQ/positions/index.php3 (accessed 20 March 2002).
10 The petition is hosted at www.petitiononline.com/tromafig 'as a public service' (accessed 26 May 2002).
11 See http://store.choppingmaul.com. The sole product which is obviously a hoax is the 'Preserved Body of V.I. Lenin,' available at a cost of $8 million. 'An historical oddity,' the site advises, and it '[c]omes in a unique display coffin and a 2-year supply of embalming fluid' (accessed 20 March 2002).
12 See MacKinnon 1984 and Levy 1991.
13 See Avineri and de-Shalit 1996; see also Daly 1994. Margaret Jane Kidnie in her analysis of *Tromeo and Juliet*, employs the work of social theorist Ulrich Beck and the idea of a 'risk society':

> [W]e are now entering a period of late industrial capitalism in the western world in which priority is no longer placed on survival, but on attempting to control the latent hazards inherent in industrial production. Instead of interpreting western society as postmodern, Beck sees it as moving into an advanced state of modernization, in which . . . [people have become] aware of society's potential for mass destruction (2000: 104).

14 www.toxicavenger.com/news/varietyreview.html; and www.variety.com (accessed 20 June 2002).
15 For fans' nostalgic recollections of the series see www.yesterdayland.com/popopedia/memories/show_mem.php?ID=SA1576 (accessed 20 March 2002). In 1996, Troma released a 76-minute animated film, *Toxic Crusaders: The Movie*, which combined 4 of the original 13 episodes, and in 1997 it released *Toxic Crusaders 2: The Revenge of Dr. Killemoff*.
16 *The Toxic Crusaders* was first broadcast on British television, on BBC1, weekly from 7 June 1993 to 6 September 1993.
17 For further discussion of *The Toxic Crusaders*, especially regarding business decisions, see Kaufman and Gunn 1998: 261–7.
18 See *ibid.* 1998: 166.
19 See www.troma.com/lk2/nader/index.php3 (accessed 26 June 2002).

Bibliography

Avineri, S. and de-Shalit, A. (eds.) (1996) *Communitarianism and Individualism*, Oxford and New York: Oxford University Press.

Bukatman, S. (1994) 'X-Bodies (The Torment of the Mutant Superhero),' in R. Sappington and T. Stallings (eds.), *Uncontrollable Bodies: Testimonies of Identity and Culture*, Seattle, WA: Bay Press, 92–129.

Daly, M. (1994) *Communitarianism: A New Public Ethics*, Belmont, CA: Wadsworth Publishing.

Ferrara, A. (1995) 'Universalisms: Procedural, Contextualist and Prudential,' in D. Rasmussen (ed.), *Universalism vs. Communitarianism: Contemporary Debates in Ethics*, Cambridge, MA: MIT Press, 11–37.

Kaufman, L. and Gunn, J. (1998) *All I Need to Know about Filmmaking I Learned from The Toxic Avenger*, New York: Berkley Boulevard Books.

Kidnie, M.J. (2000) ' "The Way the World Is Now": Love in the Troma Zone,' in M.T. Burnett and R. Wray (eds.), *Shakespeare, Film, Fin de Siècle*, Basingstoke: Macmillan, 102–20.

Levy, E. (1991) *Small-Town America in Film: The Decline and Fall of Community*, New York: Continuum.

MacKinnon, K. (1984) *Hollywood's Small Towns: An Introduction to the American Small-Town Movie*, Metuchen, NJ, and London: Scarecrow Press.

Nesselson, L. (2001) 'Citizen Toxic: *The Toxic Avenger IV*,' *Variety*, Cannes daily edition, 18 May, online:

www.toxicavenger.com/news/varietyreview.html; and www.variety.com (accessed 20 June 2002).

Quarles, M. (1993) *Down and Dirty: Hollywood's Exploitation Filmmakers and Their Movies*, Jefferson, NC: McFarland.

Ray, F.O. (1991) *The New Poverty Row: Independent Filmmakers as Distributors*, Jefferson, NC: McFarland.

Sconce, J. (1995) ' "Trashing" the Academy: Taste, Excess, and an Emerging Politics of Cinematic Style,' *Screen*, 36, 4: 371–93.

Part III

Iconoclasts and auteurs

Chapter 11

John Sayles, independent filmmaker
'Bet on yourself'

Diane Carson

John Sayles did not invent independent filmmaking, but he has championed it longer and practiced it better than anyone else. His works boast an unparalleled diversity of genres and issues, geographical locations and historical frameworks. While writing, directing, and editing thematically daring films for more than two decades, Sayles has successfully financed and distributed his works, an exceptional achievement in any arena. As tribute to his accomplishments and longevity, Sayles has become an icon, the 'virtual godfather of independent film,'[1] among filmmakers and art-house audiences for his determined autonomy and his challenging content.[2] Moreover, he has earned a reputation for his strong encouragement of, and financial assistance to, other filmmakers. Perhaps ironically, to support his own films Sayles contributes as a 'writer for hire' to mainstream projects. A foot in both the independent and mainstream camps, he eludes easy categorization himself, embodying these overlapping worlds while maintaining a distinctive voice. This is a positive stance for Sayles, not a reactive one; that is, he does not define himself or his films by their rejection of conventions, but rather by the authentic, uncompromised demands of his own artistic responsibility. This chapter examines Sayles's self-proclaimed, distinctive ideas about independent filmmaking as well as the thematic and stylistic qualities of his multifaceted career, a career sustained because, as he says, 'I'm willing to throw the dice and bet on myself' (Sayles 1999a).

Sayles's films

Sayles's admirers cite his preference for complex, flawed communities rather than oversimplified heroic individuals; his strong sense of place as opposed to homogenous or interchangeable locations; and his believable, sometimes even halting, dialogue delivered by realistic individuals instead of artificially clever 'written' banter by insubstantial characters in contrived situations. Rejecting distracting histrionics and indulgent sentimentality, Sayles deals seriously with an impressive array of issues. *Matewan* (1987) explores corporate exploitation of 1920s' Appalachian coalminers and company-sanctioned violent retaliation against workers' unionizing.

Using the 1919 'Black Sox' baseball scandal as its catalyst, *Eight Men Out* (1988) dramatizes the individual compromise of principles and loss of integrity prompted by greed and vindictive retaliation. Using a contemporary urban setting, *City of Hope* (1991) depicts the enervating tribalism within communities and the self-defeating quandary of city politics. *The Secret of Roan Inish* (1994) elucidates the sustaining power of myth, while *Lone Star* (1996) indicts the stultifying effect of cultural icons through revelations concerning the revered past sheriff and a murder. *Hombres Armados/Men with Guns* (1997) surveys the destructiveness of civil strife, the impact of willful ignorance, and the impossible position of those caught in the middle. *Limbo* (1999) critiques the theme-park mentality regarding nature, the struggle for people to make themselves vulnerable, and the courage necessary to reconnect with others. Expansive in their scrutiny, several significant motifs recur, in various guises, with more emphatic treatment in one or another of the works: for example, political disenchantment dominates *Return of the Secaucus Seven* (1980) and *City of Hope* (1991); the nature of racial prejudice undergirds *The Brother from Another Planet* (1984); the impact of class weighs heavily in *Baby, It's You* (1983); and gender issues and sexual preference drive *Lianna* (1983).

Whether addressing race or class, gender or community politics, violence or corruption, Sayles refuses to simplify the issues or to capitulate to an uncomplicated solution. In an age when mainstream films pursue quick fixes to unambiguous problems, he has tenaciously adhered to his unpopular position: that is, intricate situations resist tidy resolutions. In fact, over the decades, Sayles has posited increasingly open-ended, even perplexing, conclusions, frustrating some audience members while inviting others to pursue the ideas and problems beyond the cinema.

From Sayles's first film, his narrative themes as well as his production practices have defined him as a daring independent pursuing his own intellectual challenges and using his own financial resources. Sayles made a characteristically unprecedented decision in his 1997 *Hombres Armados/Men with Guns*. Set in an unnamed Latin American country, elderly Dr. Humberto Fuentes (Federico Luppi) undertakes a disconcerting journey of discovery into rural areas. After his wife's death, in need of reassurance and still proud of the medical students he's trained over the years, Dr. Fuentes decides to visit them in the small villages to which they've dispersed. At first rejecting the alarming events he hears about, eventually, after his exposure to the conflict, he must accept the students' disappearances and deaths at the hands of soldiers and guerrillas who ravage the land. During his journey, Fuentes encounters a cross section of society: a priest, a young boy, a woman silent since her rape, an army deserter and thief. Though a road movie,

Figure 11.1 Chief of Police Sid Hatfield (David Strathairn) confronts coal company agents in *Matewan* (Sayles, 1987; Red Dog Films, Inc.).

Men with Guns atypically moves from ignorance to dismay. Violence takes place offscreen or is described rather than visually exploited as in mainstream productions. More unusually, to maintain narrative integrity, almost all the characters speak Spanish, though Sayles knows the reduced US exhibition opportunities for a subtitled film. In other words, Sayles makes the exceptional choices of a principled individual, sacrificing potential income, adhering to the integrity of his central character and the disheartening truths this individual reluctantly, but ultimately, confronts. Sayles doesn't pander; he won't compromise his vision.

Countering Sayles's admirable thematic achievements, his detractors point to a serviceable, but never elegant, aesthetic sensibility and an unsatisfying approach to intractable difficulties. Critics argue that Sayles's plots rely on predominantly linear narratives, with easy-to-follow flashbacks when they do exist, as illustrated in *The Secret of Roan Inish* and *Lone Star*. Even in *Limbo*, only the stunning conclusion dares to disrupt, thoroughly and abruptly, an otherwise straightforward narrative, albeit one with a hairpin turn in the middle. Characters' motives remain clear cut; good is easily distinguishable from more compromised values; and editing patterns follow traditional expectations. Use of these conventional cinematic elements makes the atypical content more inviting to a wider audience, making Sayles accessible, even ideologically reassuring. Those who expect independents to propose thoroughly confrontational alternatives would like Sayles to push his sociopolitical critique further, desire more adamant arguments for progressive change, and crave more provocative controversy over deeply perplexing issues. For while Sayles refuses to endorse pat answers, he does, at times, resort to familiar questions. For example, we all recognize the corruption and influence-peddling dramatized in *City of Hope*, yet the film fails to envision realistic, constructive, effective strategies to counter perplexing social transgressions.

Those who believe independents must embrace daring stylistic inventiveness also find Sayles wanting. Dismissed by critics as a mediocre stylist, described as lacking in 'visual flair' (Levy 1999: 85), Sayles rejects montage editing, self-conscious angles, flashy effects, and other trappings of the 'style is everything' school. This puts him in Ingmar Bergman's camp: the landscape of the face and the drama of human reactions dominate his compositions. His directions to his cinematographers concentrate on their understanding the emotional register of the scene and complementing, if not intensifying, it: 'I leave the lens and lighting up to them' (Sayles 1999b). Refusing to capitulate to the supremacy of ostentatious images, Sayles has never allowed superficial appearance to overwhelm substance. He highlights the more subtle contributions and diversity of framing and rhythm. No one would mistake the look and feel of *The Secret of Roan Inish* for *Matewan* or, for a more equivalent comparison, *Men with Guns* for *Lone Star*. Sayles uses camera distance to establish intimacy with or separation from his characters. Similarly, his editing rhythms echo the accelerated drive or meditative calm of characters. If Sayles has a signature shot, it is the camera's leaving one or more characters, as they continue their discussions, to intercept and move off with another individual. This intertwining of lives, however oblivious the characters may be to their connections and impact upon one another, undergirds the modern urban landscape of *City of Hope*. It is, in fact, exactly the point of the film, featuring 38 characters and more than 50 speaking parts.

Sayles's admirers and critics alike make valid points.[3] Though not an auteur who promotes or makes avant-garde works, nor one who advocates radical social agendas via his films' content or style or who promotes political causes through explicit advocacy, Sayles does distinguish himself as an independent in many other ways. While he may not satisfy all that his critics yearn for, Sayles travels a less defined path, raising political, cultural, and social issues long since abandoned for serious scrutiny by conformist cinema. And however much we may want more revolutionary form and even stronger radical content, Sayles's work unmistakably originates from outside the Hollywood mentality. Neither technically flamboyant nor narratively hip, Sayles has diligently avoided trendiness, even forswearing digital capturing and digital editing of images.

Sayles's definition of independent cinema

Addressing the debated, highly whimsical, definitions of independent filmmaking,[4] Sayles explains his thinking, championing aesthetic integrity over budgetary considerations. To counter the pervasive erroneous notion that a small budget equals independence, Sayles says:

> No matter how it's financed, no matter how high or low the budget, for me an independent film emerges when filmmakers started out with a story they wanted to tell and found a way to make that story. If they ended up doing it in the studio system and it's the story they wanted to tell, that's fine. If they ended up getting their money from independent sources, if they ended up using their mother's credit card, that doesn't matter (Carson 1999a).

To illustrate his conviction, Sayles cites an eclectic mix of directors who make his kind of independent movies, among them Spike Lee, Martin Scorsese, Tim Burton, Steven Soderbergh, and Jim Jarmusch. For Sayles, only adherence to narrative integrity, above all else and regardless of budget, qualifies *any* director as *independent*. 'Independent distributors who see new talent moving on to make studio films for larger budgets just love to wag their fingers at those youngsters and bemoan the fact that none of them has the integrity and purity of John Sayles' (Pierson 1995: 18). The crucial difference remains a refusal to conform to a numbingly monotonous uniformity. Commendable directors do not surrender their 'idiosyncratic mindset, the stamp of truly independent filmmakers like Steven Soderbergh, John Sayles, Hal Hartley, and Todd Haynes, who stubbornly stick to their eccentric sensibilities' (Levy 1999: 2).

Sayles and others with his experience in the trenches know that this usually means a small budget. But 'studios don't allow you or not allow you to make a movie; they either give you the money or they don't. So if you want to tell the story, find a way that it doesn't cost $20 million. You can talk about anybody for $25,000' (Sayles 1999a). Even so, Sayles believes lack of knowledge about a subject must give a director reason for pause, and he specifies his own 'cultural restrictions' as one crucial limiting factor. 'There are people I wouldn't make a movie about because I don't know enough about them. . . . Studios have their blind spots too. Female directors get stuck in the "women's pictures" bag' (ibid.). Sayles believes that even when a woman director makes a profitable action film and she gets offered the opportunity to direct more, 'it isn't going to apply to other women' (ibid.). And every independent filmmaker better realize, as Sayles does, that 'the bottom line gets used like any statistic to reinforce what they [the studios] are interested in' (ibid.), by which he means that producers will brandish the profit motive and employ accountability as the weapons with which to co-opt nonconformity. The pressure to repeat oneself, to reach a pre-sold audience and to eschew challenging originality, has restrained and defeated more than one promising director.

Sayles adamantly rejects such categorizing or repetition for himself. While themes of community and individual responsibility thread their way through Sayles's films, more than any other independent director he has refused to repeat settings, genres, or narrative contexts. This makes difficult the acquiring of easy capital, though, he argues, some films make poor candidates for any studio involvement – he cites his own *Men with Guns* as totally inappropriate for studio financing or distribution: in addition to being almost exclusively in Spanish, as noted earlier, the lead actors are virtually unknown to American audiences, though Federico Luppi is a star in Argentina and admired by fans of Spanish-speaking cinema. With marketing expertise, Sayles saves time by correctly assessing a project. He notes: 'We didn't even try them [studios] first. We went straight to my pocket, and then luckily Maggie [Renzi, Sayles's long-time producer] could find an independent investor' (Carson 1997). Fortunately, that investor, Sony Pictures Classics, has extensive experience marketing niche films, helping meet the challenge of devising a distribution strategy for a difficult product.

This exhibition–marketing relationship with Sony Pictures provided a welcome financial security that contrasts with the way Sayles made and distributed films before the 1997 release of *Men with Guns*.[5] Earlier he had relied on his own resources and his producers' creative ideas. As a result of his films' diversity and the difficulty of pigeonholing them, no single entity felt comfortable channeling Sayles's output into a promotional network with little adaptability for idiosyncratic work. And so Sayles 'sold his films one by one resulting in his [first] nine features being distributed by six different independents, one so-called mini-major (Orion), and one major' (Pierson 1995: 19). With *City of Hope*, considered a strong theatrical contender with a compelling story and relevant urban concerns, Sayles and his distributor expected higher grosses than it earned, proving again the uphill battle for financial success with nonconformist fare.[6] Discussing *City of Hope*'s low box-office revenues, Sayles notes that 'almost every review started with the word "grim" and so it's no surprise the film did badly' (Sayles 1999b). But sincerely and convincingly Sayles adds: 'I always felt good about my movies [because] I made the movies I wanted to make, told the stories I wanted to tell' (*ibid.*). This resolute stance equates not with indifference but with integrity. As he told *The Progressive*: 'I'm *not* nonchalant. I'm interested in the stuff I do being seen as widely as possible – but I'm not interested enough to lie. There comes a time in any story when you say, "I know how to make this more popular." But then, it's bullshit' (Carson 1999b: 143). For audiences dissatisfied with repetitious studio offerings, Sayles thus offers a refreshing alternative as a successful independent who recognizes and accepts his self-defined position.

Sayles's financing

Sayles relies on a simple strategy for dealing with one of the most daunting hurdles to all independent production – financing. Sayles possesses the courage, has the talent, and makes the connections to finance his own films. He then takes them completed to various distributors and studios for 'pickup.' But working this way and succeeding are two very different things. First, few can follow Sayles's solution, and he knows it. 'I have a good bread job, which is I'm a screenwriter for hire and I write fast and I write a lot' (Carson 1997). The year he made *The Brother from Another Planet*, which he financed himself and which eventually cost $400,000, he wrote five other screenplays, four or five drafts for each, leaving himself one week to write his own movie. An actor as well, when finances necessitate, Sayles can earn additional money in this way, though never as much as when writing for others. By contrast, many of the aspiring filmmakers he knows 'are waiting tables, are working as largely unemployed actors, semi-employed grips and gaffers. They just don't make that much money.' He reports that as a scriptwriter he's made 'as much as $800,000 in one year and I put it all into my movies' (Sayles 1999a).

On more than one occasion, Sayles began production without necessary financing in place, confident that he 'could write some more things. I made the movie with my own money without the post production and then kept writing screenplays in order to rent the editing machine.' Sayles realizes that he has the good fortune to be in demand, writing, for example, for *Mimic* (Del Toro, 1997) – about giant cockroaches – for approximately $100,000. He's also contributed to *Apollo 13* (Howard, 1995), *The Quick and the Dead* (Raimi, 1995), and a host of other distinguished films, plus an equal number of forgettable ones.[7] On occasion, Sayles felt he had to begin shooting or lose the opportunity to do so: 'If the weather is going to change and we'll have to wait a whole year or an actor is not going to be available, I've just started making the movie' (Sayles 1999a). For example, he lacked two-thirds of the budget for *The Secret of Roan Inish* when he began scouting and prepping in Ireland. Proceeding under such conditions, Sayles knew he might lose the money he invested. Nevertheless, while the producers looked for the rest of the financing, Sayles had progressed two weeks into shooting. With only $10,000 left in his bank account, producers Sarah Green and Maggi Renzi secured funding. Sayles's actions testify to his optimism that, once the project begins, an investor will find it attractive or he'll rely on his own bank account as long as possible. Sayles talks about taking risks, makes movies about risk (*Limbo*), and takes them himself. He puts his money where his mouth is.

Editing his own films is another cost-saving advantage for Sayles. Knowing what he needs, he does not do multiple takes of a scene even if an actor flubs a line (Sayles 1987: 101). When the actor expresses concern that he has not delivered the dialogue all the way through once without mistakes, Sayles will explain: 'Yeah, but you botched a different line each time. I've already cut the scene in my head and I know I've got everything we need. You just have to trust me' (Carson 1999a). Only someone who writes, directs, and then edits his own work can streamline production to this extent, eliminating 'coverage' of scenes that will end up on the cutting-room floor. Not all directors have the special talent needed for multitasking on their own films.

Sayles has another trick up his sleeve when it comes to maximum exposure on a minuscule publicity budget. As he puts it, 'I carry my own bucket,' doing, by his own estimation, 300–400 interviews per film. 'It's been necessary. We've so rarely had big-name stars' (Carson 1999a). Levy (1999: 14) verifies Sayles's observation: 'Despite his stature in the indie world, John Sayles could not always get the actors he wanted for his films. For years, agents would not even show his scripts to their top actors.' This certainly accounts for Sayles's surprise and delight when James Earl Jones agreed to appear in *Matewan*, as Sayles reports in his account of that film's production history (Sayles 1987: 51). As Few Clothes, scab coalminer-turned-union supporter, Jones's charismatic presence and flawless acting intensify interaction with union organizer Joe Kenehan (Chris Cooper), while Jones's admirable reputation boosts sales. But Sayles realizes that stars do not necessarily improve a film in the incomparable ways Jones did, though they do help publicity by garnering attention.[8] Without such bankable leads, Sayles goes to work, spending weeks, perhaps months, promoting his film through 'free' publicity via feature articles and reviews. Through this press exposure and 'hoping you've built up some kind of an audience,' Sayles aims to 'get a critical mass of people to come in the first couple weeks because we will never have and have never had the money to advertise on television and open wide. We hope that the word-of-mouth starts moving, and that doesn't cost you any money' (Carson 1997). This worked with his popular *Lone Star*, which appealed to audiences because it contains 'more iconic things that are familiar to people who don't usually go to non-Hollywood movies. There was a badge, a sheriff, a gun, a murder, and that was their way into the picture' (*ibid.*).

More often, in myriad ways, Sayles's films shout their difference from the status quo: 'The difficulty of our movies – and they are difficult to a certain extent – is that they're complex. For most movies, the whole point is to make life *less* complex and more dramatic. Because of that, you have clear "good guys" and "bad guys" ' (Carson 1999b: 141). In doctoring scripts, Sayles says, one of his chores is to establish a clearer delineation between the heroes and the villains, to 'iron out the wrinkles. So you have the bad guy kick a dog or a small child in the first act' (*ibid.*: 222–4). For his own films, he employs several strategies to make his characters more than two-dimensional props or shallow ploys to nudge the story along. As Sayles reports it, the first thing many character actors ask when they read the script is: 'Where's the rest of me? What ammunition and evidence do I have for who this *person* is, not just his function?' (Carson 1999a).

Sayles counters the limited approach by giving minor characters 'even an extra line or two so we know who they are as well as what they're doing in the scene' (*ibid.*). When Sayles's characters enter, they not only imagine a back story but may even introduce some fragment of it into the central plot line. For example, in *Passion Fish*, Chantelle (Alfre Woodard) becomes May-Alice's (Mary McDonnell's) caretaker after several women have quit in disgust. But Chantelle has her own history with Luther (Tom Wright), her cocaine-addicted ex-boyfriend, who visits her new Louisiana home. Chantelle's developing romantic relationship with Sugar (Vondie Curtis-Hall) gains resonance because, though a supporting player, she possesses three-dimensional qualities and a past she tows with her. Similarly, in *Eight Men Out*, about the 1919 'Black Sox' scandal, each ballplayer delivers dialogue conveying his humanity and struggles. Moreover, each player has his own specific reasons for agreeing, however reluctantly for some, to throw the 1919 World Series. As Sayles has joked on more than one occasion, a mainstream film would have had *One Man Out* or, at most, *One-and-a-Half Men Out* instead of *Eight Men Out*.

Sayles's thematic and narrative challenges

In the final analysis, above all other considerations, the heart and soul of Sayles's uniqueness rest in his atypical themes and his thoughtful treatment of them, as noted earlier: coalminers' unrest and unionizing (*Matewan*); the greed and power plays of baseball management (*Eight Men Out*); a married woman discovering her attraction to another woman long before lesbian topics were openly addressed in the movies (*Lianna*); a woman becoming a paraplegic after an automobile accident (*Passion Fish*); and a respected medical doctor confronting tragic truths in the civil conflict in his country (*Men with Guns*). Into each of these examples, Sayles consistently and insistently inserts a sociopolitical critique that inhabits 'his study of a particular milieu or situation' (Andrew 1999: 74).

A recurrent thread shows Sayles questioning traditional religion. Self-described as a 'Catholic atheist,' Sayles presents moral choices in shades of gray, that is, with the complexity they pose in real life.[9] Moral issues span a continuum. From the fire-and-brimstone preacher in *Matewan* professing his repressive religious belief to the educated Dr. Fuentes in *Men with Guns* asserting his irrelevant faith in science, Sayles interrogates the religious and the secular. Also in *Men with Guns*, ethical dilemmas test the priest with his 'portable god,'[10] a god he carries with him in his heart and soul, one that allows the priest to abandon his village in peril, while the peasants, whose spirituality is tied to their land, enjoy no such luxury. In *Lone Star* myth supplants truth, sustaining a crippled social order. *Men with Guns* holds up a mirror to all those 'ugly American' tourists, those Teflon travelers who pass through foreign lands, immune and indifferent to the local crisis. *The Brother from Another Planet* indicts racial prejudice in both humorous and serious ways through the Brother (Joe Morton), a fugitive black slave from outer space, being chased by white (alien) bounty hunters to Harlem. In a community struggling with white drug dealers and authoritarian policemen (Ryan 1998: 101), welfare and urban decay, the Brother finds a refuge in Odell's (Steve James's) bar. More comically, when the two aliens (Sayles and David Strathairn) looking for the Brother challenge Fly (Daryl Edwards), one of the regulars in Odell's, to produce his green card, Fly makes clear: 'My people built this country, Jim.' And when the two white Iowa men, in New York for a self-actualization conference, take a wrong turn and end up in Odell's, their nervous attempts at communication reveal their racial insensitivity and ignorance. In all of these films, Sayles's criticism, embedded in characters integral to the plot, ranges from mild jesting to scathing denunciation.

One of the most hotly debated topics and most exploited elements of contemporary film is violence. Sayles argues thus:

> There is violence, and then there is violence. Over the last ten years we've all seen too many shootouts with automatic weapons and great squibs and blood and people flying through the air John Woo-style. I can't top that and astonish people, so what I'll say is what we haven't seen: three-dimensional characters whom you meet and start to feel something for the way you would a real person in a violent situation – humanistic violence which is much more upsetting (Carson 1997).

Put another way, the violence emerges from the story, is earned, and deeply felt. Sayles foregoes momentary sensationalistic thrills in order to emphasize the impact and the devastating consequences, from Joe Kenehan's murder in *Matewan* to the peasants sacrificed in *Men with Guns*.

Nor do stereotypical gender dichotomies dominate Sayles's works. His writing and casting choices consistently involve men whose experiences have left them alienated, less than idealistic though clinging to principle, verbally and physically passive, thoughtful, self-aware, and soft spoken. These men do not define themselves through conflict with other men or competition for women, the hackneyed components of conventional fare. His most memorable leading men include Chris Cooper, David Strathairn, Joe Morton, Federico Luppi, Vincent Spano, and Mick Lally. To varying degrees, they come across as sensitive and accessible, sometimes unusually so. At their best, they exhibit a responsiveness to others, a dignity that does not slide into sentimentality, a complexity that acknowledges fragility and fear, a decency.

Their female counterparts possess similar attributes, though with few exceptions (*Lianna*, *Passion Fish*, and *Roan Inish*) they seldom dominate narratives the way men do. More often, the adult women exhibit a measure of restraint, escaping many of the insulting Hollywood caricatures of male–female relationships, though sometimes, as in, for example, *City of Hope* and *Lone Star*, women still focus on romance as their anchor. Most admirably, men and women do not succumb to the 'mood of detachment' (Connor 1992: 135) that defines the postmodern, nor do they affect the superior smugness that belies a defensive posture.

The case of *Limbo*

Sayles compares most films to roller coaster rides – a simulation of peril:

> At the end of the roller coaster ride the bar comes up, you walk off, and you may forget you took the ride. It's a consumable item like a meal at McDonald's . . . a little more challenging or more interesting movie is something that, even if you didn't expect the ending or weren't satisfied by it, it makes you ask the question, 'Why did it end that way?'[11] (Carson 1999a).

Limbo epitomizes Sayles's determination to indict predictable conformist cinema through its unexpected plot developments and an implicitly scathing commentary on the Disneyfication of nature. Alaskan (or any) wilderness does not exist to entertain, welcome, or even accommodate people, despite the theme-park approach that persists in enticements to the great outdoors. *Limbo*'s opening video seeks to lure tourists to places like Alaska. There (as in film viewing) they can indulge the illusion of danger and seek frontier encounters that thrill but never threaten. Invalidating this attitude, *Limbo* will depict the consequences for ill-prepared individuals who stumble into real-life danger in the wilds.

Joe Gastineau (David Strathairn) becomes romantically involved with Donna De Angelo (Mary Elizabeth Mastrantonio), both of them haunted by quite dissimilar, but equally unnerving, past mistakes – Donna's many dysfunctional relationships and Joe's involvement in a freak boating accident twenty-five years earlier that killed two people. Donna's teenage daughter Noelle (Vanessa Martinez) struggles with her own insecurities that erupt in angry outbursts or self-mutilation. When the three become stranded on an island, their emotional and physical struggle involves fierce confrontations and, eventually, the summoning of the courage necessary for reconciliation and emotional healing. But the film ends abruptly without our knowing if they are physically rescued or not.

Figure 11.2 Donna De Angelo (Mary Elizabeth Mastrantonio), Noelle De Angelo (Vanessa Martinez), and Joe Gastineau (David Strathairn) in *Limbo* (Sayles, 1999). © 1999 Global Entertainment Productions GmbH & Co. Medien KG and SPE German Finance Co., Ltd. All rights reserved. Courtesy of Columbia Pictures.

Limbo, Sayles's most hotly debated film, testifies to his refusal to capitulate to expectations. It requires its viewer to live viscerally, not just endorse intellectually, its concluding jolt. When *Limbo* premiered at the 1999 Cannes International Film Festival,[12] critics, shocked by the startling cut to a black screen at the film's conclusion, voiced their displeasure by booing loud and long. Sayles defends his film: 'I don't think the ending is open. I think these three people, who have a lot of problems, a lot of fears, have managed to become a family facing a very uncertain future' (Sayles 1999b). Sayles believes, 'You can cop out and have a happy ending you didn't earn, something lightweight, or you can tack on a heavy, serious ending you don't deserve as many did in the 1970s. I want an ending that asks people to think about the movie a little bit' (Carson 1999a). In a film about taking risks, Sayles deliberately took one by avoiding any semblance of a scripted conclusion. He also asks his audience, many unwilling or unnerved, to take one with him.[13]

By contrast, mainstream films will not leave their central characters hanging. Stars will not, in the long run, be punished for emotional or physical trauma. But as *Limbo* ends, pilot Smilin' Jack (Kris Kristofferson) arrives to either rescue or deliver someone to murder the stranded trio. A crucial question remains unanswered: 'Who's on that plane?' Even Kristofferson asked Sayles about this, to no avail (Sayles 1999a). The uncertainty extends beyond the film's narrative limits to invite reflection on *Limbo* itself and the nature of our conditioned expectations.

Limbo joins *Lone Star*, which has its own surprising but shrewd conclusion.[14] Its dramatization of multicultural conflict confronts racial, intergenerational, and legal complexities seldom considered in mainstream film, much less in one tightly woven narrative combining music, language, and family in a multifaceted story. The legacy of the past and its impact on the present challenge all the borders defined in the film.[15] Pilar and Sam also cross an extreme sociosexual border in the final scene, though their decision is not the only element defying the norm. Sayles is characteristically atypical in his presentation of religion, violence, race, gender, class and political content.

Everyone conversant with Sayles's films agrees that, as Levy puts it, 'all of John Sayles's films are about outsiders' (1999: 52). How could it be otherwise, when Sayles is himself the ultimate outsider: outside Hollywood, outside hypocrisy, outside materialism, and outside monotony. Ironically, the one constant needed for support of independent cinema – past, present and future – is 'adventurous audiences . . . risk-taking viewers' (*ibid.*: 502). An issue beyond the scope of this chapter, but one that merits serious discussion, is how to nurture audiences to be open to a disruption of conventions. We have learned to accept flashy stylistic flourishes but not truly unsettling, narrative challenges. There are too few adventurous viewers today, too many who want preconceptions reinforced with films like suburban landscapes and strip malls – mindlessly homogenous. Too few bet on themselves.

Notes

1 As recently as the 1999 Cannes International Film Festival, a panel on independent cinema, hosted by *Variety* and moderated by Roger Ebert, reiterated this flattering designation. The panel included Ron Howard (*Edtv*, 1999), Spike Lee (*Summer of Sam*, 1999), Alex Winter (*Fever*, 1999), and Daniel Myrick and Eduardo Sánchez (*Blair Witch Project*, 1999).

2 The Library of Congress established the National Film Preservation Board in 1988 to preserve films that are 'culturally, historically, or aesthetically important.' Beginning in 1989 and each year thereafter, the Board selects twenty-five films to honor by adding them to the National Film Registry. In 1997 the National Film Preservation Board selected Sayles's first film, *Return of the Secaucus Seven* (1980), for the US National Film Registry.

3 For an array of opinions, see, for example, Levy 1999, Molyneaux 2000, Pierson 1995, and Ryan 1998.

4 See especially Levy's 'Introduction' (1999: 1–12) in this regard.

5 This relationship continued through the 2002 release of *Sunshine State*.

6 Samuel Goldwyn caught 'festival frenzy' at the 1991 Sundance Film Festival, paid $2.5 million for distribution without video rights, and recouped less than half the price it paid (Pierson 1995: 138).

7 Early in his career, Sayles wrote scripts for Roger Corman, among them *Piranha* (1978), *The Lady in Red* (1979), and *Battle Beyond the Stars* (1980). He can also count *Alligator* (1980) among his credits.

8 For the six years I've been a journalist covering Cannes, mob scenes of critics pushing and shoving greet the press conferences for every big-name Hollywood star: Sean Connery, Sharon Stone, John Travolta, Bruce Willis, among others. For all its love–hate relationship with Hollywood, Cannes cannot resist the siren call of fame and fantasy. European, Asian, and Latin American celebrities garner much less attention. I've walked casually into half-filled press conferences with Jean-Luc Godard, Shohei Imamura, Nagisa Oshima, and Manuel de Oliveira, among other legendary directors.

9 See my interview with him in Carson 1999b, especially p. 229 and his comments on the choices in *City of Hope*.

10 As Sayles described it, the priest can choose to run because he takes his god with him. It isn't so easy for the peasants whose spirituality is tied to the land; see Carson 1999b: 224.

11 At the *Variety* panel discussion, when the integrity of endings and pressure to conform to unacceptably compromised scenarios came up, Spike Lee used *Do the Right Thing* as his prime example. One studio vehemently objected to the ending, wanting the characters to shake hands and make up. Universal gave Lee *carte blanche*, and told him that he had $6 million, but no more, to do whatever he wanted. Lee agreed, maintaining his artistic integrity and the only ending *Do the Right Thing* could include.

12 *Limbo* competed with twenty-one other international films for the prestigious Palme d'Or, which the French film *Rosetta* won. *Limbo* won no awards from the jury, headed by David Cronenberg with jurors Dominique Blanc, Doris Dorrie, Jeff Goldblum,

Barbara Hendricks, Holly Hunter, George Miller (the Australian director of *Mad Max*), Maurizio Nichetti, André Téchiné, and Yasmina Reza.

13 By Sayles's own estimate, approximately one-third of an audience finds the ending satisfactory.

14 Having learned that they have the same father, Pilar and Sam decide nonetheless to continue their sexual relationship.

15 Particularly provocative in this regard are David and Womack 1998: 471–85, Limon 1997: 598–616, and Montoya 1997: 223–40.

Bibliography

Andrew, G. (1999) *Stranger than Paradise: Maverick Filmmakers in Recent American Cinema*, New York: Limelight.

Carson, D. (1997) Personal interview with John Sayles at the Toronto Film Festival, 8 September 1997.

—— (1999a) Personal interview with John Sayles at the Cannes International Film Festival, 22 May 1999.

—— (ed.) (1999b) *John Sayles: Interviews*, Jackson, MS: University Press of Mississippi.

Connor, S. (1992) *Postmodernist Culture: An Introduction to Theories of the Contemporary*, Oxford, UK: Blackwell.

David, T.F. and Womack, K. (1998) 'Forget the Alamo: Reading the Ethics of Style in John Sayles's *Lone Star*,' *Style*, 32, 3: 471–85.

Dreifus, C. (1991) 'John Sayles,' *The Progressive*, 55, 11: 30–3; reprinted in D. Carson (ed.) (1999) *John Sayles: Interviews*, Jackson, MS: University Press of Mississippi.

Johnston, T. (1993) 'Sayles Talk,' *Sight and Sound*, 3, 9: 26–9; reprinted in D. Carson (ed.) (1999) *John Sayles: Interviews*, Jackson, MS: University Press of Mississippi.

Levy, E. (1999) *Cinema of Outsiders: The Rise of American Independent Film*, New York: New York University Press.

Limon, J.E. (1997) 'Tex-Sex-Mex: American Identities, Lone Stars, and the Politics of Racialized Sexuality,' *American Literary History*, 9, 3: 598–616.

Molyneaux, G. (2000) *John Sayles: An Unauthorized Biography of the Pioneering Indie Filmmaker*, Los Angeles: Renaissance.

Montoya, M.E. (1997) 'Lines of Demarcation in a Town Called *Frontera*: A Review of John Sayles' Movie *Lone Star*,' *New Mexico Law Review*, 27: 223–40.

Pierson, J. (1995) *Spike, Mike, Slackers, & Dykes: A Guided Tour Across a Decade of American Independent Cinema*, New York: Hyperion.

Ryan, J. (1998) *John Sayles, Filmmaker*, Jefferson, NC: McFarland & Co., Inc.

Sayles, J. (1987) *Thinking in Pictures: The Making of the Movie 'Matewan,'* Boston, MA: Houghton Mifflin.

—— (1999a) *Variety* Panel Discussion on Independent Filmmaking, Cannes International Film Festival, 18 May 1999.

—— (1999b) *Limbo* Press Conference, Cannes International Film Festival, 22 May 1999.

Chapter 12

Haile Gerima

'Sacred shield of culture'

Mark A. Reid

Haile Gerima's twenty-five year plus career as an independent filmmaker, producer, and distributor–owner of Mypheduh Films, Inc., provides American film
history and world cinema with a fertile example of the deterministic limits of
multinational capitalism and mainstream tastes. Though the film and distribution
career of William Greaves dates earlier and might seem as, if not more, important
to any discussion of black independent cinema (Reid 1993:126–7), Gerima stands
out on the contemporary scene both because he controls the production and
distribution of his films and because he helps make African diasporic connections
possible, distributing work by other African and African diasporic artists and
mentoring future generations of filmmakers and film scholars as well.

Born in Gondar, Ethiopia in 1946, Gerima is the son of a writer and a teacher,
and the second of eight children. Although many know him as Haile, his father
formally gave him the name 'Mypheduh,' which means 'sacred shield of culture'
in the Ethiopian 'Geze' language group. In 1967, he left for the US, studying
theater at the Goodman School of Drama in Chicago. Later, he moved to
Los Angeles and enrolled in the MFA film production program at the University
of California at Los Angeles. Since 1975 he has been a tenured professor of film in
the School of Communications at Howard University in Washington, DC. He also
heads Mypheduh Films, Inc., which he founded in 1982, and the Sankofa Video
and Bookstore, established in 1996.

Although Gerima spent twenty-one years in Ethiopia, he identifies himself as an
African filmmaker having a shared heritage with African diasporic people. He says:
'Even if I were to return to Africa, I would always protect my direct links with
black America. It has given me the courage to discover myself. . . . At first,
I considered myself Ethiopian rather than connected to black America. Black
America helped to humanize me' (Marcorelles 1984: 11).

With fourteen films to his credit – ten completed, two in production, two
others produced and edited – Gerima's commitment to shielding African
and African American culture is clear.[1] I focus in what follows on two of his

feature-length fiction films, *Bush Mama* (1976) and *Sankofa* (1993). The former I consider important because, in making it, Haile Gerima became the first member of a group of Los Angeles-based university-trained filmmakers to produce an independent feature film which helped establish a womanist independent film practice.[2] *Sankofa*, Gerima's fifth feature, was made almost twenty years later than *Bush Mama*, and in it Gerima takes *Bush Mama's* womanist heroine back to her Afrocentric roots, enriched and empowered African American consciousness. Stylistically quite different, both films are thus strongly woman-centric.

Bush Mama and African American womanist ethics and issues

According to independent filmmaker St. Clair Bourne, Gerima's films epitomize the non-linear, black, independent, narrative films from the West Coast (Bourne 1982: 104–5). *Bush Mama* tells the story of the wakening consciousness of Dorothy (Barbara O. Jones), a welfare mother whose husband, TC (Johnny Weathers), is imprisoned for a crime he did not commit.

Dorothy must raise her daughter (Susan Williams) in Watts, a Los Angeles inner-city neighborhood. Returning home, Dorothy discovers a white police officer (Chris Clay) attempting to rape her daughter. Like the character Sweetback

Figure 12.1 Dorothy (Barbara O. Jones) in *Bush Mama* (Gerima, 1976). Courtesy of Mypheduh Films.

(Melvin van Peebles), who in *Sweet Sweetback's Baadasssss Song* (Van Peebles, 1971) assaults two police officers to protect Mu-Mu (Hubert Scales), a young black revolutionary, Dorothy protects her next generation and in doing so kills the police officer. Dorothy's violence, similar to that of Sweetback, is self-protective and leads to her wakening consciousness.

While it is important to note the specific ways in which *Bush Mama* typifies the black independent family film, it is also important to differentiate this film both from the many mainstream and independent studio-distributed black action films and from black family films.[3] I find three major differences between *Bush Mama* and studio-distributed black action and black family films. First, studio-distributed black action films portray interracial violence between black and white men, while women are restricted to passive roles, the sexual partners of these violence-prone men. In contrast, Dorothy's violence protects her daughter from a sexual assault.

Second, it is significant that Dorothy's violence empowers the mother–daughter relationship. This is in complete opposition to typical Hollywood black action films that feature individualistic and masculinist empowered heroes like Sweetback, Shaft (Richard Roundtree), and Priest (Ron O'Neal), the main protagonist in *Super Fly* (Parks, 1972). Unlike these black Hollywood heroes, the independent maternal–black action hero Dorothy does not escape her socioeconomic environment through retaliatory violence or successful drug deals.

Third, and unlike most studio-produced black family films, *Bush Mama* uses violence as an act that protects and sustains the African American family. Thereby, the film establishes Dorothy's maternal aspects without denying the 'by any means necessary' self-defensive act of violence. Her violence is restricted to one act, whereas both whites and blacks constantly assault her. Here I am stressing the distinction between conventional constructions of black heroes produced for mainstream consumption and hero(ine)s, such as Dorothy, who are developed by independent black filmmakers like Gerima. Dorothy exemplifies a black liberation hero(ine) in the manner in which she arrives at a political consciousness that shields her daughter from further physical and sociopsychic assault.[4]

Violent spectacle is not the central focus of *Bush Mama* as it would be had it been a 1970s' studio-distributed black-action film or, for that matter, F. Gary Gray's black female heist film *Set It Off* (1996). Violence here shows only that Dorothy will no longer passively endure psychological and physical abuses directed at her and her family. Dorothy becomes an agent rather than an object and victim ripe for the pity of those mainstream film-goers who usually admit lower-class women like Dorothy into their homes as house-cleaners and caretakers.

Though black family films such as *A Raisin in the Sun* (Petrie, 1961), *The Learning Tree* (Parks, 1969), *Sounder* (Ritt, 1972), *Claudine* (Berry, 1974), and *The River Niger* (Shah, 1976) portray injustices, they either avoid or make the development of the hero(ine)'s political consciousness as limited to passivity and static images of victimization. Black family films produced in Hollywood restrict certain forms of agency. Most actions are confined to the psychological sphere, such as Dorothy's growing awareness. It is rare when a mainstream black-oriented film dramatizes retaliatory violence as a respectable option in resisting physical threats from racist and/or sexist villains.

Gerima avoids the stereotypes still circulating as the sole currency in American popular films: Dorothy is not a sexless mammy, an over-sexed exotic primitive, a swaggering gun-totting operative or a passively enduring black woman. Of equal importance, she is not linked to a husband or lover who resembles a sexless coon, an ebony saint or an over-sexed, demanding tyrant.

Many, if not most, pre-1975 independent and studio black-oriented films portray black heroines who nobly and selflessly endure socioeconomic hardships and sociopsychic abuses. For instance, one finds this black female type in most pre-1960 films that feature black women in major roles. Included in this group are such actresses and films as Abbey Lincoln in *Nothing But a Man* (Roemer, 1964), Cicely Tyson in *A Man Called Adam* (Penn, 1966), and Tyson's later roles in *Sounder* and *Claudine*. In contrast, Gerima's *Bush Mama* suggests that a black heroine who proudly endures dehumanizing situations should not be idolized, and as a result *Bush Mama*, and Gerima as its screenwriter–director, resist conventional closures that would re-unite Dorothy's family or would permit her to escape her socioeconomic conditions. Gerima expresses, through his film, the sentiment that permanent changes in the social system will not result within a fictional narrative. Yes, Dorothy retaliates against black-on-black crime, insensitive welfare workers, and police brutality. However, Gerima insists that Dorothy's struggle be against institutions, like the welfare *office* and the police *force*; he seeks to indite institutions by criticizing actions of the individuals who work for them.

It is characteristic of Gerima's generation of black filmmakers that their independent film praxis requires a resolute struggle against the classical Hollywood narrative form and its bourgeois ideological content. Avant-garde and experimental camera techniques deter the recurrent critical and spectatorial relationships that classical narratives usually enjoy.[5] *Bush Mama*'s non-linear narrative style, as apparent in the use of collage and abrupt editing, evokes a self-reflexive form that disrupts the spectator's pleasurable and seamless identification with story and protagonist. Charles Burnett, Larry Clark, and Alile Sharon Larkin use this technique for similar political purposes. Although one must bear in mind that the largest black audiences grew fat from consuming dominant narrative forms and stereotypes of themselves and others, it is nevertheless more advantageous if a filmmaker's work attracts and engages large audiences by manipulating various styles – classical, avant-garde, and experimental – to produce an interesting cinematic form while still articulating politically sensitive but appropriate issues and themes.[6]

Gerima began production of *Bush Mama* in 1973, and by 1975 he had received the finished print of what was a very early, if not actually the first, West Coast feature produced, directed, edited, and personally distributed by a university-trained black independent filmmaker. *Bush Mama*, Charles Burnett's *Killer of Sheep* (1977), Larry Clark's *Passing Through* (1977) and Julie Dash's *Illusions* (1982) typify the new black independent features and shorts made on the West Coast in the late 1970s and early 1980s. During the early 1990s, Burnett, Dash, Gerima, and a 1980s generation of university-trained black filmmakers, like John Singleton, have used different modes of production and distribution to produce a distinctive blues-inflected African American cinema. Many of their films exhibit a slow pace due to the use of long duration shots and minimal editing. I am particularly thinking of Burnett's *To Sleep with Anger* (1990), Dash's *Daughters of the Dust* (1991), Singleton's *Boyz N the Hood* (1991), and Gerima's *Sankofa* (1993).

Sweet Sweetback's Baadasssss Song established a new heroic paradigm for the black cinematic hero as sexual, individualistic, and violent. However, Sweetback's violent actions haphazardly connect him to a young black radical; his individuality links him to the black community, while his sexual activity is a means by which to escape life-threatening encounters. *Sweetback* and other similarly produced and distributed black independent films provide instances of a sociocultural moment which permitted a free-zone for independent work. Van Peebles' film attracted a large black following whose more radical members gave opposing receptions to the film and its hero. In the 1990s, Dash's *Daughters of the Dust* and Gerima's *Sankofa* were similarly popular with black audiences. Unlike *Sweetback*, however, both are black female-centered.

Gerima's marketing success with *Sankofa* showed once more that a truly independently produced and distributed black film could be successfully marketed to large audiences, if the story addressed the sociocultural and psychological needs of its people. Dialogic zones of free exchange exist and are in constant flux, and can enable formerly silenced discourses. Gerima successfully produced and distributed *Sankofa* with the marketing and distribution originality of the black independents of the 1910s and 1920s. Since its release at the Magic Johnson Theater in Los Angeles in 1995, the film has grossed over $5 million.

Sankofa: a Hollywood narrative or something not yet identifiable?

The word *sankofa* derives from an Akan West African word meaning 'one must return to the past in order to move forward,' and, as Gerima informs us in his film, the Sankofa bird is known as the 'bird of passage.' Here the 'return to the past in order to move forward' takes the main protagonist Mona/Shola

(Oyafunmike Ogunlano) through the historical trajectory of the middle passage and returns her with an 'enlightened' black consciousness equal to that of the heroine Dorothy in *Bush Mama*.

The film opens with drumbeats over images of African art objects and the credits' sequence. A medium close-up of a wooden Sankofa bird appears as the drumming continues and a voice-over monologue begins:

> Spirits of the dead rise up, lingering spirits of the dead rise up . . . and possess your vessel. Those Africans shackled in leg irons and enslaved, step out of the acres of cane fields and cotton fields and tell your story.
> . . . Those lynched in the magnolias, swinging on the limbs of weeping willows, rotting food for the vultures, step down and claim your story.
> . . . Those tied, bound and whipped from Brazil to Mississippi. . . .
> Those in Jamaica, in the fields of Cuba, in the swamps of Florida, the rice fields of Carolina, you waiting Africans step out and tell your story.

Crosscutting between the cane-fields and the divine drummer Sankofa (Kofi Ghanaba), visually enhances the monologue and cinematically introduces Gerima's compelling story about the African holocaust. The recurring image of a buzzard and Sankofa's rhythmic drumming connect to a series of visually stunning medium close-ups of the white-powdered drummer who implores, 'Africa, listen.'

The next shot presents a contemporary African coastal area busy with anglers. The shot that follows contrasts with the preceding naturalistic images of the African coast and shows Mona, a scantily clad black female, posing in a swimsuit as a white male photographer goads her to pose in a more erotic manner. A tall, slender, middle-aged African man holding a wooden Sankofa staff looks angrily at them and frightens Mona, the African American model. This man is the human equivalent of Sankofa, as is the African drummer whose drumbeats and chants introduce the film. The following scenes establish Mona's centrality to the African Holocaust narrative by showing her branded and chained in the Cape Coast's castle dungeon. She cries to her captors: 'Wait a minute! You're making a mistake. . . . Don't you recognize me? I'm Mona. I'm an American!' Her entreaty is lost on her captors, who confine her with the other slaves. The historical time has shifted, yet the slavers still hold Mona captive in the dungeon of the castle. She must now honor the drummer Sankofa's earlier admonishment of 'Africa, listen.' The film thus begins its story of Mona's African American double Shola, a house-servant who was born on a Lafayette sugarcane plantation. Shola's master constantly rapes her, and when she looks to the Catholic priest, Father Raphael (Reginald Carter), for spiritual help he tells her to seek refuge in prayer. However, her lover Shango (Mutabaruka), an Afro-Caribbean field slave, entreats her to reject Christianity and accept African spirituality. Shango argues that the white man's religion offers no escape from rape and physical enslavement. After Shola accepts African spirituality, Shango offers her a wooden carved Sankofa bird that his father had given him. This weds together Shango and Shola and leads to Shola's physical return to Africa and Mona's spiritual return to her African roots. In a voice-over narrative accompanied by a chanting chorus and crane-shots moving over cane fields and a large body of water, Shola describes her spiritual passage from slavery to freedom.

> Guns, horses, head slaves, I can still hear it all now. . . . I heard the guns go off again. . . . The dogs, I heard them as they scrunched one of us. I heard his voice. *Keep runnin' sister.* . . . Suddenly I heard another one go down. They were right on our heels. . . . I knew I was next. One cried out to me to go on as the dogs feasted on him. *Keep runnin' sister.* . . . Then I had this feelin', this light feelin'. And there wasn't no more pains in my feet. This big buzzard was flyin' next to me and he spread his wings and scooped me up and up. . . . Just like what Shango said. The buzzard brought me.

As Shola, Mona must witness the humiliation and physical abuse that most, if not all, African slave women experienced in the New World. The final sequence presents Mona in African garb. She walks out of the dungeon and joins the black people who sit observing the performance of the white-powdered Sankofa drummer chanting the 'Spirits of the Dead' monologue that had introduced the film.

Sankofa: independent production, distribution, and exhibition

Initially, American film distributors and theaters refused to market Gerima's *Sankofa*. As Oscar Micheaux had done over seventy years earlier, Gerima took his film all around the US, offering screenings accompanied by lectures. He traveled to thirty-five cities, where he screened *Sankofa* in churches, community spaces, and rented theaters. Thanks to his efforts, by 1995 *Sankofa* had already grossed more than $3 million. Gerima reports: 'Churches and schools came in busloads to see *Sankofa*'; and he understood their attraction to his film as reflecting a desire for films that are rarely available to the black community. He added:

> Most black movies make black people look very bizarre, hopelessly bizarre; this is unacceptable. Commercial filmmakers sometimes leave the community unfulfilled and demoralized, asking itself: 'Is this all that blacks are capable of?' Church people complain that the romanticism and

glamor associated with violence in mainstream black films trickle back into the community. While Hollywood continues to select and produce films that reflect its own view of what the black community is, this contradiction will continue (1995).

Gerima had faced local and international rebuffs when seeking financing and distribution for *Sankofa*. Recalling these instances, which he calls censorship at the pre- and post-production phases, he explained:

> In America, slavery is a very sensitive topic. The moment I wanted to make *Sankofa* my credentials in the USA vanished, because I was

Figure 12.2 Noble Ali (Afemo Omilemi) and Nunu (Alexandra Duah) in *Sankofa* (Gerima, 1993). Courtesy of Mypheduh Films.

venturing into forbidden territory. The resource centers were closed to
me. I couldn't get funding. Censorship became a reality; the funding
agencies for cultural development shut their doors. They'd talk about
timing: 'This year's budget is nearly spent. You're too late or too early.'
Nobody comes out with it straight and says that the subject matter is
wrong. The press is much the same: they wouldn't touch *Sankofa* at
Berlin, though it was in competition with big-budget movies. They cen-
sor you by making you non-existent. We went to Montreal and Toronto
[in September 1993]: they skipped us, didn't even talk to us. They
thought we were finished (Crémieux 2001).

According to Gerima, the international press that covered film festivals in Berlin,
Montreal, and Toronto in 1993 avoided discussing his film. He took their rebuff as
a form of censorship in which their lack of coverage made his film non-existent to
distributors and potential audiences. He willingly acknowledges that slavery is a
topic which is rarely welcomed, and one that is even less so when filmed, as
Gerima films it, in a particularly non-classical style. Although Steven Spielberg's
Amistad (1997) treated a similar history and had lackluster box-office receipts, it
did have the benefit of having a linear narrative that appeals to audiences versed in
classical narrative film style. Because of Steven Spielberg's power within the film
industry, his film also enjoyed wide domestic and international distribution and
press coverage. This was certainly not the case with Haile Gerima's *Sankofa* – or,
for that matter, any other of his eight feature films.

While some critics might find *Sankofa*'s sentimentality too closely resembles
contemporary classical Hollywood melodramas, black communities celebrated
Sankofa as a genuine articulation of the African holocaust. When it premiered in
cities throughout the nation, black audiences packed the screenings. Still, no US
distributors were interested. Undaunted by the cold reception his film received
from the press and distributors, in New York City Gerima gathered together
twenty local community activists; they opened a local theater for regular screenings of the film. After *Sankofa*'s box-office receipts established it as a popular film
with the local black community, the New York Cineplex Theater agreed to a
rental agreement.

Exceptionally, in 1995, United Artist Theaters screened and distributed
Sankofa on the West Coast. Nevertheless, the UA Theaters' schedule for *Sankofa*
deteriorated into irregular screenings in smaller rooms, discouraging much of the
film's potential audience. However, the most courageous and flexible film-goer
did get to see the film during its three-week engagement. After the UA
bamboozle, the Magic Johnson Theaters booked *Sankofa* for the rest of the 1995
summer with regular screenings in spacious rooms. Consequently, the film
grossed more than $5 million. According to Eric Martin, the manager at Magic

Johnson Theaters, the daily takes out-performed *Judge Dredd* (Cannon, 1995) and *Apollo 13* (Howard, 1995) which were also being shown at the theater chain. (It is important to note that the Magic Johnson Theaters is a Los Angeles black-owned and operated theater chain that screens black-oriented films as well as conventional Hollywood mainstream fare such as *Apollo 13*.)

Nonetheless, the Blockbuster chain, one of the largest and certainly the most important video distribution chain in the US, would not stock Gerima's *Sankofa*. Again, Gerima was undaunted by attempts to forestall the wider distribution of his film. He took the profits that he had made from the theatrical distribution of *Sankofa* and made a down-payment on a building in which he opened Sankofa Video and Bookstore. Gerima's building also has conference rooms and post-production facilities. It was here that Shirikiana Aina, his wife and the vice-president of Mypheduh Films, Inc., edited her first feature-length film, *Through the Door of No Return* (1997). Later, in 1999, Haile used the editing facilities for his feature film *Adwa*. Gerima explains:

> That's why you see so many black independent filmmakers playing [*sic*] in with Hollywood and making bizarre 'shoot 'em up and kill' movies. Black people respect Spike Lee, especially for his shrewd ability to function in that mega world; he brings many black talents into his productions. Our people see Spike walking the commercial tightrope to make something serious, and more dignified. He's at a critical stage now, and we are waiting to see what happens next [. . .] *Sankofa* may well be a milestone linking African cinema to African American cinema. It is the first time two [West] African countries, Ghana and Burkina Faso, have collaborated on a film about slavery. But to talk of African cinema is sometimes very hard: even Ousmane Sembene, the father of African social cinema, has to wait 10 to 15 years between films, and I know 20 filmmakers in Ethiopia who have not made a film in five years (1995).

Sankofa's remarkable box-office success might leave one optimistic about the future of black independent filmmaking. I am not, however, all that hopeful about the future of black independent cinema. Multinational companies with little interest in the visual arts control film production, distribution, and exhibition. Their control leaves little room for independent filmmakers like Gerima. Several critically successful black independent filmmakers, among them Julie Dash, Cheryl Dunye and Charles Burnett, have had only one (relatively) widely distributed and successful independent movie. For the most part, black independent filmmakers are relegated to film festivals and college campuses. The general public has no knowledge of independent black film culture, the alternative (non-)narrative styles or the sociopolitical worlds that many of their films explore.

Nevertheless, Gerima's international reputation as an independent filmmaker, producer, and writer makes him a formidable example of what consistency and purpose can accomplish. His work expresses a distinct type of womanist ethics that makes it a worthy subject of any discussion of independent American cinema. At the same time, Gerima's experience of marketing his films in the US unearths the stratified layers of institutional racism and the general problems that American-based independent filmmakers face. Gerima's case is of singular importance since, for almost three decades, he has worked steadily in the independent film arena and steadfastly made films that express black female empowerment. Though different, both *Bush Mama* and *Sankofa* utilize a heroic narrative form. The psychological and physical acts of Mona/Shola further Haile Gerima's development of a womanist film aesthetic of black female empowerment, and *Sankota* can be seen as a sequel to *Bush Mama*. As heroine, Mona/Shola in particular is similar in stature to a historical figure like Malcolm X. Malcolm Little's travels as Malcolm X to African nations and his pilgrimage to Mecca equal the imaginative and spiritual travels of Mona as the enslaved, then liberated, Shola.

Notes

1 For the most part, Gerima has worked in 16mm, but *Hour Glass* (1971) was shot in Super 8, *Sankofa* (1993) in 35mm. His other films are *Child of Resistance* (1972), *Bush Mama* (1975), *Harvest: 3000 Years* (1976), *Wilmington 10-USA 10,000* (1978), *Ashes & Embers* (1982), *After Winter: Sterling Brown* (1985), *Imperfect Journey* (1994), and *Adwa – An African Victory* (2001). *Ashes & Embers, Harvest 300 Years, Bush Mama, Child of Resistance* and *Sankofa* are available for rental and purchase through Mypheduh Films, Inc. or the Sankofa website at www.sankofa.com

2 I take the term 'womanist' from Alice Walker, who defines it thus:

> A woman who loves other women, sexually and/or nonsexually. Appreciates and prefers women's culture, women's emotional flexibility . . . and women's strength. Sometimes loves individual men, sexually and/or nonsexually. Committed to survival and wholeness of entire people, male and female. Not a separatist, except periodically, for health. Traditionally universalist, as in 'Mama, why are we brown, pink, and yellow, and our cousins are white, being and black?' (Walker 1983: xi).

See further Reid 1993: 109–24.

3 The black action films I'm thinking of are Warner Bros.' *Cleopatra Jones* (Starrett, 1973) and *Cleopatra Jones and the Casino of Gold* (Bail, 1974); American International's *Coffy* (Hill, 1973), *Foxy Brown* (Hill, 1974), and *Friday Foster* (Marks, 1975). In a general sense one might also include Twentieth Century–Fox's *Trouble Man* (Dixon, 1972), MGM's *Shaft* (Parks, 1971), *Shaft's Big Score* (Parks, 1972), *Shaft in Africa* (Guillermin, 1973), and others. See further Reid 1993: 86–91.

4 Gerima says:

If I was interested in her violent act, the next logical scene would be prison. . . . However, the stages of her assertion were more entertaining. In the first stage of her consciousness, a young person snatches her purse. She is incapable of even defending her purse from a little kid. The second stage is the oppressive woman who represents the state [a clerk at the welfare agency] and commits silent violence against her; Dorothy retaliates in fantasy by breaking a bottle over the woman's head. The third level was when it affected her daughter. My obsessive theme deals with consciousness. . . . When do you begin to become aware of the fact that the world has to be changed, and what are the processes that lead towards that awareness? For Dorothy, when the oppressive tool came down on her daughter . . . [s]he stood her ground and asserted herself in very physical terms . . . it is with her consciousness that I ended the film and not at the logical conclusion of a conventional drama that would show that she went to jail (quoted in Howard 1985: 29).

5 In an interview with *Le Monde Diplomatique*, Gerima commented:

Traditional film narrative techniques require that filmmakers narrate their film in a similar style. Implicit in this requirement is the assumption that there exists only one narrative style. . . . Thus, we have a responsibility to reproduce this style. If black filmmakers perpetuate this Hollywood style for all the world . . . black film will be judged and evaluated according to the Anglo-Saxon cinematic tradition. It is not sufficient to merely reject these conventions, the struggle must be carried on within the film's narrative itself. (1984: 5; translation mine).

6 As Kobena Mercer argues, 'the issue is not the expression of some lost origin or some uncontaminated essence in black film language, but the adoption of a critical "voice" that promotes consciousness of the collision of cultures and histories that constitutes our very conditions of existence' (1990: 24–5).

Bibliography

Bourne, St. C. (1982) 'The Development of the Contemporary Black Film Movement,' in G.L. Yearwood (ed.), *Black Cinema Aesthetics: Issues in Independent Black Filmmaking*, Athens, Ohio University Center for African American Studies, 93–105.

Crémieux, A. (2001) 'Interview with Haile Gerima,' online: www.africultures.com/actualites/sorties/anglais/gerima.html (accessed 6 September 2001).

Gerima, H. (1984) 'Haile Gerima: Pour un Mouvement de Libération culturelle,' *Le Monde diplomatique*, 364: 5.

—— (1995) 'Haile Gerima: Images of Africa,' *Index on Censorship* 6, online: www.oneworld.org/index_oc/issue695/hailegerima.html (accessed 11 August 2001).

Howard, S. (1985) 'A Cinema of Transformation: The Films of Haile Gerima,' *Cineaste*, 14 (May): 28, 29, 39.

Marcorelles, L. (1984) 'Haile Gerima: "J'Appartiens à la fois à l'Ethiopie et à l'Amérique noire," ' *Le Monde*, 7 July: 11.

Mercer, K. (1990) 'Diaspora Culture and the Dialogic Imagination: The Aesthetics of Black Independent Film in Britain,' in M. Alvarado and J.O. Thompson (eds.), *The Media Reader*, London: British Film Institute, 24–35.

Reid, M.A. (1993) *Redefining Black Film*, Berkeley and Los Angeles: University of California Press.

Walker, A. (1983) *In Search of Our Mothers' Gardens: Womanist Prose by Alice Walker*, New York: Harcourt Brace Joavanovich Publishers, 1983, xi–xii.

Chapter 13

Seminal fantasies

Wakefield Poole, pornography, independent cinema and the avant-garde

José B. Capino

The winter before *Deep Throat* (Damiano, 1972) made pornography chic, a former ballet dancer named Wakefield Poole leased a small movie theater on 55th Street in Manhattan to screen the ninety-minute porn film he had shot the preceding summer at his friends' Fire Island haunts. In sharp contrast to the grimy urban 'sleaze' of gay porn's peep-show fare, Poole's *Boys in the Sand* (1971) proffered a veritable Eden of handsome studs who cavorted romantically in sun-drenched beaches and posh island dwellings. In lieu of a moan-and-groan soundtrack, Poole's actors made love to an elegant instrumental score embellished with strains of classical music. In place of hackneyed scenarios involving sailors and rough trade, Poole created three self-reflexive episodes that dramatize the sexual fantasies of an attractive but lonesome Fire Island dweller. The episodes, which combine mystery, eroticism, and humor, include enigmatic encounters with a sex god who emerges from the depths of the bay, an African American lineman who haunts a bourgeois stud, and a mustachioed muscle-man who appears when a palm-sized tablet is dissolved into a swimming pool.

To promote the film, Poole and his business partner (an accountant named Marvin Shulman) made modest advertising placements in gay-interest and mainstream publications. The $8,000 film grossed an impressive $24,655 on a single-screen run during its opening weekend. It made another $20,100 during its second weekend, grossing more money per screen than the current number one hit, the James Bond film *Diamonds Are Forever* (Hamilton, 1971).[1] *Boys* landed a spot in *Variety*'s national top-50 chart for three consecutive weeks, merited long runs in major American gay capitals, and enjoyed a robust afterlife in the 8mm home-movie market.[2]

The first-time filmmaker received a lot of press attention from mainstream and gay-interest publications, not only for the film's breakthrough success but for its signal departure from the 'shoddy fare' (Verill 1977: 20) playing in America's red-light districts. Poole gladly cultivated the recognition of his film as a sophisticated answer to erotic cinema. In an interview with *The Advocate*, for instance,

Poole characterized *Boys in the Sand*'s conspicuous aesthetization of gay pornography as something of a political gesture: 'I wanted [to make] a film that gay
people could look at and say, "I don't mind being gay – it's beautiful to see those
people do what they're doing." ' (Teal 1972a: 17). Poole also managed to convincingly intellectualize his approach to pornography. To critics who disliked, for
instance, *Boys'* abundance of cruising scenes, he explained that the long walking
scenes in the film were purposeful and in fact expressed his unique sensitivity to
the relationship between form and content in staging gay sexuality in film pornography: 'That's three quarters of gay life. Even at the baths and movie houses you
walk – you're afraid you're going to miss something.'[3] Poole further distanced
himself from the sleaziness of the red-light district by publicizing his interest in
the fine arts. For his interviews in *The Advocate* and *Andy Warhol's Interview*, the
filmmaker posed naked for publicity shots in front of his collection of Claes
Oldenburg sculptures and Warhol's Marilyn Monroe paintings.

Placing pornography

The breakthrough commercial success of *Boys in the Sand* and its inevitable categorization as a 'skin flick' tend to obscure the fact that it was produced, exhibited,
and publicized in much the same manner as independent films of the present. *Boys
in the Sand* was the work of an aspiring artist, financed by credit-card debts, made
without the prospect of financial gain, privately distributed through four-wall
deals, pushed by taste-makers for its unique vision and progressive politics, and
fervently supported by a subculture.

If it is already a stretch to see *Boys in the Sand* as an independent venture, it is
even more difficult to recognize Poole's affinity to the underground tradition of
American avant-garde cinema. Such ties to the avant-garde were strengthened
during the course of his decade-long career, beginning with his second film, *Bijou*
(1972), a hardcore feature about a 'straight' construction worker's exploration
of his bisexual desires inside a mysterious sexual fun-house. Poole described the
film in *Andy Warhol's Interview* as 'an abstract pornographic movie. I want to get
every element of pornography, not just gay pornography, into this film. You
know, audible pornography, visual pornography' (quoted in Colaciello 1972: 22).
To simulate the world of the construction worker's 'dark drop down a gay
White Rabbit's fantasy hole,' Poole lined his spacious apartment with black
velvet, mounted illuminated signs at skewed angles, surrounded the actors
with mirrors, sprayed artificial fog, and used matte shots to create gigantic sets
out of small sculptures. The film's *piece de resistance* is a multimedia spectacle
comprised of slides and footage of various sexual creatures (including the filmmaker himself) striking seductive poses in front of the bewildered protagonist.
The attraction's purported diegetic function was to dramatize the lead character's

complex sexuality, but it was also used to strengthen the discourse around Poole's artistic inclination by referring to his involvement in New York's multimedia performance scene.[4]

Although *Variety* declared that 'Poole's accomplishment does not live up to its pretensions about creating abstract pornography' (Verill 1972: 18), the film was rightfully commended by *The Advocate* for its 'care and nuance to visual detail' and its 'artsy, sometimes multimedia technique that brings to mind Andy Warhol's *Chelsea Girls*' (Teal 1972b: 25).

Poole's unusual body of work and the discourse of artistry that he and the press cultivated around his *oeuvre* present a number of interesting problems (and discoveries) for film historians. These problems range from the hackneyed dilemma of differentiating between the erotic and the pornographic, to the more provocative enterprise of mapping the areas in which the traditions of avant-garde filmmaking overlap independent cinema. In consideration of Poole's relative obscurity, this chapter proposes a more modest research program. It defers a detailed theoretical investigation of the large issues raised by his work in favor of a preliminary survey of his corpus and career that is also designed to identify their affinities to independent cinema and, more specifically, to the avant-garde. Such double-duty attempts tend to fall short of fulfilling either goal, but they are strategic for making knotty arguments about understudied films and figures. What

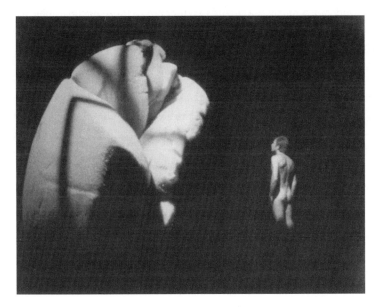

Figure 13.1 A construction worker (Bill Harrison) explores his sexuality in the surreal, self-reflexive, movie theater/dreamscape of *Bijou* (Poole, 1972). Courtesy of Anthology Film Archives.

is at stake in this effort to win recognition for Poole's work as independent cinema and an avant-garde corpus is not the elevation of a pornographic work into two more desirable traditions; on the contrary, my aim, to put it somewhat sheepishly, is to *rescue* independent cinema from the art-house by recuperating the heady intermingling of cinematic practices and discourses that attended the emergence of pornography during the 1970s. By eliciting a discussion of alternative/ independent film practices outside the constricting political–economic registers of their opposition to the studio system and their establishment of a domestic art-house cinema, I am angling to expand the discipline of film studies' understanding of independent cinema and the avant-garde.

Pornography and the practice of independence

By examining Poole's corpus of films in relation to the circumstances of their production and reception, we may recognize the parallels between his cinematic practice and independent cinema's. The artistic merits of Poole's films considerably ease this rather counter-intuitive suggestion, especially in light of the mistaken impression that pornography's status as a 'bad object' is contradictory of the lofty artistic goals of independent cinema. But I wish to go even further and venture that, if we were to distinguish independent films based on their mode of production and distribution, the recognition of certain pornographic films as works of independent cinema should extend even to those pornographic films that are not generally deemed to be artistically meritorious. Of course, our ability to distinguish what constitutes independent cinema hinges on the way we choose to define what constitutes a practice of independence and what makes a work of cinema an independent film.

In its most current incarnation, the independent cinema of *sex, lies & videotape* (Soderbergh, 1989) and Sundance circulate a discourse of difference based on an oppositional practice that is supposedly unfettered by the commercialism and the bloated production values of the blockbuster-oriented studio system.[5] The oppositional nature of this practice is carefully circumscribed, however, by the strictures of art-house exhibition standards.[6] To use an analogy from the theater, the content and the form of contemporary independent film occupy the same imaginary middle ground as off-Broadway plays. Independent films, like off-Broadway plays, are poised to cross over into mainstream venues whenever the opportunity arises. Off-off-Broadway plays, on the other hand, are like underground films in their occupation of unconventional spaces that are homologous to their radical disavowal of the mainstream's most cherished conventions.[7] Looking back at the first decade of the 'New American Cinema,' filmmaker Jon Jost decried its coziness with Hollywood, and described the American Independent Feature as 'bastard child of Hollywood, standing at the gates, yearning for intimacy.'[8]

Interestingly, the successful marketing of the notion of independent cinema is forcing an expansion of the term to encompass practically all film and videomaking practices outside the sponsorship of Hollywood, network television, and corporate America. The popularizing of the term – accelerated in the present by one-day film schools and manufacturers of 'prosumer' videography equipment – is such that all film and video enthusiasts with access to production equipment can now rightfully call themselves independent filmmakers. The hardcore feature emerged and prospered at a time when, similarly, numerous film enthusiasts were engaged in the production of small-gauge films (16mm and 8mm); when the boundaries between modes of cinema (e.g. documentary, narrative, experimental, pornography) were less rigid; when the distance between high and low art was being closed by the likes of Andy Warhol; when filmmaking practices outside the Hollywood system ranged from the ciné poems of Stan Brakhage to the raunchy comedies of Russ Meyer, and from the sordid experimental non-fiction of Curt McDowell to the racialized theatrics of blaxploitation.

From the very beginning, most of pornography's pioneers operated as independent filmmakers. They began their filmmaking careers by producing 'homemade' pornographic films (called 'loops') and selling them to larger mail-order companies and to franchisers of lucrative coin-operated peep shows. Bill Osco, the director of *Mona The Virgin Nymph* (1970), co-founded his company Griffith Films with a capital of $80, which he grew by making and selling 'Beaver' flicks (short films exhibiting female genitalia). When the $7,000-budgeted *Mona* grossed over $2 million, Osco and his partner Howard Ziehm embarked on bigger filmmaking ventures (Turan and Zito 1974: 137). The same is true of Gerard Damiano, who wrote, directed, and co-produced *Deep Throat* for $25,000 and would have earned a third of the film's estimated $30 million gross had it not been bought out, allegedly by the mob (see Blumenthal 1973: 31 and Weiner 1997: 6). Some independent filmmakers, such as the Mitchell brothers, grew their backyard porn loop operations into small independent studios that maintained a core group of managers, creative personnel, and, in some cases, its own movie houses.

The hardcore feature's popularity, its relative ease of production, and the lack of competition from Hollywood cultivated a practice of independent filmmaking that was prolific and immensely profitable. It was a practice that also encouraged experiments across genres, produced transgressive parodies and appropriations of Hollywood cinema, employed legions of amateurs and professionals, spawned a network of alternative theaters and spectatorial practices, and promoted the construction of a progressive, sex-positive, culture for adults. As film historian Jon Lewis argues in *Hollywood v. Hardcore* (2000), pornography was the strain of independent filmmaking that most effectively challenged (and changed) the business of Hollywood.

For most of his career, Wakefield Poole enjoyed a level of independence that was even greater than that of others who worked within the porn industry. He made films on such a small scale that he exercised almost complete creative control, personally attending to their conceptualization, scripting, directing, cinematography, and editing. The first four of his ten films were co-produced with his friend and accountant Marvin Shulman, who gave him a free hand in the creative process. When their partnership ended, Poole obtained financing from moonlighting producers. Except for his fifth film, *Hotshots* (1981), Poole managed to stay clear of full-scale porn studios – the kind that distributed their products through a national network of adult theaters and thus carefully supervised the creative and technical aspects of their films.[9]

Figure 13.2 Wakefield Poole directs adult superstar Casey Donovan in *Hotshots* (Poole, 1981). Courtesy of Anthology Film Archives.

Like any of the valorized independent filmmakers, Poole recruited friends and lovers to perform in his films, to build sets, and to tide him through the ups and downs of both the production process itself and the life of a creative artist. We shall see later that, as in the case of Warhol and Cassavetes, the imprint of a filmmaker's relationships with creative collaborators/loved ones – rather than the handiwork of some studio executive – is legible in Poole's films. In addition, the much-prized feature of the independent film, the filmmaker's 'personal vision,' is evident in Poole's corpus. In sharp contrast to the formulaic concoctions of Hollywood in the blockbuster era, Poole drew and dreamt up his film fantasies from the wellspring of his active sex life in the post-liberation gay milieux of New York and San Francisco. Even in his most conscious attempt to make a commercially successful film, Poole's quirky instincts and unique personal vision could produce only his biggest box-office disaster: a heterosexual softcore adaptation of the Bible that failed to take off after two premieres.

The distribution and exhibition of his films was another site of struggle for Poole, as it is for any independent filmmaker. The handful of organizations that ran national networks of adult theaters either insisted on buying out all the rights to a film or simply distributed pirated copies of independent hits. Because of this, Poole was often very closely involved in publicizing, marketing, and exhibiting his films. This required forming personal and professional relationships with adult-magazine correspondents and owners of gay adult theaters. It also required Poole to pay for the repair of a cinema's air conditioning unit, to paint the lobby of a theater, and to mount a burlesque show for the owner of San Francisco's Nob Hill Theater.

Thus far, I have discussed how Poole's filmmaking practice may be posited as independent cinema not only in relation to Hollywood but to the world of motion-picture pornography. In the next section, I locate Poole's place within the rarefied domain of avant-garde cinema, a domain that I understand to overlap significantly with that of independent cinema. The distinction between 'independent' and 'avant-garde' is decidedly hazy, and depends significantly on how one defines those terms. If we characterize 'independent cinema' as a *practice* that encompasses all works created outside the Hollywood studio system, then we may consider all avant-garde films as independent cinema. However, if we define independent cinema on a different register, as a *corpus* of theater-exhibited feature films patterned after the stylistic and financial models employed by the likes of John Cassavetes, then we might say that 'independent cinema,' like its predecessors (e.g. the 'New American Cinema' of the 1960s; 'No Wave'/'New Narrative' Cinema of the 1970s and 1980s), is a distinct strain in the larger history of the American avant-garde.[10] For the purpose of this discussion, I make the distinction between the two terms on the level of stylistics: in other words, I limit avant-garde cinema to the popular notion of 'experimental film,' to a corpus of art films that evinces a central preoccupation with form. I finesse this definition later in the chapter, when I discuss why Poole's films have not been admitted into the avant-garde.

By positioning Poole's corpus within the avant-garde in the next section, I am effectively touting the artistic merits of his films and simultaneously continuing this affirmation of their pedigree of independence by showing how Poole satisfies another element of independent cinema's discourse of uniqueness.

Pornography and its avant-garde

Poole's heady fusion of experimental film and pornography had many precedents. From the various camps of avant-garde cinema (whether identified as underground, experimental, or independent), the likes of Andy Warhol, Jack Smith and Curt McDowell had already been making films with explicit (homo)sexual themes and situations before Poole entered the scene. (Poole acknowledged Warhol's influence.) Gay sailors, rough trade, urban hustlers, and sexually aggressive Oriental fairies populated the avant-garde screen before pornographic shorts flourished in red-light districts. The 'deviant' sexual candor of these experimental films matched their oppositional modes of production and circulation, constituting a cinematic practice in which art and (gay) identity politics were articulated in a single gesture of celebration and defiance.[11]

Around the time that Poole was assembling his debut film, a West Coast filmmaker named Fred Halsted was making *L.A. Plays Itself* (1972), a feature-length film that staged uncommon sexual situations through the expressive language of avant-garde cinema. Halsted's earlier film *The Sex Garage* (1971), touted by its publicists as the first 'trisexual porno film,' used artful sound design, editing, and camera work in showing, among other things, a sexual encounter between a biker and the exhaust pipe of his bike. Like Poole, Halsted touted the artistic orientation of his film, filling his ads with blurbs from such critics as Jonas Mekas and quoting celebrities such as William S. Burroughs.

Although Halsted blasted Poole's films – he described *Bijou* as 'artsy craftsy, closety faggot stuff' – the two were decidedly peers in an unusual filmmaking practice that defiantly traversed the discursive boundary between art and pornography, and between the institutions of experimental cinema and pornographic film (Siebenand 1975: 203). At first glance, the films of Poole (and of Halsted) seem to gesture towards an *avant-garde of pornography*, an oppositional practice which critics may locate within pornography itself (or closely teetering on its margins). By an *avant-garde of pornography*, I wish to conjure a fleeting vision of an elusive corpus of artistic erotica – not the so-called 'chateau fuck-films' that simply dress up mechanically executed coitus with opulent scenery and costumes, but the fugitive kind that reproduce the aesthetic qualities of sex through the expressive possibilities of cinema. Alternatively, Poole's films could also be considered as *avant-garde pornography*. On this view, his films are inscribed squarely within the boundaries of the avant-garde and its tradition of explicit sexual representation. If breaking the taboo on sexuality was, as Parker Tyler (1970) suggested, a prevalent feature of underground cinema, Poole's work seems to register an extreme manifestation of experimental cinema's predilection for sexually explicit representations.

Between the two terms, I prefer *avant-garde pornography* as a descriptor of Poole's and Halsted's films because it honors the contiguities between the underground film tradition of the avant-garde and the seminal works of moving-image picture pornography. These contiguities are not limited to Poole's and Halsted's conscious appropriation of avant-garde stylistics: they also reflect experimental cinema and hardcore pornography's shared programmatic objective of supplanting mainstream cinema. To locate their films within an *avant-garde of pornography* is to engage in the project of establishing an avant-garde *for* pornography – a project that is ultimately designed to insulate the avant-garde (a good object) from the (bad object) of pornography.

The films that I envision as belonging to avant-garde pornography, along with Poole's corpus, include Curt McDowell's sexually explicit profiles of his friends and lovers, *Nudes: A Sketchbook* (1974) and *Ronnie* (1972); and Rinse Dream's pornographic alien film, *Café Flesh* (1982).

An avant-garde corpus, an independent practice

In trying to understand Poole's *oeuvre* as an avant-garde corpus, it is useful to think of his project as a filmmaker in terms of his exploration of the possibilities of gay pornographic cinema in all three registers: gay, pornography, and cinema.

His first film, *Boys in the Sand*, offered a poetics of hardcore pornography that privileged fantasy over documentation. In his use of Fire Island, which he effectively designated as gay pornography's cinematic Eden, Poole defined this new cinema as a site for generating and sharing collective sexual fantasies. Poole claimed that he made the film in response to the dismal quality of all-male pornographic films circulating at the time. 'There was no challenge to the head at all,' he complained in an interview with *The Advocate* (Teal 1972a: 16). It is clear from the resulting film that by 'head' he meant not so much the intellect as the imagination. Indeed, *Boys in the Sand* is literally built on a series of intense imaginings: the film is structured as an elaboration of three sexual fantasies.

The primacy of consciousness in *Boys in the Sand* makes it remarkably different from contemporaneous films, especially in its address to the spectator and in the vocabulary of expressive techniques that Poole employed to represent consciousness. The film externalizes the process of intense imagination through its avoidance of dialogue and ambient sound, its strategic disavowal of continuity editing, and its deployment of expressive cinematic devices (e.g. to denote the passage of time in the second episode, the pages of a calendar are simultaneously incinerated and carried away by the agitated waves of the swimming pool). Taken as a poetics of gay pornography, the film posits gay porn as a wellspring of fantasy, not as a mere site for visible documents of sexual congress (upon which film loops, with their focus on the sexual act, seem premised). A good pornographic film, Poole seems to suggest, is one that enjoins spectators to participate in the collective and personal fantasies available to them through the cinema. Like avant-garde film-makers who demand a more intense engagement with their spectators, Poole sought to make a film that offered something 'to the heads' of the spectators, inviting them to engage not only their bodies but their minds. One also finds in *Boys*, as in many of Poole's succeeding films, distinct echoes of the American avant-garde's formative tradition of the psychodramatic trance film. As in Deren's *At Land* and *Meshes of the Afternoon*, or Brakhage's *Flesh of Morning*, the central figures in Poole's films engage in what Sitney (1974: 18) describes as a 'quest for sexual identity' enacted through surrealistic, somnambulistic journeys across domestic spaces and evocative landscapes. Even the common motifs of the psychodrama – the ubiquity of mirrors, the relentlessly mobile protagonist, and the performance of ritualistic acts – are conspicuously present in Poole's films.

Bijou, Poole's second feature, is both his most unabashedly psychodramatic film and the early apex of his career-long exploration of pornography's cinematic specificity. Clearly mounted as an attempt to live up to the commercial success of *Boys in the Sand* and to the artistic reputation he was consciously cultivating in the press, *Bijou* – produced at nearly thrice the cost of Poole's first film and replete with innovative visual effects – is so intensely experimental that it is practically unrecognizable as a gay porn film.[12]

The film begins like a low-budget thriller: a slender woman in a fur coat is run-over by a car. A construction worker (Bill Harrison) who witnesses the accident makes off with the woman's purse instead of helping her. Back at his apartment, the man examines the purse and finds a ticket to a 7 p.m. affair at a place called 'Bijou.' He takes a long shower during which he masturbates to thoughts of nude female centerfolds, and afterwards proceeds to the enigmatic venue. Like the protagonist of *Alice in Wonderland*, he navigates a space inhabited by different creatures and objects – phallic sculptures, yonic flowers, a multitude of gigantic lips, illuminated signs, mirrors. After sodomizing a long-haired individual (whom he later discovers is a man), he wakes up to a multimedia slideshow (described by critics as an homage to Warhol's two-screen film *The Chelsea Girls*) that visualizes a complex matrix of male sexual desire.

According to Poole, the film's innovative style runs parallel to his attempt to depict the fluidity of (gay male) sexuality: 'He's turned on by tits, by hips, by high heels, by women. But there are no women involved. . . . It's all men. . . . It will be of the moment, it will be total sex. It's [about] the opportunity to express yourself totally with freedom, even though it's alien to your makeup' (Colaciello 1972: 22).

Bijou was both a critical and commercial success. Critics from a wide range of publications praised Poole's unique artistry. Audiences in New York showed their appreciation by supporting the film's six-month run.

In his next film, Poole juggled several ambitions: to venture into softcore pornography, court a heterosexual audience, make a grand costume-drama in the camp tradition, and produce a commercially viable project. Responding to the Federal Government's crackdown on film pornography, Poole and his business partner, Marvin Shulman, decided to produce a straight softcore porn film based on three episodes of the Bible 'told from a woman's point-of-view' (Poole 2000: 190). Though the film has neither gay sex nor explicit sex, both elements are sublimated into the conceptual realm: high blasphemy proxies for explicit sex, and 'gayness' is expressed through the film's camp aesthetic. Poole and Shulman reportedly spent $100,000 on *Bible!* (1973; also released under the title *Wakefield Poole's Scandals*), shooting on location in the Caribbean and investing in decent sets and costumes. To boost the film's appeal to straight audiences, the duo cast Georgina Spelvin fresh from her successful porn debut in Gerard Damiano's *The Devil in Miss Jones* (1973).

Poole's attempt to incorporate some of elements of mainstream adult films was undermined, however, by his refusal to adopt the codes of classical Hollywood narratives, which were already normative in hardcore features. His intent to keep one foot within the familiar realm of the avant-garde is evident in his description of the film: 'I wanted to make this film with no dialogue but storied and staged to an entire musical composition: an adult *Fantasia.*' By all accounts, the film turned into a rather audaciously lurid camp tribute to Cecil B. DeMille's silent biblical spectacles.

Clinging on to their hype as purveyors of legitimate erotica, Poole and Shulman placed advertisements in mainstream publications, threw press screenings, and exhibited *Bible!* at the Lincoln Art Theater in a 35mm print blown up from the film's original 16mm format. The film's advertisements in mainstream papers elicited a storm of protest – normally good in stimulating sales – but *Bible!* earned only enough at the tills to make rent.

Burned by the failure of *Bible!* Poole and Shulman decided to produce a film that was supposed to go straight to the lucrative home-movie market. But *Moving* (1974), according to Poole, turned out to be 'so good it was released theatrically.' Perhaps the most interesting aspect of the film is its successful transposition of the elements of *Boys in the Sand* into the milieu of San Francisco's gay subculture. The film registers Poole's brief move to San Francisco and his attempt to start over after his career had hit the doldrums in New York. Like *Boys in the Sand*, the film features three self-reflexive scenarios tied by a common motif (the theme of changing abodes replaces *Boys in the Sand*'s unifying locale of Fire Island). The third episode most closely evokes Poole's debut film: instead of a lonely cruiser who finds a stud in a magic tablet, *Moving* features an apartment hunter who employs the force of his intense desire to make a life-size drawing of a tattooed muscle-man spring to life and fulfill his sexual desires. But the episode also marked a profound departure from the 'candor' of Poole's earlier films. It included an extremely graphic fisting scene that was extensively promoted in the film's advertisements.[13]

Poole's professional relationship with Marvin Shulman ended after *Moving*, when their friendship grew cold and when the latter turned Broadway impresario. Bereft of his financial backer, Poole teamed up with an acquaintance who owned a film production studio in San Francisco and invited a friend from Los Angeles to invest in his fifth film, a 'docufantasy' entitled *Take One* (1977). Inspired by the warm reception accorded his documentary project on the San Francisco Gay Pride March, Poole interviewed numerous gay men about their individual sexual fantasies. He then chose a handful of subjects, filmed the interview and staged the sexual fantasies using the interviewees themselves. The film – which was seized by Poole's financial partners soon after its release – is no longer available for study, but is vividly described in the filmmaker's biography and in various reviews and articles. *Variety* mentions that one of the erotic scenarios 'includes a young man having sex with his car,' and another 'involves an incest session with twin [sic] brothers.' In a 1978 interview, Poole insisted that 'the two brothers ball for the first time in their lives'; he also admitted to heightening the scene's transgressiveness by embedding a barely decodable message on the film's soundtrack: 'I scored in on the soundtrack the noise of kids on a playground and if you listen really closely, you can hear the last words on the track saying, "Hey, you got one just like mine!"'(Fritscher 1978: 14–22).

Take One was by no means the first hybrid of pornography and documentary. Numerous 'marriage manual films' and self-reflexive documentaries about the history of pornography preceded the debut of the hardcore feature and paved the way for the gradual acceptance of the latter's non-moralized, non-scientific, depiction of sexuality. What sets Poole's film apart from its precedents is its inspired incorporation of fantasy within documentary and the film's audacious sexual transgressions, including the much-advertised incest scene. Touted by Poole at the time of its release as the piece of his *oeuvre* with the most sex and 'at least twenty come shots,' the film predictably fell foul of the censors and did good business in San Francisco and New York, closing prematurely in the latter only because of problems with the theater's air-conditioning system.

Out of work and money in 1981, Poole wrote and directed *Hotshots* (1981), a film that adheres to all the conventions of the typical hardcore feature and marked the entrance of dialogue in his films. Casey Donovan plays a lusty chauffeur who imagines (and reads aloud) three scenarios described in a mail-order catalogue of gay adult films. Even in his most lethargic effort, Poole's fine sense of what is cinematic and erotic is displayed in the film's silent introductory dream sequence. In his dreams Donovan imagines himself as the boss who is chauffeured around the city in his Rolls-Royce after attending a concert with a female companion. As he undresses in his plush apartment, Donovan sees an imaginary reflection of his driver's naked chest and torso in the mirror. The reflection (which looks like projected black-and-white film) either follows his desires or teaches him how to desire. The film's self-reflexivity and its rehash of elements from *Bijou* seem lazy, but the virtual inscription of fantasy, which recurs in his succeeding films and indeed in most of his corpus, does seem to emerge as a stylistic signature of his *oeuvre*.

In yet another take at self-reflexivity, Poole explores the dynamics of sexual performance in *Split Images* (1984), his first feature shot on video. It was produced by Male Express, the tiny porn studio where Poole – cash-strapped and recovering from drug addiction – had found employment supervising photo layouts and shooting porn. Poole appears in the bookend scenario as a photographer–pornographer who draws erotic looks and poses out of three adult models. Each of the three sex scenes that ensue dramatizes the fantasies employed by the models to psyche themselves during the shoot.

Poorly executed but strongly conceptualized, the video exposes the mechanics of erotic performance: how the pornographer elicits and captures a sex act and how actors internalize the fantasies they embody. He articulated a similar set of ideas about pornographic performance in magazine interviews conducted earlier in his career: 'I like to film people . . . so they can see not only how they look but [also] how I see them when they do some really beautifully basic personal things. They never see what I see when they're jerking off into the mirror. When they see the footage, that's the big surprise' (quotes in Fritscher 1978:14). Poole's conviction that erotic performance should draw upon an authentic sexual experience (rather than a simple kinesthetic activity conducted for the benefit of the camera) generously ascribes agency to both the director and the actors. In this sense, the pornographic film's production and reception are posited as a ritual in which members of a subculture participate. The idea is compatible with underground cinema's role as a venue for the performance of subcultural rituals.

In the same year, Poole made *The Hustlers* (1984), an 'all-talking' hybrid of soap-opera and video pornography. He weaves a narrative around the exploits of two gay lovers who meet at a sex club and enter into a personal and financial partner-ship. In the film's most interesting scene, the couple hires an older professional hustler who shares the story of his sexual encounter with a transvestite. The scene is staged through voice-over narration and a succession of still images of the encounter. Poole uses stills instead of video to make the sex 'more palatable'

(Poole 2000: 266) but the device also registers as an interesting artistic touch, a throwback to the hypnotic flicker of motion pictures. The inclusion of the transvestite encounter also expands the range of gay sexuality portrayed in Poole's corpus. (He was criticized earlier in his career for portraying only vanilla sex, but had vowed to heed the suggestion by casting different sexual types and depicting a wider variety of sex acts.)

Inspired by the creative success of *The Hustlers*, Poole decided to form a part-nership with the video's financier Bill Adkins. They would jointly produce videos and distribute them through their own mail-order company. It was, for Poole, a return to the vertically integrated practice that had brought him and Shulman considerable financial success. It was also an attempt to regain his independence (and hopefully, his vision) as a filmmaker. To jump-start the company, they decided to produce a sequel to *Boys in the Sand*.

Boys in the Sand II (1984) is, to be precise, an unusual hybrid of sequel and re-make. It revisits the scenarios of the 1972 film, emphasizing rather than muting its continuities and discontinuities with the original. The passing of time registers in a succession of aerial shots (taken from a helicopter) that close in on Fire Island. On the bushes where it had all begun, a very mature Casey Donovan recreates his tryst with a full-bearded beach-bum. In the following scene, Donovan comes home to find notice of an early morning meeting with a stranger. When he shows up at the beach at the appointed time, a young blonde stud (Pat Allen) emerges from the depths of the bay in the same way he had done more than two decades earlier. After coitus, the relay between Donovan and Fisk in the 1972 film is repeated. Donovan runs into the water, taking his appointed place in the oblivion of the bay's abyss, dramatically affirming the end of film pornography's carefree days.

Poole tried to drum up publicity for the straight-to-video release by arranging for a pictorial and an article in a gay adult magazine, but the sudden death of his new producing partner resulted in an eighteen-month delay and a court case that cost Poole $8,000. Cash-strapped again, he decided to co-produce another video that was to piggy-back on *Boys II*'s release. *One, Two, Three* was conceived on the basis of nothing more than a strong marketing premise: 'shoot a movie with six people who would travel around the country on a personal appearance tour along with the movie. The opening night in each city would benefit AIDS research and the video would be sold in the theater' (Poole 2000: 279–80). The film's title also dictated its structure: three sex scenes performed by a succession of one, two, and three actors.

> Part 1 starred J.D. Slater . . . talk[ing] directly to the camera while bringing himself to orgasm. Part 2 featured . . . sex accompanied by a voice-over reading [of] a sexually explicit story unrelated to [the] . . . sex scene . . . .. [In] Part 3, the dialogue was spoken by Ryder [Hanson] who

stood on the sidelines, instructing Ron and Tom on what to do with each other (Poole 2000: 280).

In his biography, Poole reveals that he liked the video ('It's a terrific movie, and the guys are all great'), though it appears to be the least artistically successful piece in his *oeuvre*. Conceptually interesting is the video's employment of different levels of verbal pornography (dialogue, narration, audible 'stage' directions) articulated in different modes of address (first-person, third-person and second-person, respectively) and thus in varying relationships to the spectator.

After the video wrapped shooting, a disaster struck that killed both its lead star and Poole's filmmaking career. Porn actor Dave Connors overdosed on sleeping pills after being diagnosed with AIDS. *One, Two Three*, along with *Boys II*, was quietly released by a distribution partner that never paid any royalties to the director. Poole quit filmmaking altogether following an angry phone call from a porn actor he had never worked with who accused him of casting someone he knew was HIV-positive. Poole denied that he knew of Connors' infection but was deeply burned by the tirade. Not too long after the traumatic experience, Poole enrolled in a French culinary institute and began a new career as a chef at La Caravelle.

The sentence of (film) history

If Poole was such a remarkable experimentalist, why does he need to be claimed for the avant-garde?

We may begin by scrutinizing the rubric 'avant-garde,' which seems to exist on three different registers.[14] First, experimental cinema is an oppositional film-making *practice* that engages, while remaining defiantly outside, the mainstream of commercial cinema. Because the mainstream is constant flux, experimental cinema dynamically regenerates itself, advancing forward as the mainstream inches toward the position formerly occupied by the advance guard (the avant-garde). Second, 'experimental cinema' refers to the oppositional 'look,' the shorthand of sonic and visual codes associated with the corpus of experimental cinema. It comprises the (often rough) surface created by a film's mode of production and its maker's oppositional (often economical) aesthetic practices. Because they have become quite familiar, these codes are easily simulated, as in the case of music videos with relentless visual fugues and comedic parodies of bad video art. The third register of experimental cinema pertains to its *institutional dimension*: the self-confirming community of critics, filmmakers and audiences who define the terms of inclusion within the domain.

A close appraisal of Poole's career and *oeuvre* evinces his fulfillment of the first two registers of the avant-garde. He prided himself in creating art outside the system of commercial pornography, and many of his films bear the imprint of avant-garde film's techniques. His fulfillment of the third criterion is more complicated, for although Poole recognized himself as an artist standing at the vanguard of erotic cinema, his work did not gain recognition from the avant-garde's community of critics. It is important to stress, however, that critics from the mainstream press and the alternative (gay) press instantly recognized the difference between his work and the garden variety pornography being peddled by his peers. *Variety* described *Boys in the Sand* as an 'artsy-craftsy romantic fantasy' and *Bijou* called it a 'head picture, part ersatz Kubrick, part raunchy Disney.' Even after the commercial fiasco of Poole's softcore adaptation of the Bible, the same publication acknowledged the integrity of his artistic vision: 'Per usual in Poole's work, *Bible*[!] is notable for a tactile awareness for [*sic*] the human form and a heady visual sense not found in most sexploitation features' (Verill 1974: 18). On the release of Poole's feature-length documentary, *Take One, Variety* affirmed his consistent passion for innovation: 'Poole continues to experiment within the confines of gay erotic films and his pix offer much more than the meat-rack gymnastics of his competition. *Take One* is overly long at 98 minutes but it's heads above the shoddy fare that dominates in the field' (Verill 1977: 20).

Critics from adult magazines and gay publications showed even more enthusiasm in praising Poole. The gay press embraced *Boys in the Sand* as an instant classic: 'What distinguishes . . . the entire film is a care and nuance to visual detail; the kaleidoscopic music track . . . is more sensitively integrated with image, which has an ambitious design that is more controlled and expressive than in any erotic film I have ever seen' (*Gay Sunshine* 1973: 7). Al Goldstein, the influential editor of *Screw* magazine, proclaimed Poole's second film, *Bijou*, as the best (pornographic) picture of 1972: 'All the gay guys who like their filmic sex surreal . . . will have to pack a lunch to stand in line to wait for a chance to buy a ticket to the most ambitious and successful hardcore film to emerge from the porno underground. The gay Masterpiece of Masterpieces is *Bijou*.'[15] (Interestingly, he also cites *Boys in the Sand* in the same article as the worst film of the year.)

In every review mentioned above, Poole's films are claimed as innovative and meritorious in relation to the delimited rubrics of erotic film and gay cinema, but never in relation to experimental cinema itself. The non-admittance of Poole's *oeuvre* to the domain of the avant-garde simply because critics of the time did not deem it necessary or appropriate to do so is not, however, a sufficient reason. If one were to stay true to the spirit of avant-gardism, the range of oppositional cinematic practices should never be constricted or proscribed – indeed the establishment of such criteria should be indefinitely deferred in order to give audiences and critics a generous grace period in which to catch up with the strides of visionary artists. While the artistic merits of Poole's films are subject to debate, his conscious aspiration towards the refinement of erotic film is well documented. To be sure, it is only in Poole's work and in his words that one may find a clearly articulated poetics of gay erotica and a sustained exploration of cinema's pornographic possibilities.

The ancillary issue of Poole's worthiness as an independent filmmaker is, I hope, put to rest by this lengthy articulation of his predominantly artisanal mode of production outside the legitimate and adult studio systems, his stylistic innovations, and the discourse of difference which the filmmaker, his audience, and some critics cultivate about his work. The aim of this chapter – to sell the idea of a pornographer as an independent and experimental filmmaker – is a tough sell, because both labels are applied not solely on the basis of the cinematic practice they denote but, perhaps more importantly, on their romantic purchase as the artistic and non-commercial guardian angels of American cinema. As film critic Annette Insdorf argued in her article 'Ordinary People, European Style,' a real indie film is distinguished by a complex of 'such elements as casting, pace, cinematic style, and social or moral vision' (1981: 58). If the romance of a purely artistic, commercially and morally untainted independent cinema must be maintained in order to serve as the symbolic conscience of American film in the face of Hollywood's rampaging commercialism, artistic dearth and moral bankruptcy, then Poole and his hardcore contemporaries (we may call them 'the red-light indies') don't even have a prayer.

Notes

Thanks to L.S. Kim, Chuck Kleinhans, Wakefield Poole, and Justin Wyatt for commenting on various drafts of this chapter. The films are available on DVD from TLA video (1–800–333–8521). 'Unauthorized,' and in some cases, expurgated versions of most of Poole's work are available on VHS through Bijou Video (1–800–932–7111).

1　The budget is mentioned in an interview with Poole in Turan and Zito (1974: 197). The opening week's figures are provided by Teal (1972a: 16–17). *Variety* reports the film's second and third week grosses: see Standard Data Corporation 1972a and 1972b. The 55th Street theater had a 250-seat capacity, and Poole charged a $5.00 admission fee which was consistent with the ticket price for adult films; the typical ticket price for mainstream films in 1971 was about $3.00.

2　For a quarter-page advertisement of the film indicating screenings in Los Angeles, San Francisco and Chicago, see *The Advocate* 1972.

3　In a much later interview Poole makes an impressive argument for the aesthetization of fisting: 'In *Moving*, when Peter [Fisk] pulls his hand out of Terry's ass, audiences gasp at the juices and fluids that come running out. When we were editing, I said to Peter: "That's not blood. That's not scat. Those are juices, life fluids. . . . That's one interpretation of reality related man-to-man" ' (quotes in Fritscher 1978: 22).

4　Poole created a well-received multimedia spectacle based on the work of theater-poster designer David Byrd at the Triton Gallery which was owned by Poole's then lover Peter Fisk.

5　In his book on independent cinema, film critic Donald Lyons (1994: xi) defines independence on two registers: the *way* Hollywood makes movies ('expensive, increasingly agent-driven . . . succeeded by executive and marketing interference') and *what* Hollywood makes ('infantile – at best adolescent').

6 Annette Insdorf (1981: 57–60) defines independent film as an American version of European art cinema. She argues that it is the independent filmmakers' ability to 'treat inherently American concerns with primarily European style' that truly differentiates independent features from 'commercial films.'

7 Insdorf excludes independently produced films of the non-art-house variety from her definition of independent film, characterizing them as '"portfolio" films made for the purpose of hopping to Hollywood' (*ibid.*: 58).

8 See Jost (1989: 42–5).

9 Turan and Zito (1974) provide a detailed overview of the porn industry's production, distribution and exhibition models during the early 1970s in *Sinema*. They elucidate the operation of adult theater chains such as the Pussycat cinemas, and they profile entrepreneurs who operated adult cinemas and peep-show cubicles in adult bookstores across the country.

10 For a historical overview of the 'New American Cinema,' see Barrett (1973: 103–12).

11 Richard Dyer (1990: 172–3) argued that 'underground film was the space in which gay cinema could emerge, at that time, in the USA . . . partly because of the overlaps of the avant-garde and gay milieux and the importance of homosexual imagery in what informed the underground (Freudanism, the novel of alienation, camp and pop art) but, above all, because of underground cinema's definition of cinema as "personal"' (1990: 172–3).

12 The film reportedly cost $22,000. Turan and Zito (1974: 192).

13 The scene was excised from the version (distributed by Bijou Video) that I saw.

14 I assume that 'experimental' and 'avant-garde' are equivalent, although I acknowledge P. Adams Sitney's suggestion (1974: vi–viii) that the former – like 'underground' cinema – is a more historically specific term.

15 The blurb from Goldstein is quoted in an advertisement for the film (*Screw* 1972: 9).

Bibliography

Barrett, G.R. (1973) 'Jonas Mekas: Interview,' *Film/Literature Quarterly*, 1, 2 (spring): 103–12.

Blumenthal, R. (1973) 'Porno Chic,' *New York Times Magazine*, 21 January: 28, 30–3.

Colaciello, R. (1972) 'Wakefield Poole: Passionate Pornographer,' *Andy Warhol's Interview*, May: 22.

Dyer, R. (1990) *Now You See It: Studies on Lesbian and Gay Film*, London and New York: Routledge.

Fritscher, J. (1978) 'Dirty Poole: Everything You Fantasized about Wakefield Poole but Were Too Wrecked to Ask,' *Drummer*, 27: 14–22.

Gay Sunshine (1973) 'The Fantasy World of Wakefield Poole,' 17 (March–April): 7.

Insdorf, A. (1981) 'Ordinary people, European Style: or how to spot an independent feature,' *American Film*, 6, 10 (10 September): 57–60.

Jost, J. (1989) 'End of the Indies,' *Film Comment*, 25, 1 (January–February): 42–5.

Lewis, J. (2000) *Hollywood v. Hardcore*, New York: New York University Press.

Lyons, D. (1994) *Independent Visions*, New York: Ballantine.

Poole, W. (2000) *Dirty Poole: The Autobiography of a Gay Porn Pioneer*, Los Angeles: Alyson.

Siebenand, P.A. (1975) 'The Beginnings of Gay Cinema in Los Angeles: The Industry and its Audience,' Ph.D. dissertation, University of Southern California.

Sitney, P.A. (1974) *Visionary Film: The American Avant-garde 1943–1978*, New York: Oxford University Press.

Standard Data Corporation (1972a) '50 Top Grossing Films: Week Ending January 12,' *Variety*, 19 January: 17.

—— (1972b) '50 Top Grossing Films: Week Ending January 19,' *Variety*, 26 January: 9.

Screw (1972) 'Surrealistic Homosex,' 6 November: 9.

Teal, D. (1972a) ' "No Degradation": Wakefield Poole Adds New Dimension to Porn,' *The Advocate*, 1 March: 16–17.

—— (1972b) 'Bijou Offers Multimedia Hardcore,' *The Advocate*, 22 November: 25.

The Advocate (1972) Advertisement for *Boys in the Sand*, 29 March: 25.

Turan, K. and Zito, S. (1974) *Sinema: American Pornographic Films and the People Who Make Them*, New York: Praeger.

Tyler, P. (1970) *Underground Film: A Critical History*, New York: Grove Press.

Verill, A. (1972) 'Bijou,' *Variety*, 18 October: 18.

—— (1974) 'Bible,' *Variety*, 20 March: 18.

—— (1977) 'Take One,' *Variety*, 17 August: 20.

Weiner, R. (1997) 'Sore from "Throat",' *Variety*, 18 August: 6.

Part IV

Identity hooks ⇔ cultural binds

Chapter 14

Generation Q's ABCs
Queer kids and 1990s' independent films

Chris Holmlund

Queer subjects in a fairy kingdom

Meet little Stevie (Evan Bonifant), age 6¾ (he's quite precise about it). Stevie spearheads Todd Haynes's queer reframing of Freud's case study, 'A Child Is Being Beaten' in the 1993 short *Dottie Gets Spanked*.[1] Growing up in a 1960s' household that does not believe in spanking, Stevie's fascinated by it. Following Freud, who analyzed the beating fantasies of six young girls and boys in 'A Child Is Being Beaten,' Haynes demonstrates how, in fantasy, gender roles bend, viewing positions shift, and power stations alter.[2] Additionally, he ruminates on the importance of media models for gay kids: his little hero idolizes Dottie (Julie Halston), an *I Love Lucy*-type star. A budding artist, he makes sketch after sketch of her as he watches her show.

But, Stevie learns, *girls*, not boys, like Dottie. In compensation, he moves from reality – his comfortable suburban home – to fantasy – an expressionist black-and-white cardboard kingdom – which he literally rules. Asleep, he watches children *and* adults get spanked; awake, he wins a ticket to a *Dottie* episode where Dottie gets walloped, too. To his father's disapproval and his mother's dismay, the drawings Stevie makes of Dottie become more graphic. Finally Stevie dreams of his own beating by the strongest man in his fairy kingdom. Frightened but stimulated, he wakes, takes from a drawer his sketch of Dottie getting spanked, folds it, wraps it in foil, and buries it outside, patting (spanking . . .?) down the earth around it.

For little Stevie, queer childhood is impossible: he must leave his beating fantasies behind and watch football with his dad. But, as Freud has shown, 'gone' is not forgotten: the adult Haynes remembers and offers up (his own) sissy childhood through his character. And Haynes/Stevie are not alone: other gay artists, too – among them, argues Michael Moon, Henry James and Andy Warhol – also learned to recognize their queer desires thanks to 'the production and transmission' of images and narratives (1998: 3).

Many in the US, however, including many in the mainstream movie industry, find the idea that children might be sexual – and especially that they might be homosexual – unthinkable. 'Out' queer kid characters aged seventeen and under are rare indeed in 1990s' studio films: in his comprehensive study, Tim Shary (2002: 59, 66) finds only *Pump Up the Volume* (Moyle, 1990) and *Clueless* (Heckerling, 1995).[3] In earlier decades, young gay characters were even less visible: usually closeted, always troubled, they often died as well: witness *Rebel without a Cause* (Ray, 1955), *Tea and Sympathy* (Minnelli, 1956), *Ode to Billy Joe* (Baer, 1976), and *Fame* (Parker, 1980).[4]

In contrast, *nine* full-length 'independent' films featuring queer kids aged seventeen and under, in *lead* as well as secondary roles, were released between 1995 and 1999; the phenomenon continues today.[5] Most are centered on lesbian and gay topics, and made by 'out' directors who, born between 1960 and 1970, are part of Generation 'Q'; their films participate in what B. Ruby Rich heralded as the 'New Queer Cinema' (1992). Some of these nine 'queer kid' movies fit niche marketing labels less neatly, however, for reasons discussed below. The majority (five) are distributed by small companies, but three are products of 'mini-majors' and/or studio independent 'art' arms – Fine Line for *The Incredibly True Adventure of Two Girls in Love* (Maggenti, 1995) and *All Over Me* (Sichel, 1997); Lions Gate for *But I'm a Cheerleader* (Babbitt, 1999)[6] – and one, *Election* (Payne 1999), was made and released through a major studio (Paramount). Because *Election* won three 'Independent Spirit' awards and was comparatively inexpensive ($8.5 million), I consider it here also as an independent.[7]

Though but a tiny fraction of total 'indie' output (one executive estimated that 1,100 'indies' were finished in 1998 alone[8]), that all nine films appeared in the space of five years testifies to growing recognition of a new demographic group, queer youth under eighteen years of age. How to evaluate the emergence of 'queer kid' indie features? Jacqueline Rose's 1984 study *The Case of Peter Pan or The Impossibility of Children's Literature* is instructive. Using that most mythical and queer of children Peter Pan as touchstone (remember: 'all children, save one, grow up'), Rose makes three principal points:

- At the heart of children's literature is the (scandalous) desire of the *adult for* the child: children do not write these books.[9] Memory and fantasy are key.
- To define children's literature as literature *about* children is 'to fall into a trap,' suppressing Freud's insights about childhood and, by extension, adulthood, as polymorphously perverse (*Rose* 1984: 3). Facile unities – 'childhood,' 'the child,' 'children' – paper over identifications and identities that are deliciously fraught, fabulously fragmentary.
- Children's literature is neither timeless nor singular. Audiences and address change; media and marketing matter.

The nine films studied here all represent returns to (queer) childhood and adolescence by adult 'instigators.' By no means solely 'about' queer kids, all nonetheless reference a demographic group barely noticeable in the 1980s. Significantly, where 70 percent of US lesbian, gay, bi- and transsexual adults report feeling 'different' at a young age (Owen 1998: 17), queers have only recently been able to 'come out' while in high school. The number of youth now identifying as queer – an estimated 3 million in 1998 (Owen 1998: 10) – is thus remarkable: internal conflict and external opposition are intense. Grouping these films thus testifies to the ability of independent features to address new topics and engage new audiences. At the same time it facilitates analysis of the issues which they raise – and how, and the issues which they avoid – and why.

With an eye to moving future independent work further 'out there,' I position 'my' nine films in relation to three sets of contemporaneous 'independent' films about queer kids: foreign features; US documentaries; and experimental shorts. I subdivide my observations into three sections. The first is called '"Indie" mood for love' because five of these films revolve around teenage love and/or sex. Building on the lesbian romances of the 1980s and 1990s and the queer road movies of the early 1990s, *The Delta* (Sachs, 1995), *The Incredibly True Adventure of Two Girls in Love, The Toilers and the Wayfarers* (Froehlich, 1996), *All Over Me*, and *Edge of Seventeen* (Moreton, 1998) are all basically 'realist,' making comparisons with documentaries and foreign 'realist' romances pertinent. Both the documentaries and the foreign features bring out aspects of queer lives that US independent features downplay or shun.

The second section, 'Schooling camp followers,' focuses on two films which highlight school and feature 'camp': *Election* and *But I'm a Cheerleader*. True, *Incredibly True Adventure*, *Edge of Seventeen*, and *Happiness* (Solondz, 1998) also present 'camp' moments,[10] but *Election* and *But I'm a Cheerleader* are consistently parodic, mimicking – in kinder, gentler ways – John Waters' raunchier early independent films. Given the importance of Fassbinder and von Prauheim to gay film, camp is amazingly absent from most foreign features. Only US experimental shorts more pointedly play with style and performance; often they are politically 'edgier,' too.

The third section, 'Child and Family Values,' links two films which are stylistically poles apart: Todd Solondz's acerbic comedy *Happiness* and Su Friedrich's experimental fiction/documentary mix *Hide and Seek* (1996).[11] By including the latter, this essay again stretches the limits of what constitutes an independent feature, since even though the main story is fictional (it's scripted by Friedrich and Cathy Ann Quinlan) *Hide and Seek* screened at Sundance as a 'documentary.' Exceptionally, both *Happiness* and *Hide and Seek* include queer pre-teens. Very few foreign features or US documentaries and only a few experimental shorts similarly showcase queer children: that *children* could be queer is viewed as really risky business, especially by 'Indiewood.'

In conclusion I look at how rating constraints and distribution strategies of the late 1990s affected the representations and receptions given 'queer' teens and kids. Following Thomas Waugh's lead in 'Walking on Tippy Toes,' I argue here for a return to the past, a 'Rainbow Revival' if you will,[12] because like Waugh I believe that Generation Q's black-sheep aunties and funny uncles – i.e. the documentary and experimental makers of the late 1970s and early 1980s – can still provide giddy guidance for anyone engaged in inventing and presenting queer kid fairy tales.

'Indie' mood for love

That the majority of queer kid 'indie' features should foreground romance and showcase sex is not surprising: sexuality is, after all, central to queer identities; more importantly, 'risqué business' sells. Per trademark independent 'regionalist' tradition, locations and moods of the five discussed here vary widely.[13]

Shot in black-and-white, one-third in German, *The Toilers and the Wayfarers* is the bleakest of the five. The loose-knit narrative follows Philip (Andrew Woodhouse) and Dieter (Matt Klemp) as they escape from high school persecution and parental abuse in small-town Minnesota to an independent life of prostitution, destitution, and, in Philip's case, disease in the Twin Cities.

'A moody film set in muggy Memphis' (Stack 1997), *The Delta* focuses on a 'sexually confused,' well-to-do white boy named Linc (Shayne Gray) who has a casual affair with an Afro-Vietnamese man named John/Minh (Thang Chan). In *LA Weekly*, reviewer Ernest Hardy's gave a terse summation:

> John is attractive but has the weary air of an old whore. He also has her lingo: 'You so cute, boy. You want to love me?'. . . . The problem is, [he] is absolutely sincere, and Linc ends up first beating, then rejecting him, returning – however temporarily – to his white middle class home and white middle class girlfriend (1997).

The other three films offer happy endings and energetic sound tracks. *All Over Me* concentrates on the conflicts Claude (Alison Folland) encounters as a result of her friendship with and love for the self-destructive Ellen (Tara Subkoff) in Hell's Kitchen, New York. Eventually Claude transfers her affections to Lucy (Leisha Hailey), a riot grrrl who, like her, reveres Patti Smith, Ani di Franco, and Sleater Kinney. *The Incredibly True Adventure of Two Girls in Love* pairs working-class baby butch Randy (Laurel Holloman) with upper-class African American Evie (Nicole Parker) in upstate New York. The two gradually fall in love and, on Evie's eighteenth birthday, finally 'do it.' A John Hughes romantic comedy with a Bronski Beat, *Edge of Seventeen* combines coming-of-age with coming-out, in 1984

Sandusky, Ohio. Although Eric (Chris Stafford) is dumped by his college-age first lover Rod (Andersen Gabrych), by film's end Eric has hooked up with a boy his own age.

By integrating 'homosexual teen characters into [their] plots,' do these films 'normalize gay lifestyles?' (Shary 2002: 246). Tim Shary and Patricia White feel that *All Over Me* and *The Incredibly True Adventure* do.[14] But what to make of the fact that many leads are not *exclusively* lesbian or gay? Dieter and Philip are gay; a third character, Uno (Ralf Schirg) may be bisexual (he turns gay tricks in exchange for alcohol). John is gay; Linc is bisexual. Randy is a dyke; Evie tells her friends, 'I didn't say I was gay, I said I was in love.'[15] Eric comes out as gay, but tries to 'turn the page' en route by sleeping with his best friend, Maggie (Tina Holmes). Ellen is clearly heterosexual; Claude and Lucy avoid using labels.

Obviously this fluidity is in part a cross-over marketing ploy. As Shary (2002: 246) points out, moreover, *All Over Me* 'de-emphasize[s] the pursuit of sex'; the same could be said of *The Incredibly True Adventure*.[16] Both — recall — are released by Fine Line. But the three 'boy' films — all released by smaller companies[17] — make a point of showing sexual acts. *The Toilers and the Wayfarers* portrays hustling and includes several shots of Dieter nude. *The Delta* documents encounters in hotel rooms, cars, and arcades. And *Edge of Seventeen* shows Eric's sexual initiation (both boys are naked); later, his face presses against the glass of a car as he engages in (condom-protected) anal intercourse with a pick-up.

Most importantly, however, all five films insist on the right to be queer in the face of straight oppression, and even the most cheerful acknowledges that being

Figure 14.1 Ellen (Tara Subkoff) and Claude (Alison Folland) in *All Over Me* (Sichel, 1997). Courtesy of Fine Line/Kobal Collection.

young and queer is tougher than being young and straight. Evie's friends ditch her; Randy's Operation Rescue-fanatic mom kicks her out; Ellen's boyfriend (Cole Hauser) and male friends are murderous homophobes; Dieter's dad (Jerome Samuelson) refuses to let him come home. Most of the films also include scenes where queer teenagers are verbally harassed.

Unsurprisingly, US documentaries and foreign features proffer bleaker pictures. *Reaching Out to Lesbian, Gay and Bisexual Youth* (Rohab, 1997) notes that 97 percent of queer teens regularly hear homophobic remarks; that 45 percent of boys and 20 percent of girls have been attacked; that 42 percent of all homeless youth self-identify as lesbian or gay; that prostitution and AIDS are rife. The gay LA teens of *Surviving Friendly Fire* (Nelson, 1997–99) talk about prostitution, AIDS, alcohol use, and parental abuse as they prepare and perform a play in a shelter. *School's Out: Lesbian and Gay Youth* (Spalding, 1993) turns on the fact that 28 percent of queer teens leave high school. All three films reference the inordinately high (30 percent) suicide rate among queer kids.[18] Significantly, all three documentaries include queer teens of color – characters missing in most independent features – and show their subjects as survivors, not just as victims.

Tellingly, however, most of the kids interviewed in these documentaries describe themselves as 'born' lesbian or gay. Terms like 'queer,' 'transgendered,' and 'bisexual' are rarely used: to admit fluidity or acknowledge choice is deemed dangerous. I find Eve Sedgwick's comment in 'How to Bring Your Kids Up Gay' (1993: 163) ominously relevant: 'Even outside the mental health professions and within more authentically gay-affirmative discourses, the theoretical space for supporting gay development is . . . narrow. . . . Conceptualizing an unalterably *homosexual body* seems a safer place from which to proceed.'

Like the majority of US 'queer kid' indie features, foreign features – among them Sweden's *Show Me Love* (Moodysson, 1999) and the UK's *Beautiful Thing* (Macdonald, 1996) and *Get Real* (Shore, 1999) – usually revolve around older teens and coming-out stories. Unlike all the 'indie' features I study except *Hide and Seek*, however, three other foreign films – the French *Wild Reeds* (Téchiné, 1995), Canadian *Set Me Free* (Pool, 1999), and Dutch *For a Lost Soldier* (Kerboesch, 1993) – explore queer life in earlier decades (the first two take place in the 1960s, the third in the 1940s).[19] Also unlike US indie features, all three of these films position the personal issues they explore within larger political contexts: *Wild Reeds* references the Algerian War; *Set Me Free* mentions the Quebec independence movement; *For a Lost Soldier* uses the Canadian liberation of Holland as backdrop for the sexual 'liberation' of a Dutch teen (Maarten Smit) by a handsome Canadian soldier (Andrew Kelley).

Almost all foreign queer kid features are, as I mentioned earlier, 'realist' romances. No one in Europe or elsewhere seems to have adopted continental camp for kids. In contrast, a significant portion of US queer kid independent work does build on 'camp' traditions of 'irony, aestheticism, theatricality, and humor' (Babuscio 1999: 119).

Schooling camp followers

But I'm a Cheerleader and Election in particular use camp comedy to send up high school horror. Both also showcase over-the-top acting, tongue-in-cheek casting, tacky sets, crazy costumes, kitsch props, off-the-wall editing, and silly sound.

A low-budget 'high concept' film, But I'm a Cheerleader is higher on style than on plot. Sets are color-packed, costumes gender-tuned. Occasional montage sequences whip through 'gender-appropriate' motions or linger on 'gender-inappropriate' dreams. Only a love scene between cheerleading heroine Megan (Natasha Lyonne) and a punk named Graham (Clea DuVall) plays without pastiche. Casting is key: Dad is Bud Cort of Harold and Maude (Ashby, 1972) fame; Mom is the John Waters diva Mink Stole; gay pop-star RuPaul Charles plays an 'ex-gay' camp employee.[20]

The drama centers on Megan's 'wrongful' desires. She has a boyfriend, but hates his sloppy kisses; she fantasizes instead about her girl teammates' thighs, panties, and breasts. Yet she can't understand why her born-again father and mother, friends, and boyfriend should one day announce, 'Honey, we think you're a lesbian,' then hustle her off to 'True Directions' boot camp for a five-step 'heterosexual' cure. All's well that end's well: Megan meets Graham, and the rest is 'herstory.' The film's finale has her parents adjust their attitudes, not their daughter's, attending a PFLAG (Parents and Friends of Lesbians and Gays) meeting with her.

Election's message is more complex, but the film similarly relies on screwy visuals (optical inserts, unflattering freeze-frames, tacky rear projection), unconventional sound effects (dueling voice-overs, absurd musical choices), exaggerated acting, and evocative casting (for starters, 'Ferris Bueller' – Matthew Broderick – turned high school history teacher 'Mr. M'). Its queerest kid is a supporting character, a high school sophomore named Tammy (Jessica Campbell), who decides to run for school president against her older brother (Chris Klein) and obnoxious over-achiever Tracy Flick (Reese Witherspoon). Tammy's speech ('Who cares about this stupid election? We all know it doesn't matter. Vote for me because I don't even want to go to college . . . and so none of us will ever have to sit through these stupid assemblies again!') so electrifies the student body that the principal has her suspended. Much to her delight, her parents send her off to a Catholic all-girl school; there she finally meets her Ms. Right.

Noteworthy – and 'new' – is that both films make their straight characters more ridiculous and less likable than the queers. The moms and dads of the True

Directions' kids are clowns; the camp director (Cathy Moriarty) is more of a menace. Mr. M. watches cheerleader porn and fantasizes he's Marcello Mastroianni; Tracy's brother bumbles on about blow-jobs; Tracy screeches and schemes, jumping for joy when she wins, jumping to destroy when she loses. By comparison, Tammy easily becomes the most likeable, 'normal,' well-rounded character.

In both films, moreover, queer identity is multifaceted. *Election* case in point: a scene where Tammy insists, 'It's not like I'm a lesbian or anything. I'm attracted to the person. It's just that all the people I happen to be attracted to are girls.' Among the queerer examples in *But I'm a Cheerleader*: two older gay men assure Megan that 'there's no one way to be a lesbian.'

Yet experimental shorts take camp performance *much* further. To name just three: Sadie Benning's *Jollies* (1990) and *It Wasn't Love* (1992) delight in sexual stretching and gender bending; Julie Zando's *Apparent Trap* (1999) marries Vito Acconci's *Pryings* (1971) to Walt Disney's *The Parent Trap* (Swift, 1961).[21] In the last video, especially, performance is everywhere, situated literally and figuratively in camp: Zando and collaborator Jo Anstey divide Hayley Mills's double role as arch rivals and unwitting sisters between them; Zando attempts to pry open Anstey's eyes in the woods; stern camp counselor Miss Inch is played by a man in drag.

Yet Hayley Mills wasn't queer, was she? Is she queer here because reframed through adult lesbian desire, against and through Acconci's reflections on voyeurism? Crucially, and unlike the majority of US independent or foreign features, all three experimental shorts center on queer pre-teens; perhaps a dozen others do so as well. In contrast, only two feature-length independent films have to date showcased queer children, and one encountered distribution problems, the other right-wing complaints.

Child and family values

Eve Sedgwick again: 'That one woman, *as a woman*, might desire another; that one man, *as a man*, might desire another: the indispensable need to make these powerful, subversive assertions has seemed . . . to require a relative de-emphasis of the links between gay adults and gender-nonconforming children' (1993: 157). Only *Happiness* dares pair its young sissy, eleven-year-old Johnny (Evan Silverberg), with an adult, pedophile and psychiatrist Dr. Bill Maplewood (Dylan Baker). Post a Little League game where Johnny performs less than brilliantly, his tough-guy dad confides to Dr. Bill: 'I think he's gay. What if I get him a professional? A hooker to break him in?' Bill protests: 'But he's eleven.' Johnny's dad replies: 'You're right. It's too late. He is what he is.'

Bill's late night 'poaching' when Johnny sleeps over is thus partially 'excused': Johnny is already gay. And Bill is likeable; he has a great relationship with his own son, Billy (Rufus Read), reassuring him, for example, when Billy worries that his penis is too small. A second rape of a young boy lands Bill in jail. In a reserved but moving scene, Billy asks his dad 'why?' 'It felt great,' says Bill simply. Crying, Billy continues: 'Dad, would you ever fuck me?' Still calmly but now crying himself, Bill responds: 'No, I'd jerk off instead.'

Yet Bill is not the only disturbed character in the film: *all* the adult characters in this film are perverse. There's a rapist, a murderer, a pill-popping divorcee, a maker of obscene phonecalls, and more. Casting involving prior roles (especially Ben Gazzara as the divorcing Lenny, Louise Lasser as his wife Mona; Elizabeth Ashley as his girlfriend Diane), off-the-wall dialogue, dead-pan acting, a syrupy sound track, occasional flashback and fantasy inserts, and Maryse Alberti's oppressively attentive, claustrophobically framed cinematography combine to further 'queer' everyone. As *New Statesman*'s Jonathan Romney writes: 'If its characters are all fucked up, *Happiness* implies, it's because we all are. . . . It may be the most genuinely psychoanalytical fiction that American cinema has yet produced' (1999: 37).

Solondz did no research on psychoanalysis or pedophiles, however. Instead he gives as impetus for the film *Megan's Law*, which requires law enforcement officials to notify residents when a convicted pedophile moves into the neighborhood, and the Russian case of 'Citizen X,' a man who murdered more than fifty children, yet was married and had kids of his own.[22] In contrast, *Hide and Seek* is grounded in Su Friedrich's protests at a grade school in Queens, where she and other activists wore purple T-shirts saying 'I was a lesbian child' and carried balloons for the kids, to most parents' consternation.[23] Her film intercuts archival footage (from a pre-war Italian film and a silent movie about a woman explorer who lives with lions in Africa) with documentary reminiscences by twenty women from the New York area. The principal story centers on two pre-teen girl friends (Chels Holland and Ariel Mara), at least one of them a budding lesbian. The fictional narrative concentrates on the girls' interactions with each other and with other friends; the documentary interviewees posit that in childhood *everyone* experiments with different forms of sexuality.

Hide and Seek thus emphasizes how fluid sexuality is during childhood. So, too, do several experimental shorts about queer girls: additional examples include Sadie Benning's *Flat Is Beautiful* (1998), Donna Carter's *Tomboy* (1997), Julie Zando's *Let's Play Prisoners* (1991), Megan Siler's *First Base* (1991), and Andrea Stoop's *Adam* (1996).[24] In contrast, films about boys typically depict queer sissyhood as damnably different: 'You're a feminino!' taunts a girl in *Dottie Gets Spanked*; in *Tongues Untied* (1989) Marlon Riggs recalls that, when he was a boy, epithets like 'Punk!' and 'Faggot!' were hurled at him. Rough treatment is accorded effeminate boys in *The Smell of Burning Ants* (Rosenblatt, 1994) and *Trevor* (Rajski, 1994), too.[25]

Figure 14.2 Maureen (Alicia Manta), Betsy (Ariel Mara) and Lou (Chels Holland) in *Hide and Seek* (Friedrich, 1996). Courtesy of Su Friedrich.

Fewer 'talking head' documentaries tackle the problems faced by young queers: to my knowledge, there's only Debra Chasnoff and Helen Cohen's *It's Elementary* (1996).[26] Two foreign features, *A Room for Romeo Brass* (Meadows, UK, 2000) and *My Life in Pink* (Berliner, Belgium, 1997), do, however, feature young queer characters. Yet even though the latter contains no nudity, no simulated sex, no violence, and no graphic language, it earned an R rating from the MPAA.[27] Ever intent on controlling arts funding, anti-NEA factions charged that *Hide and Seek* was 'obscene' and 'pornographic,' as well.

Rainbow Revival

So how to summarize industry's relationships to queer teenager and kid identities? What to suggest to independent feature makers of the future?

It's hard to generalize on the basis of nine very different films, however supplemented by US documentaries, experimental shorts, and foreign features. Nonetheless it is safe to say that in all cases identity 'tags' matter. Producers, reviewers, and marketers tend to pigeonhole 'queer' product in lesbian and gay niche markets: queer audience members are eager to see queer characters. Not surprisingly, therefore, press coverage made much of the autobiographical and biographical memories that underpin all films except *Happiness* and *Election*.[28]

But how many queer *kids* see these movies? Not many, unless they sneak into theaters with fake IDs, watch them on DVD or video, or catch them on cable. MPAA ratings rule: same-sex romance is for adults only. Those films released by a major or mini-majors are R-rated – in the case of *But I'm a Cheerleader* only after several cuts.[29] All others are unrated.

Nor did these films reach most adults – whether gay or straight – in theaters, at least. The $8.5 million *Election* grossed less than $1.8 million at the box office: Paramount did not know how to handle a smaller film.[30] *Happiness* presents an even unhappier distribution story: despite winning the International Critics Prize at Cannes and a Golden Globe nomination, the new parent company of October Films, Universal Pictures, forced October to drop the picture. *Happiness* was released only because its production company, Good Machine, took on domestic as well as foreign distribution.[31]

Final tally, then? Do these films net 'equal rights in film-world clichés,' as *New Republic*'s Stanley Kauffmann wrote of *Incredibly True Adventure*? (1995). Have 'the past 30 years of the gay rights struggle [taken] place primarily to ensure homosexuals' rights to the same mediocre entertainment as straight people,' as *Buffalo News*' Ronald Ehmke lamented of *Edge of Seventeen*? (1999).

My survey and my comparisons with foreign features, experimental shorts, and documentaries indicate that many of the problems real queer kids face today are un- or under-explored in indie feature films, and this is particularly true of those released by mini-majors and majors. Queer pre-teens and queer teens of color are barely visible; pre-Stonewall queer kids are missing in all except *Hide and Seek*. My overview *does* show, however, that *some* controversial material is 'coming out,' if largely to niche markets, with cable channels like Sundance and IFC providing additional access. Smaller independent producers like Christine Vachon, Andrea Sperling, Ted Hope, and James Schamus (now, however, working for Universal's Focus Features), and distributors like Marcus Hu at Strand Releasing, have often been key. As Hu famously reassures filmmakers: 'we suck so that you don't have to' (Vachon and Edelstein 1998: 292).

But these films should not be measured solely in terms of the 'real life' experiences they tap or avoid. As Rose says: '[T]he story of Peter Pan cannot be fitted into a framework which sees the child as a historical entity which literature reflects. It shows history as a divided entity which is given a false unity in the image of the child' (1984: 143). At the same time, however, as Maggenti points out, while a movie can 'give comfort to a young [queer] who feels isolated . . . it will not allow her to walk down the hallways of her school that much more safely. Unless other things are in place' (quoted in Guthmann 1995).

It is nevertheless urgent that we find ways to move feature-length independent cinema further 'out there.' How to make it a 'minor cinema' that promotes difference while producing solidarity, per Deleuze and Guattari's sense of 'minor literature'?[32] How to 'deterritorialize sexuality' (Deleuze and Guattari 1986: 18) so that 'queer kids' are not cordoned off as niche characters but rather offer liberation *from* labels to *all* kids, and to adults as well?

For me, as for White, Hildebrand, and Waugh, Generation Q's experimental shorts together with queer work from the 1970s and 1980s constitute valuable 'shots from a queer canon' that drill away at convention (Waugh 1997: 122). Teaching Waugh's essay last year, I re-encountered a gem. Move over *Happiness* and man–boy love; make way for young 'lezzie' lust! In the penultimate episode, 'Child Molester,' of Jan Oxenberg's 1974 camp classic *A Comedy in Six Unnatural Acts*, an adult lesbian dons a girl scout uniform, then stuffs her pockets with girl scout cookies, all the better to seduce little lasses. Much to her surprise, the seven-year-olds she encounters – one white, one black – are not tempted: although they wave at her, they hug and kiss, join hands and skip off, happy to be *together*.

And yet a coda, lest you think I do not appreciate the many contributions made by today's big and little US independent and foreign features. As someone who grew up in the 1950s and 1960s – watching films like *The Children's Hour*, no wonder I fixated on Mary Martin as Peter Pan! – I *do* value even the most candy-coated of Generation Q's ABCs. Though a girl, I cheer the cheeky optimism of *Get Real*. As *its* video jacket promises: 'School's out! So is Stephen! Boy meets boy! Boy likes boy! Boy oh boy!'

Notes

Thanks to Lucas Hildebrand, Tim Shary, and Patricia White for sharing their research, and to Bob Eberwein, Kelly Dorsey, and Sara Nash for suggestions and comments. Frameline, Cinema Guild, Women Make Movies, and Video Data Bank generously provided videos.

1 *Dottie Gets Spanked* is available from Zeitgeist Films (www.zeitgeistfilms.com).
2 Freud finds that all six children disguise masturbatory sexual urges as beating scenarios. He also posits an unconscious incestuous stage which, for the two boys, is homosexual. See Freud 1963; see further Rodowick 1991.
3 Shary (2002: 68) also mentions *Election* (Payne, 1999). For reasons discussed in the text and in note 7, I count it here as an 'independent.'
4 See further Considine 1985: 235–45.
5 Examples include *L.I.E.* (Cuesta, 2001) and *Flush* (MacCubbin, 2001).
6 Fine Line was designated by Turner as mini-major New Line's 'art' arm; when Turner merged with Time–Warner in 1996, both became part of the Warner Brothers family; Lions Gate remains one of two big stand-alone independents.
7 In 1999, the 'Independent Spirit' awards were opened to *all* films made in a 'spirit' of independence – i.e. on a small budget with challenging, confrontational, and thought-provoking themes. *Election* won best film, best director, and best screenplay. Budgets for the other films discussed in this chapter range from $3.2 million (*Happiness*) to $1 million (*All Over Me*) to $300,000 (*Hide and Seek*).

8 Of these, 150–70 films saw some form of distribution but only 20 or so received significant exposure and made money (Handy 1998).

9 Nor can we simply speak of literature *for* children: *what* children read is not co-terminous with what is written for them: see Wojcik-Andrews 2000: 6.

10 In *The Incredibly True Adventure* Randy's married girlfriend (Maggie Moore) is costumed *à la* Zsa Zsa Gabor and Anita Ekberg; the lead of *Edge of Seventeen* patterns himself on camp icon Boy George. Campy aspects of *Happiness* are discussed in the penultimate section of this essay.

11 *Hide and Seek* is distributed by Women Make Movies (www.wmm.com). Home video copies can be ordered from Friedrich directly (e-mail: Sufried@princeton.edu).

12 See Waugh 1997.

13 On 'regionalism' and independents, see for example Levy 1999.

14 See White 2001.

15 'Many in the film move comfortably between same-sex and other-sex relationships' (Michel 1995: 46). When the film opens, Randy is involved with a married woman; her aunt played by (Kate Stafford Rebecca's) ex-lover moves in after breaking up with her boyfriend; near the end, two old women dressed in nightgowns peer out of a hotel doorway and ask: 'Did our husbands send you?'

16 See also Halberstam 1998: 126 and Hollinger 1998: 181 and 241.

17 *The Delta* and *Edge of Seventeen* are distributed by Strand; *Toilers and Wayfarers* by Outsider Enterprises.

18 *Homoteens* (Jubela, 1993) and *Out Loud* (Gaulke, 1995) offer similar statistics. Both, like *Surviving Friendly Fire*, are available from Frameline (www.frameline.org). *Reaching Out to Lesbian, Gay and Bisexual Youth* and *School's Out* is available from Cinema Guild (www.cinemaguild.org). *School's Out: Lesbian and Gay Youth* is available from Facets (www.facets.org).

19 More recent foreign features include *Lost and Delirious* (Pool, Canada, 2000) and *Memento Mori* (Young and Dong, Korea, 1999).

20 Character names are campy, too. How *could* girls named 'Hilary' and 'Graham' be sure of their 'core gender identity?' Behind 'Rock' (Eddie Cibrian) lurks, of course, Rock Hudson.

21 See Holmlund 1997 on performances in Benning's work. Benning's early videos are available both from Women Make Movies and from Video Data Bank (www.vdb.org); *Apparent Trap* is available from Video Data Bank. The online description says the piece looks at 'the violence that erupts when one is confronted with one's mirror image, the "trap" of identification with the Other. . . . Acconci's *Pryings* . . . is reinterpreted as a search for recognition, rather than simply a rape scene' (2002).

22 See Feinstein 1999.

23 The demonstration is documented in *Lesbian Avengers Eat Fire Too* (Baus and Friedrich, 1993).

24 *Flat Is Beautiful, Tomboy*, and *Adam* are available from Frameline, as – earlier but no longer – was *First Base; Let's Play Prisoners* is available from Video Data Bank.

25 *Tongues Untied* is available from Frameline; *Trevor* from Facets. *The Smell of Burning Ants* is available on 16mm from Canyon Cinema (www.canyoncinema.com) and on video from Transit Media (info@transitcinema.net).

26 *It's Elementary* is available from New Day Films (www.newday.com).

27 *My Life in Pink* received the equivalent of a G rating in Europe: see Hildebrand 2001.

28 *Edge of Seventeen* draws on writer Todd Stephens's boyhood and was partially shot in his

parents' home; Chris Stafford even wore Stephens' old clothes. *Incredibly True Adventure* is dedicated to Maggenti's first girlfriend. *All Over Me* draws indirectly on Sylvia and Alex Sichel's girlhoods. *Hide and Seek* plumbs Friedrich's, Quinlan's, and inter- viewees' memories. *The Delta* taps Sachs's Memphis haunts. *But I'm a Cheerleader* is partially based on the life of Lyn Duff, who, after coming out to her mother, found herself in a psychiatric hospital in Utah 'where doctors tried to change her sexual orientation. Her treatment included heavy doses of psychiatric medication, being locked in a seclusion room . . . and being forced to smell ammonia while being shown pornographic pictures of lesbian sex' (Duff 2000). All four women directors (most of them lesbian) pitched their films as 'universal,' not as 'lesbian,' however. The video jacket of *Hide and Seek* is typical, promising that the film is 'for every woman who's been to a slumber party and every man who wonders what went on at one.' In interviews, many expressed ambivalence about the benefits of identifying as lesbian. Alex Sichel's response was typical: 'I'm out as a lesbian. It's only important if there are girls trying to figure out what they're doing.' Long-time lesbian Maria Maggenti's answer was more complicated: involved with a man, she refused the term 'bisexual' and continued to claim the label 'lesbian,' saying, 'put me down as lesbian . . . they need the numbers' (1995: 25).

29 Babbitt angrily provided details: 'I had to take out a two-second shot of Clea's hand sweeping across Natasha's body on top of her clothes . . . And I had to eliminate the pan up Natasha's body in the scene where she's masturbating. I could only use the close-up of her face.' Babbitt also removed a line explaining that Natasha was expelled from camp 'because [she] ate Graham out' (quoted in Taubin 1999: 57).

30 Sony's *Go* and Buena Vista's *Rushmore* did badly at the box office for similar reasons: see Klawans 1999: 31.

31 For Solondz, this solution was positive: he did not want to make cuts to gain an R rating: see Tunison 1998.

32 My invocation of Deleuze and Guattari is sparked by White's 2001 paper 'Lesbian Minor Cinema.'

Bibliography

Babuscio, J. (1999) 'The Cinema of Camp,' in F. Cleto (ed.), *Camp: Queer Aesthetics and the Performing Subject: A Reader*, Ann Arbor: University of Michigan Press, 117–36.

Considine, D. (1985) *The Cinema of Adolescence*, Jefferson, MO, and London: McFarland.

Deleuze, G. and Guattari, F. (1986) *Kafka: Toward a Minor Literature*, trans. D. Polan, Minneapolis and London: University of Minnesota Press.

Duff, L. (2000) 'Sexual Switcheroos,' *New Times LA*, 24 August: n.p.

Ehmke, R. (1999) 'One Moment in Time,' *Buffalo News*, 13 August: G16.

Feinstein, H. (1999) 'A Tender Comedy about Child Abuse?' *Guardian*, 26 March: n.p.

Freud, S. (1963) '"A Child Is Being Beaten": A Contribution to the Origin of Sexual Perversions,' in S. Freud, *Sexuality and the Psychology of Love*, New York: Macmillan, 107–32.

Guthmann, E. (1995) 'Maria Maggenti's *Two Girls in Love*,' *San Francisco Chronicle*, 25 June: 37.

Halberstam, J. (1998) *Female Masculinity*, Durham, NC, and London: Duke University Press.

Handy, B. (1998) 'Truly Independent Cinema,' *Time Magazine*, 26 October: 93.

Hardy, E. (1997) 'Cruising: *The Delta*'s Independent Mien,' *LA Weekly*, 15–21 August: 39.

Hildebrand, L. (2001) 'Mediating Queer Childhood,' paper presented at the 'Persistent Vision' conference, San Francisco, June.

Hollinger, K. (1998) *In the Company of Women*, Minneapolis and London: University of Minnesota Press.

Holmlund, C. (1997) 'When Autobiography Meets Ethnography and Girl Meets Girl: The "Dyke Docs" of Sadie Benning and Su Friedrich,' in C. Holmlund and C. Fuchs (eds.), *Between the Sheets, In the Streets: Queer, Lesbian, Gay Documentary*, Minneapolis: University of Minnesota Press, 127–43.

Kauffmann, S. (1995) 'The Incredibly True Adventure of Two Girls in Love,' *New Republic*, 213, 5 (31 July): 26.

Klawans, S. (1999) 'Fast Times at Carver High,' *The Nation*, 268, 24: 31–3.

Levy, E. (1999) *Cinema of Outsiders: The Rise of American Independent Film*, New York and London: New York University Press.

Maggenti, M. (1995) 'Falling for a Guy: A Lesbian Adventure,' *Village Voice*, 27 June: 25.

Michel, F. (1995) 'The Incredibly True Adventures of Two Girls in Love,' *Cineaste*, 21, 4: 41–2, 46.

Moon, M. (1998) *A Small Boy and Others: Imitation and Initiation in American Culture from Henry James to Andy Warhol*, Durham, NC, and London: Duke University Press.

Owen, R.E. (1998) *Queer Kids: The Challenges and Promise for Lesbian, Gay, and Bisexual Youth*, New York and London: Harrington Park Press.

Rich, B.R. (1992) 'The New Queer Wave,' *Sight and Sound*, 2, 5 (September): 30–4.

Rodowick, D.N. (1991) *The Difficulty of Difference: Psychoanalysis, Sexual Difference and Film Theory*, New York: Routledge.

Romney, J. (1999) 'La Condition américaine,' *New Statesman*, 12, 550 (9 April): 37–8.

Rose, J. (1984) *The Case of Peter Pan or The Impossibility of Children's Fiction*, London: Macmillan.

Sedgwick, E.K. (1993) *Tendencies*, Durham, NC: Duke University Press.

Shary, T. (2002) *Generation Multiplex*, Austin: University of Texas Press.

Stack, P. (1997) 'Pleasure, Peril on *The Delta*/Moody Tale of Secret Love,' *San Francisco Chronicle*, 7 November: C3.

Taubin, A. (1999) 'Erasure Police,' *Village Voice*, 3 August: 57.

Tunison, M. (1998) 'Welcome to the Hot Seat,' *Entertainment Today*, 16 October: 8, 21.

Vachon, C. and Edelstein, D. (1998) *Shooting to Kill: How an Independent Producer Blasts Through the Barriers to Make Movies that Matter*, New York: Avon Books.

Video Data Bank (2002) '*Apparent Trap*,' online: www.vdb.org (accessed 22 June 2002).

Waugh, T. (1997) 'Walking on Tippy Toes: Lesbian and Gay Liberation Documentary of the Post-Stonewall Period 1969–84,' in C. Holmlund and C. Fuchs (eds.), *Between the Sheets, In the Streets: Queer, Lesbian, Gay Documentary*, Minneapolis: University of Minnesota Press, 107–26.

White, P. (2001) 'Lesbian Minor Cinema,' paper presented at the Persistent Vision conference, San Francisco, June.

Wojcik-Andrews, I. (2000) *Children's Films: History, Ideology, Pedagogy, Theory*, New York and London: Garland.

Chapter 15

Just another girl outside the neo-indie

Christina Lane

> I'm usually reluctant to spout stuff like: 'If you're a female it's so
> much harder; if you're a male it's so much easier' — I hope it's a
> *little* more complicated than that. But I do think that the machine
> works better with boys. People are more familiar with the whole
> idea of a male director, especially when he's a maverick who's
> bucking the system.
>
> Christine Vachon, Shooting to Kill

In the winter of the year 2000, another 'Year of the Woman' was proclaimed in
the independent film scene. Reporters had either forgotten or had never known
that the Sundance Film Festival (formerly the US Film Festival) had already
celebrated the Year of the Woman in 1989, 1991, and 1993. So, for trade journalists, Sundance had hit a major milestone with its notable jump in female participants: 40 percent of the candidates in the festival's dramatic competition were
women, up from 20 percent in the previous eight years (Levy 2000: A1). And a
woman, Karyn Kusama, won the Grand Jury Prize (as well as best direction) for
her film *Girlfight*, a feminist inversion of *Rocky*, which featured a working-class
teenage girl's entrance into the world of amateur boxing. Kusama, who had
financed the $1 million film through her previous employer John Sayles and the
Independent Film Channel, sold *Girlfight* to Sony's Screen Gems for $3 million in
what was deemed the 'hottest' deal of the festival.

Around the same time, Kimberly Peirce enjoyed the success of *Boys Don't Cry*
(1999). A dramatic treatment of the real-life rape and murder of Brandon Teena, a
teenaged girl passing as a boy in Falls City, Iowa, this debut feature garnered
critical acclaim at film festivals in Toronto, Venice, London, and New York. *Boys
Don't Cry*, which Peirce had developed at Columbia University's graduate film
school and the Sundance Directors' Lab, won several highly coveted Independent
Spirit Awards as well as an Oscar and a Golden Globe Award for Hilary Swank's

Figure 15.1 Director Karyn Kusama with Michelle Rodriguez during filming of *Girlfight*. Courtesy of Columbia Tristar Home Entertainment.

performance as Brandon. A $2 million film, *Boys Don't Cry* eventually made $11.5 million in domestic box office. It had been produced by Killer Films' maverick producers Christine Vachon and Pam Koffler and then, in a rare move, purchased by Fox Searchlight before post-production had begun.

The success of Kusama and Peirce's indie debuts had a good deal to do with casting, which is not to devalue their sophisticated sense of writing and screen direction. For *Girlfight*, a publicity campaign was developed around newcomer Michelle Rodriguez who possessed little experience in either acting or boxing when she responded to an open casting call. For *Boys Don't Cry*, Hilary Swank's status as a *Beverly Hills 90210* starlet-turned-method-actor provided immediate visibility. In addition to the attention that casting could generate, these films boasted a 'high concept,' an easily synopsized 'hook' that heightened their marketability.[1] The sensational elements of *Boys Don't Cry* aided in its packaging for an audience beyond the festival circuit as did *Girlfight*'s timely connection with the popularity of women's kickboxing.

The high visibility of Peirce and Kusama's debuts would seem to set them up for enduring careers in independent film, which is where both say they would like to stay. The experiences of women directors who came before them indicate, however, that the odds do not favor Peirce or Kusama. Perhaps this historical record is what motivated Peirce to insert her authorial control over the fifteen-second interviews she gave to television reporters as she strode down the red carpet on Oscar night 2000, when she stressed that her new two-year first-look deal with New Line included a first project commitment and granted her final cut. All that those reporters would need to do to understand Peirce's motives is rewind back to 1989 and begin to chart the filmmaking careers of independent directors such as Nancy Savoca, Julie Dash, or Allison Anders.

The problem is that women who attempt to establish careers in an independent world now dominated by 'mini-major' studios often hit a plateau after their first film. These studios have squeezed out avant-garde film and, to some extent, documentary, but what of the women who decide to direct the narrative features so valued by major film festivals and mini-major distributors?[2] Why did no woman win Sundance's Grand Jury Prize in the 1990s (with Kusama finally earning one in 2000), when four women had won the award during the 1980s (Dargis 1999: 13)? What precisely are the hurdles for women filmmakers who try to parlay their 'calling card' films into passkeys for further creative possibilities in the competitive age of the mini-majors? How and when do traditional cultural assumptions figure in the world of Sundance, Miramax, New Line, and the Independent Feature Project, even as they purport to advance the causes of (gender, racial, and sexual) diversity and 'progressive' politics? What strategies of empowerment are indie women directors crafting in the narrowly circumscribed business of mini-major cinema?

This chapter examines the production–distribution context of what has become women's independent filmmaking by focusing on a number of key figures, especially Nancy Savoca, Julie Dash, Leslie Harris, Allison Anders, Rose Troche, and Lynn Hershman Leeson. It includes directors who overtly engage feminist politics as well as those who are not easily linked with feminism, for my primary interest concerns the many dilemmas confronted by women, not just feminists, given the indication of discrimination by industry statistics. This chapter is not meant to be representative nor all-inclusive but rather to make broad links between the careers of fairly visible directors. Furthermore, although my major inquiry involves how these filmmakers' status as women affects their place in major independent cinema, this focus is not meant to elide the role that their ethnic, racial, or sexual identities play in their ability to navigate the system. Indeed, the decreased visibility and number of opportunities for women of color since the 1980s suggest that while African American women such as Dash and Harris, and Latina women such as Troche, have made first films, many more women of color have been denied. The numbers of women of color in independent filmmaking were higher as contemporary mini-major cinema was forming; they began to dwindle as the movement became more institutionalized.

This chapter is divided according to separate historical periods. The first period, 1989–93, begins with the triumphal release of Steven Soderbergh's *sex, lies & videotape* by Miramax (after a highly publicized acquisition at the 1989 US

[Subsequently Sundance] Film Festival) and ends with the 1993 purchase of Miramax by Disney, which helped solidify the mini-major's status as an economic giant with supposed autonomy. This section focuses on Savoca, Dash, Harris, all of whom initiated features sometime between 1989 and 1993. Anders is also addressed here, in relation to possibilities for women in cable and digital technology, as she serves as a bridge between the early and late 1990s. While her early films launched her career, she has managed to survive major changes in the indie industry alongside more recently emerging filmmakers. The chapter's second part, which briefly discusses Rose Troche and Lynn Hershman Leeson, focuses on further breakdowns between 1993 and 2001 in definitions of independent and studio filmmaking. By the mid-1990s, nearly all federally funded arts grants had been discontinued or drastically reduced in response to pressure from conservative and religious groups. The creative decisions made by mini-majors had also been heavily impacted by the economic phenomenon of 'independent blockbusters' such as *Pulp Fiction* (Tarantino, 1994).

At times, the chapter provides a conversation with 'one-hit wonders,' films that were never made, projects that did not live up to their directors' expectations, or movies that were panned by reviewers. I would suggest, however, that it speaks volumes about the failures of contemporary independent cinema to account for those it claims to include, saying perhaps even more than the numerous success stories of certain 1990s' male directors.

Women on the verge of an indie explosion, 1989–93

Directors such as Savoca, Dash, Harris, and Anders initiated their first films on the heels of a boom in women's filmmaking that had grown out of the second-wave feminist movement. They benefited from the boundless labor and energy that women had devoted to publicizing and distributing alternative cinema and documentary in the 1970s.[3] Mini-major studios such as Miramax and New Line profited from these resources as well, taking their cue from the strategies that feminist distributors had used to constitute and institutionalize a market niche within counter cinema. The debt owed to curators – for instance, the Flaherty Women's Group (who organized the early International Women's Film Festivals); start-up distributors such as New Day Films, Iris, or Women Make Movies; as well as informal networks of scores of fledgling women filmmakers in the pre-mini-major era – goes unpaid.

Two factors, in particular, placed women directors in a weak position to compete in an increasingly commercial environment. One was the way in which a number of film festivals moved from grassroots venues into mainstream publicity events and acquisition sites for independent and (eventually) major studios. Initially a state-funded festival established to promote Utah and its Film Commission,

Sundance proved to be an explosive force in defining trends and the packaging of 'indie' films. The second major factor involved a shift in exhibition. Whereas a great deal of independent cinema, especially that made by women, had been shown in local sites such as traditional art theaters, museums, and schools, major independent studios found ways to show their product in mainstream theaters. As they became fixtures in multiplexes, many independent distributors channeled energy away from making a statement toward making a profit.

In 1989, the year that Sundance changed appreciably, Nancy Savoca's first feature *True Love* actually won the Grand Jury Prize. Savoca, an NYU film school graduate, had worked for seven years to make the film. Her partner and co-writer Richard Guay took on the role of producer and raised a $750,000 budget from private investors, among them John Sayles. Upon completion, *True Love* was bought by MGM–UA and went on to gross $1.3 million. The film casts a critical eye on the institution of marriage, following a working-class Italian-American bride (Annabella Sciorra) down the aisle. With this film, Savoca, who is half-Argentinian and half-Italian, established a reputation as a potent feminist voice and a purveyor of the emotional intimacies of Italian family life.[4]

Based on *True Love*'s relative box office success and its placement in several 'Top Ten' lists, Savoca was hired by Warner Bros.: to direct *Dogfight* (1991) (Maslin 1989: C10). This provocative polemic about conventions of female beauty helped cement her status with critics as a significant director. As Savoca sought to shape the $8 million production, however, Warners put pressure on her to change the film's conclusion to a more optimistic ending, revoking marketing support when she refused (Dargis 1999: 13). According to Savoca, the studio executives' attitude had been: ' "It's your movie, your name is on it but, P.S. we won't support it one iota with prints and advertising." It went straight to video. I got the movie I wanted but no one saw it' (Johnston 1993: 19).

Without promotional support from the studio *Dogfight* performed poorly, bringing in only $394,631. As a result, Savoca's third feature, *Household Saints* (1993), proved much more difficult to finance. With the support of executive producer Jonathan Demme, she reverted to earlier strategies, soliciting funds from private investors. An adaptation of Francine Prose's novel, *Household Saints* again detailed relationships and rituals of Italian-American family life. Picked up for distribution by Fine Line, the film received critical praise, but it, too, garnered little financial return ($574,152).

Savoca went from 1993 to 1999 before her next feature film, *The 24-Hour Woman*, was made. One of the major reasons for the extended delay was that *24-Hour Woman*, in which a TV producer juggles the demands of her job and new motherhood, is Latina-centered: 'Friends and potential backers suggested she change the character's ethnicity to something more "universal," meaning of course, white. . . . The character was [indeed] "whited out," and the filmmaker lapsed into an "angry, depressed period".' (Graham 1999: N7) But when she offered a minor role to Rosie Perez, the Oscar-nominated actor (for *Fearless*) asked to be considered for the lead and was cast as the protagonist soon thereafter. While this helped to restore the film to its original mission, Perez's attachment was not enough to carry the film, which was financed by Shooting Gallery and distributed by Artisan. *24-Hour Woman* gained little visibility, due in part to its perceived status as a particularized story that lacked 'universal' appeal. Reviewers were unsupportive and the $2.5 million film grossed a mere $109,000. A creative and aggressive marketing campaign could have been developed around *24-Hour Woman* for a niche audience – of Latinos – which was waiting to be targeted. Instead, the very institutions that poised Savoca for high visibility in the late 1980s positioned her for failure in the late 1990s.

In contrast, creative marketing was integral to the early 1990s' success of Julie Dash. Her *Daughters of the Dust* (1991) weaves together the stories of several generations of Gullah descendants who prepare to cross from Ibo Landing to the US mainland in the 1860s.[5] Because of *Daughters'* experimental narrative structure, Dash was continually asked to prove to Hollywood executives that an audience did indeed exist for her film. Ultimately, she financed its $800,000 budget through the National Endowment for the Arts, Women Make Movies, American Playhouse, and a number of regional grants (Dash 1992: 7). Then, with the help of New York-based distributor Kino International, publicity house KJM 3, and PBS's American Playhouse, Dash helped forge a new audience – of middle-class African American art cinema-goers – that white male executives had predicted simply was not there (Rhines 1996: 65–7). The grassroots publicity campaign 'arranged interviews on Black radio and television programs, placed stories in major Black mainstream and arts newspapers and magazines, and enlisted the support of many Black social and political organizations' (*ibid.*: 67).

Throughout the 1990s, Julie Dash has attempted to parlay the critical success of *Daughters of the Dust*, which earned back twice its budget, into an opportunity to direct more commercial films. She has been awarded many fellowships, a Sundance award for best cinematography for *Daughters*, and has several prestigious shorts to her credit. Yet Dash continues to struggle to gain the green light for a second feature. With little luck to date, Dash supports her efforts by directing music videos (Unterburger 1999: 107).

Similar biases against African American makers working on personal and political narratives have clearly affected Leslie Harris. Her status as an African American woman was a marketable 'hook' for Miramax in the early 1990s; but later her career languished. Like Dash, Harris culled funding for her $500,000 film *Just Another Girl on the I.R.T.* (1993) from grant organizations (the American Film Institute, the National Endowment for the Arts, the New York State Council for the Arts, and the Jerome Foundation). She also tapped individual supporters such as documentarian Michael Moore, cultural critic George Nelson, and novelist Terry McMillan. *Just Another Girl* tells the story of 'Chantel, a Brooklyn homegirl,' who contends with her unplanned pregnancy by ignoring it.[6] Given the atypical portrayal of an urban teen grappling with pregnancy, Harris appropriately ends her film with the tag 'A Film Hollywood Dared Not Do.' She won the Special Jury Prize for first feature at the 1993 Sundance Film Festival and an Open Palm Independent Feature Gotham Award. Post-production of *Just Another Girl* was financed by Miramax on the basis of its newsworthy hook. Miramax's promotional strategy – which placed Harris in national and local media more than once a day during the film's opening week – netted extensive free publicity and, in fact, worked very well (Taubin 2001: 37). But, though Harris pitched several projects (including a film focusing on a female hiphop producer) to large and small studios, she has had no luck to date in securing financing for a second feature.

As the case of Allison Anders suggests, institutional support from original cable programming has provided a solution where funding has otherwise failed. Anders' 1992 debut *Gas, Food, Lodging* traced the rites-of-passage through ado-lescence of two sisters. It performed well at festivals and garnered a New York Critics Circle Award for best new director. But Anders faced difficulties financing her next five features, in part, she claims, because '[i]t's the boy-wonder myth. . . . The girl wonder myth doesn't exist. . . . You just end up in the girl ghetto' (quoted in Spines 2000: 45). Her second feature, *Mi Vida Loca* (1993), focused on the choices confronting four Latina teenaged gang members. It was the first project made by HBO Showcase for theatrical release. When her sixth film, *Things Behind the Sun*, proved difficult to finance, she turned again to cable, selling it to Showtime for distribution.

Anders had two reasons for negotiating with a major cable network when it came to *Things Behind the Sun*. The first was pragmatic. She said of *Grace of My Heart* (1996) and the digitally shot *Sugar Town* (1999): 'Nobody saw them. They were out for two weeks and gone. It was an awful feeling' (Weinraub 2001: E1). Her second reason was the film's potential to reach a wider audience. *Things Behind the Sun* contains semi-autobiographical content related to Anders's own rape as a teenager and the resulting post-traumatic stress disorder.[7] She had already forfeited the advantage of prominent casting, losing attached star Winona Ryder and, later, Heather Graham to other projects. According to Showtime programming president Jerry Offsay, the director increased her audience tenfold by choosing the cable release over theatrical distribution (*ibid.*).[8] Although Anders' career has been celebrated for its longevity, her future remains uncertain, and in 2000 she moved to London in hope of securing European financing (Spines 2000: 47).

The most successful strategies deployed by women in their attempts to maintain the ground they gained from 1989 to 1993 have in fact occurred in cable production

Figure 15.2 Trudi (Ione Skye) and Shade (Fairuza Balk) in *Gas, Food, Lodging* (Anders, 1992). Courtesy of Cineville, Inc./Kobal Collection.

and a turn to digital filmmaking. Whereas in the 1980s directors such as Martha Coolidge, Donna Deitch, and Lizzie Borden were compelled to take work on existing cable series or low-budget made-for-TV movies in an effort to keep working, in the contemporary age of 'quality' cable programming women directors can, and often do, gain visibility and cultural cachet on television. HBO and Showtime, which rely on innovative counter-programming, have become major players at Sundance. They present themselves as the largest independent film companies in the contemporary indie market. According to Oscar-winning indie director Mira Nair, who made *Salaam Bombay!* (1988), 'HBO has become the independent filmmaker studio. . . . They respect your freedom, they respect your vision' (Rohan 2001: E1). This phenomenon presents both solutions and problems. Cable networks offer emerging women financing opportunities and creative freedom, but even premiere cable networks are sometimes portrayed within the industry as a 'female other' in relation to the 'masculine' sphere of theatrical indie film. This process might thus ultimately reinforce the 'girl ghetto' rather than counteract it.

Similarly, although the accessibility and low cost of digital equipment provides access to technology for disenfranchised groups, distribution remains uncertain. In general, little recognition has been given those digital features that are directed by women (while a male-dominated movement such as Dogme95 gained momentum). A promising exception occurred when Rebecca Miller won the 2002 Sundance Grand Jury Prize for *Personal Velocity* (shot by cinematographer Ellen Kuras). Of the initial ten films launched by InDiGent Films, the offshoot of Independent Film Channel (IFC) that produced Miller's film, however, only *Personal Velocity* was directed by a woman (Kaufman 2002). Furthermore, trade magazines such as *Wired*, which help set the standards and values for new technology movements such as microcinema and ifilms, have identified young, professional men as their target market. Technological developments alone clearly will not be enough to change gender power imbalances.[9]

The comings and goings of the up-and-coming, 1994–99

Two more factors had increasing influence over women's production and distribution in the mid to late 1990s: the rise of the producer–auteur and the intensification of commercial auteurism. Independent producers such as John Pierson and Christine Vachon became crucial links in the chain of acquisition.[10] During the late 1980s to mid-1990s, producers had nurtured important relationships not only with major studio executives but with festival curators and film reviewers, whose 'free' positive publicity made for invaluable promotion. They functioned as powerful gatekeepers who provided important access and mobility for filmmakers. The likelihood that independent directors would reach distributors became increasingly dependent on their ability to gain the committed interest of these producers. The second factor, a new brand of indie auteurism, grew as a result of the desire for festivals and independent studios to draw attention to their films by promoting the director as a maverick who had seized the reins of low-budget production and, in his own hip, cool way, made the system work for him. And it was nearly always a *him* because the traditional director's 'mystique' of auteurism pervaded the indie festivals and studios' marketing campaigns, excluding women from increasingly commercialized imagery. As the 1990s continued, it became less likely that films would be advertised on the basis of a 'woman director,' meaning that women filmmakers and 'female' genres became less marketable and less marketed, in a reciprocal spiral.[11] While occasional marketing campaigns would publicize films as 'made by women,' such as the promotion of both Nicole Holofcener and Tamara Jenkins as 'female Woody Allens,' mini-major marketing departments took little initiative to develop women's niche markets, thereby contributing to the homogenization of new indie cinema.

Rose Troche's *Go Fish* was one of the few films to be promoted via *difference* – on the basis of Troche's identities as woman and lesbian – and it proved successful.[12] In 1994, *Go Fish* gained notoriety as the first film to be sold to a distributor *during* the Sundance Film Festival. Troche, a Latina director, had teamed up with actor, editor, and co-writer Guinevere Turner, and they had pooled together their money (approximately $8,000) and resources to make an experimental lesbian feature. Their road to a Samuel Goldwyn $450,000 sale was a difficult one, though one made more manageable by producer Christine Vachon. Troche and Turner approached Vachon's company Killer Films when their limited financing ran out. After viewing their footage, she contributed $5,000 to keep them on track, eventually convincing Islet Films' John Pierson to bankroll a remaining $53,000 (Pierson 1995: 280–1; Vachon 1998: 137). Indie guru Pierson then initiated a 'buzz' campaign that culminated at Sundance. *Go Fish*, with its black-and-white low-budget aesthetic and loose narrative structure, was an unlikely candidate for indie success. A newly formed lesbian niche audience heightened its chances of visibility, however, and, through its charming sense of humor and innovative visual style, the film earned that audience's respect.

Without calling *Go Fish*'s quality and originality into question, the entrepreneurship and professional connections of Vachon and Pierson should not be underestimated. Pierson arranged a November 1993 private screening for Sundance programmers Geoff Gilmore and Cathy Schulman to help the film's chances of entry in the January 1994 festival. During the festival selection process, Schulman took an acquisitions job at Samuel Goldwyn and watched *Go Fish* carefully with an eye to purchasing it (Pierson 1995: 285–6). Pierson drummed up word of mouth and, by extension, a bidding war, which Goldwyn won when Miramax and New Line were slow to move (*ibid.*). Troche's Latina identity was (problematically) written out of the marketing campaign and the film was promoted on the basis of her gender and sexuality. And the film was released during gay pride month in June 1994, which also marked the twenty-fifth anniversary of Stonewall. After word of mouth had built in New York City, Goldwyn 'counter-programmed' the film against summer Hollywood blockbusters, exhibiting it for the most part in its own Landmark Theaters chain (*ibid.*: 297). In its opening weekend, *Go Fish* made back the purchase price ($550,000), eventually grossing $2.4 million (*ibid.*).

Troche's immediate response to studio attention was to propose a biopic on Dorothy Arzner, the 1920s and 1930s' Hollywood director who kept her lesbian identity relatively secret.[13] A studio film on Arzner might well have capitalized on the lesbian niche market; but Troche found she was stuck in the development stage. She pitched her script to numerous studios and mini-majors with little success. After a series of disenchanting development meetings with New Line, she came to the determination that '[w]omen just get chewed up by the system' (*Filmmaker* 1996; Huisman 1999).

The director eventually made the British romantic comedy *Bedrooms and Hallways* (1999), featuring several gay male characters, one of whom comes to terms with his heterosexual identity. The film, produced and distributed by the BBC and several European finance companies, disappeared after its opening weekend, making only $16,459 in the US. Troche then returned to her previous supporter, Christine Vachon, and British financiers in order to direct *The Safety of Objects* (2002), starring Glenn Close. Initial reviews were not favorable, voicing the familiar complaint that women who have something to say lapse into tones of 'didacticism.'[14]

Though Lynn Hershman Leeson approaches style and narrative differently, she too has faced charges of didacticism for attempting to weave feminist issues into her independent features. Leeson's debut feature *Conceiving Ada* (1997) stars Tilda Swinton as Victorian-era Countess Ada Augusta Byron King of Lovelace. In real life Countess Ada was the daughter of Lord Byron and the originator of computer language.[15] A contemporary female computer scientist (Francesca Faridany) devises a virtual reality mode through which to communicate with Ada, resulting in a cyber–feminist connection that reveals the precarious status of women's bodies plagued by male-dominated industry and technology. To all intents and purposes, *Conceiving Ada* was a low-budget, high concept film, in that it re-worked the 'time machine' formula into a conceptual hook using an innovative visual style.[16] The film might have lent itself to any number of aggressive marketing campaigns, including its basis in a provocative historical figure, its topicality in relation to digitality, and its dynamic graphic design.

The Independent Feature Project saw fit to include *Conceiving Ada* in its selection of 'American Independents in the Market' showcase at the Berlin Film Festival, though with little result. At Toronto, the film received little attention from distributors and none of the major independent studios showed enthusiasm at Sundance either. But Winstar Cinema, which specializes in international art cinema and academic markets, bought domestic rights to the film there. Leeson thereby lost any chance of capturing the major indie market.

Film reviewers positioned *Conceiving Ada* for negative reception, first by comparing her virtual sets derogatively with those of big-budget male directors such as James Cameron and George Lucas, and then by belittling its female-driven content and feminist politics.[17] B. Ruby Rich, a critic known for her endorsement of feminist and queer work, was the only reviewer who apparently saw this. She proclaimed *Conceiving Ada*: 'One of the Year's Ten Best. . . . Has there ever been a film so joyous about women, knowledge, and mastery? And it's even fun' (Rich 1999).[18]

Not only was *Conceiving Ada* thus unable to find its intended market but it failed to secure Leeson any further financing. She made her second feature, a cyber–vampire movie entitled *Teknolust*, through German financiers, though she still hopes to distribute it through an outlet such as Sony Pictures Classics or Fox Searchlight. Summing up what she describes as a 'heartbreaking' experience trying to promote *Conceiving Ada*, Leeson remarked: 'Remember, it was a film about a woman by a woman' (Leeson in email correspondence with the author, 9 October 2001).

Conclusion: the phenomenon of 'the Blair Bitch'

When these arduous career paths are analyzed collectively, and seen in conjunction with those of other indie women such as Nicole Holofcener, Maria Maggenti, Tamara Jenkins, Lisa Cholodenko, and Lisa Kreuger, they point strongly to the cultural gender biases that govern independent filmmaking.[19] From development to reception, the male-oriented gangster or thriller genres, and the quirky 'loser' film, have helped to condition major independent studios' ideas about what makes money and what makes film sense. The argument that independent women's films have not proven to be commercially viable does not suffice; such films might well have drawn indie audiences if they had been exposed to creative marketing campaigns and not been critically dismissed as didactic. No one will know what the ultimate impact of women's independent filmmaking of the 1990s might have been under other conditions.

The centralized role that Sundance has played in promotion and acquisition of indie films, and the festival's increasingly symbiotic relationship with Hollywood, have also been detrimental to women and their films. While Sundance has made some effort to serve the unique economic, institutional, and creative needs of female directors, the Institute has failed to become a potent site for fostering independent women's cinema. Its original mission was to work 'off-center' and non-commercial features 'into the public's consciousness,' and to compel mainstream audiences 'to want to see them' (*Scenario* 1995: 207). As it has grown, Sundance's mission has taken a detour (Young 1995: 22).[20]

There are concrete ways in which major independent studios might shift their marketing and distribution to enhance reception of these films. Historically, female genres, and other kinds of niche films typically made by indie women, have taken time to find their audience. In a marketplace determined by opening weekend box-office performance, many of the films mentioned here would appear unsuccessful. They are often films that, if given the chance, could develop 'legs,' the industry term for the process of gaining steam over time.[21] However, distributors tend to presume them 'dead' before their lives have fully played out. Indeed, because distributors and marketing departments often perceive such films to be less likely to succeed in comparison to big-budget movies or male indie fare, they often fail to put the necessary resources into independent women's films before they leave the gate. Many of these features make decent comebacks at the video-rental stage; however such financial return is rarely factored in.

In the summer of 1999, just as Kimberly Peirce's *Boys Don't Cry* was picking up some publicity, 'boy wonders' appeared yet again on the scene. This time they were Eduardo Sánchez and Daniel Myrick, co-writers and directors of *The Blair Witch Project* (1999). Their film, made for a reported $30,000 and bought by Artisan for $1 million at Sundance, would go on to gross $141 million in domestic box office and another $109 million overseas. *Blair Witch*, as many trade papers pointed out, demonstrated that there were previously untapped internet resources for cultivating word of mouth around a low-budget film. Though fewer promotional articles and reviews mentioned the fact, the success of this pseudo-documentary horror movie also indicated that the support of an institutional indie such as John Pierson could go a long way in propelling word of mouth. (Six months in advance of release date, Pierson had spread the legend of the Blair Witch on his IFC program, wondering aloud whether or not this could be a true story.)

In comparison to the industry support that benefited Sánchez and Myrick, the road for independent women's films looks a lot like the menacing scenery of the low-budget horror flick. Is it any mystery that the Sánchez–Myrick project sustains its own visibility through a singular fetishized image – that of its aspiring filmmaker–female protagonist breaking down into tears as she shines an ominous flashlight on her face and apologizes profusely for ever picking up a camera in the first place? Does she really owe us, or the male members of her crew, an apology? Did we really need to see our indie woman filmmaker reduced to a sniveling, groveling victim?

It says a lot about major independent studios, structures, and audiences that such a tear-ridden, fear-driven image of the repentant *Blair Witch* woman became an industry hit. The same 'Blame the Bitch' mentality also informs industry practices of mini-majors; if a woman's film fails, executives are more likely to attribute it to her gender than if the same fate befalls a male director. Today's festival directors, mini-major executives, and film reviewers do not realize that, as taste-makers and market-shapers, they might instead raise the cultural capital of women directors and their films. As Miramax positioned itself in the independent sector in the late 1980s, Harvey Weinstein explained that the studio's strategy was to find the marketing hook in unlikely contenders. He told the *Los Angeles Times*: 'It's the distributor's responsibility to find the audience,' criticizing major studios for neglecting to create and exploit niches (1989: F1). Whereas, during their 1980s' rise, executives felt that they could define and shape the meaning of high concept, they later presumed that high concept was an objective, external value that films either had or did not have. As studios such as Miramax grew and changed through the 1990s, the 'distributor's job' shifted into a shortsighted process of catering to young, white, male audiences. Their entrepreneurial spirit stalled when it came to finding and forging niches best targeted by women directors, reinforcing Allison Anders's claim that major independents 'really don't want to know what's in a woman's head.'

Notes

I wish to thank the participants in the 2000 Society for Cinema Studies workshop 'New American Directions/New American Directors,' namely: Robert Kolker, Jon Lewis, and Devin Orgeron. Additionally, I thank Alisa Perren for the way in which her scholarship and our conversations helped shaped this chapter. Finally, I thank Lynn Hershman Leeson and Nicole Holofcener for providing valuable insights.

1 See Wyatt 1994 and 1996.
2 Documentary had functioned as a stable economic force in the 1980s, and feminist distributors had carved out the genre of women's documentary as a stronghold in the independent sector. Feminist critic B. Ruby Rich historicizes the ghettoizing of documentary by 1990s' independent institutions in gendered terms, perceiving a distinct pattern since the 1970s whereby men are associated with narrative film and women turn to documentary and the less expensive, more readily available, medium of video (Zimmerman 2000: 136).
3 In the 1970s, women, invigorated by radical consciousness-raising endeavors and feminist networking, launched film festivals, formed film co-ops, and published 'special interest' magazines: see Rosenberg 1983: 78.
4 For critical analyses of Savoca's films, see Modleski 1998 and Nardini 1991.
5 For critical analyses of Dash's films, see Alexander 1993, Bambera 1992, Guerrero 1993, hooks 1992, Jones 1993.
6 For critical analysis of Harris's film, see Phillips 1992.
7 Anders has always drawn from personal experience in the development and production of her films; but in *Things Behind the Sun*, she went so far as to film the rape scenes in the actual house (in Cape Canaveral, Florida) where the original trauma took place: see Weinraub 2001.
8 Cheryl Dunye, who made the transition from experimental art cinema to commercial narratives in the late 1990s, turned to premiere cable production as well. She made her second feature film *The Stranger Within* (2001) for HBO with the help of C-Hundred Films. Dunye explains her decision in strategic terms: 'It took me a while – making your second feature, like all the boys, you want to make it big, broad, wide, and star-studded. But I'm not one of the boys, and the key for me was that the film was going to be seen by far more people on television and that my audience would dramatically change' (Willis 2001).
9 For a discussion of digitality's gender implications, see Bolter and Grusin 1999, Leeson 1996.
10 Though Pierson and Vachon operate in similar ways, they have very different motivations and tastes. Pierson tends to promote 'quirky' and 'cool' independents geared toward a young, straight, male audience while Vachon helped usher in the 'New Queer Cinema' era, producing more experimental and 'high art' films.
11 See Perren 1998 and Corrigan 1991.

12 For critical analysis of Troche's *Go Fish*, see Henderson 1999, Hollinger 1998.

13 See Mayne 1994.

14 See, for example, Gleiberman 2001. *Safety of Objects*, which interweaves the stories of four families confronting their disillusion with suburbia, premiered at the Toronto Film Festival in 2001.

15 For critical analysis of Leeson's work, see Popper 1997: 188–90.

16 See Rich 1999.

17 Leeson was the first person to develop the technology for 'virtual sets,' a process by which she used computer software to combine photographs of Victorian bed-and-breakfasts with footage of her actors performing against a blue screen. This technology, which she patented after working for eighteen months to perfect it, was later used in James Cameron's *Titanic* (1998). It enabled her to turn a $10 million film into a $1.2 million film: see Wingfield 1998.

18 Film reviewers negatively influenced the reception of *Conceiving Ada* by playing Leeson off against the blockbuster auteur James Cameron. In a move that obscured the large power differential between Leeson and Cameron's uses of 'virtual set' technology, one reviewer asserted that *Titanic*'s special effects far overpowered those of *Conceiving Ada*. Several others made unfair comparisons between Leeson's film and high-budget features such as *Phantom Menace* and *Tron*: see Sachs 1999 and Parks 1999.

19 See *Walking and Talking* (1996) and *Lovely and Amazing* (2002) by Nicole Holofcener; *Incredibly True Adventures of Two Girls in Love* (1995) by Maria Maggenti; *Slums of Beverly Hills* (1998) by Tamara Jenkins; *High Art* (1997) and *Laurel Canyon* (2002) by Lisa Cholodenko; and *Manny and Lo* (1996) and *Committed* (2000) by Lisa Kreuger. Notably, Holofcener shot *Lovely and Amazing* on digital video when she faced resistance from top indie companies. 'They deemed it uncommercial and hard to market,' she explains. After months of struggling for financing, once she agreed to use DV she had the necessary budget (from Blow-Up Corporation) within twenty-four hours (Holofcener in a telephone interview with the author, 13 October 2001).

20 The Screenwriters and Directors' Labs at Sundance, which enable filmmakers to build alliances with festivals and distributors, accept on average one woman for every three men: see www.sundance.org

21 I thank Jon Lewis for pointing this out during the conceptualizing of this chapter.

Bibliography

Alexander, K. (1993) 'Daughters of the Dust and a Black Aesthetic,' in Pam Cook and Phillip Dodd (eds.), *Women and Film: A Sight and Sound Reader*, Philadelphia: Temple University Press, 224–31.

Bambera, T.C. (1992) 'Preface,' in Julie Dash (ed.), *Daughters of the Dust: The Making of an African American Woman's Film*, New York: New Press, xi–xvi.

Bolter, J.D. and Grusin, R. (1999) *Remediation: Understanding New Media*, Cambridge, MA: MIT Press.

Corrigan, T. (1991) *A Cinema Without Walls: Movies and Culture after Vietnam*, New Brunswick, NJ: Rutgers University Press.

Dargis, M. (1999) 'Even in Independent Film, a Suit Is a Suit,' *New York Times*, 31 January, section 2: 13.

Dash, J. (1992) *Daughters of the Dust: The Making of an African American Woman's Film*, New York: New Press.

Dawtry, A. (1996) 'Revival of the Fittest,' *Variety*, 26 February–3 March: 169.

Ebert, R. (2001) 'Two More Treasures Unearthed at Telluride,' *Chicago Sun–Times*, September 4, online: www.chicagosun-times.com (accessed 11 October 2001).

Filmmaker (1996) 'Factory Outlet: Rose Troche Talks with Mary Harron' (spring), online: www.filmmakermagazine.com (accessed 9 September 2001).

Foster, G.A. (1995) *Women Film Directors: An International Bio-Critical Dictionary*, Westport, CT: Greenwood Press.

Gleiberman, O. (2001) 'Northern Views,' *Entertainment Weekly*, 25 September: 43–4, 46, 48.

Graham, R. (1999) 'A Mother's Film,' *Boston Globe*, 14 February: N7.

Guerrero, E. (1993) *Framing Blackness: The African American Image in Film*, Philadelphia: Temple University Press.

Henderson, L. (1999) 'Simple Pleasures: Lesbian Community and *Go Fish*,' *Signs*, 25, 1 (spring): 37–64.

Hollinger, K. (1998) *In the Company of Women: Contemporary Female Friendship Films*, Minneapolis: University of Minnesota Press.

hooks, b. (1992) *Black Looks: Race and Representation*, Boston, MA: South End Press.

Huisman, M. (1999) 'The Dearth of Dyke Cinema,' *City Pages*, 20, 984 (13 October), online: www.citypages.com (accessed 9 October 2001).

Jones, J. (1993) 'The Black South in Contemporary Film,' *African American Review*, 27, 1 (spring): 19–24.

Johnston, S. (1993) 'Nancy Savoca: So How Do You Follow That?' *Independent*, 24 September: 19.

Kaufman, A. (2002) 'Digital Video with Tangible Results,' *Indiewire*, 27 March, online: www.indiewire.com (accessed 1 May 2001).

Levy, E. (2000) 'Femme Force: Films Helmed by Women Span Fest Spectrum, Reach New High,' *Daily Variety*, 19 January: A1.

Leeson, L.H. (ed.) (1996) *Clicking In: Hot Links to a Digital Culture*, Seattle, WA: Bay Press.

Los Angeles Times (1989) 'Independent Miramax Mirrors the Majors,' 25 October: F1.

Maslin, J. (1989) '"True Love," As It Is in the Italian Bronx,' *New York Times*, 20 October: C10.

Mayne, J. (1994) *Directed by Dorothy Arzner*, Indianapolis: Indiana University Press.

Modleski, T. (1998) 'A Rose Is a Rose? Real Women and a Lost War,' in J. Lewis (ed.), *New American Cinema*, Durham, NC, and London: Duke University Press, 125–45.

Nardini, G. (1991) 'Is it True Love? Or Not? Patterns of Ethnicity and Gender in Nancy Savoca,' *VIA: Voices in Italian Americana*, 2, 1 (spring): 9–17.

Parks, L. (1999) 'Odd "Ada" Premieres Here,' *Houston Chronicle*, 21 May: 14.

Perren, A. (1998) 'Indie, Inc.: Miramax, Independent Film, and the New Hollywood,' MA thesis, University of Texas at Austin.

Phillips, J. (1992) 'Growing Up Black and Female: Leslie Harris's *Just Another Girl on the IRT*,' *Cineaste*, 19, 4 (fall): 86–7.

Pierson. J. (1995) *Spike, Mike, Slackers, & Dykes: A Guided Tour Across a Decade of American Independent Cinema*, New York: Hyperion.

Popper, F. (1993) *Art of the Electronic Age*, 2nd ed. Princeton, NJ: Prentice-Hall.

—— (1997) 'Conceiving Ada,' in A. Kroker and M. Kroker (eds.), *Digital Delirium*, New York: St. Martin's Press, 188–90.

Rich, B.R. (1999) 'High Concept: *Conceiving Ada* Reinvents the Period Film,' *San Francisco Bay Guardian*, 17 February, online: www.sfbg.com (accessed 9 October 2001).

—— (2000) 'Queer and Present Danger,' *Sight and Sound*, 10, 3 (March): 22–5.

Rhines, J.A. (1996) *Black Film / White Money*, New Brunswick, NJ: Rutgers University Press.

Rohan, V. (2001) 'A League of its Own,' *Record*, 7 October: E1.

Rosenberg, J. (1983) *Women's Reflections: The Feminist Film Movement*, Ann Arbor: University of Michigan Research Press.

Sachs, L. (1999) 'High-Tech Style Aside, Film Is Ill-Conceived,' *Chicago Sun–Times*, 12 March: 34.

Scenario (1995) 'Viewing Sundance: A Talk with Robert Redford,' 1, 3 (Summer): 3–5, 206–8.

Scenario (1996) 'A Talk with Nicole Holofcener,' 2, 3 (fall): 129–33, 190–4.

Spencer, L. (2001) 'Walking and Talking,' in J. Hillier (ed.), *American Independent Cinema: A Sight and Sound Reader*, London: British Film Institute, 140–2.

Spines, C. (2000) 'Behind Bars,' *Premiere* (November): 45–8.

Steinhauer, J. (1997) 'A Director Who Films What She Knows Best,' *New York Times*, 28 December, section 2: 7.

Taubin, A. (2001) 'Girl in the Hood,' in J. Hillier (ed.), *American Independent Cinema: A Sight and Sound Reader*, London: British Film Institute, 36–9.

Taylor, E. (1997) 'Girl Wonders,' *Sundance Institute Writers Fellowship Program*, online: www.sundance.org (accessed 5 September 2001).

Unterburger, A. (ed.) (1999) *St. James Encyclopedia of Women Filmmakers: Women on the Other Side of the Camera*, Seattle, WA: Visible Ink Press.

Vachon, C. with Edelson, D. (1998) *Shooting to Kill: How an Independent Producer Blasts Through the Barriers to Make Films that Matter*, New York: Avon Books.

Weinraub, B. (2001) 'Assault as Autobiography,' *New York Times*, 7 August: E1.

Willis, H. (1995) 'Christine Vachon,' *Daily Variety*, 25 July, online: www.variety.com (accessed 9 October 2001).

—— (2001) 'Breaking Out,' *Independent*, June, online: www.aivf.org/independent/archives (accessed 5 September 2001).

Wingfield, N. (1998) 'Let Us Entertain You,' *Wall Street Journal*, 16 November, online: www.wsj.com (accessed 9 October 2001).

Wyatt, J. (1994) *High Concept: Movies and Marketing in Hollywood*, Austin: University of Texas Press.

—— (1996) 'Economic Constraints/Economic Opportunity: Robert Altman as Auteur,' *Velvet Light Trap*, 38 (fall): 51–67.

Young, J. (1995) 'Sundown,' *New Republic*, 10 April: 22.

Zimmermann, P.R. (2000) *States of Emergency*, Minneapolis: University of Minnesota Press, 2000.

Chapter 16

Guests at *The Wedding Banquet*

The cinema of the Chinese diaspora and the rise of the American independents

Gina Marchetti

The new American independent directors and Asian American feature filmmakers have been on parallel tracks throughout the decade of the 1990s (Xing 1998). As Chuck Kleinhans has pointed out, 'each year brought forward new films and new directors and often new voices and visions that the mainstream had ignored, silenced, or pushed aside' (1998: 307). Ang Lee's *The Wedding Banquet* in particular was instrumental in bringing this trend to the fore when it outperformed (in terms of percentage of profit against costs) *Jurassic Park* at the box office in 1993 (Schamus 1998). That same year Wayne Wang, director of independent classics like *Chan Is Missing* (1982) and *Dim Sum* (1984), broke ranks with other independent directors to make *The Joy Luck Club*, based on the popular novel by Amy Tan and produced by Oliver Stone for Disney's Buena Vista. In fact, within Asian American circles throughout the decade of the 1990s, there has been considerable overlap (in the cases of Wayne Wang and Ang Lee, among others) between American independent filmmakers, mainstream commercial Hollywood, and global art cinema (financed outside the US).

These filmmakers find themselves at the border of the American independent movement in several key ways. They tend to deal in subject matter 'foreign' to mainstream Hollywood by focusing on minority communities as central, rather than ancillary, to the principal plot, and they often have one foot (financially or thematically) in another country. Scratching the surface of the American independent movement uncovers a global cinema culture that maintains a love–hate relationship with the American domination of the international market through Hollywood and, increasingly, through Hollywood's discontents within the independent environment.

While some Asian American independent filmmakers (e.g. Gregg Araki, Desmond Nakano, Karyn Kusama) have stayed away from Asian/Asian American characters and subject matter, most have embraced narratives dealing with Asian Americans in their work. Also, many (although not all) of these films rely, at least to a degree, on funding from outside the US, and these filmmakers take the international film market very seriously. *The Wedding Banquet*, for example, received a large portion of its funding from Taiwan (specifically, from an agency of the Government of the Republic of China, the Central Motion Pictures Corporation) (Marchetti 2000a; Wyatt 2001). Various agencies of the Canadian Government (Mitchell 1996), Channel 4 in Britain, and other organs of sundry national governments have funded Asian American productions in all or in part.

Thus, the new American independents and Asian American filmmakers meet on mutually beneficial turf. The independents pave the way for low-budget, small, personal films, without elaborate special effects, in the American film marketplace, and Asian American filmmakers supply the 'difference' by highlighting issues of ethnicity, or, in the case of another overlap with the New Queer Cinema, sexual orientation. As a group, these films provide product for the multiplying screens that demand far more than a diet of the latest blockbuster to satisfy satellite TV, cable, video/VCD/DVD, and, increasingly, internet viewers.

Needless to say, these films attempt a broad address to their audiences that strikes a responsive chord across national borders. Although the films fit easily into festivals dedicated to Asian American filmmaking, they are equally at home in Hong Kong movie theaters, on satellite TV, or on American cable. The films blend themes that resonate across these viewing constituencies to hit on issues that defy racial, ethnic, national, and sexual borders. Like most independents, these films deviate from Hollywood and global art cinema, while paying homage to both traditions. Sometimes they revive neglected genres like the woman's film and melodrama for the big screen, and, at other times, they engage in a postmodern play of cinematic techniques that creates a pastiche of generic forms, character types, plot situations, and ideological positions.

One of the most fecund cross-fertilizations of Asian American and American independent filmmaking involves films that deal with the Chinese diaspora. Filmmakers like Ang Lee, Wayne Wang, Peter Wang, Peter Chow, Mina Shum, Tony Chan, Quentin Lee and Justin Lin, Shirley Sun, and Evans Chan, among others, have made their mark on the independent festival circuit, and émigrés from the Hong Kong, Taiwanese, and mainland Chinese industries have contributed to American cinema from big-budget Hollywood productions to experimental shorts. A number of factors have led to this transnational cinematic phenomenon. These include the loosening of immigration laws in the US after 1965, changes in the social and economic climate in North America as a result of the civil rights movement, political upheavals and uncertainty in Hong Kong, Taiwan, the People's Republic as well as in countries like Indonesia, Vietnam, the Philippines, Malaysia, and Singapore with historically significant Chinese populations. These factors coupled with the Asian 'economic miracle' of the postwar era have led to the creation of a vibrant global Chinese culture, referred to by some as 'Greater China,' with a significant presence in the US.

This chapter looks at three films that have connections both to the American independent scene and to the cinema of the Chinese diaspora: Sylvia Chang's *Siao Yu* (aka *Shao Nu, Hsiao Yu*, 1995), Mina Shum's *Double Happiness* (1994), and Quentin Lee and Justin Lin's *Shopping for Fangs* (1997). Looking at these three films together brings to the forefront several questions that have been at the margins of many discussions of American independent filmmaking and Chinese cinema practices, including issues involving the global film culture that gave rise to and nurtures American independents, the growing impact of Chinese film culture worldwide, and the trans-national connections that enable these types of cinema practice to flourish.

Production background

Like *The Wedding Banquet*, *Siao Yu* found its way to the screen as a collaborative effort of Good Machine and the Central Motion Picture Company of Taiwan (Shen 2001). Aided by director Sylvia Chang – an established actress, filmmaker, and chanteuse in the Chinese-speaking world – and author Yan Geling, who wrote the short story on which the film is based (Yan 1999), Ang Lee and James Schamus collaborated on the screenplay to produce a balance between Mandarin and English dialogue comparable to *The Wedding Banquet*'s script. Both films, set in New York City, revolve around a green card marriage. However, unlike *The Wedding Banquet*, *Siao Yu* plays as straight melodrama, and it eliminates both the lighter aspects of *The Wedding Banquet* and that film's gay theme. In this production configuration, a mainland perspective is brought into the mix with the addition of Shanghai-born writer Yan Geling, who went to study at Columbia University after 1989. Yan's interest in female characters is strengthened by Sylvia Chang's long career in Chinese melodrama and 'the woman's film.' Thus, an independent American production company enables talent from both sides of the Taiwan Strait to work together on a project in the US.

As a Canadian film, *Double Happiness* is, by definition, at the edges of American independent filmmaking. Although picked up by New Line for distribution, *Double Happiness*, unlike its US fellows, owes its existence to several agencies of the Canadian Government, including the National Film Board of Canada, its provincial sister organization in British Columbia, the Canada Council for Media Arts, and its sister office devoted to multiculturalism in Canada. Telefilm Canada and the Canadian Film Centre were also involved. Just as *The Wedding Banquet* was independent of Hollywood, but not the Taiwanese Government, *Double Happiness* finds itself in a similar situation as solidly backed by a specific national cultural program.

The inclusion of the *Double Happiness*, a Canadian production, in this discussion of American independent filmmaking and the Chinese diaspora makes good sense. Given the parallel histories of the exploitation of Chinese labor followed by exclusionary laws in both the US and Canada, the Chinese American communities in both countries share important roots. Although immigration laws now differ, a bond exists between the two communities, and Canadian Asian films find routine acceptance at Asian American film festivals in the US. Thus, *Double Happiness* played in many of the same venues as did its American independent cousins, and it shares an important cultural history with the other films under discussion here.

Arising out of a UCLA film school friendship, *Shopping for Fangs* seems to have the best shot at American independent credentials with Los Angeles' suburban locations, a budget under $100,000, and a twenty-one-day shooting schedule (Locke n.d.). However, as Quentin Lee is a Canadian citizen, about 30 percent of the $100,000 did, indeed, come from the Canadian Council[1] (Hong 1998). Also, unlike many other independent projects that tend to be the 'vision' of an individual aspiring auteur, the directorial duties of *Shopping for Fangs* are fairly evenly divided between Taiwan-born Justin Lin, who shot the scenes involving Phil (Radmar Jao), a sexually frustrated Asian American accountant who may also be a werewolf, and Hong Kong-born Quentin Lee, who handled the scenes involving frigid housewife Katherine/outspoken lesbian waitress Trinh (Jeanne Chin) (see Li 1997). However, as a self-styled GenerAsian X film, *Shopping for Fangs*, like many indie features, does draw on several clearly identified market niches, including youth, Asian Americans, B-movie fans, queer viewers (O'Neill 1997), as well as audiences from Greater China (covered broadly by the two directors, who come from Taipei and Hong Kong).

White knight redux

One strategy all these films use to draw in a domestic American as well as an international audience involves interracial romance. The 'white knight' (Marchetti 1993) fantasy, in which Asian women are 'saved' from the excesses of the Chinese patriarchy by Anglo-American heroes, has been particularly popular in Hollywood cinema. Similar narratives about women attempting to free themselves from feudal Chinese marriage customs also have deep roots in Chinese cinema, going back to the progressive tradition of the silent era and continuing through the present-day in films like Zhang Yi-Mou's *Ju Dou* (1990) and *Raise the Red Lantern* (1991). For example, *Siao Yu* revolves around the arranged green card marriage of Italian-American Mario Moretti (Daniel J. Travanti) and illegal-immigrant sweatshop worker Siao Yu (Liu Joyin, aka Rene Lao) that takes the Asian woman away from her Chinese childhood sweetheart and 'saves her' from an abusive relationship. In *Double Happiness*, Jade (Sandra Oh) uses her liaison with white Canadian Mark (Callum Keith Rennie) to give her the strength to escape from the expectations of her traditional father. Similarly, a good portion of the narrative in *Shopping for Fangs* revolves around comparisons made between Phil and his sister's white boyfriend and the relationship between Katherine and her white psychiatrist.

Siao Yu, for example, follows a familiar 'white knight' formula. Working illegally in a sweatshop, Siao Yu suffers from the drudgery, low wages, and substandard working conditions of a non-unionized garment factory as well as from the constant threat of deportation by the INS. Also, as characteristic of the 'white knight' scenario, Siao Yu's Asian boyfriend Giang Wei (Chunghua Tou) tends to be insensitive to her suffering, agreeing to 'sell' Siao Yu in an arranged marriage that will eventually result in his obtaining a green card through her, and he threatens to leave her if she refuses to go along with the scheme. When Siao Yu takes up residency to prove to the INS the validity of her marriage to Mario, the selfish Giang Wei wastes little time establishing a romantic liaison with his house-mate's girlfriend. Despite his own infidelity, however, Giang Wei expects absolute loyalty from Siao Yu, even if she is technically married to another man and cohabiting with him.

Like many 'white knights' in commercial films, Mario is a flawed hero in need of some recuperation by his bride. In addition to becoming a bigamist after the wedding, Mario has a number of vices and serious flaws, including compulsive gambling, alcoholism, a ruined career as a progressive journalist, and a general inability to get and keep a job. Just as Mario saves Siao Yu from the insensitive Giang Wei, Siao Yu saves Mario from a dysfunctional marriage to an independent white woman, Rita (Marj Dusay). Thus, as is common, the white knight romance saves both the exploited Asian woman and the hapless white man. Even though Mario dies at the end of the film, Siao Yu has found enough strength, through the relationship, to declare her independence from Giang Wei. In the penultimate scene, Siao Yu remains with the body of her white husband rather than driving off under the orders of her Chinese fiancé. The white knight has liberated her from the strictures of the Chinese male and, presumably, enabled her to find her own way in the 'land of liberty' by teaching her to be a 'good' American housewife.

The plot of *Double Happiness*[2] parallels 'white knight' stories like those in *Siao Yu* as well as the queer triangulations that structure *The Wedding Banquet*. The title of the film refers to the Chinese character for marital bliss (i.e. a doubling of the character for happiness) that adorns spaces associated with Chinese nuptials like the banquet hall, the bridal suite, and the newlyweds' first home. The film's plot revolves around Jade's parents' attempts to get their aspiring actress daughter to make 'a good match' with a Chinese professional who promises some upward mobility for the working-class family. The pressure to conform to a normative Chinese heterosexuality is presented as misguided and irrational, more the result of blind tradition than a reaction to racism. The Li parents insist on a Chinese husband for Jade even though their own experiences of Chinese patriarchy are presented as less than pleasant.

Double Happiness adds another element to the equation by comically offering the gay Andrew (Johnny Mah) as the most suitable Chinese suitor. In *Double Happiness*, Jade is positioned between gay Chinese Canadian Andrew and white heterosexual Mark, just as Wei-Wei is positioned between Wai-Tung and Simon in *The Wedding Banquet*. However, in the case of *Double Happiness*, the white male saves the Chinese woman, Jade, rather than the Chinese man, Wai-Tung, from the strictures of the Chinese patriarchy.

If Andrew represents the impossibility of finding happiness with a 'nice Chinese boy,' Mark promises the freedom from convention and the celebration of individuality that Chinese tradition abhors. *Double Happiness* compares Mark favorably to Robert, the 'rice king' boyfriend whom Jade's friend Lisa (Claudette Carracedo) has in tow. Although he does not appear in the film, Robert's presence manifests itself in his apartment, which is filled with a motley collection of Asian bric-à-brac, and Lisa does point out that he practices *tai chi* and drinks only Tsing Tao beer from China. When Lisa says she would not mind living with Robert, Jade is appalled and calls the apartment an 'Oriental love den.' For Jade, a romance with a white Canadian must represent a break with Chinese patriarchy and all it represents. Clearly, a 'rice king' looking for a 'traditional' Asian woman would not be right for Jade, who yearns for self-determination and personal liberation.

In fact, when Jade first meets Mark, she suspects that his interest is in the image her race conjures up in his mind of a submissive 'lotus blossom.' After pretending not to speak English, Jade finally takes pity on the vulnerable Mark and goes off with him. Throughout the course of *Double Happiness*, Jade's and Mark's positions in the film gradually change. As Jade's vulnerability becomes more apparent through the difficulties of her career as an actress and the pressures of family life, Mark emerges as a quiet pillar of strength, who woos Jade with flowers, thoughtful gestures, and tender kisses. Although Jade gives in to pressure from her father to give up Mark, it becomes clear that her decision to leave her family home, estrange herself from her father, and live in her own apartment comes as much from a desire for the forbidden romance as from a desire for personal emancipation. Although *Double Happiness* does not hold out a definitive promise of romantic bliss and acceptance within white society, Jade's first phone call from her apartment does reach out to Mark. Although Jade reaches only his answering machine, the avenue for further communication and potential romantic happiness has been opened, and Jade has established herself, through Mark, as free from the constraints of Chinese tradition.

In *Shopping for Fangs*, the 'white knight,' embodied by two figures of scientific authority, becomes a less potent element of the narrative. Katherine's relationship with her white psychiatrist, Dr. Suleri (Daniel Twyman), parallels Phil's relationship with his sister's white boyfriend, Matt (Scott Eberlein), a specialist in paranormal phenomena, including lycanthropy. While the film presents each character as a figure of white male authority at the beginning of the narrative, these two characters, unlike Mario and Mark, prove woefully inadequate as saviors of either Phil or Katherine. While Matt's race shores up his masculine identity, Phil cannot seem to find any women interested in dating an Asian man. Testosterone out of control, Phil works out incessantly, shaves constantly, but still cannot seem to get rid of his five o'clock shadow. He tries to pick up girls at discos, and even agrees to go to a Christian Bible study meeting in return for some female company. While his white female doctor diagnoses his problem as raging hormones, Phil begins to think he may be a werewolf. Because the white medical establishment and Christianity seem unable to 'save' Phil, he turns to Matt in a final attempt to cure his condition. However, this 'white knight', tightly under the thumb of the bossy Naomi (Lela Lee, author of the comic-strip *Angry Little Girls*), also proves inadequate. Even after Phil has hoisted the much larger Matt up against a wall, Matt refuses to recognize Phil as a werewolf and offers little solace and no remedy.

In contrast to his nerdy co-worker Phil, Katherine's husband Jim (Clint Jung) epitomizes Asian machismo. Tall, elegantly dressed, and worldly, Jim, Phil's superior at the office, does not, however, have the same control in the domestic sphere. Shunned by the frigid Katherine, Jim is actually as frustrated as is Phil. In contrast to Phil, who eventually proves his prowess in the bedroom, Jim remains alone to masturbate in an empty house. Mistakenly, Jim sees his chief rival as Katherine's white psychiatrist Dr. Suleri, to whom she goes for help, though he proves inadequate for her salvation. During hypnosis, Katherine relives the trauma of her voyage out of Vietnam and attacks Suleri, calling him a 'bloody rapist.' Given that Katherine had been attacked by Southeast Asian pirates, this transference may be too easily explained away as a result of the psychoanalytic relationship as opposed to a revelation that the 'white knight' syndrome, associated with US involvement in Vietnam, led not only to the rape of her country but to the specific circumstances in which she had been raped as a young girl. Thus, Katherine's outburst turns the tables on the myth of the American soldier as 'white knight' in Vietnam, attempting to 'save' the country from communism by domesticating the Asian woman through romance. In *Shopping for Fangs*, this romance becomes a rape, and the 'white knight' loses his power over the Vietnamese woman, and, analogously, over Asia itself.

Symbolically killing off white male authority and knocking traditional Asian patriarchy to its knees, *Shopping for Fangs* frees its protagonists from the strictures of sexism and enforced heterosexuality. Unlike *Siao Yu* and *Double Happiness*, in which the white knight is cleansed of his sexism and racism in order to take a firm stance against Chinese patriarchy, *Shopping for Fangs* moves away from white knight fantasies to empower the repressed Katherine and the emasculated Phil. Thus, *Shopping for Fangs* quotes, but does not uncritically reproduce, the 'white knight' romance for its GenerAsian X audience.

Ethnic trouble

When Katherine confronts her husband she is masquerading as Trinh, a lesbian waitress, wearing a blonde wig and sunglasses like the unnamed drug runner (Brigitte Lin Ching-Hsia) in Wong Kar-Wai's *Chungking Express* (1994). Not only does she take on the trappings of this powerful character from the well-known Hong Kong film, but she, like the drug runner, takes on an identity that mimics 'whiteness.' In blonde wig, sunglasses, waitress uniform, and second-hand dresses, Katherine ironically empowers herself with symbols of white American women's oppression. Starting with Marilyn Monroe, whose working-class roots (emblematized by the waitress uniform), need for anonymity (symbolized by the dark glasses), desire for glamour (concretized by the chic used-clothing), and vulnerability created an image that mingled sexually available white-trash allure with a naive innocence, Trinh adds the Chinese folk heroine popularized by actresses like Brigitte Lin who portray *gung fu* adepts, assassins, and characters with supernatural martial prowess.

Living in a hotel room that emphasizes her working-class persona and provisional status, and moves her away from Jim's settled, bourgeois, suburban home, the hybridized figure of Katherine/Trinh represents identity in flux within the Asian diaspora. She suffers as a victim of male violence as Katherine and vanquishes her oppressor as Trinh, and she does this by blending masks associated with the working class, femininity, and Chinese ethnicity. Jim dispatched, Katherine can shed Trinh and pass her on to her gay friend Clarence

Figure 16.1 Trinh/Katherine (Jeanne Chin) and Jim (Clint Jung) in *Shopping for Fangs* (Lee and Lin, 1997). Courtesy and © 1997 Margin Films.

(John Cho). Like Wai-Tung in *The Wedding Banquet* and Andrew in *Double Happiness*, Clarence marks a meeting of the Chinese and the queer diasporas. In a Taipei-style shaved-ice parlor, Clarence tells Trinh about his background. He went to California from Taiwan to go to high school, studied photography in college, and stayed on illegally. Although his boyfriend has returned to Asia, Clarence has 'gotten used' to life in the US (Ong 1999). Gay sons, like Wai-tung and Clarence, may be in America to further family interests by establishing a base for future immigration and/or business expansion, but they soon find a welcome place within what has been called, inspired by Arjun Appadurai, the 'queerscape' or 'homoscape,' that global space shaped by the possibility of queer identity and desire (Waugh 1998; Leung 2001; Marchetti 2001).

In *Shopping for Fangs*, the blonde wig and dark glasses condense postcolonial mimicry (Bhabha 1994) with queer considerations of gender as parody and performance (Butler 1990; Holmlund 2003). The wig and sunglasses do not simply denote a specific type of femininity but point to a particularly white and American femininity defined by consumer commodities. The reference moves beyond Monroe to Brigitte Lin, and, with it, conjures up a critique of British colonialism and American cultural imperialism in Asia by referring to *Chungking Express* (Marchetti 2000b). The allusion goes beyond a knowing wink to the cognoscenti in the audience and creates an important bridge between the textual politics of Hong Kong cinema and American independents. When Katherine/Trinh has her stand-off/*pas-de-deux* with Jim, as guns shift from threatening heads to torsos, the allusion to John Woo's famous gun fight choreography goes beyond a simple reference for fans to draw *Shopping for Fangs* into the orbit of Chinese cinema and the political ramifications of Woo's appropriation of Sergio Leone's quotation of John Ford to critique Hollywood figurations of power, masculinity, and imperial expansionism.

Although her only love interest is herself as Katherine, Trinh proudly takes on a lesbian persona, openly telling Clarence and her co-workers she is a lesbian, in order to combat the stifling heterosexual norms her husband represents. Throughout *Shopping for Fangs* issues of identity revolve around sexual, gender, ethnic, national, and racial plays of power. Clarence, Katherine, and Phil all struggle to escape from the strictures of rigid gender roles and heterosexual norms that are inflected by American racism and the legacy of colonialism globally. Phil struggles against the asexual, brainy, 'model minority' Charlie Chan, Katherine against the simpering 'lotus blossom,' and Clarence against the accommodating 'houseboy' (Fung 1991).

Thus, exiled by American ideology and queer proclivities, Katherine/Trinh and Clarence pair up in California as 'soul mates' chafing at the need to play 'feminine,' 'masculine,' and 'Asian' roles in a racist, sexist, and homophobic society. Not surprisingly, as Clarence takes up where Trinh left off in her parody

Figure 16.2 Trinh/Katherine (Jeanne Chin) and Clarence (John Cho) in *Shopping for Fangs* (Lee and Lin, 1997). Courtesy and © 1997 Margin Films.

of Monroe/Lin, Katherine and Phil move on to another American movie genre, leaving the werewolf B-horror film, the action film, and the melodrama behind to drive off into a road movie and the freedom from convention that genre promises.

Double Happiness's Jade, as an aspiring actress, is also no stranger to gender parody and ethnic mimicry. As Korean Canadian actress Sandra Oh takes up the clapboard to begin the film by taking on the role of Hong Kong-born actress Jade Li, she directly addresses the camera and says: 'I said I would never make a big deal about being Chinese . . . but I want to tell you about my family, and they are very Chinese, if you know what I mean.' With this, she recognizes the roles she plays as 'Chinese' within a predominantly white Canadian society and as 'female' in her role as dutiful daughter within the Chinese Canadian household.

Self-conscious about role-playing, Jade begins pondering why her family could not be the Brady Bunch, and concludes that the Brady Bunch 'didn't need subtitles.' However, every member of the family is 'typecast,' and, through the course of the film, the difficulty of maintaining these roles is revealed; i.e. ethnic pain uncovered under the comic veneer of quaint accents and charming cultural differences. Although the rebellious Jade's affinity for the closeted Andrew needs no explanation, the fact that all the apparently guileless characters in *Double Happiness* are also 'in the closet' draws the homophobic Chinese patriarchal family closer to Andrew as an icon who can hide his 'Chinese-ness' under a veneer of assimilation in dress, speech, and demeanor, and who can hide his sexual orientation under a façade of apparent heterosexual masculinity.

The two scenes in which Jade auditions for parts indicate her inability to fit in with ethnic expectations for her performance. In the first, confronted by a panel of white judges, Jade is asked to deliver her lines with an accent. Jokingly, she offers a Parisian accent and, then, seriously delivers a 'very good' Chinese accent. As Edward R. O'Neill (1997: 57) notes:

> In this scene, Jade performs her assigned ethnic and gender role so that she can destroy that role by revealing it to have been a performance, a stereotype mimicked in advance of the other's expectations. Cultural identity here becomes part of a complex strategic interaction ritual in which each player anticipates the other's expectation so that it can be acted out as a bluff and as bait for a trap.

Later, when the scene that features Jade as a waitress plays on a TV soap-opera. Jade's voice, without a Chinese accent, remains an offscreen presence. She has visually been eliminated from the frame. Since the assimilated voice does not go with the racially marked body, the body goes, and the disembodied Jade misses a chance to further her career with a television appearance.[3]

However, Jade has equal difficulty dealing with Chinese media. After losing a chance at a Connie Chung news anchor role because, as her African American agent says, 'They're looking for a Filipina,' Jade gets a shot at a Hong Kong production planned for filming in Vancouver. Although she initially impresses the woman producer, Jade again fails to pull off the role because she is insufficiently 'Chinese.' While her ability to speak Cantonese makes the grade, Jade cannot read, and her illiteracy in Chinese prompts the producer to ask with contempt: 'Are you really Chinese?' When Jade, crestfallen, whispers 'Yes' in Cantonese, the producer simply exhales cigarette smoke with a look of utter exasperation.

While always expected to play a Chinese role, Jade can never be 'Chinese' enough for her family or potential employers. Like Trinh, the aspiring actress Jade is associated with the glamour and tragedy of Monroe's white sexuality and vulnerability early in the film when some friends of the family jokingly belittle her theatrical ambitions by saying she aspires to be Marilyn Monroe. In fact, Jade takes on roles associated with white femininity under siege. Tennessee Williams's Blanche DuBois from *A Streetcar Named Desire* is doomed by her own unattainable desires and self-deluded dreams, and the French martyr Joan of Arc burns at the stake for daring to take on the trappings of male attire to follow the will of God into battle. Imitating these hopeless figures, Jade takes on the transgressions of tragically misunderstood and vilified white women. Just as Blanche DuBois and Joan of Arc step over the boundaries set for their gender and suffer the consequences, Jade crosses the racial and gender line to break free from the roles assigned to her that she simply could not perform.

Siao Yu's journey from exploited illegal alien to liberated American woman and Mario's transformation from a failed husband and writer to a reinvigorated champion of the rights of the downtrodden involve playing and discarding a number of racial, ethnic, and gender roles as well. Ironically, the roles they play most convincingly and 'naturally' involve portraying man and wife for the benefit of the INS. Unlike *The Wedding Banquet*, which presents the wedding night as the consummation of an unlikely comedy of errors, *Siao Yu* presents the chaste marriage of its protagonists as the road to their salvation. Mario sets aside his persona of Italian-American low life in order to become the social crusader he missed becoming because he was 'too old for Woodstock and too young for the Lincoln Brigade.' Although he only manages to liberate a single soul other than his own, Mario redeems himself as the embodiment of bourgeois American values of individual liberty and justice. To do this, Mario must play the sensitive, liberated man, who can keep his wife domesticated, liberated from sweatshop labor, happy to have chosen her subordinate status, and clearly better off than in China or married to a Chinese husband. Siao Yu finds herself in this construction of a heterosexual union as well, and she remains loyal to her white American husband to his dying day.

Given that the marriage begins as a sham but ends as a transcendent union, *Siao Yu* underscores the power these roles have to shape reality above and beyond the actual motives behind the relationship. Although fear of the INS and the Mafia bring Siao Yu and Mario together as man and wife, the institution of marriage transforms them into a heterosexual couple who embody bourgeois values of hard work and individuality. Actually, the fact that a marriage between an unemployed, aging, white American male and a young, working-class, Chinese immigrant woman should seem so 'natural' to the INS as well as the viewer, given the highly unlikely circumstances of their marriage of convenience, points to the tremendous staying power of the imperialist myth of the 'white knight' paired with the Asian woman. The improbable becomes possible, even inevitable, and the attraction of a childhood sweetheart with whom one shares a home, a language, a culture, a history, and a nation pales in comparison to the allure of even the most flawed white American.

Conclusion

All three of these films situate themselves as 'American' through the treatment of issues of concern within North American society, ranging from immigration, labor, class inequities, racism, ethnic exclusionism, sexism, and homophobia. However, in each case, China also exerts a considerable narrative, dramatic, and emotional pull. Although the films shy away from any direct discussion of contemporary Chinese politics (specifically, the events of May–June 1989 in Tian'anmen Square), all three films recognize the influence of China – and all the varied and contradictory things China represents – on the overseas Chinese. New immigrants as well as those removed from the mainland by one or two generations still negotiate 'Chinese-ness' as racial difference, questionable national loyalties, economic expectations, as well as prescribed gender roles, familial obligations, and sexual restrictions. Thus, the nation (China/America) becomes inextricably linked with the body (its gender, its age, its color, its desires) and torn asunder by the strains of the social, the economic, and the political, as well as the personal, vicissitudes of a global culture. Currently, 'China' and 'patriarchy' are both under assault from the hybridized edges of a 'Greater China' that includes independent women, lesbians, gays, and a younger generation comfortable with being Chinese and Asian American, or refusing to be either.

As the American independents draw in minority perspectives to criss-cross global markets looking for those niche audiences that will bring in the profits, the cinemas of Greater China move outside the Chinese-speaking world into the realm of the diaspora and filmmakers move back and forth between Chinese and English, straddling nation states and industries, in order to escape the constraints of both Hollywood and Taipei or Hong Kong. These films reflect ambivalence about identity that strikes a responsive chord across colonial history, economic hierarchies, racial, ethnic, and national identities. Made by filmmakers in transit about people, like themselves, 'flexible' in their approach to nationality, ethnicity, gender, sexuality, and class, these films appeal to audiences that find themselves increasingly on the move physically (as tourists, émigrés, refugees, exiles, etc.) or mentally (surfing the internet, sending a fax, or making an intercontinental phone call).

Collapsing time and space, in their postmodern play with genre and narrative conventions, the American independent meets the international art film within the context of Greater China, and it becomes increasingly difficult to look at the American independent without recognizing the impact of Chinese cinema on it as a trans-national, rather than purely domestic, phenomenon. While *Siao Yu* and *Double Happiness* stick with formulae familiar to more general audiences, *Shopping for Fangs* moves closer to the edge to target GenerAsian X viewers with inside references that specify the dilemmas faced by Asian American youth and gay and lesbian Chinese within the diaspora. Attempting to realign the audience, the independent American film works in tandem with a Greater China youth culture to create a hybrid that works on global screens.

Looking at these three features within the context of American independent film production as well as the Chinese diaspora brings several key factors to the surface. First recognized as a phenomenon in Europe, defined by filmmakers born outside of the US, funded by foreign governments and overseas capital, aesthetically bound to the international art cinema, the American independent film exhibits the vigor of the hybrid. Thus, in a world in which transnational ventures define global screen culture, the 'American,' as well as the 'independent,' and, in the digital age, the 'film' of the phenomenon must never be taken as self-evident. Similarly, the 'Chinese' aspect of Greater Chinese screen culture should also be considered within the specificity of Asian American life and media arts. As the American independent continues to rub shoulders with the cinema of the Chinese diaspora, questions of economic, political, linguistic, social, and cultural borders will continue to disturb easy categorization, and it would be a serious mistake to look at these films as less 'American' or 'independent' than others, when the margins that define the American independent cinema may never be able to contain the global mix of which it is comprised.

Notes

1 Both filmmakers have continued in the independent vein: Lin showed *Better Luck Tomorrow* at Sundance in 2002, and it has been picked up by MTV for distribution; Lee made the independent feature *Drift* in 2001.
2 For more on this film, see Erens 2000 and Levitin 1997.
3 The students in my seminar 'Senior Topics in Film Studies: The Cinemas of China and the Chinese Diaspora,' Ithaca College, spring 2000, insisted that the threatening mole in the soap-opera in *Double Happiness* refers directly to fellow-Canadian Helen Lee's *Sally's Beauty Spot*, and I am happy to pass on that observation here.

Bibliography

Bhabha, H.K. (1994) *The Location of Culture*, New York: Routledge.

Butler, J. (1990) *Gender Trouble: Feminism and the Subversion of Identity*, New York: Routledge.

Erens, P.B. (2000) 'Mina Shum's *Double Happiness* and Women's Immigrant Writing,' paper presented at the Society for Cinema Studies conference, Chicago, IL, 11 March.

Fung, R. (1991) 'Looking for My Penis: The Eroticized Asian in Gay Video Porn,' in Bad Object-Choices (eds.), *How Do I Look? Queer Film and Video*, Seattle, WA: Bay Press.

Holmlund, C. (2003) *Impossible Bodies: Femininity and Masculinity at the Movies*, New York: Routledge.

Hong, P.Y. (1998) 'New Voices Emerge to Tell the Story of Ordinary Americans,' *Los Angeles Times*, 23 May: 2, online: www.sound2cb.com/education/teaching/ucla/voices.html (accessed 28 May 2003).

Kleinhans, C. (1998) 'Independent Features: Hopes and Dreams,' in J. Lewis (ed.), *The New American Cinema*, Durham, NC Duke University Press, 307–27.

Leung, H.H. (2001) 'Queerscapes in Contemporary Hong Kong Cinema,' *positions: east asia cultures critique*, 9, 2: 423–47.

Levitin, J. (1997) 'Making Film in the Diaspora: *Double Happiness* and Difference,' paper presented at the Asian Cinema Studies Society conference, Trent University, Canada, 23 August.

Li, W. (1997) 'UCLA Graduate Students Collaborate to Create GenerAsian X Thriller,' *Daily Bruin*, 22 September, online: www.dailybruin.ucla.edu/DB/issues/97/09.22/ae.fangs.html (accessed 28 May 2003).

Locke, C. (n.d.) '*Shopping for Fangs* Helps Usher in the New School of Asian American Filmmaking,' *Hardboiled*, online: www.hardboiled.org/1–4/shopping.html (accessed 28 May 2003).

Marchetti, G. (1993) *Romance and the 'Yellow Peril': Race, Sex, and Discursive Strategies in Hollywood Fiction*, Berkeley: University of California Press.

—— (2000a) '*The Wedding Banquet*: Global Chinese Cinema and the Asian American Experience,' in D.Y. Hamamoto and S. Liu (eds.), *Countervisions: Asian American Film Criticism*, Philadelphia: Temple University Press, 275–97.

—— (2000b) 'Buying American, Consuming Hong Kong: Cultural Commerce, Fantasies of Identity, and the Cinema,' in P.S. Fu and D. Desser (eds.), *The Cinema of Hong Kong: History, Arts, Identity*, New York: Cambridge University Press, 289–313.

—— (2001) 'Cinema Frames, Videoscapes, and Cyberspace: Exploring Shu Lea Cheang's *Fresh Kill*,' *positions: east asia cultures critique*, 9:2: 401–22.

Mitchell, K. (1996) 'In Whose Interest? Trans-national Capital and the Production of Multiculturalism in Canada,' in R. Wilson and W. Dissanayake (eds.), *Global/Local: Cultural Production and the Trans-national Imaginary*, Durham, NC: Duke University Press.

Ong, A. (1999) *Flexible Citizenship: The Cultural Logics of Transnationality*, Durham, NC: Duke University Press.

O'Neill, E. (1997) 'Asian American Filmmakers: The Next Generation? Identity, Mimicry and Transtextuality in Mina Shum's *Double Happiness* and Quentin Lee and Justin Lin's *Shopping for Fangs*,' *CineAction*, 42: 50–62.

Schamus, J. (1998) 'To the Rear of the Back End: The Economics of Independent Cinema,' in S. Neale and M. Smith (eds.), *Contemporary Hollywood Cinema*, New York: Routledge, 91–105.

Shen, S.Y. (2001) 'Locating Feminine Writing in Taiwan Cinema: A Study of Yang Hui-Shan's Body and Sylvia Chang's *Siao Yu*,' *Postscript*, 20, 2–3: 115–23.

Waugh, T. (1998) 'Good Clean Fung,' *Wide Angle*, 20, 2: 164–75.

Wyatt, J. (2001) 'Marketing Marginalized Cultures: *The Wedding Banquet*, Cultural Identities, and Independent Cinema of the 1990s,' in J. Lewis (ed.), *The End of Cinema as We Know It: American Film in the Nineties*, New York: New York University Press, 61–71.

Xing, J. (1998) *Asian America Through the Lens: History, Representations, and Identity*, Walnut Creek, CA: Alta Mira/Sage.

Yan, G.L. (1999) *White Snake and Other Stories*, San Francisco, CA: Aunt Lute Press.

Part V

Shifting markets, changing media

Chapter 17

Revisiting 1970s' independent distribution and marketing strategies

Justin Wyatt

The 1970s is often characterized as a decade in which mainstream film distribution shifted from platform to wide releases. Each successive summer offered a larger number of screens for summer blockbusters, and this shift soon led the way for all releases opening in substantial numbers of screens. In many ways, the opening of *Matrix Reloaded* on 3,603 screens in 2003 can be traced back to the 'wide' release of *Jaws* in 409 screens back in 1975. As this trajectory became clear through the mid- to late 1970s, the implication was evident to the major studios – for any film with moderate to high marketability, open as widely as possible and position the movie in the marketplace as strongly as possible through TV advertising.

Of course, the independent film world was somewhat exempt from this strategy, at least initially. Nevertheless, even in the 1970s, there were consequences for the independents given this shift in distribution. Suddenly, independent distributors were under pressure to find 'A' theaters and quality bookings, both always a challenge for independents who often settled for less attractive theaters and drive-in bookings. With this distribution shift in the mainstream film world, independent distributors were forced to be more creative in their strategies for distribution. Four-wall engagements, in which the independent rented the 'four walls' of the theater outright and saturated the airwaves with targeted TV spots, became very successful in the wake of Tom Laughlin's *Billy Jack* (1971). In particular, this strategy became standard (and successful) practice for the sensationalistic 'true-story' Sunn Family Classics films, such as *The Mysterious Monsters* (Gunette, 1975), *The Outer Space Connection* (Warshofsky, 1975) and *In Search of Noah's Ark* (Conway, 1977) (Moses 1975: 22).

But four-walling was just one approach favored by the independents to gain a foothold in the crowded marketplace. On occasion, independents employed more drastic means to position and place their product. George C. Scott's melodrama *The Savage Is Loose* (1974) and Joe Camp's family film *Benji* (1974) are two cases of independents attempting to rethink standard distribution and marketing practice during this period. While there are some similarities between their approaches, there are also key differences, particularly in terms of time frame. While ultimately unsuccessful, George C. Scott's approach nevertheless was influential as a short-run marketing tactic for independents. Scott was able to manipulate a disputed MPAA rating and devise a highly marketable distribution mechanism for his film. Of course, both strategies were helped immeasurably by Scott's star power and the specific elements of his star image. Joe Camp's distribution and marketing approach, on the other hand, capitalized on an under-served market – the G-rated family film. Rather than relying on 'stunt' marketing and distribution, *à la* Scott, Camp attempted an intervention in terms of quality in the almost barren family market. Camp's strategy had long-run consequences for the independents that, to this day, are able to benefit from market segments ignored by the major studios. Both Scott and Camp deserve a place in the annals of independent film history for their contributions to the business.

Revisiting these contributions demonstrates just how innovative and entrepreneurial independents had to be in this period, decades before the relative safety and comfort offered by the Disney-owned Miramax, the Vivendi–Universal-owned Focus Features, and Viacom-owned Paramount Classics. Nowadays, stars such as Sean Penn are able to make the occasional indie film, such as *The Crossing Guard* (1995) for Miramax, and support these assignments with more mainstream starring roles in *I Am Sam* (Nelson, 2001), and *Mystic River* (Eastwood, 2003). There is no need for a star–director like Penn to work outside the institutionalized independents, as predecessors Scott and John Cassavetes had found it necessary to do.

Selling through media mayhem: *The Savage Is Loose*

To focus on a short-run strategy as a start, consider George C. Scott's marketing and distribution of *The Savage Is Loose*. Scott's approach is tied to the MPAA ratings system and, more specifically, to the inconsistencies and fissures within the system. President Jack Valenti describes the primary function of the MPAA ratings system as a guide – 'to offer to parents some advance information about movies so that parents can decide what movies they want their children to see or not to see.' Regardless, since its inception in 1968 the voluntary ratings system has served another significant purpose: to gain publicity for movies lacking 'conventional' marketing assets. *The Savage Is Loose* is an early and influential example of this appropriation and exploitation of both the specific ratings and the media battles with the MPAA for marketing purposes.

Set up as a four-ply system (G/M/R/X) initially, with the X ratings barring without qualification those under sixteen, the MPAA hoped that the replacement

Figure 17.1 Director Joe Camp and star Benji (Camp, 1974).

for the Production Code Administration would satisfy a range of constituents: the far right would applaud the censorship potential within the system; the conservatives would favor the efforts at self-policing without governmental interference; and filmmakers would be able to experiment with 'freer' themes since children's admission would be limited to certain films (*Variety* 1968: 5). Under the MPAA system, non-member distributors were welcome to self-apply X ratings, but not the less restrictive ratings (*Variety* 1969a: 3). Even before the new system had been instituted, independent distributors lobbied against exhibitors playing only films with MPAA ratings. Since the majority of the independent films were directed at 'adult' audiences, the independents felt that their films would have little to gain by having an MPAA rating (*Variety* 1966: 7). Many of these distributors also balked at the cost of submitting the film to the MPAA for a rating that would have no bearing on their potential audience.

By 1970, independent distributors began to complain about the double standard that seemed to apply within the ratings system: MPAA members' releases (i.e. the studios) were apparently receiving more lenient ratings than non-members'. For instance, ABC Pictures Corporation lost its appeal on the R rating for *Lovers and Other Strangers* (Howard, 1970) despite relatively minor thematic elements: the plot concerned the confusion ensuing from the decision of a young couple, living together secretly for a year, to get married. In an article about the failed appeal titled 'Hollywood Indies Mutter that Code Is More Strict Against MPAA Outsiders,' *Variety* described several studio films – *Halls of Anger* (Bogart, 1970, for United Artists), *Hello-Goodbye* (Neame, 1970, for Fox), *Start the Revolution Without Me* (Yorkin, 1970, for Warner Brothers) – with just as explicit content which received a GP (PG) rating (*Variety* 1970: 23). While the pressure to ensure an R rating over the X rating was well documented, perhaps more urgent was the desire for a PG rating over an R rating. In the first six years of the MPAA ratings system, majors and 'mini-majors' released more PG movies than any other category, with the percentage rising from 42 percent in the first year of the system to 50 percent in the sixth year (Murphy 1974: 30).

The confusion over the PG–R divide and the overwhelming popularity of PG as a ratings category were evident with *The Savage Is Loose*. To understand why the ratings battle ensued, it is worth considering the film's background. Released in November 1974, *The Savage Is Loose* concerns a couple (played by Scott and wife Trish Van Devere) and their young son David who are stranded on a South Seas' island with little hope of ever being rescued. Described by one reviewer as 'Swiss Family Oedipus,' the plot revolves around a difference in parenting philosophy between mother and father: Dad believes that David must be raised to survive in the violent jungle, while mom wants to reinforce the benefits of a civilized upbringing. Patriarchy wins out, and, after a fifteen-year sojourn on the island, David's sexual maturation is complicated by his survival-of-the-fittest approach to life. The second half of the film explores the fractured relationship between father, mother, and son, with the increasingly explicit sexual overturnes of son to mother. After a botched attempt to kill his father, the distraught David confronts his mother who is clutching a knife behind her back. In the resolution, she drops the knife and, despite the presence of her wounded husband, proceeds to give her son a full-mouthed kiss. Reviews were, at best, mixed, ranging from *Variety*'s rave ('an excellent survival drama') (Murf 1974: 14) to Pauline Kael's devastating *New Yorker* pan ('about as agonizing as any two hours I've spent at the movies') (1974: 183).

Producer–director–star Scott developed a unique plan for the distribution and exhibition of his film. Choosing to return to a method commonly used in early film sales, Scott self-distributed and licensed prints 'in perpetuity' direct to individual theaters for unlimited showings (Pryor 1974: 48). Scott demanded cash up front in advance of delivering the print. Each license agreement for a particular theater included the use of a single print and a complete advertising and promotion campaign. Scott's intent was to cut the middleman, the distributor, out of the equation. As he commented at the time: 'This can be the beginning of a continuing relationship between – and I hope that others besides myself will do it – the people who make the films and the people who get the films out to be seen' (*ibid.*). In addition, by coordinating all advertising and promotion (with the help of PR expert Jim Mahoney) for the film, Scott circumvented the usual distribution of advertising materials through the National Screen Service (NSS). Instead of renting advertising materials through NSS, Scott provided free-of-charge stills, posters, radio spots, and two different versions of the trailer.

Certainly Scott's uncommon distribution, marketing and exhibition plans for his film were augmented greatly by his own fiercely independent star image. While Scott's stardom bolstered public interest in his projects, the specific components of his star image dovetailed ingeniously with this film. Scott's image can be succinctly captured by the title of the cover article in *Time* which ran a month prior to the Academy Awards in April 1971: "An Actor's Art: Rage Beneath the Surface." Scott was at the pinnacle of his career with his Oscar-nominated (and ultimately winning) performance in *Patton* (Schaffner, 1970). Cocks's article foregrounds both his perfectionism in his craft (chameleon-like performances, thorough research, attention to physical detail) and his volatile personality – 'Always, just below the surface, there is an incessant drumbeat of anger,' followed by descriptions of his 'self-hatred,' heavy drinking, and his intimidation of co-stars (Cocks 1971: 63).

Defiance was almost certainly the defining characteristic. This traced all the way back to Scott's declining an Oscar nomination in 1962 for his supporting role in *The Hustler* (Rossen, 1961). At that point, Scott was the first person in the organization's thirty-five-year history to state publicly his lack of interest in being nominated. He commented: 'I did not send the telegram out of petulance or impudence. I meant it as a constructive rather than destructive move' (quoted in Weiler 1962: 31). The public diatribes against the Oscars were covered widely in the press, particularly at the time of the *Patton* nomination as Scott was the leading contender for the award. His defiance, added to public reports of his 'reckless' behavior, only enhanced a portfolio of roles that depended on a strain of individuality and iconoclasm: General Buck Turgidson in Stanley Kubrick's *Dr. Strangelove* (1964), the philandering doctor in Richard Lester's *Petulia* (1968), the slithering prosecutor in *Anatomy of a Murder* (Preminger, 1959), and, of course, the perfect match between star persona and character as the stubborn George S. 'Blood and Guts' Patton. Appropriately enough, Scott's debut effort as a director was a thriller titled *Rage* (1972).

Scott's star persona certainly meshed perfectly with the untraditional manner in which *The Savage Is Loose* was placed into the market. Further, the media controversy surrounding the film's rating only augmented the unique distribution strategy. Recall that Scott was handling all the advertising for the film and that he was no stranger to media controversy (which, to that point, had only solidified his star image). *The Savage Is Loose* received an R rating from the MPAA for 'its strong and developing theme of incest.' Scott's response was to hold a press conference at which he ridiculed the MPAA's position, that incest was 'a major theme.' Somewhat disingenuously, Scott countered that the sexual aspect was secondary, and 'that not only sexual values must change, but we must change. That's the theme of the picture – mankind is on an island.' Scott had already failed to have the rating reversed on appeal to the MPAA. Arguing that his film possessed 'taste and inherent decency,' Scott suggested at the press conference that the ratings code be adjusted for the film: '*The Savage Is Loose* is the ideal instrument to facilitate a change in methodology – when I requested a special category such as "thematic R" or PG with specific admonition to parents and children alike – we were met with shrugs and vague apologies' (quoted in McBride 1974: 5).

Scott encouraged potential exhibitors to run the film without the disputed rating. In addition, he revealed a new advertising campaign to be run in nine test cities offering money-back guarantees for any parent who found the film unsuitable for family viewing: as the ad proclaimed, 'I'm putting my picture in your hands and my money on the line' (Kael 1974: 183). Scott followed the press conference with extensive appearances on national television talk shows to publicize his film and his offer to the public. Scott's appearance on the *Mike Douglas Show* with MPAA president Jack Valenti was most visible within the trades. Valenti, expressing admiration for the 'exciting' and 'superbly done' film, reiterated that the theme of incest would be of concern to most parents and that the R rating was therefore justified. Scott stated that the R rating signified a much stronger film in terms of content, terming it 'ridiculous' for his film to receive the same rating as *The Texas Chainsaw Massacre* (Hooper, 1974) (Harris 1974: 26). Valenti responded: 'You can't take one picture and give it a special waiver.' Valenti's position on the *Mike Douglas Show* reflected the public statements made by Richard Heffner, the MPAA's rating board chairman. Heffner contended that Scott was falling into a typical fallacy about the ratings system, namely, the belief that because films have a common rating they somehow share thematic elements (*Variety* 1974a: 7). As would be expected, the *Mike Douglas Show* debate created no progress between the participants in *The Savage Is Loose* case.

Fueling the publicity fire, religious groups chimed in with opinions on the ratings battle: the US Catholic Conference placed the film on its 'Condemned' list indicating that it was morally objectionable for Catholics. The *Catholic Film Newsletter* elaborated on the decision by mentioning the 'morally unsupportable resolution' that would be severely disturbing to youngsters, 'particularly those wrestling with their own sudden awareness of sexuality' (*Variety* 1974b: 64). The National Council of Churches of Christ, an umbrella organization representing several Protestant denominations, deplored Scott's actions urging people to disregard the rating, stating that, 'rules that are broken finally weaken the overall structure. Anarchy can tear down a system faster than a voluntary democracy can build it' (*Variety* 1974c: 26).

Understanding that *Variety* is often described as an extension of the studios' publicity departments and therefore deeply complicit in the institutional structures and supports within the industry, the industry trades reported widespread aversion to Scott's plight and his plea for exhibitors to show the film without advertising a rating. Samuel Z. Arkoff, head of American International Pictures (AIP), warned a National Association of Theater Owners convention in Atlanta of the dangers involved should exhibitors disregard the rating – in particular, that the legislature and the public would question the film industry's ability to police itself, opening up further entries for censorship. Arkoff pointedly mentioned that Scott has 'shamed the industry on its proudest night' by refusing to accept the Academy Award and that his actions with the MPAA simply represented additional 'rule-breaking and anarchy' (*Variety* 1974d: 5). Joseph E. Levine, producer of the expensive flop *The Day of the Dolphin* (Nichols, 1973), also starring Scott, took the opportunity to chime in with 'he's a jerk,' due mainly to Scott's publicizing *The Savage Is Loose* so extensively while entirely ignoring the promotion of *The Day of the Dolphin* (*Variety* 1974e: 26).

The resentment of Arkoff, a formidable advertising and exploitation expert, may have been merely disguised jealousy over Scott's marketing ingenuity. As well as the TV and media coverage of the ratings disagreement, the issue generated local press around the decision of local theaters to use the rating. In the *Houston Chronicle* (1975: 25), for instance, the film's advertisement was augmented by the following statement:

> Notice: This is the picture you've probably heard about and which George C. Scott asked theaters to show without a rating. We agree that it is a beautiful film, but its subject matter is so sensitive that we feel obliged to the people of Houston to restrict it to persons under 17 unless accompanied by a parent or adult guardian.

While the accepted view seems to be that *The Savage Is Loose* was a box-office bomb, this is not really the case at all. In fact, sales to exhibitors, prior to opening, generated about $3 million on a negative cost of $750,000. In *Variety*'s sample of top-grossing films, *The Savage Is Loose* opened strongly (peaking at $325,700 in 55 theaters), but the decline was steep and sudden – indicating strong marketability for the opening, yet poor playability for the disappointing final gross. Regardless, thirty years on, the film stands as a testament to the power of entrepreneurial spirit and the ways through which independents were able to carve out marketing, publicity, and distribution space. Admittedly, the tactics seized by Scott, namely the controversy surrounding ratings and censorship, were specific to that film, yet they did serve as an effective means to position it in the marketplace, especially in conjunction with Scott's star image. The impact of Scott's strategy is primarily short-run: adequate as a way to generate publicity and curiosity, but less so as a long-term strategy to maintain the film in the market. Nevertheless, Scott paved the way for several other campaigns centered on ratings skirmishes, especially for Miramax films in the 1980s.

Another case study from the same year presents a sturdier model for long-term independent survival through identifying a missed audience segment and developing an integrated marketing and distribution campaign. Moving to a much different kind of 'family film,' Joe Camp's *Benji* was instrumental in targeting the 'missing' family audience in the early 1970s.

Reclaiming an audience segment: *Benji*

Interestingly, the impact of independent auteur Joe Camp can also be traced back initially to the MPAA ratings system. Just as Scott was able to capitalize on a ratings 'inequity,' *Benji* auteur Joe Camp benefitted from a stigmatized, and under-served, ratings category – the G rating. With the introduction of the MPAA system, the number of R and GP/PG movies jumped year on year, while G ratings dwindled during this period. For instance, in the first six months of 1970, only 35 movies out of 205 were rated G, with 10 of these 35 G pictures actually re-issues (Schickel 1970: 10). G-rated movies were 'missing' due to the youth revolution, with Hollywood focused on trying to reach the lucrative alienated teens and young adults, rather than families. Even Jack Valenti claimed that G-pictures were box-office poison: 'I could show you a lot of G movies that died horrible deaths. There's no lack of family movies; there's a lack of family audiences' (*Variety* 1969b: 3).

Many producers claimed that Walt Disney Productions monopolized the market for family movies, yet even Disney was going through a rough period. With the death of Walt Disney in 1966 and that of his successor Roy O. Disney in 1971, the company essentially went on auto-pilot for the next several years. As president and CEO, E. Cardon Walker commented (*Time* 1973: 64): 'We haven't gone in any new directions. The name has become a guarantee. If it says Walt Disney Productions, a family can be assured that they're not going to be shocked in any way – bored, maybe sometimes, but never shocked.' Boredom actually became a major issue for these family movie-goers with the Disney product. Disney began to rely too heavily on its strategy of re-releasing its classics, such as *Bambi* (Hand, 1942), *Pinocchio* (Luske and Sharpsteen, 1940) and *Snow White and the Seven Dwarves* (Sears and Creedon, 1937) every seven years. It moved away from ani-mated production and toward insipid live-action comedies such as *The Barefoot Executive* (Butler, 1971), *The Computer Who Wore Tennis Shoes* (Butler, 1969), and *The Boatniks* (Tokar, 1970). Between 1966 and 1973, only two new animated features were released, *The Aristocats* (Reitherman, 1970) and *Robin Hood* (Reitherman, 1973), the former being already in preparation when Walt Disney died. The shift away from animated production was both a financial decision (too cost prohibitive) and a pragmatic one (shortage of good animators).

As a company, Disney became so reliant on theme-park and merchandising revenue that stockholders suggested relocating the company headquarters to Florida, close to Walt Disney World (Davis 1980: 144). Revenues from Disney's film and television arm dropped from 50 percent of total profits in 1971 to less than a third in 1977. Therefore, with Disney in flux post-Walt and in the throes of theme-park success, the emphasis on producing high quality family films became lost in the shuffle. As critic Richard Schickel (1973: 65) amusingly commented about Disney film product: 'The typical Disney movie today is static, over-reliant on low-grade verbal humor and ill-conceived comic situations – cars and chim-panzees that are almost human which is more than you can say for the people who appear in support of them.' Schickel attributed the lethargy at Disney to its monopolization of the family market, essentially saying that the lack of competition generated tired, outdated product.

To fill the space in its distribution schedule, Disney resorted to packaging older releases as a 'Walt Disney Summer Festival of Pictures.' Buena Vista programmed eight sets of two older Disney movies, along with two 'first run' engagements in its 1974 festival. Disney was therefore attempting to wring the last dollar from combinations of such played-out films as *Old Yeller* (Stevenson, 1957) and *The Incredible Journey* (Markle, 1963), *Snowball Express* (Tokar, 1972) and *The World's Greatest Athlete* (Scheerer, 1973).

It is unsurprising that this last-ditch attempt represented an opportunity for smaller independents. Over time some of this potential was realized. The four-wall independent distributors were particularly interested in this market. Renting theaters outright, these companies would conduct massive TV and newspaper campaigns and collect revenues directly from the theaters. The range of four-wall family films ran the gamut from wilderness sagas (Pacific International Enter-prises' *The Adventures of the Wilderness Family* [Raffill, 1975]) and animal pictures (Doty-Dayton Productions' *Where the Red Fern Grows* [Tokar, 1974], *Baker's Hawk* [Dayton, 1976]) to quasi-scientific/religious pictures (Sunn Family Classic's *In Search of Noah's Ark, Beyond and Back* [Conway, 1978], *The Outer Space Connection*). These films found their largest audiences in the south and the midwest. Doty-

Dayton's *Baker's Hawk*, for example, premiered in markets such as Salt Lake City, Savannah, Boise, and Topeka, rather than New York, San Francisco, and Boston (*Time* 1977: 74). Over time, however, four-wall family movies also made a dent in large urban markets. *The Adventures of the Wilderness Family*, for example, generated a substantial $2 million from the New York City market alone, and a total gross of $30 million – all based on a total production cost of under $2 million (Jeffries 1978: 50).

Advertising executive-turned-filmmaker Joe Camp is a particularly noteworthy figure in this period of the smaller independents muscling in on the territory of the 'major independent,' Walt Disney Productions. Camp started his career as copywriter in Houston, albeit also a frustrated screenwriter who started writing each day at 4 a.m. before going to work at the advertising agency. With cinematographer James Nicodemus and the help of seven investors, Camp formed Mulberry Square Productions in January 1971. Rather presumptuously, given their utter lack of a track record, the partners sponsored an ad in *Variety* the following August publicizing their company: 'A few years from now you probably won't remember where you first heard of Mulberry Square Productions. A sincere little outfit making some pretty big waves with some unusually nice philosophies' (*Variety* 1972: 9). His Dallas-based company eventually focused on the notion of a high quality family film. Camp claimed that the market for G had been tainted by 'four-wall fast buck distributors.' Camp said of this phenomenon: 'It has become an industry-caused thing, but the G rated classification has to some degree become "if it's G, it can't be for me"' (*Variety* 1977: 35). He claimed that the issue was not with G, but rather the low-grade family pictures presented by the four-wall companies. His solution was to make an intervention in terms of quality in the G market.

Camp's answer was a script inspired by watching Disney's *Lady and the Tramp* (Geronimi, Jackson and Luske, 1955). The idea of a live action tale told from a dog's point of view intrigued Camp (Primeau 1987: E1). Starring a mongrel named Higgins, a veteran of the TV series *Petticoat Junction, Benji* was filmed over a twelve-week period in 1973 from a script written and directed by Camp. After all of the majors (including Twentieth Century–Fox, Warner Brothers, MGM, Disney, and Paramount) turned down the film for distribution, Camp was faced only with an offer from K-Tel International, best known for aggressive mail-order record sales. Instead of acquiescing to a less than ideal alternative, Camp decided to form his own distribution company, Mulberry Square Releasing, Inc. At the time, he contended that family films were not being marketed effectively, despite the burgeoning force of four-wall family pictures:

> I'm not advocating four-wall distribution as the answer, but I am a firm believer in hardhitting grassroots promotion. I'm a firm believer in

selling a picture, as opposed to sending it down the pipelines with a few reviews and a couple of ad mats and then letting it lie there to see what happens – or, in the words of one distribution executive, letting it stand on its own two feet (quoted in Barker 1974: 28).

Camp's distribution strategy was, in fact, the opposite of four-wall distribution. Rather than 'hit-and-run' distribution, Camp wanted *Benji* to play only in the top quality first-run houses. He believed that the public knew that 'good' films play in 'good' theaters. The top quality, or 'A', theaters were dominated by the major distributors, with independents allowed little access to these most desirable theaters. Consequently, for *Benji*'s premiere Camp tried for only two theaters in the Dallas region, and ended up opening on 24 May 1974 at the North Park Cinema, then the leading theater in Dallas for the General Cinema theater chain. Camp was careful to position the film in its opening engagement as a story told through a dog's perspective, rather than as merely a kidnapping caper in which the canine saves the day. The film's souvenir program, for instance, included a section titled 'Critics Praise Benji's Acting' and, curiously, made no mention of the human actors at all. Such a positioning depended on Benji making appearances for the press so that the writers could fall in love with the mutt, and put critical guidelines aside, before their reviews were finished. As much as possible, Camp and Benji toured market-by-market doing the rounds of talk shows, radio shows and interviews. With this approach, *Benji* proved to be very successful with a rather surprising demographic: while Camp had thought that the film would be more successful in rural markets, actually *Benji* played best in urban markets and, surprisingly, with an adult to child ratio of 2 to 1 (Camp 1993: 217).

Rather than compromise on this strategy, Camp took the somewhat unusual stand of withdrawing the film from distribution at the end of the summer rather than risk lower grosses in the less desirable fall season. By the end of the 1974 summer, *Benji* had amassed $5 million on his initial investment of $500,000 to make the film. Strategizing during the intervening months, Camp was able to re-open *Benji* on 4 June 1975 to even stronger grosses – around $12 million by the end of July, most amazingly half of which was derived from repeat runs in either the same theaters or the same towns as the year before (Jacobson 1975: 12). Even in markets like New York, with a history of low family film grosses, Camp was able to develop a grassroots marketing approach for *Benji*. With no bookings forthcoming, Camp bought a *New York Times* ad heralding the arrival of *Benji* to New York. The audacity of the ad (after all, Camp did not even have a New York booking for the film) caught the interest of Norman Elison, owner of the Guild Theater. When the film set box-office records at the Guild, Elison asked Camp to allow him to play the film for a year (Bender 1975: E1). Through the same careful market-by-market sales approach, *Benji* eventually built to a $46 million

Figure 17.2 Publicity still of Benji (Camp, 1974).

worldwide gross. Ironically, Camp borrowed his final distribution tactic from veteran Disney: he intended to withdraw the film from distribution and re-release it seven years later, just like the Disney animated classics.

Camp followed *Benji* with a series of family films: *Hawmps* (1976), a western based on the first camel cavalry, the inevitable sequel, *For the Love of Benji* (1977), and the suspense thriller *The Double McGuffin* (1979). With the exception of the *Benji* sequel, Camp's other films were financial disappointments. Realizing the franchise appeal of *Benji*, by the end of the decade Camp was in the difficult position of feeling alienated from the market he had helped to identify and exploit. As Camp explained in 1978:

> You see, back in 1974 part of *Benji's* success was timing. So many producers had jumped into the hard PG and R film that the public was ready for a film they could enjoy as a family. Today I think the pendulum has started to swing back to more family-type movies, but society has changed and the rating code has splintered audiences (quoted in Jeffries 1978: 54).

Rather than maintain *Benji* as a family franchise, Camp made the bold, and ultimately foolish, move of trying to extend 'Benji' into 'adult' comedy – matching him with Chevy Chase, Jane Seymour and Omar Sharif in the PG-rated *Oh, Heavenly*

Dog! (1980). Watching Benji jump into Jane Seymour's bubble bath while Chevy Chase offered leering voice-over apparently had limited appeal – the film was an utter critical and financial failure. Camp was unable to resurrect *Benji* until 1987, with the family oriented *Benji the Hunted*, distributed by Disney's Buena Vista Productions (Summers 1987: 16).

Independent lessons from a maverick and a mutt

Thirty years on, the landscape of independent film has changed so irrevocably that the value of these two case studies might seem limited. Nevertheless, the contributions of Scott and Camp to marketing and distribution have rippled throughout the independent world over the years. Scott's careful manipulation of the MPAA ratings and the perceived inequities of ratings for independents vs. majors have been replicated several times over the ensuing years. Miramax's Weinstein brothers maximized the publicity of challenging the X rating for *The Cook, the Thief, His Wife and Her Lover* (Greenaway, 1989) and *Tie Me Up! Tie Me Down!* (Almódovar, 1989). Disingenuously, the brothers in the end chose to release both films unrated. Despite this final decision, Miramax foregrounded the X in the advertising of *The Cook* by using a quote from *Time*'s Richard Corliss – ' "X" as in excellent, exciting, exemplary and extraordinary' – with a shot of a scantily clad Helen Mirren (Wyatt 1998: 80).

Similarly, the identification and exploitation of a market underserved by the majors has been a venerable independent tactic many times since Camp's *Benji* family market strategy. Consider, for instance, the relative success of *Go Fish* (Troche, 1994), a black-and-white 16mm art film that tapped into the almost ignored lesbian market: on a cost of only $15,000, the film grossed $2.4 million domestically. Producer Christine Vachon employed the same strategy as Camp – realizing that the so-called 'Queer Cinema' explosion was primarily a male phenomenon, Vachon seized on the chance of releasing a film for the lesbian market (Hirschberg 1997: 104).

Nevertheless, even with these parallels, the possibility of another Joe Camp or George C. Scott shifting the 'rules' of independent film distribution is increasingly unlikely. The ability to *re-invent* independent cinema has become much less pressing as independent cinema has been institutionalized over the past three decades. Despite the impact of both Scott and Camp, by the 1990s there was less room for the entrepreneur or innovator in the independent film world – and much less need – due, in part, to the shifting definition of independent film in that decade. Today 'independent film' is a veritable catch phrase, and the parameters bounding it are increasingly elastic: witness the rise of video stores classifying titles under 'independent cinema' instead of the older rubric of 'art cinema,' video selections in the Book-of-the-Month Club gathered under the umbrella 'independents day,' and, of course, the development and public awareness of film festivals and cable channels devoted to independent film.

Many critics trace the birth of this enthusiasm to Steven Soderbergh's breakthrough commercial success *sex, lies & videotape* in 1989. A more crucial turning point for public awareness of independent film may have been the 1996 Oscar race, with four of the five 'Best Picture' nominees – *The English Patient* (Minghella), *Fargo* (Coen and Coen), *Secrets & Lies* (Leigh), *Shine* (Hicks) – released by independents. *Variety* proclaimed 'Oscar Rings in New Era of Indie Chic,' while *Time* also adopted the title of 'Independents Day,' subtitling their story: 'With 20 Oscar nominations, the Weinsteins of Miramax are leading a small revolution' (Corliss and Harbinger 1997: 62). After that point, independent cinema was branded by journalists and the independent companies' publicity and marketing departments as an attractive way to signify creativity, vision, and innovation. A small marker of this branding and the capacity of independent film to embody transgressive behavior can be seen in the rather hyperbolic reaction to Monica Lewinsky, en route to her Senate testimony hearing in January 1999, wearing a cap emblazoned with 'TSG' for the independent film production company The Shooting Gallery. After appearing on the cover of the *New York Times*, The Shooting Gallery received 'hundreds of phone calls asking for the cap.' Of course, representatives of TSG were quick to add that caps could be purchased for $17 on the company's website (*Entertainment Weekly* 1999: 14).

The public and the media focus on independent film has created a marketplace in which the separation between the independent and the commercial has largely dissolved. In his discussion of the terminology (avant-garde, experimental, personal, individual, and independent films) surrounding non-Hollywood production, Jonas Mekas suggested that the most distinctive characteristic separating independent film from Hollywood was commercial: he described formally experimental independent films as non-commercial and of appeal to only limited audiences. Inverting the usual terms of the debate, Mekas claimed further: 'It's the commercial film that is on the margins of the art of the cinema and that needs a proper and clear term to describe it' (1978: 39). In locating the key determinant of independent film as a lack of commitment to a commercial imperative, Mekas anticipates a key shift on the part of contemporary critics, many of whom believe that the independent film of the 1990s became *the* commercial category helping to save Hollywood. This fascination derives from the increased publicity around the term 'independent cinema' and from the structural ties between the majors and independent film distributors. Perhaps even more significant is the raising of the box-office 'bar' for independent films – from *sex, lies & videotape* to *The Crying Game* (Jordan, 1992) to *Pulp Fiction* (Tarantino, 1994) to *The Blair Witch Project* (Myrick–Sánchez, 1999). All of these were, of course, produced at a fraction of the cost of a typical Hollywood feature.

With independent cinema becoming more and more oriented around commercial concerns and, indeed, becoming a commercial marketing category in itself, the possibilities of shifting distribution and marketing in the manner of Scott or Camp are rather remote. While independent cinema has relied on the entrepreneurs and the visionaries, both artistically and commercially, in the current environment they are much less significant – independent cinema can support itself through its own marketing apparatus by arguing, however tenuously, that 'independent' is superior to studio output. Ultimately, as James Schamus (2001: 253) suggests, the economics of independents are merely 'studio economics' at this point. Consequently, 'innovation' in marketing and distribution is just as likely to be derived from the majors as from the independents. With this apparent complacency and sense of 'belonging,' aspiring independents should not forget the lessons from a maverick and a mutt from thirty years ago – independent film should also be searching for new ways to enter the marketplace, challenging business norms just as much as aesthetic and social ones. Only through such an agenda will independent cinema have long-lasting commercial impact.

Bibliography

Barker, B. (1974) ' "Benji" Prod. Asserts Family Pix Can Be Sold; Forms Distrib Co,' *Variety*, 5 June: 28.

Bender, M. (1975) 'Benji: A Doghouse Hero,' *New York Times*, 31 August: E1.

Camp, J. (1993) *Underdog*, Marietta, GA: Longstreet Press.

Cocks, J. (1971) 'George C. Scott: Tempering a Terrible Fire,' *Time*, 22 March: 63–8.

Corliss, R. and Harbison, G. (1997) 'Independents' Day,' *Time*, 149, 8: 62–6.

Davis, S. (1980) 'Wishing upon a Falling Star at Disney,' *New York Times*, 16 November: 144–52.

Entertainment Weekly (1999) 'Head's Up,' 5 February: 14.

Harris, H. (1974) Column, *Variety*, 13 November: 26.

Hirschberg, L. (1997) 'The Producers: Lawrence Gordon/Christine Vachon,' *New York Times Magazine*, 16 November: 104–6.

Houston Chronicle (1975) Advertisement for *The Savage Is Loose*, Digest, 12 January: 25.

Jacobson, H. (1975) 'Benji and Three Dallas Guys Thrive with Indie Film Against Major-Ruled Topmost Tracks,' *Variety*, 30 July: 12.

Jeffries, G. (1978) 'The Problem with G,' *American Film*, June: 50–7.

Kael, P. (1974) 'Review of *The Savage Is Loose*,' *New Yorker*, 25 November: 183.

McBride, J. (1974) 'George C. Scott Excoriates MPAA on His *Savage Is Loose*; Tells Exhibs to Ignore Rating,' *Variety*, 9 October: 5.

Mekas, J. (1978) 'Independence for Independents,' *American Film*, September: 39.

Moses, R. (1975) 'The Rise, Fall and Second Coming of Four-Walling,' *Variety*, 8 January: 22.

Murf. (1974) 'Review of *The Savage Is Loose*,' *Variety*, 16 October: 14.

Murphy, A.D. (1974) 'Code Ratings Analysis Since '68: Self-Imposed X's Outside Record,' *Variety*, 6 November: 30.

Primeau, M. (1987) 'High Profile: Joe Camp,' *Dallas Morning News*, 17 May: E1–3.

Pryor, T. (1974) 'George C. Scott Cuts Off Distribs at Pass,' *Variety*, 15 May: 48.

Schamus, J. (2001) 'A Rant,' in J. Lewis (ed.) *The End of Cinema as We Know It*, New York: New York University Press: 253–60.

Schickel, R. (1970) 'Whatever Became of the Family Movie?' *Life*, 11 September: 10.

—— (1973) 'The Films: No Longer for the Jung at Heart,' *Time*, 30 July: 65.

Summers, J. (1987) 'Benji's Back and Disney's Got Him,' *Boxoffice*, June: 16–17.

Time (1973) 'Disney After Walt Is a Family Affair,' 30 July: 64.

—— (1977) 'G Is for Gold,' 3 January: 74.

Variety (1966) '"Classification" by Indies?' 31 August: 7.

—— (1968) '"Ratings" an All-Things Thing,' 18 September: 5.

—— (1969a) 'X Marks the Spot (Self-Interest),' 28 April: 3.

—— (1969b) 'Valenti Sez Sex Becoming Old Hat in Pix, but There's No Family Aud,' 15 October: 3.

—— (1970) 'Hollywood Indies Mutter that Code Is More Strict Against MPAA Outsiders,' 6 September: 23.

—— (1972) Mulberry Square Productions advertisement, 9 August: 29.

—— (1974a) 'All Kinds, Qualities of Pics Under R, Heffner Re: Scott,' 30 October: 7.

—— (1974b) 'Scott's Refund Offer Latest Ploy in Feud Over Savage; Catholic Echo of MPAA Rating,' 6 November: 64.

—— (1974c) 'Protestants Rue "Rule-Breaker" George C. Scott as to MPAA Tag,' 13 November: 26.

—— (1974d) 'Arkoff Berates Scott's "Anarchy,"' 9 October: 5.

—— (1974e) 'Disrespects Paid Scott by Levine,' 13 November: 26.

—— (1977) 'Camp Guesses That "G" Rating Is Carrying Goody-Goody Stigma,' 6 July: 35.

Weiler, A.H. (1962) 'George C. Scott Declines an Oscar Nomination,' *New York Times*, 6 March: 31.

Wyatt, J. (1998) 'The Formation of the "Major Independent": Miramax, New Line, and the New Hollywood,' in S. Neale and M. Smith (eds.), *Contemporary Hollywood Cinema*, New York: Routledge: 74–90.

Chapter 18

Digital deployment(s)

Patricia R. Zimmermann

Deployments

In the twenty-first century, the term 'independent film' requires a serious over-haul and a cogent updating. Digital interfaces, platforms, technologies, and pro-grams both continue older entertainment industry economic models, with its focus on distribution–exhibition, and also open up new formations such as online festivals, Flash, and streaming that reconfigure the relationship between shorts and the feature-film industry. In a multiplatformed media landscape that spans film, video, broadcasting, video on demand, satellite, CD ROM games, and the inter-net, the divisions between technologies are blurred as works migrate between different platforms, with different interfaces. This migration of media productions across technologies, where the transnational media corporations function as dis-tributors–exhibitors rather than producers, has also blurred the borders and debates that defined the term 'independent film' in the previous thirty years: it is not so easy to draw a line between dominant and oppositional, profit and non-profit, film and video, analog and digital, as it might have been in 1974. A quarter of a century ago, independent media could be identified through its structural, aesthetic, and ideological differences from corporate media: oppositional, polit-ical, non-profit, different voices, different aesthetic strategies, new narrative structures.

Now, independent film forms a vital part of the entertainment industry as a way to outsource risk, innovation, and project development. As a result of con-centration, conglomeration, and risk aversion, the transnational media corporate economy has increasingly utilized a more horizontal, business model based on exploiting this transindustrial and transtechnological environment where flexi-bility is achieved through outsourcing production and where production costs are reduced through endless repurposing of archives into different platforms. Media in all forms, whether corporate or independent or oppositional, now functions in circulatory networks typified by constant movement between platforms, between users, and between different economies of scale such as big-budget tentpole films, independent features, and digital shorts. The independent film sector has transformed into a vital part of the transnational entertainment industry, integral to both innovation and to outsourcing risk to achieve higher profit margins.

This chapter attempts a very provisional redefinition of independent film by triangulating four intersecting salient formations of exhibition within this trans-industrial economy. In each case I look at how independent narrative modes interact with and depend on new formations within this new, complex, multilayered, digital environment. In what follows, I examine:

- the interdependence that exists between the media transnationals and the independent film sector;
- the reinstitution of exhibition as a major feature of the transnational media sector's retailing of media products;
- Flash animation as an extremely pervasive software program unique to the web as well as streaming technologies as sites to look at how the digital conflates production, distribution and exhibition; and
- how digital distribution may provide more access for independents through point to point exhibition practices.

Each of these four sectors provides different altitudes from which to assess the changes in distribution and exhibition as the analog and digital combine. Each of these sectors demonstrates that independent narrative film needs to perhaps be rethought as a form of cinema that moves across different platforms and through different audiences and economies, rather than the more static model of a feature-length film on celluloid that plays in theaters and film festivals. They also help us to understand the impact and realignments new digital technologies precipitate in the indie landscape, offering a contradictory environment of increased concentration mixed with increased access. Flash and streaming, as two digital modalities unique to digital networked media of the internet, are important because they help to chart the imagined broadening of the indie scene from features to shorts. These two technologies also suggest how the retail aspect of film exhibition is not only multiplatformed across analog and digital interfaces but multiple in terms of how it addresses spectators as either groups or individuals sitting at their computer terminals.

This new horizontally networked universe that sprawls between the analog world of theaters and the digital domains of online festivals, Flash and streaming presents an overwhelmingly vast landscape that is simultaneously global, regional, local, and individual. One way to track its operations and practices is to focus on how the events of September 11 and the subsequent war on terror have been represented by independent filmmakers. These digital interfaces offer a rapid response to world events, where media artists can enlist digital platforms as means by which to insert their point of view into the horizontal circulatory networks of transnational media practices, a major difference from previous political events like the Gulf War, the civil wars in Central America, or the Vietnam War where the independent media networks worked in opposition to the absences of the dominant media by creating different networks of production and distribution that often operated like parallel universes to the entertainment industry.

Although a feature-length narrative on the events and responses of September 11 in the US has yet to emerge, many media artists have produced a variety of documentary and experimental shorts to memorialize the trauma of the attack and the ensuing war on terror, such as curator Jay Rosenblatt's *Underground Zero* (2002) project, a four-hour compilation of short narrative, documentary, and experimental media artists responses to the World Trade Center and Pentagon bombings. The enlistment of these digital interfaces – by both anti-war and pro-war movements – demonstrates how digital technologies together with net-worked communications can offer rapid response to world events within the circulatory networks via Flash animation, streaming, and websites. But we must not read these new technologies and new interfaces as simply new ways for progressive voices and cultural difference to be heard. As this discussion shows, these technologies have also functioned as a kind of a return of the repressed, expressing racism and xenophobia prohibited in corporate multiculturalized domains of the commercial media, a warning to media theorists to avoid investing political hope in technologies as opposed to social and political movements.

'Dependies'

A significant reorganization between the American independent film movement and the corporate entertainment industry happened in the 1990s as mergers created media corporations with economies larger than many nations'. It is important to unpack the new relationship between the independent film sector and the transnational media sector in order to begin to see how this horizontal business model has created more fluid, less bounded, exchanges between different economic sectors of media production. With the advent of digital video (DV), it would appear that anyone can make a feature, a fantasy of a newly democratized realm of previously inaccessible feature production that enlisted lightweight, small, digital technology.

In the early twenty-first century, the independent film scene in the US has morphed into a multifaceted, diverse sector of the entertainment economy. In the decades since *The War at Home* (Brown and Silber, 1979) and *Northern Lights* (Hanson and Nilsson, 1978) utilized a four-walling theatrical exhibition strategy, the independent film scene has grown exponentially. It defines American film, and operates as a testing ground for new technologies like video, digital video, streaming, gaming, and digital interfaces. DV is viewed as providing low-cost access to democratize the means of film production, with many feature-length narratives and documentaries produced in this format and then dumped to 35mm for distribution, like Lars von Trier's *Dancer in the Dark* (2000) or Mike Figgis's *Time Code* (1999). In the independent feature realm, DV productions have increased significantly: at the 2000 Independent Feature Film Market, 43 percent of the works were DV (Cheever 2000).

DV is often designated – at least in the DV magazines[1] – as a new technology lowering the barriers to entry to make independents competitive with the studios and networks. However, the history of amateur media technologies suggests that although low-end technologies extend production beyond corporations, larger social and economic contexts interlace with these technologies to create significant contradictions (Zimmermann 1995). On the one hand, DV is cheaper and of lighter weight than 35mm Panavision; on the other hand, the transnational media corporations exert a stranglehold: as global cartels, they cordon off access to distribution and exhibition because they own every form of interface, from theaters, video stores, DVD, cable, and even internet portals (Miller *et al.* 2001: 146–71). No matter how many DV cameras circulate and how many new film festivals sprout up, capacity to compete against this massive global distribution oligopoly in terms of print costs, marketing, advertising, and product tie-ins is chimerical.

With foreign films and art cinemas in precipitous decline due to multiplexing and increased nationalizing of exhibition, independent exhibitors call American indie films 'art films without subtitles.' According to Kenneth Turan (2002) fewer foreign language films unspool on American screens than at any time in US history. Yet, compared to two decades ago, more independent films screen in former art cinemas than ever before. Film festivals – functioning more and more as alternative exhibition networks – have mushroomed, with almost every major city in the US hosting one (*ibid.*: 31–48, 160–8). Rather than thinking in terms of binary oppositions of corporate entertainment versus indie films – a hangover from the 1970s' vision of dominant and alternative media – it might be more structurally illuminating to move towards a metaphor of a 3D integrated digital structure, with constantly moving, interdependent layers.

In a vertically and horizontally integrated entertainment economy (in finance, organization, integration, and operation), indies serve a dual purpose: on the one hand, they are the farm team for entry to the majors – and big money as a director/producer; on the other hand, the indie discourse of entertainment shrouds its acquisitive careerism in its *outré* status. Much indie narrative flaunts its character development and represses digital imaging that so defines the visual look of contemporary media – but not the digital tools like DV, Avids, Final Cut Pro. In opposition to the plot-less, special effects-laden, blockbuster tentpole film with marketing tie-ins, like *Minority Report* (Spielberg, 2002) or *Spider-Man* (Raimi, 2002), indie narrative film sustains the myth that characters, dialogue, and narrative actually matter, a reactionary specter of the golden age of Hollywood where studio-based writers and directors created films with real actors, dialogue, and plot.

However, a digital divide exists in the entertainment industry between transnational corporate technological innovation for global market domination and independent feature production. According to *Variety*, digitality assumes two forms in the entertainment industry. Virtually all special effects in major studio productions are digital. Cost savings and labor management factors to control the post-production process are attractive to studio financial analysts. The studios have deployed digital technology primarily for post production and special effects, solidifying corporate control and protecting their global market through high barriers to entry. Historically, studios viewed technological innovation in terms of profit maximization. Digital special effects continue this trajectory. For independent features, DV operates, according to *Variety*, as a grassroots movement for access to low-budget narrative. Thomas Vinterberg (*The Celebration*, 2002), Gary Winick (*Tadpole*, 2002), Steven Soderbergh, and Spike Lee accentuate emotional realism with DV (Bing 2002b: 1, 24).

Transnational entertainment complexes have been reorganized into global distribution entities operating across technologies. In this context, independent narrative film outsources production risk and cultivates new talent and product without investment. A recent article in *Variety* detailing the deal between James Schamus of Good Machine (the indie art-film producer of *The Ice Storm* [Lee, 1997], and *Crouching Tiger, Hidden Dragon* [Lee, 2000]) and Universal to form a new entity called Focus points out that:

> major studios continue to invest in the specialty arena and not just for the prestige factor. At a time when production and marketing costs are spiraling upwards, they're nixing midrange pics in favor of event films that cost more than $80 million and nice films that cost less than $10 million, many of which come with foreign financing and minimal risk (Bing 2002a: 1).

Because media transnationals hit niche markets through low-budget indie film and because no independent feature can recoup costs without corporate distribution, *Variety* mused that indies are the new 'dependies' (Lyons 2002: 1, 11).

But beyond distribution deals for niche fare, a more variegated independent film political economy has evolved over the last decade. This new rapidly changing eco-system is not easy to track. My argument is that the independent scene has to be more *interdependent* than the trade papers suggest to begin to provisionally plot the relationships between corporate media, independent ventures, new exhibition formations, new technologies and the public media sector. Neither the hyperbole of the incipient online democratic vistas nor 'end of cinemas as we know it' negativity sufficiently understands the relationship between digitality and independent cinema.

In this second decade, digitalization solidifies older transnational media formations but also offers new public media possibilities. Thus, the independent media sector has changed significantly from the late 1970s. Twenty years ago, indies fought to gain access to public television and screens, public monies supported production and infrastructure, and independent meant oppositional to dominant culture.

The indie scene combines both commercial and non-profit media, ranging from films produced by fêted art-cinema directors like Jane Campion, Sam Mendes, Todd Haynes, Ang Lee to low-end digital video/streaming features like *The Last Broadcast* (Avalos and Weiler, 1998), the first film to be digitally exhibited (www.tebweb.com/lastbroadcast). Political documentaries employing new digital technologies are self-distributed through websites such as *Zapatista*, *This Is What Democracy Looks Like* and *9/11 (2001)* from the Big Noise Film Collective (www.bignoisefilms.com). Short three-minute live action and Flash animation works crowd online film festivals. A range of political and experimental work in documentary, narrative, and hybrid forms also migrate across technologies and distribution platforms. The lines of demarcation between these quite different filmic practices, however, are fluid. For example, the Independent Television Service (ITVS) and HBO, a subsidiary of AOL – Time Warner financed a large number of award-winning features and documentaries at the prestigious 2002 Sundance Film Festival.[2]

Consequently, it is misleading to navigate the independent film scene with terms like profit/not-for-profit, film/video, or analog/digital. New technologies, distribution platforms, political communities, and fluidity between formerly distinct sectors have erased these binaries. The online film festival world provides a case study. Parodies of commercial media ranging from *Star Wars* (Lucas, 1977) to almost any mainstream release have emerged as a salient genre online, suggesting that binary oppositions are no longer usefully descriptive. Instead, all media productions – even independent film – repurpose and remediate themselves across a range of formats, interfaces, and forms for various niche market segments across multiplatformed media environments.

Retail

Exhibition forms an important node for an analysis of the shifting terrain of independent film in relation to digitality. Despite the mass-produced fantasies

Figure 18.1 Website for www.bignoisefilms.com. Courtesy of www.bignoisefilms.com.

manufactured by film schools and film magazines that production is the most exciting and important part of the independent film world, exhibition has, since the early days of the film studios, been the economic powerhouse of the entertainment industry, producing profit. With the infusion of digital platforms in the 1990s and the early twenty-first century, exhibition platforms have also multiplied beyond the brick-and-mortar hard-top theaters in multiplexes into DVD, VCD, and internet-based festivals which deliver point-to-point access to media. Although digital delivery within the context of the transnational media industry is still unclear and still forming, there is no question that the industry's interest in broadband is directly connected to its knowledge of the importance of multiple exhibition venues.

Film exhibition is the retail end of the film business. With twenty-first century convergence and proliferating analog and digital platforms, film exhibition is no longer about selling movies in a theater – films are no longer the end product. Rather, films are the nodal points of circulating commodities: *Variety* refers to the James Bond films as a 'franchise' product; large blockbusters with product tie-ins are dubbed 'tentpoles.' The difference between a studio production and an independent production resides no longer in production values, narrative structure, or casting, but in distribution, exhibition, marketing, and product tie-ins. The major studios are massive marketing machines insuring global product domination, tie-ins and screens, while independent works are simply films, confined to limited distribution and exhibition. Within this economy, the short films of the late 1990s' boom were simultaneously calling-card films and 18–34-year-old white male niche marketing.

Digital technologies like Flash animation, DV and streaming blur the borders between production, distribution, and exhibition. Although digital technologies lower distribution and exhibition barriers, they are plagued by moving-image compression for streaming, limited broadband access, and slow downloads. However, these technical limitations have stimulated short film internet exhibition: three-minute films load faster and conform better to internet surfing. The short film environment should not be confused with art cinema, the avant-garde, or underground film, however: it is more congruent with pop songs and popular culture (Sterritt 2000: 13). As Dion Algeri (2000) of the now defunct www.shortbuzz.com has argued, internet films not only appeal to teenage boys, but serve as anti-TV entertainment, focusing on sex, violence, and humor unsuitable for commercial TV or cable.

The online festival sector is distinct from the independent film festival circuit. It focuses almost exclusively on shorts of under three minutes, adapting to technological limitations and reception issues unique to computing. Although the online sites feature primarily work by unknown directors without studio affiliation, many feature-film directors like Spike Lee, James Brooks, David Lynch, Tim Burton, Barry Sonnenfield, and Mike Figgis have directed works specifically for the online environment, their cult status providing a marketing cachet to these sites (Houston 2000).

Most significantly, the online cinema business models illustrate the intertwining of independent work and commercial trans-national studios, as well as digital and analog exhibition. Atom Films not only runs shorts online, but sells them to HBO, Warner Bros., Continental Airlines, Blockbuster, and the Sundance Channel. The company has worked with Lucasfilm to encourage fans to submit *Star Wars* spoofs on their site without fear of cease-and-desist letters (Webdale 2001). However, it would be misleading to characterize Atom Films as a stand-alone independent: although it functions like an old media studio with distribution to a variety of markets, it operates more like a 'dependie.' Warner Bros., merchant bank Allen & Company, and former Viacom and Universal Studios CEO Frank Biondi provided financial backing (Harding 1999). Ifilm (www.ifilm.com), a prominent online cinema site, moved from San Francisco to Los Angeles in 2000, financed by Microsoft Corporation billionaire Paul Allen,

Sony, Kodak Corporation, and Shamrock Capital Advisors, the investment vehicle
for Roy O. Disney (Miller 2000).

As many scholars of exhibition have argued, exhibition constitutes the retail
end of the film business, the place where people meet the screen and money
meets the film business at the point of sale. Film exhibition is one of the only
capitalist products where the customer pays in advance before using the commodity (Waller 2002; Gomery 1992). However, according to Janet Wasko (1994), in
the post-merger environments of the late 1990s, exhibition, distribution, and
exhibition across different technologies, platforms and spaces are the key to media
trans-national economic power. On the one hand, digital technology's ease of
lossless reproduction presents a major threat to copyright, currently the largest
US export (Siwek 2000). On the other hand, digitalization of production in
Hollywood big-budget production has augmented labor power for producers who
can control the image in post production and reduce labor costs.

Aida Hozic (2002) has argued that the historiography of Hollywood's entertainment industry can be reconceptualized as a relationship between space and
power, rather than simply product differentiation. She identifies three periods of
Hollywood hegemony: Hollywood in the Studio; Hollywood on Location; and
Hollywood in Cyberspace. Hozic's theorizing of a political economy of the entertainment industry has moved from an analysis of industry practices such as business operations, film aesthetics, marketing, and reception towards the specificity
of spatial relations as material mappings of hegemonic power. Spatial relationship
'defines the boundaries of what is private and what is public; what is visible and
what is concealed, of what is imagined and what is real,' marking 'the boundaries
of politics' (ibid.: 27).

The studio period featured mass production, controlled environments, social
control of actors, self-regulation, censorship, surveillance, and the Fordist structures of the vertically integrated major studio. The location period signaled a shift
towards more dispersed locales for more horizontally integrated firms post-
Second World War due to increased labor costs, the 1948 Paramount decrees,
crisis in export markets, and the rise of agents in the 1950s and 1960s. For Hozic,
the third period of Hollywood hegemony, Hollywood in Cyberspace, marks a
distinct shift away from location to cyberspace, where Hollywood and the military
merge in digital technologies for special effects, now dubbed 'dual purpose' technologies for both civilian and military usage. She argues that the entertainment
industry's digital conversions arose out of conflict between producers on the one
hand and financiers, distributors and agents on the other. For example, George
Lucas and Steven Spielberg were early adopters of digital technologies in the
science-fiction realm, a genre the studios ignored. They asserted producers' rights
by replacing stars with digital special effects. They spurred industry digitalization
by demonstrating how digital effects render unnecessary the most expensive part

of the production process (sets, costumes, stunts, location shooting). Following Wasko, Hozic emphasizes that the 'Hollywood in Cyberspace' period is organized around distribution rather than production technologies (*ibid.*: 133–63).

Although theatrical digital exhibition appears to be years away, given high conversion costs, home digital projection has advanced at record rates with the accelerated penetration of DVD. New technologies are not so much a threat to celluloid as they are indications of the almost exponential multiplication of exhibition into many formats. Consequently, the much-heralded possibilities of DV to lower barriers to entry into commercial production may be exaggerated, despite increasing numbers of DV works blown up to 35mm, as evidenced at the 2002 Sundance Film Festival. Despite the proliferation of DV, the large media transnationals still control the retail end of the business in all sectors, making it difficult for any kind of independent filmmaker to penetrate (Miller *et al.* 2001: 146–71).

In public media outside the domains of the corporate media transnationals – the universities, media arts centers, museums, film festivals that promote public culture and artistic/intellectual exchange rather than commodity exchange – digital conversion has challenged production, distribution, and exhibition. A major Ford Foundation study sponsored by the National Alliance for Media Arts and Culture (NAMAC) called *Digital Directions: Conversion Planning for the Media Arts* (2000) convened independent producers and public media programmers from across the country to debate the impact of digital conversion on the independent sector. Because technologies change so rapidly and the start-up costs are so expensive, technological change threatens to further destabilize the chronically underfunded public media sector.

Media arts organizations now confront shifts from their former mission to show work not typically accessible in commercial culture and to provide media services to the underserved. Their missions have broadened from aesthetics and access to media to more hybrid sources of education and training in new technologies for underserved communities. The digital divide refers to more than just equipment: it now signifies access to digital and computer knowledge. Partnerships and collaborations are necessary. Consequently, new digital economies for the public media sector may require development of public–private partnerships. Further, networked communications creates fluidities between local, national, and global organizations. New infrastructures for broadband, servers and routes for interactive communications need to be developed (*ibid.*). In the new independent media environment, the boundaries between public and private, between digital and analog, and between production and distribution are twisted together, creating new unexplored territories for independent production.

In the new media environment, the construct of the director making an artisanal work is perhaps as outdated as the Fordist feature-film production line in

Hollywood. Horizontally organized teams, cross-fertilization between people with different skills and knowledge, flexible and fluid organizational models, and multiple distribution and exhibition modes have mutated the independent media landscape from the film–video product to a multiplicity of iterations and interfaces in a range of exhibition environments (*ibid.*: 69–81).

The media trans-nationals have been slow to enter the online or by-demand digital sector because of limited broadband access. However, a major legislative and political battle is unfolding between independent producers, media activists and the Federal Communications Commission over two central issues: media concentration, which limits the diversity of voices and opportunities for independents as rulings on ownership are revoked; and media trans-nationals, particularly cable companies', entry into broadband, which threatens open access and unlimited, uncensored voices on the internet. The American Civil Liberties Union (ACLU) and the Center for Digital Democracy have argued that 'broadband is the free speech issue of the 21st century' (Zimmermann 2002: 7). Independent producers, scholars, media reformers, and media activists have formed broad-based coalitions to fight concentration and cable companies' broadband control which narrow outlets for independents and inhibit a diversity of viewpoints as they advance corporate monoculture.[3]

Flash wars

While online festivals for independent analog shorts that have been digitized have presented a new exhibition formation within the digital networks for independent shorts' producers, another digital formation in exhibition is emerging that conflates production and distribution into a software created specifically to bypass the reality of slow downloads for moving images on the internet as broadband is debated: Flash. Flash appears on almost every website where images move; it is one of the most pervasive software systems on the internet. Most importantly, the quick downloads of Flash works and their ability to circulate virally through email networks have functioned as an important manifestation of the independent media response to the war on terror. They allow for a rapid response to events utilizing point-to-point peer networks circulated through forwarded emails and online websites that serve as portals.

One to three minutes long to adjust to streaming capabilities, online films frequently use Flash animation with easily downloadable files. Atomfilms.com, ifilms.com and madblast.com offer independently produced racist shorts about Osama Bin Laden, the war in Afghanistan, the war against terror, and Arabs. The war on terror and patriotism have transformed into speciality narrow-casting markets that parallel the lesbian, gay, sci-fi, comedy, and movie-spoof genres that proliferate in online indie short film sites. Bin Laden, Al Qaeda and the Taliban are not only enemies of the US, but distinctive genres with identifiable characteristics and narrative patterns in online environments. Many of these shorts mobilize a revengeful–jingoistic patriotism. They install an America versus the other narrative structure. They demonize Arabs, the Middle East, the Taliban, and Osama Bin Laden as inept primitives. They visualize Bush's and Rumsfeld's covert racialized revenge fantasies that heads of state are unable to state.

Slow downloads, lack of general availability of broadband, and problems transferring between platforms and different software applications plague both studio websites pumping up blockbuster anticipation and indie online festivals. Flash animation software resolves the problem of creating moving-image media with sound in this transitional digital environment. Flash is vector-based on mathematical formulas rather than pixels, facilitating easy download. It can transfer between the internet, mobile phones, movie screens, broadcast, and gaming platforms (Delgado 2002).

Unlike video, Flash streams better over a modem because it is not compressed and has infinite resolution. It was designed specifically for the internet in order to provide the most television-like appearance (Sachs and Fox 2002). It was shown at the 1995 Siggraph Conference, an annual gathering of computer artists and animators, and sold to Future Wave Software and then Macromedia in 1996. Currently, Macromedia Flash is the most distributed software in the history of the internet, with 96 percent of web desktops using some Flash;[4] Flash appears on many commercial websites. It has also attracted an underground cult following among college students, office workers' and political activists.

Flash animations tend towards bawdy comedy and visual jokes. Using bold primary colors and simple drawings, Flash does not lend itself easily to social realist documentaries or complex argumentation. Its strength lies in making things move with bare-bones narrative causality, with music for affect. The software was designed to attract PC surfers. Much Flash animation on the internet is humorous. Some more conceptual, artistic work such as pieces produced by freerangegraphics.com for progressive political groups like Greenpeace and the ACLU has emerged to great impact. Many Flash animators, such as freerangegraphics.com or Mark Fiore, originate from graphic design and political cartooning. Flash animation's flat images differs significantly from the commercial digital animation of *Toy Story* (Lasseter, 1995) or *Antz* (Darnell and Johnson, 1998), which continue tropes of cinematic realism and immediacy through 3D modeling, depth, texture, lighting, and an adherence to narrative cinematic language in shot design and story editing (Manovich 1997: 5–15).

War on terror Flash animations represent the most recent iteration of wartime Hollywood propaganda animation. During the Second World War, when most studio production was aligned with the US Government, Warner Bros.' animations applied a similar reductionist–simplistic schemata to mobilize patriotic goals in Bugs Bunny and Daffy Duck wartime cartoons. Frank Capra's 1943 *Prelude to War* utilized Disney animation of black ink spreading across the globe to illustrate Axis expansion (Barnouw 1983: 139–72; Schatz 1988: 297–407).

Flash animations about the war on terror remediate historical propaganda modes to marshal pro-nationalist sentiment. Bolter and Grusin (2000) define remediation as reprocessing and incorporating legacy media into digital works for critical intervention or refashioning. Remediation invokes the real with emotional responses and repression of interface. Remediation resides less in postmodern surface play than in repurposing older, more analog, media forms (Bolter and Grusin 2000: 20–80). Flash animations about the war on terror repurpose nineteenth-century flat graphic newspaper-style cartoons and re-enlist classical Hollywood narrative structure from Second World War studio cartoons. The films simplify complex geopolitics into a reductionist narrative, and, although addressing the current crisis, they stimulate an emotional response by reprocessing historical propaganda forms from the war. However, their interactive, privatized, multimedia distribution platforms suggest that their exhibition interface rather than their software distinguishes them as digital works.

The most pro-war, anti-Arab, narratives have appeared on Madblast.com, a flash animation portal. Unlike a conventional four-wall theater, Madblast Flash movies arrive on your computer in viral interfaces to create wide market diffusion through personal networks. Each Flash piece ends with an option to forward to a friend by clicking a box and inserting an email address. Most Madblast Flash animations are two-minute-long visual jokes about sex, violence, bodily functions or gender stereotypes, with titles like *Beefcake for the Ladies*, *Mona Lisa's Naughty Secret*, *The Groovin' Granny Song*, *Sending You Some Crap*, *Let's Be Naughty Like Adam and Eve*.

The war on terror has supplied Madblast with a cartoon cast of characters – Osama Bin Laden, Al Qaeda, and the Taliban. Anti-Bin Laden and anti-Taliban Flash have been featured prominently on the homepage since early October 2001, portraying a stereotypical Arab iconography of beards and flowing robes. They link these racialized, reductive, iconic representations to US military power: nearly every Flash on the war concludes with the destruction of Bin Laden or the Taliban. In a post 9/11 psychic landscape where out-of-control technology and terror looms invisibly large, these works facilitate a compensationary fantasy of control, revenge, and imaging.

Dubbed 'classic Flash' and featured in an NPR story and many online festival websites, *Bin Laden Nowhere to Run, Nowhere to Hide* emerged as a notorious response to the war on terror. The three-minute animation spliced the calypso-inspired Harry Belafonte song 'Day-O' with new pro-war lyrics. The narrative straddles a racialized binary opposition. Bush plays congas while Colin Powell croons about the war. This image intercuts with Osama Bin Laden hopping between hills and caves. Bush, Powell, and Bin Laden are produced by splicing analog photos to digital bodies. Parallel editing between Colin Powell/Bush and Bin Laden in Afghanistan maps binary oppositions between the US and Afghanistan, Bush and Bin Laden, high technology and primitive caves.

The storyline purges psychoanalytic repression: kill Bin Laden. The song exclaims: 'George Bush say revenge come, daylight come and we drop the bomb. Come Mr. Taliban hand over Bin Laden, Colin Powell going to bomb his home, cruise missile knocking at your door.' The narrative concludes with the obliteration of the other: in the final image, a missile destroys the earth. Afterwards, a box pops up to forward the flash animation. *Nowhere to Run, Nowhere to Hide* translates, visualizes, popularizes, and animates Bush's war on terror. It sutures hatred for fantasies of active agency and control over the future, nationalizing psychic economics of military superiority. *Nowhere to Run, Nowhere to Hide* dangerously conflates narrative resolution, sexual climax, mouse movement, violence, and xenophobic patriotism into one large blast.

The Madblast animations suggest how independent cinema in the new media era splices together old media screens with new media screens as a way to create stability within the flux of multiple windows, constant interaction, and the migration of data between computers and databases. Lev Manovich (1997) has argued that the construct of the screen has undergone three periods of change: the classical screen of perspectival painting; the dynamic screen of the first 100 years of cinema; and the interactive screen of the computer, with its emphasis on interface and multiple screens. These Flash animations straddle the classical screen and the interactive screen. On the one hand, their visual design and narrative structures deploy binary oppositions and suture a nationalism, evoking classical Hollywood narrative to suggest a more stable – and predictable – historical modality. Similarly, their short form recalls the early years of primitive cinema one-reelers. On the other hand, their interface is a node within the new media environment of networked circulatory media, where images migrate between multiple screens. Their narrative structures connote the historical past of classical cinema. Their interface traces the historical present of interactive networked computer media. And their imaginary ironic scenarios project a history of the future.

Streaming indies

While online festivals serve as clearing houses for a range of analog and digital video shorts and Flash operates as a way to present moving images without download problems latent in networks, streaming technologies present another sector of exhibition that offers new and different possibilities for independents, particularly in the context of the war on terror, because they mix analog and digital, cyberspace and real space. For anti-war and anti-racist media activists, streaming offers a way to traverse different sectors of the media environment to address different kinds of audiences and communities without resorting to broadcasting or more traditional exhibition.

As exemplified in *Nowhere to Run, Nowhere to Hide* as well as myriad other sites with shorts on the nationalistic response to the war on terror, clear, linear, resolved storylines – condensed classical Hollywood narrative cinema – drive most of the online screen world in Flash and gaming sites. They sadistically project a US-dominated future of infinite war. They express the revenge and hatred mass media's distanced discourse of sobriety suppresses. While CNN and Fox may run 3D digitally composited layers of flags and weaponry, they do not openly state racialized hatreds. However, it is critical to remember that the online independent environment is not confined to militaristic, nationalistic, racism, which might lead theorists and analysts to link digitality to regressive reactionary politics, but also includes investigative journalism, interrogations into racism, and alternative news and documentaries, modes which recoup the potentialities of the digital for democratization of media access and the pluralization of discourses.

In response to the war on terrorism, a plethora of independent media projects in documentary and muckraking journalism genres has emerged. This work is realist documentary rather than imaginary narrative projections. Its epistemological structure de-emphasizes unity, hatred, racism, binary oppositions. Instead, it elaborates the complexities and pluralities of difference through regions, ethnic groups, national identities, histories. Rather than focusing on an imaginary future, these works shift towards connecting historical understanding with the present.

This work is streamed video, not Flash animation. Streaming refers to the conversion of analog media (movies or audio) for internet communications. Due to moving images' large file size, files must be compressed to be viewed, converting information into the smallest size to reduce artifacts. Streaming allows a file to be played before the download is completed. Although constantly confronting lost image parts, slow downloads, and length, streaming provides independent media as distribution and exhibition advantage as it moves towards a model of narrowcasting (Monaco 1999: 237). Because broadband internet – which has the capacity for large files – has not yet penetrated, streaming poses difficulties for exhibiting moving images and audio on the internet to achieve wider distribution. For example, 80 per cent of computer users use dial-up, with lower capacity for larger image and sound files than broadband on T1, DSL, or cable modem. Before the digital environment emerged in the late 1990s, independent distribution relied on shipping video and film to venues like video stores or theaters, posing a significant barrier to entry. Although only short narratives appear to have what internet marketers terms 'sticky eyeballs,' in another sense streaming allows the sampling of short independent films on the internet. This process creates a model based on shareware or freeware rather than commodity exchange: the point is the circulation of the independent narrative rather than exchanging exhibition for profit. As John Carr, founder of www.konscious.com, an independent media site, explains: 'Streaming allows you to bypass the traditional means of distribution' (phone interview with the author 2002).

Three different initiatives emerging in the post-9/11 environment point to streaming's potential to create viral environments for anti-war and anti-racist work outside mass-media distribution. Streaming has the potential to generate political consciousness and action by producing networked exhibition. As an interface, it offers an expandable archive of accessible, downloadable, and mutable media. In 2002, the Independent Television Service (ITVS 2002), one of the largest funders of independent film in the US, commissioned nine independent producers (Dan Bergin, Lena Carr, Louis Massiah's Termite TV Collective, Hector Galan, Joan Mandell, Sam Pollard, Ellen Spiro–Karen Bernstein, and Kyung Sun Yu) to produce minute-long responses entitled *A 9/11 Moment*. The press release notes: 'we are re-defining ways of looking at ourselves as American and at others in our global community. To promote understanding and compassion in our communities around the country, we look to independent media producers to speak about the sudden changes in our lives' (*ibid.*). Thirty-four one-minute spots were offered to PBS stations to air by 23 November 2002 (the spots are also streamed on www.itvs.org).

The 9/11 'moments' project a variety of multicultural voices across the US who express outrage, fear, sadness, pain, loss, mapping a complexity of responses. Navajo filmmaker Lena Carr produced *Quintera Yazzie*, where an eleven-year-old Navajo girl reflects on the events she witnessed at school. Joan Mandell, an artist with extensive experience taping Arab communities, made *Scout Leader*, where a Michigan boy-scout leader, Khalil Baydoun, and his teenage scouts describe being unjustly accused of being suspicious characters. In Ellen Spiro and Karen Bernstein's, *This Is Not a John Wayne Movie* (Molly Ivins), columnist Molly Ivins comments on the support of America's European allies around 9/11, despite the vast cultural differences between Texans and the French. Louis Massiah's *Flag* interviews Philadelphians pondering the varied meanings of flags displayed after 9/11. These spots elaborate the multicultural pluralities of American responses in contrast to cable and network militaristic jingoism. They function as historical records of the multiplicity of voices responding to these events. The short form facilitates streaming for an internet distribution system traveling between digital and analog: the spots are available online for preview, and can also be broadcast on public television between programs.

The www.konscious.com site called *9/11 and Beyond: Independent Voices Speak*, identified as 'voices of the people, from the streets,' includes 25 streamed pieces ranging from 2 minutes to 28 minutes from Konscious, the War and Peace D-Word Collaborative Project, and the Third World Newsreel Call to Media Action. Downtown Community Television's trailer *Afghanistan: From Ground Zero to Ground Zero* tracks a young Afghani woman who travels from New York to Afghanistan to confront deaths from US bombings. *Invisible Girl*, by Angela Alston, looks at how a Palestinian American girl in New York confronts the after-effects of the World Trade Center bombings. From the Third World Newsreel collection, Kevin Lee's *New York Chinatown 9/11* looks at how the World Trade Center bombings affected Chinatown.

Konscious.com functions as a portal – a gateway for other related sites – for works made in response to the war on terror. Their special feature on 9/11 attracted the most hits of any project on their alternative progressive website. However, like ITVS, the Konscious strategy is not limited to the internet but includes a move to real spaces. Konscious has curated selections from its web-site for Anthology Film Archives, for the Culture Project, and for Manhattan Neighborhood Network, and has shared programs with the Free Speech network to upload the videos to satellite. Unlike the more rabid pro-war Flash animations that survive only in the privatized internet netherworld, these anti-war works migrate between screens and exhibition venues, between digital and analog, building multiple public spaces.

Stories from the ground that counteract the commercial news media's war hysteria muckrake the proposed war. A project by independent journalists Jeremy Scahill and Jacquie Soohen in conjunction with WORT in Madison, Wisconsin (website: www.iraqjournal.org) collapses together production, distribution, exhibition, and reception. As the world community debates war in Iraq and Congress authorizes war, iraqjournal.org webcasts from inside Iraq. The web page supplies a different story from that of the anti-Osama Flash animations that mobilize hatred, concentrating on the specifics of everyday life in Iraq as a result of the sanctions. The site features downloadable text-based news stories, deep background, audio reports, and video reports.

An evidentiary cinema, these digital videos shot in a cinema vérité style weave an alternative archive to the images of weapons' inspection, creating representations from inside 'enemy' territory, dislodging nationalistic revenge fantasies. With iraqjournal.org, digital warfare occupies networks to circulate stories that connect people across the globe using viral marketing techniques of passing on websites and Flash animations via email – an assault against the mobil-ization of hatred in other online environments that torques new technologies for a new political agency. Iraqjournal.org suggests that information, documentary visions, and new technologies are instruments of hope rather than machines of death.

Targets

Digital technologies, as this chapter has argued, both refortify old patterns in the entertainment industry that secure profit through control of exhibition *and* create new spaces for a different kind of independent producer outside the system to create different discourses within different interfaces. Digital technologies, then, simultaneously solidify concentration in the exhibition sector while they open up and expand the exhibition sector with online festivals, Flash, and streaming. The relationship of interdependence between independent film and the media trans-nationals suggests that media critics need to look as closely at the economic structures and business models of these new entertainment industry behemoths that feed on indie work as they do at narrative and theoretical models to analyze the films themselves. It is no longer possible to talk about the film industry as a stand-alone entity; nor is it possible to conflate independent film with feature-length filmmaking. Digital technologies, from DV to Flash to streaming to online festivals to web portals, demonstrate the importance of thinking *across*

Figure 18.2 Website advertising *The Fourth World War*. Courtesy of www.bignoisefilms. com.

technologies, sectors, industries, and audience formations. In other words, the trans-industrial media environment of multiple platforms and re-purposed, re-mediated media migrating across and between different formations requires that indie media be reconceptualized within a multiplicity of production and exhibition interfaces and forms. To understand the significance of independent film, both analog and digital, feature and short, pro-war and anti-war, it is necessary to see that the indie sectors, which are themselves multiple, are now in constant movement, migration, and mix, rather than in one location of opposition.

In the context of the war on terror, digitality has offered a means of rapid response formerly available only to the commercial networks with their vast resources. Digitality has also presented a different model of exhibition that is point-to-point narrow-casting rather than broadcasting, and circulatory as it employs viral marketing rather than mass marketing. However, unlike computers, which can delete archives and history, it is important to be sober about the possibilities that digitality offers to indies. Although the oppositions between dominant and alternative media that fueled the anti-war movements during Vietnam, the incursions in Central America and the Gulf War no longer help us to triangulate and map the much more variegated and complex indie media scene of the twenty-first century, their histories of successes and failures in mobilizing public opinion and widening debate are sober reminders that, in the end, technologies are only as significant as the social and political movements that deploy them and re-imagine their use, for peace.

Notes

1   See for example www.dv.com/magazine.
2   See www.cpb.org and www.hbo.com/films.
3   See www.reclaimthemedia.org and www.democraticmedia.org.
4   See http://untoldhistory.weblogs.com.

Bibliography

Algeri, D. (2002) 'Economics of Short Film Distribution on the Internet,' paper presented at the Digital Cinema Conference, Cambridge, Massachusetts Institute of Technology, November.

Barnouw, E. (1983) *Documentary: A History of the Non Fiction Film*, Oxford: Oxford University Press, 139–72.

Bing, J. (2002a) 'Will U's Focus Prove Blurry?' *Variety*, 13–19 May: 1, 11.

—— (2002b) 'H'W'D's Old Spool Ties,' *Variety*, 19–25 August: 1, 24.

Bolter, J.D. and Grusin, R. (2000) *Remediation: Understanding New Media*, Cambridge: MIT Press.

Carr, J. (2002) Telephone interview with the author, 19 October.

Cheever, B. (2002) 'Dfilm and Internet Distribution,' paper presented at Digital Cinema Symposium, Cambridge, Massachusetts Institute of Technology, November.

Delgado, L. (2002) 'Lots of Flash, Even More Sizzle,' *Wired*, online: www.wired.com (accessed 25 July).

Gay, J. (2002) 'The History of Flash,' online: http://untoldhistory.weblogs.com (accessed 25 July).

Gomery, D. (1992) *Shared Pleasures: A History of Movie Presentation in the United States*, Madison: University of Wisconsin Press.

Harding, M.L. (1999) 'Now Showing: Shorts,' *New Media Age*, 30 September: 3.

Houston, F. (2000) 'Hollywood Flirts with Short Films on the Web,' *New York Times*, 15 June: G13.

Hozic, A. (2002) *Hollyworld: Space, Power, and Fantasy in the American Economy*, Ithaca, NY: Cornell University Press.

ITVS (2002) Press Release: 'ITVS Presents *A 9/11 Moment*,' January.

Lyons, C. (2002) 'New Machine Comes into Focus,' *Variety*, 13–18 May: 1, 11.

Manovich, L. (1997) ' "Reality" Effects in Computer Animation,' in J. Pilley (ed.), *A Reader in Animation Studies*, London: John Libbey, 5–15.

Miller, G. (2000) 'Internet Movie Firm Shifts Focus to LA: New Media Flush with $35 Million in New Investment Capital,' *Los Angeles Times*, 25 January: C1.

Miller, T., Govil, N., McMurria, J., and Maxwell, R. (2001) *Global Hollywood*, London: BFI Publishing, 146–71.

Monaco, J. (1999) *The Dictionary of New Media*, New York: Harbor Electronic Publishing.

National Association for Media Arts and Culture (2000) *Digital Directions: Conversion Planning for the Media Arts*, San Francisco, CA: NAMAC–Ford Foundation.

Sachs, J., and Fox, L. (2002) (founders of www.freerangegraphics.com) Telephone interview with the author, 1 August.

Schatz, T. (1988) *The Genius of the System: Hollywood Filmmaking in the Studio Era*, New York: Pantheon Books.

Siwek, S.E. (2000) *Copyright Industries in the US Economy: The 2000 Report*, International Intellectual Property Alliance, Washington, DC.

Sterritt, D. (2000) 'Short Film Festival: Quick Flicks Are No Longer Getting the Short End of the Stick Thanks to Internet Exposure,' *Christian Science Monitor*, 11 August: 13.

Turan, K. (2002) *Sundance to Sarajevo: Film Festivals and the World They Made*, Berkeley: University of California Press.

Waller, G.A. (ed.) 2002, *Moviegoing in America*, Malden, MA: Blackwell Press.

Wasko, J. (1994) *Hollywood in the Information Age*, Austin: University of Texas Press.

Webdale, J. (2001) 'Atom Films Hopes to Deliver a Shock to the Media System,' *New Media Age*, 1 March: 36.

Zimmermann, P.R. (1995) *Reel Families: A Social History of Amateur Film*, Bloomington: Indiana University Press.

—— (2002) 'Media Democracy Day(s),' *Independent*, September: 7.

Chapter 19

The IFC and Sundance
Channeling independence

Robert Eberwein

On the weekend of 3–5 May 2002 Sam Raimi's *Spider-Man*, estimated to have cost between $120 and $130 million dollars, opened in 3,615 theaters on approximately 7,500 screens. Its second-day take ($43.7 million), (three-day) weekend receipts ($114 million), and the speed with which it surpassed the $100 million mark all set records (Grove 2002). It eventually earned $821.6 million ($403.7 domestic; $417.9 foreign) (*Variety* 2003: 32). It's unlikely that the collective production budgets of any ten of the most expensive films playing that same weekend on the Independent Film Channel (IFC) and the Sundance Channel (Sundance) could match the estimated cost of *Spider-Man*, and even less likely that the total gross of those same films could approach its eventual earnings.[1] It's doubtful that *Spider-Man* will ever be shown on these channels because their special function in our intellectual economy is to offer audiences a way to see films made by independent filmmakers who do not compete for box-office records.

Consideration of the importance and value of the IFC and Sundance seems particularly appropriate at a time when the enormous budgets of Hollywood productions throw into dismal (and dismaying) relief the desperate experiences of independent filmmakers in getting funds to make their films. Even when a work can be funded, made, and shown at a film festival, there may be no exposure for it through ordinary distribution in theaters. This is one of the many areas where, as this chapter points out, both channels are of considerable valuable. Moreover, although seeing a film on a TV screen is less satisfactory than viewing it on an actual screen in a theater, it is better than watching a tiny image on a computer screen, the fate of many films and videos made by independent artists whose work is available solely on the internet.

As will be apparent, IFC and Sundance are vitally important sources of films about race and gender that could never be shown on commercial network TV or even the Public Broadcasting Service. Moreover, given their focus on film art, it is not surprising that a great deal of their documentary programming focuses on filmmakers. They have been a significant force in funding film and video artists in general, and offering those working in the medium of digital video venues for displaying their work. My aims in this chapter are to provide a brief history of both channels; to describe their programming practices; and to comment on some economic and social implications of their operations.

History

This section presents information about the origins of both channels, gives consideration to their rivalry and perceived differences, and offers commentary on some of their marketing tactics. The IFC began transmission on 1 September 1994 to an initial audience of 1 million satellite and cable viewers. It was not the first time independent film had been aired on television; earlier, Cinemax's Vanguard Cinema had shown independent films once a week, for example Todd Haynes's *Poison* (1991). Moreover, Bravo Networks, for all practical purposes the immediate predecessor of the IFC, had also afforded independent filmmakers a venue. Bravo, at that time a division of Rainbow Media Holdings, which is a subsidiary of the Cablevision Systems Corporation, began in 1980 as a commercial free channel carried on added-pay tiers. When Bravo became part of various bundled basic packages for cable subscribers and was included with other add-ons like the Disney Channel, it had to adjust to the wider viewership. Hence, it began editing movies for potentially objectionable content.

Amy Taubin's account of IFC's origins credits Martin Scorsese's importance in particular. She quotes Jonathan Sehring, then the programming vice president at Bravo, who reports: 'Martin Scorsese was irate when we edited *Who's That Knocking at My Door?* [1968.] When we explained the situation [about censorship], he said, "We've got to do something about this"' (Taubin 1994: 62). Scorsese was an original member of the IFC's board, which included other independent filmmakers (Joel and Ethan Coen, Robert Altman, Spike Lee, Steven Soderbergh, and Martha Coolidge) as well as a university advisory board. From its beginnings, IFC had access to Bravo's existing film library. Swire (1995: 20) describes several of the initial categories of its original offerings:

> [T]he 'New Voices' category showcases 'today's efforts of tomorrow's stars' (*Slacker*, [Richard Linklater, 1991], *Straight Out of Brooklyn* [Matty Rich, 1991]); while 'The Masters' is devoted to studying the work of cinema's greatest directors (Orson Welles, Michael Powell, Nicholas Ray), and 'Cult Classics' focuses on movies too bizarre or taboo for more mainstream programming.

In addition, it had licensing arrangements with production studios like Sony and Janus (Taubin 1994: 62). The IFC's first president Kathleen Dore emphasized that it would not be just a ' "multiplex" of Bravo with a time shifted schedule' (Walley 1994: 18).

The number of current subscribers to both the IFC and Sundance is not completely clear since both are available in many more households than actually subscribe. In June 2001, the IFC's website indicated that it 'reaches 23 million homes on a full-time basis.' In March 2001 David Lipke said it 'is seen in 30 million households' (2001: 61); in November 2001 Jim McConville put the number of subscribers at 20.5 million (2001: 96); as of September 2002, John Demsey says that the 'IFC reaches 24 million households, Sundance 16 million' (2002: 21).

Reports about the origins of the Sundance Channel often make the inevitable connection between it and the Sundance Festival, founded in 1986 by Robert Redford, a co-owner of the channel with Showtime (a division of Viacom) and Vivendi-Universal. Before he established his financial venture with Showtime, Redford had first approached Bravo and proposed that Sundance be affiliated with the IFC. Redford wanted creative control over the programming. According to David Finnigan and Doris Tourmarkine, 'the channel would have been called Sundance/IFC.' They indicate that Dore had said the idea of the linkage 'did not score well with test audiences and that the Sundance title ignores other fine festivals.' Moreover, she saw a gap between the spirit of independent filmmaking and the Hollywood–corporate links of Redford. 'The Sundance channel, Dore said, "will certainly be the Hollywood studio version of independent filmmaking. I mean, Showtime is owned by Viacom, which owns Paramount" '(Finnigan and Tourmarkine 1995: 137). In contrast, Redford claimed that the affiliation with Showtime would be a means of guaranteeing creative freedom and, according to a subsequent article by Tourmarkine (1995: 8), 'of creating a television environment for independent film, a development that "completes a circle" that began in 1980 with his effort to develop more independent works through his Sundance Institute.' Redford stressed this connection between the festival and channel to Duane Byrge (1995: 8): 'What you see here at the festival is going to be transferred over as a look and feel process of the channel.' Sundance finally launched on 29 February 1996, showing as its first major feature a film that had opened the 1995 Sundance Festival: *Before Sunrise* (Linklater, 1995).

From the beginning there has been discernible rivalry between the two channels, which would have been just one channel had Redford succeeded. It is not really accurate to see the discourse of antagonism as part of a scenario that has a fiercely independent IFC facing off against the corporate world of Hollywood, as represented by Redford. What really drove the rivalry in the early years, from 1996 to 1998, was the competition for space on cable systems. Prior to the widespread availability and adoption of broadband digital technology by cable providers, individual cable systems had a limited capacity for channels, usually a maximum of 70–80. Although IFC and Sundance were available on satellite systems that had the capacity to carry hundreds of channels, there were many fewer subscribers to this mode of delivery. Thus IFC and Sundance were in constant competition for carriage.

The rivalry received a lot of attention in the media. Around the time of Sundance's launch, trade journals were headlining 'The War of Independents' (Forkan 1996: 42); 'Sundance Ready to Face Off vs. IFC,' (Katz 1996: 18); a 'Marketing Duel' (Paikert 1996a: 48); and 'IFC Counterpunches with New Campaign' in a 'furious marketing battle' (Paikert 1996b: 38). The competition 'in the war' reached an ironic point the following year, according to Thomas Goetz, when the Coen brothers found themselves 'the battleground.' *Fargo* (1996), directed by the Coens, original board members of the IFC, was to be shown on Sundance in conjunction with a sweepstake having as its prize attendance at the Sundance Festival: 'Their names may be in their ads [for the IFC], Sundance Channel spokeswoman Sarah Eaton says, but we're showing their films' (Goetz 1997: 74).[2]

In their early years, both channels used other venues to give visibility to their presence and offerings. For example, in 1996, the IFC made an agreement with BMG Independents to include trailers for the channel in its initial advertisements

Figure 19.1 Marge Gunderson (Frances McDormand) in *Fargo* (Coen and Coen, 1996). Courtesy of Working Title/Polygram/Kobal Collection/Michael Teckett.

on videotapes. In turn, the IFC presented advertisements for independent films released on BMG Video (*Billboard* 1996: 50). In 2000, passengers on select Northwest Airlines flights were able to watch films from the IFC. Landmark Theaters have been advertised on IFC. In turn, the chain has aired varied humourous advertisements for IFC that also appear on the channel. These began in 1997 with spots featuring 'Christie,' a precocious child who speaks about the value of independent film. Later the IFC added 'Boris,' a gruff Russian filmmaker–teacher. Monica Hogan reports: 'The IFC-created Boris character teaches film students to "never go Hollywood"' (1999: 34); among the 'students' were Illeana Douglas and Christian Slater. One of the spots introduced in the 2001–2 advertising campaign featured an aspiring stuntman named 'Mike Jablonski' who works his way into the buffet being served to individuals making a film. According to Kathleen Sampey: 'In the 5–8 spots that will comprise the effort, Jablonski gets shot at, set on fire and thrown from a building' (2001: 27).

Shelly Gabert reports that after launching, Sundance initiated a connection with Blockbuster by which it 'developed a list of 100 independent films and then promoted them with "Sundance Channel Recommends" promotional cards at 2500 Blockbuster Video stores' (1996: 24). Like Showtime, a division of Viacom, Blockbuster has devoted shelf space to Sundance Festival films. According to *Cable World* (1998: 20), in 1998, when Sundance was the sponsor of the 34th Chicago International Film Festival, it joined with US Satellite Broadcasting 'in a promotional campaign focused on driving digital satellite system sales. A ticket stub from the festival goes toward a 5 percent discount at Montgomery Ward off the price of DSS.' Obviously stimulating satellite sales could potentially increase the number of subscribers to the channel. Another promotional deal with Joe Boxer in 2000 offered new subscribers free clothing. According to Monica Hogan (2000: 60): 'After somewhat racier spots were nixed, the Sundance marketing team came up with the campaign's tag line: "Take a peek at our shorts." The pun promotes the premium channel's short films – especially its "Short Stop" hour.'

Programming

Examination of the programming practices of both channels allows one to understand their similarities and particular emphases; in addition, I consider their relation to streaming video websites, and the channels' roles in the production of independent films.

Although the rivalry in the first two years was driven by the limited channel space available on cable systems, the substantive issue that informed both the earlier and later competition was programming. Each channel was described as having a particular niche that made it unique and, hence, was a desirable addition for people who are serious about watching independent film. At the time of its launch, Sundance was perceived as having 'a first-play distribution strategy using fresh movie titles' as opposed to the IFC's strategy, described by Dore, of using films from its library: ' "Our feeling has always been that this isn't about windows. . . . By placing yourself in a first-play window you are limiting yourself in the diversity of programming that you can play" ' (McConville 1996: 48). Even before its launch, Richard Katz (1996: 18) noted that IFC's Sehring 'derided Sundance's schedule. "We looked at all of the pictures [Sundance is running in March] a year ago and passed on 95 percent of those deals. . . . The other ones weren't worth the money that was being asked. They're approaching the channel like they're running a film festival, but there are lot of bad films run at film festivals." ' Three years later, the two were still perceived as having different emphases, sufficient to suggest to Lewis Beale in the *New York Daily News* that the channels offered service

> in radically different ways. IFC . . . primarily programs small art-house films that have had theatrical distribution. . . . The channel also shows older foreign and American independent features by filmmakers like John Cassavetes and Akira Kurosawa that have influenced the work of con- temporary artists. And IFC offers original programming like *Split Screen*.

In contrast, Sundance's focus is 'more toward American independent films that enjoyed little, if any, theatrical distribution' – like McCarthy's *Floundering* (1994). It 'shows more well-known movies, like *Big Night* [Tucci, 1997] and *Afterglow* [Rudolph, 1997], and is strongly committed to short films, documentaries and work from other countries' (Beale 1999: 8).

Beale observed that 'their different programming philosophies mean they actu- ally complement each other' (*ibid.*). The general perception that Sundance offers more independent films that have had minimum visibility is accurate, but even a cursory examination of their offerings demonstrates that both channels premiere new independent films. Both show many American and foreign works that have had limited theatrical release or, as in some cases, still await distribution. They present short films, documentaries, and the occasional classic. In addition, both offer ori- ginal programming. The greatest difference between the two is in regard to their roles in film production. Sundance helps filmmakers financially at the Sundance Institute, while the IFC is actually involved with film production and distribution, creating and supporting the kind of products that are shown at the festival.

Both companies acquire features in three ways. First, they negotiate with film companies and distributors. Second, teams from the channels attend the major film festivals such as Sundance, Toronto, SXSW (Austin), and Cannes in search of films to license. Third, they accept submissions from individual filmmakers (information about individual submissions is available on the channels' websites: www.ifctv.com; www.sundancechannel.com).

Although Sundance is much the more dominant force in this regard, both channels premiere works in two senses: initial showing on television and, in some cases, first presentation after festivals or, occasionally, anywhere. For example, the IFC's presentation of Thomas Vinterberg's *The Celebration* (1998) was the first time this work, produced by a founder of the Dogme95 group of filmmakers, had been shown on television. The same week on *DV Theater* the IFC premiered Caveh Zahedi's *The Bathtub of the World* (2001), shot on digital video, in which the filmmaker presents one-minute clips of his life during 1999. Sundance scored a coup in 2000 by showing the complete *Decalogue* (1997), Krzysztof Kieslowski's ten-hour masterpiece that had received limited theatrical release. The same year Sundance premiered two films that had been presented at the 1999 festival and which then went into theatrical release shortly after their initial showings: Lisanne Skyler's *Getting to Know You* (2000), and Cuban filmmaker Fernando Pérez's *Life Is to Whistle* (1998). In July 2001, Sundance premiered Michael Haneke's *Code Inconnu* (2000), a French film shown at the 2000 New York Film Festival that had failed to get an US distributor. The film was finally shown in New York in November 2001, at the Quad Cinema. Interestingly, the review in the *New York Times* reproduced excerpts from the earlier review Anita Gates (2001: 18) had given the film when it appeared on the Sundance Channel, rather than the review that was published when the film was shown at the festival. Most recently, Christopher Munch's *The Sleepy Time Gal* (2001), shown at the Sundance Festival in 2001, did not get a distributor. But, as B. Ruby Rich (2002: 29) explained, it was selected to be part of the 'Film Comment Selects' series at the Walter Reade Theater in New York, in February 2002, prior to being shown on the Sundance Channel in March. She quotes Paola Fraccero, vice president for acquisitions at the Sundance Channel: 'It's our purpose to rescue films that deserve audiences but that get lost in the shuffle.' In showing films that have not been distributed or that are unlikely to make it to video (much less DVD), even if they do get some kind of theatrical release, both the IFC and Sundance offer their viewers invaluable exposure to independent filmmakers, both American and foreign.

Sometimes relatively unseen or unavailable independent feature-length films are presented as part of a programming festival or series on the IFC and Sundance. In February 2001, the IFC staged a Black Heritage Week Festival that included *Do the Right Thing* (1989), the widely seen film by Spike Lee, and the less well-known *Straight Out of Brooklyn* and *To Sleep With Anger* (Burnett, 1990). In July 2001 the IFC showed a documentary it had produced on sex in independent cinema, *Indie Sex: Taboos* (Ades and Klainberg, 2001). This documentary was followed by a series that included not only the highly publicized *Crash* by David Cronenberg (1996) but the relatively unknown *Kissed* (1996), Lynne Stopkewich's disturbing study of necrophilia that received hardly any commercial release.

Sundance has regularly run a series devoted to gay issues during June, Gay Pride month, that includes both fictional and documentary films. Offerings in 2001 included Ira Sachs's *The Delta* (1996), a work about a closeted gay teen shown at the 1997 festival, and Nonny de la Penna's documentary *The Jaundiced Eye* (1999), about two men wrongfully imprisoned for child abuse. Although both are available in video, neither has received much, if any, theatrical exposure. In 2003, during Gay Pride Month, Sundance offered the first television showing of *Trembling Before G-D* (DuBowski, 2001), a documentary about gay and lesbian Orthodox Jews and the problems they encounter. The film premiered at the 2001 Sundance Festival and has won many awards, including the GLAAD (Gay and Lesbian Alliance Against Defamation) 2003 Media Award for Outstanding Documentary of the year. Given its limited release pattern, the film appears to have received its widest exposure to date on Sundance.

Still, films devoted to race, gender, and ethnicity appear throughout the programming year and are not consigned only to festivals or particular months. For example, although February is Black Awareness Month, in August 1998 Sundance ran a series *Representing Soul* in which both new and established filmmakers were represented. Included were Cheryl Dunye's *The Watermelon Woman* (1997), now better known than it was then because of the filmmaker's growing reputation, and *Sweet Sweetback's Baadasssss Song* (1971), Melvin van Peebles's groundbreaking blaxploitation work. Recently it showed Zeinabu irene Davis's *Compensation* (1999), a film about two African American couples in Chicago. Although set in different periods (the early twentieth century and today), the wife in each marriage is deaf. In September 2001 Sundance initiated a series on Latin American films, including *F**CKLAND* (Marquès, 2000), and *Te Amo (Made in Chile)* (Castilla, 2001).

Occasional programming is coordinated wittily with (or against) a particular institution or holiday. For example, the IFC celebrated Christmas 1999 by devoting a show to David Lynch: *The Lynch Who Stole Christmas*. Sundance has shown films about dysfunctional families on Thanksgiving and aired nothing but short films on 21 December.

Both channels are important sources of short independent films. Some of the shorts are presented at the conclusion of feature-length films and in certain cases are listed in the program guides published by the channels on their websites. Both channels also program individual shows devoted specifically to shorts. Sundance sometimes devotes programs to a group of filmmakers, such as films by women (*She Said Shorts*) and Latinos (*Latino Shorts*). An hour of shorts appears every Sunday night, connected, when appropriate, to the month's programming theme. Thus June's shows are devoted to the gay *Shorts Out Loud*.

The websites of both channels have also provided direct or linked access to short films. For a time the IFC was streaming eight short films. One of them,

Das Clown (Brown, 1999), was also being shown on the channel (www.ifctv.com/films). Access to the short films shown at the Sundance Festival is available beginning sometime in December and extending for a short period of time after the festival ends on the website (www.Sundanceonlinefilmfestival.org/sundance).

Earlier the Sundance Channel had an association with SkyyVodka. Skyy streams short films by established filmmakers, such as Agznieszka Holland's *The Wedding* (2001), on its website (www.skyyvodka.com), as well as running a contest for independent filmmakers. For a brief period the winning shorts were streamed on the Skyy website and broadcast on the Sundance Channel. One of the earlier winners of the contest still available on Sundance is the animated *Luz* (Martínez, 2001).

Some short films and videos that have won awards at the Outfest Queer Short Movie Award contest on PopcornQ are streamed on that website (www.planetout.com/pno) and on ifilm.com, a co-sponsor. In at least two cases recently, the winners have been shown on the Sundance Channel, although neither was shown at the festival itself: Robert Kennedy's *Hi, I'm Steve* (1999), a comedy about trying to find a companion, and Stephen Patrick Forey's *Family* (1998), a documentary video about a teenager's coming out.[3]

Such documentaries make up a significant part of their programming. The IFC's August 2001 line-up included Errol Morris's *First Person* in which the well-known documentarian profiled four individuals. Noted filmmaker Albert Maysles presented four films in December 2001 on Martin Scorsese, Wes Anderson, Robert Duvall, and Jane Campion: *With the Filmmaker: Portraits by Albert Maysles*. Sundance has had a series on Monday nights, *Matters of Fact*, devoted to documentary film. In August 2001 the channel gave a TV premiere to Tim Kirkman's probing study *Dear Jesse* (1996), in which the gay filmmaker explores the presence and impact of Jesse Helms. Beginning in March 2003, Sundance initiated 'DocDay' on Mondays, on which the programming is devoted to documentaries.

IFC presents many documentaries that it has produced itself. These include works about issues, such as *Indie Sex: Taboos*, mentioned earlier; about genres, such as *American Nightmare* (Simon, 2000), on horror films; and about filmmakers. In the latter category is *The Name of This Film Is Dogme95* (Metzstein, 2000), the first work to be made about the Danish collective of filmmakers that includes Thomas Vinterberg and Lars von Trier. The very first film that the IFC produced was Adam Simon's documentary *The Typewriter, the Rifle, and the Movie Camera* (1996), a remarkable work about independent giant Sam Fuller.

Most importantly, both channels offer original programming. Besides the kinds of special programs mentioned above, the IFC presents ongoing series, one of the most rewarding of which was *Split Screen*, hosted by John Pierson, one of the more important forces in independent film production. The series, which ran for four years, gave viewers a chance to see filmmakers like Kevin Smith interacting casually with this significant producer and supporter of independent film. Seeing the unassuming Pierson with various filmmakers who owe their visibility (and funding) to his initial enthusiasm gave viewers a chance to observe the independent film version counterpart of a major Hollywood mogul like Jerry Bruckheimer. Earlier the IFC ran a series *IFILM@IFC* that provided news and updates on activities in the world of independent film. IFC regularly covers the Sundance Film Festival and showcases informative materials and photographs about the films on its web page. In addition, the IFC presents *Escape from Hollywood*, a series highlighting films by noted independent filmmakers such as David Lynch and Alan Rudolph. This show appears on Wednesday and Sunday nights, hosted by John Cameron Mitchell, the noted indie filmmaker who made *Hedwig and the Angry Inch* (2001).

One of the newest original programs on the IFC is *Dinner For Five*, created and hosted by Jon Favreau. This weekly show, now in its third season, was modeled, according to the IFC website, on the Algonquin Hotel's 'round table.' Favreau is the gregarious and funny host who assembles a group of guests likely to generate a lot of information about the industry and recent films. On the first episode of the 2003 season, he hosted Kevin Smith, Ben Affleck, Jennifer Garner, and Colin Farrell. The generally hilarious conversations were partly about *Daredevil* (Johnson, 2003) in which the latter three starred, and partly about the friendship of Smith and Affleck. Clips from *Dinner For Five* are available on the IFC website.

Two of Sundance's current original programs are *Anatomy of a Scene* and *24 Frame News*. The first explores filming history of a particular scene in a current film: for example, the musical confrontation scene between Hedwig and Tommy in John Cameron Mitchell's *Hedwig and the Angry Inch* was shown as the director explained various aspects of its production. Films and scenes treated recently include *Buffalo Soldiers* (Jordan, 2001) and *28 Days Later* (Boyle, 2003). Given the long-standing problems with distribution of *Buffalo Soldiers* because of post 9/11 concerns about its story (American soldiers involved in the black market in 1989 Berlin prior to the Wall coming down), this offered audiences a brief look at a film whose ultimate distribution fortunes were at that time uncertain. Hosted by Jake Tapper, *24 Frame News* offers information about current releases and directors. In addition, for a time Sundance offered *Conversations in World Cinema* in which independent directors like Chantal Akerman and Ang Lee talked about their films.

One area that distinguishes the IFC from Sundance has been the former's involvement in film production through a number of divisions. First, before it was terminated, IFC Next Wave Films was conceived of as providing 'finishing funds' of up to $75,000–125,000 for filmmakers who need money to complete their films. One of its recipients was Kate Davis whose *Southern Comfort* (2000) presents the story of Robert Eads, a female-to-male transsexual dying of ovarian cancer.

This documentary, shown at the Sundance Festival, was nominated for an Academy Award and premiered commercially on HBO in 2001.

Four divisions remain active. First is IFC Productions, described by the IFC's website as 'a feature film company that provides financing for select independent film projects,' including such as works as Adam Simon's documentary about Sam Fuller, mentioned earlier, Steven Soderbergh's *Gray's Anatomy* (1996), and Kimberly Peirce's *Boys Don't Cry* (1999), for which Hilary Swank won an Oscar. Second, InDigEnt (Independent Digital Entertainment) is a division of IFC Productions that makes digital films. As of June 2003, that unit had produced seven films, including *Chelsea Walls* (Hawk, 2001) and *Tape* (Linklater, 2001). Third, the IFC Originals Division creates films for showing on IFC, such as *American Nightmare*, mentioned earlier. Fourth, IFC Films is described on the website as a 'theatrical film distribution company'; it was involved in the distribution of the wildly successful *My Big Fat Greek Wedding* (Zwick, 2002) and the less well-known *The King Is Alive* (Levring, 2000), a Dogme95 film.

Although Sundance does have some involvement with distribution, such as with *Getting to Know You* and *Life Is to Whistle*, mentioned earlier, Sundance has no

Figure 19.2 Brandon Teena (Hilary Swank) in *Boys Don't Cry* (Peirce, 1999). Courtesy of Fox Searchlight/Kobal Collection, Bill J. Matlock.

direct role in production comparable to that of the IFC. Nonetheless, the non-profit Sundance Institute is an important source of support for independent filmmakers. The Institute offers screenwriting and filmmaking laboratories that, according to the website (htt://institute.sundance.org), are 'designed to offer emerging screenwriters and directors the opportunity to develop new work . . . under the guidance of experienced filmmakers.' Among the advisors in the 2003 session were Miguel Arteta, Antonia Bird, Keith Gordon, Joan Tewksbury, and Stanley Tucci. Some recent films that received support from the Feature Film Program are *Raising Victor Vargas* (Sollett, 2002), *Laurel Canyon* (Cholodenko, 2002), *The Laramie Project* (Kaufman, 2002), and *The Slaughter Rule* (Smith and Smith, 2002).

Economic and social issues

The relation of IFC and Sundance to the media industry and to their potential audiences receives consideration in this final section. In the case of the IFC, but not of Sundance, mergers and a divestiture have raised questions about the potential impact on programming. First, developments in 2000 and 2001 raise some concerns about the place of the IFC in the total operations of Rainbow Media Holdings and the impact of that on its offerings. The IFC is one of several channels and operations in the Rainbow division of Cablevision; some of the others are American Movie Classics (AMC), Women's Entertainment (WE, formerly Romance Classics), and Rainbow Sports. Cablevision has twice put up parts of Rainbow for sale. The first time, in 1997, Robert Murdoch's News Corporation was a potential buyer for 40 percent of it, a deal that would have increased Murdoch's role in sports programming (McConville 1997: 1). The deal did not happen, and now Rainbow has a 50 percent partnership in Murdoch's Fox Sports Net. When Cablevision put Rainbow up for sale in 2000, one of the bidders was Barry Diller, owner of the USA Network, the Sci-Fi Channel, and Home Shopping Network; a majority owner of Diller's operations is Vivendi-Universal. Viacom was another of the bidders, as was NBC, which already owned about one-third of Rainbow. Diller did not succeed, for various reasons, while Viacom's bid was well under the $4.2 billion price expected for the Rainbow Group. Eventually MGM bought 20 percent of the Rainbow Group for $825 million. Had Diller's or Viacom's bid succeeded, the IFC would have had a corporate connection to Sundance, thus bringing the two together at last in a quintessential example of the labyrinthine linkages that characterize the economics of cable system ownership.

David Lieberman's analysis (2001) of the implications of the partial sale to MGM is relevant to anyone concerned about the continued health and integrity of the IFC. He wonders if future financial actions involving Rainbow will affect the nature of programming:

A message to movie fans: Pay attention to the on-again, off-again sales talks involving Rainbow Media. The outcome could determine whether cable – which is crammed with awful B-movies – will also sustain a few havens for classic and avant-garde fare. . . . If the wrong buyer steps in, it could be goodbye to Spike Lee, *Rashomon* [Kurosawa, 1950], the Three Stooges (hey, they're classics) and *Inside the Actors Studio* [a Bravo show] . . . and hello to, oh, *Dude, Where's My Car?* [Leiner, 2000] (Lieberman 2001: 2B).

Mike Farrell wondered at the time what impact MGM's ownership of 20 percent of Rainbow would have on the group's future. According to Farrell, 'the deal does not give Cablevison access to MGM's film library. But Rainbow's CEO Josh Sapan said . . . that could change' and that 'the deal allows Rainbow to pay down debt and provides cash "to expand and accrete our activities, [including] improvement of programming on the channels"' (Farrell 2001: 1). As it happens, in June 2003 Cablevision repurchased the 20 percent it had sold to MGM. But the economic situation remains fluid and unsettled. Rainbow, which owns the IFC, was partially detached from Cablevision because the larger company saw an opportunity to get cash. The transactions had no effect on programming. But it is clear that the IFC has no special status as one of the channels caught up in the financial actions. This initial sign of vulnerability for one of two vital sources of independent film is unsettling; and it has been made even more so by the sale, in August 2002, of Bravo to NBC. Thus the channel from which the IFC evolved has been jettisoned.

In contrast, Sundance's corporate status at this point seems healthier and much less problematical. In fact, at the 2002 festival, Redford announced that he was adding a new channel devoted entirely to documentary film and establishing a fund to support documentary filmmaking. Redford explained the need for this channel to Eugene Hernandez: '"The way it is now documentarians are just tossed to the dogs" explained Redford. There will be no formal tie between the new station, the institute and the festival, but when Redford was asked if there would be any spill-over between the three, he replied, "I hope so!"'(Hernandez, Schiller, and Kersnowski 2002). This plan has not materialized as yet, though, as noted above, beginning in March 2003 Sundance instituted 'DocDay' every Monday on which only documentary films are shown.

At the time of the channels' launches, Richard Turner wrote a thoughtful commentary suggesting that the IFC and Sundance offered cable operators 'the foie gras part of the menu when they're trying to wire new homes. They're Trojan horses for the lumpen USA Network. . . . They also provide cover. Cable operators can tell Congress not to regulate their rates because they're offering wonderful, pro-social material' (1995: 22–3). He mentioned a *Wall Street Journal* editorial that had used the existence of such channels as a way to challenge the continued existence of public funding for the PBS. The logic was that the PBS should, like any other private channel, compete for viewers rather than ask for government support. As far as I know, the various right-wing foes of the PBS are not currently using this argument to deny funding. But Turner's commentary raises an important issue that needs to be considered: who watches these channels?

As noted earlier, the initial heated rivalry between the IFC and Sundance was driven by their competition for a limited number of channels on the pre-broadband cable systems. According to Jim Rutenberg in the *New York Times*, as of August 2001, 12 million of the 70 million cable customers now have broadband (2001: C1). It is difficult to ascertain the exact number of such customers at this time because statistics are bound up with other information about the expanded role of cable companies in delivering combined phone, internet and TV services. No matter how much expansion there has been, for various reasons the expanded capacity for channels does not necessarily translate into subscriptions to the IFC or to Sundance. First, a system, whether or not it has broadband, may not offer either channel; for example, according to Deborah McAdams, Cablevision (owner of the IFC) was not carrying Sundance on any of its subsidiaries as late as May 2000 (2000: 42). Second, even if a system provides the IFC and/or Sundance, not every subscriber takes them. Since the most basic cable service can easily cost well over $20 a month, many people cannot afford even the added tiers that include non-premium channels like AMC and A&E (Arts and Entertainment), much less the more expensive packages with premium channels. Neither channel is by itself in the same price range as HBO or Showtime ($12.95+), but the particular charge for each is hard to determine, and will vary according to the provider. Each used to cost $5.95 on my Media One system, but that charge was reduced when they were bundled with a package that added all the premium channels (including multiple channels of HBO, Showtime, and STARZ). Now my system is operated by Comcast on which the cost for Sundance, with both a west and east coast feed, is part of a special digital tier, while the IFC is factored separately.

Although it is possible to determine the approximate number of actual sub-scribers to the IFC and Sundance, acquiring extensive data on the demographics of the viewership for the channels is not easily done. Using data from the IFC, Lipke (2001: 62) found its viewers 'more likely to live in smaller markets, such as St. Louis, Orlando, and Phoenix. Only 24 percent . . . live in the five largest television markets, while 26 percent live in the next 15 largest markets. . . . 34 percent are 18–34 years old, 29 percent are college grads, and 43 percent have annual household incomes of $60,000 and more.' In contrast, Sundance's viewers 'tend to be younger, more urban and suburban (as opposed to rural), more likely to have Web access, more likely to buy things through the internet, and more ethnically diverse than the average cable customer' (*ibid.*) But knowing that the IFC's viewers are living in smaller markets is of limited value when we consider that some larger markets, such as parts of New York City, may not have access to the channel as yet.

Granting the absence of more complete information about viewers and the varied reasons why some have or have not subscribed to either channel, I still think it is possible to consider the ideological implications of the limited access to the IFC and Sundance. In effect, those of us who do and others who don't have access to them are participants in a cultural class system tied significantly (but not solely) to economics in a way that deprives many the opportunity to view the work of independent filmmakers. This is unfortunate for two reasons. First, some are missing exposure to exciting new art and to some of the works that helped form the current generation of filmmakers. Second, the features, documentaries, and short films that focus on race, gender, and ethnicity deserve a much larger audience, including both those who are the subjects of the works and those who could learn in a way that raises consciousness and sensitivity to the needs and lives of others in society. Sadly, the 'wonderful pro-social material' Turner (1995) spoke of is going unseen by too many people.

Still, by making it possible to view independent films previously available only at film festivals and in limited theatrical release, the IFC and Sundance have broadened the potential base of viewership significantly. We would be the losers if either one of them ceased to operate.

Notes

1 The following feature-length documentary and narrative films were shown on the IFC and Sundance Channel, 3–5 May 2002. (* = repeated)

IFC

Autumn Tale (Eric Rohmer, 1998); *Boys Don't Cry** (Peirce, 1999); *Eye of God* (Tim Blake Nelson, 1997); *The Grass Harp* (Matthau, 1995); *The Hi-Lo Country** (Stephen Frears, 1998); *The Indian Runner* (Penn, 1999); *Johnny Stecchino* (Benigni, 1991); *A Life Less Ordinary* (Danny Boyle, 1997); *Martha & Ethyl* (Jyll Johnstone, 1994); *Mi Vida Loca* (Anders, 1993); *The Minus Man** (Hampton Fancher, 1999); *Mystery Train** (Jim Jarmusch, 1989); *Re-Animator** (Stuart Gorden, 1985); *Savages* (James Ivory, 1972); *Shadows and Fog* (Woody Allen, 1992); *The Sweet Hereafter** (Atom Egoyan, 1997); *Your Friends and Neighbors* (Neil LaBute, 1998)

Sundance Channel

American Pimp (Hughes and Hughes, 1999); *Before Sunrise** (Linklater, 1995); *Claire Dolan* (Kerrigan, 1998); *F**KLAND* (Marquès, 2000); *Funny Bones* (Chelsom, 1995); *Genghis*

*Blues** (Belic, 1999); *George Washington** (Green, 2000); *Happiness** (Solondz, 1998); *House of Games** (Mamet, 1987); *The Man Who Bought Mustique* (Bullman, 2000); *Nights of Cabiria** (Fellini, 1957); *Signs and Wonders* (Nossiter, 2000); *Someone Else's America* (Paskaljevik, 1995); *Swimming to Cambodia* (Demme, 1987); *The Swindle** (Chabrol, 1997); *Theremin: An Electronic Odyssey** (Martin, 1993); *Time Regained* (Ruíz, 1999); *The Trip to Bountiful* (Masterson, 1995); *Two Hands** (Jordan, 1999); *Wages of Fear* (Clouzot, 1953); *Waking the Dead** (Gordon, 2001); *Without You I'm Nothing* (Boskovich, 1990); *Women in Love* (Russell, 1969).

2 According to John Demsey, the issue of competition has shifted to a different field, given the arrival of Starz Cinema in 1999. The latter, one of the channels in the STARZ system, has access to more films through its corporate links (Miramax, Fine Line, New Line, Universal Focus) and better financing. But all share the following: 'The problem facing all three nets is that the number of people who gravitate to both foreign films and independent American movies on cable television is tiny judged by the standards of Nielsen's household ratings; Sundance, IFC and Starz Cinema have not convinced cable operators that there's room in the marketplace for all three' (Demsey 2002: 21).

3 Watching the video on the Sundance Channel is much more effective than seeing it streamed on ifilm.com. Because there is no option to enlarge this particular video to full screen (there is with some), the 5 × 4 in. image must be viewed with the distracting clutter of other visual information. Nonetheless, free sites such as ifilm.com and atom.com give budding artists much needed venues. In some cases, a film streamed on the web can be a breakthrough for a filmmaker, as happened with Joe Nussbaum's *George Lucas in Love* (1999), which became so popular that it is for sale on VHS and DVD and can no longer be viewed free on the internet. Another enormously popular streaming video, *405* (Banit and Hunt, 2000), had over 4.6 million hits by June 2003. The popularity of the digitally created work, a comedy about a driver on Highway 405 who finds himself in front of a jumbo jet trying to land on the freeway, has led to the creation of a website, 405Themovie.com, as well as a video for sale.

Bibliography

Beale, L. (1999) 'Small Films Find Big Following on Cable Channels,' *New York Daily News*, 24 January: 8.

Billboard (1996) 'Picture This: Home Vid Data: A Lot of Baloney? A Truce in Cable/Tape Movie War: Friendly Enemies,' 20 July: 50.

Byrge, D. (1995) 'Redford Gives His Vision of Indie Channel,' *Hollywood Reporter*, 30 January: 8.

Cable World (1998) 'Mighty Moves: Sundance Channel,' 5 October: 20.

Demsey, J. (2002) 'Starz Hitches Wagon to Niche,' *Variety*, 9–15 September: 21.

Farrell, M. (2001) 'MGM Buys 20% Slice of Four Rainbow Nets,' *Multichannel News*, 5 February: 1.

Finnigan, D. and Tourmarkine, D. (1995) 'Showtime Gets Sundance Pact,' *Hollywood Reporter*, 1, 17 January: 1, 137.

Forkan, J. (1996) 'The War of Independents,' *Cable Vision*, 19 February: 42.

Gabert, S. (1996) 'Get a Load of the Competition,' *Independent Film–Video Monthly* (August–September): 24–7.

Gates, A. (2001) 'Film in Review: "Code Unknown," ' *New York Times*, 30 November, Section E, Part 1: 18.

Goetz, T. (1997) 'Cable Guys: Indie Film Channels Vie for Airtime,' *The Village Voice*, 3 June: 74.

Grove, M.A. (2002) 'Box Office Analysis: *Spider-Man* Snares Box Office Record,' 5 May, online: www.Hollywood.com (accessed 18 September 2003).

Hernandez, E., Schiller, J.L. and Kersnowski, M. (2002) 'Redford Announces Major Doc Initiative,' 14 January, online: www.indiewire.com (accessed 10 February 2002).

Hogan, M. (1999) 'IFC Sends "Boris" to Movies,' *Multichannel News*, 19 July: 34.

—— (2000) 'Sundance Looks to Humor to Draw Subs,' *Multichannel News*, 1 May: 60.

Katz, R. (1996) 'Sundance Ready to Face Off vs. IFC,' *Multichannel News*, 2 February: 18.

Lieberman, D. (2001) 'Battle Over Rainbow Media Could Determine Quality of Cable Offerings,' *USA Today*, 5 February: 2B.

Lipke, D. (2001) 'Independence Day,' *American Demographics*, 23, 3 (March): 61–4.

McAdams, D.D. (2000) 'Bucks, Capacity, and the Sundance Kid,' *Broadcasting & Cable*, 8 May: 42.

McConville, J. (1996) 'IFC on the Move,' *Broadcasting & Cable*, 26 February: 48.

—— (1997) 'Murdoch Chases Cable Sports Deal,' *Electronic Media*, 23 June: 1.

—— (2001) 'Favreau Chatfest Has Place Set at IFC "Dinner" Table,' *Hollywood Reporter*, 27 November: 4, 96.

Paikert, C. (1996a) 'IFC, Sundance Begin Marketing Duel,' *Multichannel News*, 4 March: 48.

—— (1996b) 'IFC Counterpunches with New Campaign,' *Multichannel News*, 20 May: 38.

Rich, B.R. (2002) 'Adventures of an Indie Gem on its Way to the Screen,' *New York Times*, 10 February, Section 2: 29.

Rutenberg, J. (2001) 'Cable Networks Look for Ways to Stand Out,' *New York Times*, 20 August, Section C, Part 1: 9.

Sampey, K. (2001) 'Film Flam,' *ADWEEK*, 23 July: 27.

Swire, B. (1995) 'Independent Film Channel,' *Filmmaker* (summer): 20–1 [included as interior column in Willis, H. and Macaulay, S. (1995) 'Four Arguments for the Continuation of Television': 19–24].

Taubin, A. (1994) 'Another New York Blackout,' *The Village Voice*, 6 September: 62.

Tourmarkine, D. (1995) 'Redford: Sundance Net Lured by Showtime "Clout",' *Hollywood Reporter*, 18 January: 8.

Turner, R. (1995) 'The Highbrow Ghetto,' *New York*, 6 November: 22–3.

Variety (2003) 'Top 125 Worldwide,' 13–19 January: 32.

Walley, W. (1994) 'Bravo to Launch Premium Service,' *Electronic Media*, 9 May: 18.

Index

eBooks – at www.eBookstore.tandf.co.uk

A library at your fingertips!

eBooks are electronic versions of printed books. You can store them on your PC/laptop or browse them online.

They have advantages for anyone needing rapid access to a wide variety of published, copyright information.

eBooks can help your research by enabling you to bookmark chapters, annotate text and use instant searches to find specific words or phrases. Several eBook files would fit on even a small laptop or PDA.

NEW: Save money by eSubscribing: cheap, online access to any eBook for as long as you need it.

Annual subscription packages

We now offer special low-cost bulk subscriptions to packages of eBooks in certain subject areas. These are available to libraries or to individuals.

For more information please contact webmaster.ebooks@tandf.co.uk

We're continually developing the eBook concept, so keep up to date by visiting the website.

www.eBookstore.tandf.co.uk